M000235114

Beginner's Croatian

with Online Audio

Beginner's
Croatian

with **Online Audio**

Aida Vidan
and
Robert Niebuhr

Hippocrene Books, Inc.
New York

Audio files available at www.hippocrenebooks.com

Online audio edition, 2020

Text copyright © 2009 Aida Vidan and Robert Niebuhr
Audio copyright © 2009 Hippocrene Books, Inc.

All rights reserved.

For information, address:
Hippocrene Books, Inc.
171 Madison Ave.
New York, NY 10016
www.hippocrenebooks.com

Cataloging-in-Publication Data available from the Library of Congress

ISBN 978-0-7818-1408-9
Previous edition ISBN: 978-0-7818-1232-0

Printed in the United States of America.

Contents

Foreword xi
Introduction: **Croatian History 101** 1
List of Abbreviations 9
The Croatian Alphabet and Pronunciation Guide 11

Lesson 1: Tko je Marijana? *Who is Marijana?* 15
Pragamatics: Introducing oneself 16
Vocabulary 18
Verb List 18
Greetings 19
Grammar: noun gender; personal and possessive pronouns; verb types and conjugations; irregular verbs **biti** *to be* and **moći** *to be able to*; verb negation I; interrogative forms 19
Exercises 24

Lesson 2: Marijana, Darko i Ivan razgovaraju *Marijana, Darko and Ivan talk* 27
Pragmatics: Conducting a simple conversation 28
Vocabulary 32
Verb List 33
Useful Expressions 34
Grammar: introduction to cases; nominative case; noun plurals; *fleeting -a*; verb **htjeti** *to want* and **e**-type verbs; verb negation II; negative pronouns; reflexive verbs 34
Exercises 40

Lesson 3: Vožnja *Driving* 45
Pragmatics: Simple description & colors 46
Vocabulary 48
Verb List 48
Useful Expressions 49
Useful Adjective Pairs 49
Grammar: adjectives (short & long), voicing assimilation; nominative singular and plural of adjectives; interrogative question words; adverbs; plural of possessive pronouns; demonstrative pronouns 50
Exercises 55

Lesson 4: Marijana posjećuje zagrebački restoran *Marijana visits a Zagreb restaurant* 59
Pragmatics: Ordering food in a restaurant 60
Vocabulary 64
Verb List 64
Useful Expressions 65
Sample Menu 66
Grammar: verb **imati** *to have*; accusative case—direct object, nouns, adjectives, possessive & personal pronouns; accusative prepositions; days of the week; vocative case; conjunction **da** *that* 67
Exercises 74

Lesson 5: Kako naći stan? *How to find an apartment?* 79
Pragmatics: Renting an apartment 80
Vocabulary 84
Verb List 85
Useful Expressions 85
Grammar: genitive case—nouns, adjectives, possessive pronouns; pointer words; quantifiers & genitive; prepositions & genitive; verbs **bojati se** *to be afraid of* and **sjećati se** *to remember* & genitive; colors & genitive; personal pronouns in the genitive; possessive forms of names; conjunctions **i, a, ali, pa, ili, ni, niti, jer, ako** 86
Exercises 94

Lesson 6: Kupovina *Shopping* 99
Pragmatics: Buying food; telling time & giving the date 100
Vocabulary 104
Verb List 105
Useful Expressions 105
Grammar: cardinal & ordinal numerals; the rule of 5; dates; months; seasons; telling time 106
Appendix: collective numbers & other numeral forms 113
Exercises 114

Lesson 7: Na poslovnom sastanku *At a business meeting* 119
Pragmatics: Using the phone; business expressions; professions 120
Vocabulary 124
Verb List 124
Useful Expressions 125
Professions 126

Grammar: dative and locative cases—nouns, adjectives, possessive and personal pronouns; dative usage—indirect object, verbs **sviđati se** *to like* and **trebati** *to need*, impersonal and idiomatic dative expressions, dative of possession, dative prepositions; locative usage—locative prepositions, **na/u** and locale designations; tag questions 126
Exercises 133

Lesson 8: Marijana ide na zabavu *Marijana goes to a party* 139
Pragmatics: Social interaction 140
Vocabulary 144
Verb List 144
Useful Expressions 145
Grammar: instrumental case—nouns, adjectives, possessive and personal pronouns; instrumental usage—prepositions, transportation, instrument, spatial designation, temporal marker; interrogative, affirmative, neutral and negative pronouns; prepositional objects; impersonal **"se"** constructions; reflexive pronouns (personal & possessive) 145
Exercises 152

Lesson 9: Vrlo važna poruka *A very important message* 157
Pragmatics: Writing a personal message/letter 158
Vocabulary 162
Verb List 162
Useful Expressions 163
Grammar: past tense; negative and interrogative statements in past tense; impersonal sentences in past tense; past-time markers; numbers in past tense; reported speech; word order; expressions **sve** *all/everything*, **svi** *all/everybody*, **takav** *such*, **ovakav** *this kind*, and **onakav** *that kind* 163
Exercises 170

Lesson 10: Put na jug *A journey to the South* 175
Pragmatics: Discussing future plans 176
Vocabulary 180
Verb List 180
Useful Expressions 180
Compass Directions 181
Grammar: future tense; negative and interrogative statements in future tense; impersonal sentences in future tense; future time expressions; relative pronouns 181
Exercises 186

Lesson 11: Izgubljene isprave *Lost documents* 193
Pragmatics: Reporting lost documents; interacting with officials 194
Vocabulary 198
Verb List 198
Useful Expressions 199
Grammar: the preposition **po** and the particle **po**; verb aspect—imperfective & perfective, practical use of aspect, formation of perfective and imperfective verbs; motion and transportation verbs; verbs of perception & expression, bi-aspectual verbs 199
Exercises 209

Lesson 12: Marijana u gradu cara Dioklecijana *Marijana in Emperor Diocletian's city* 215
Pragmatics: Giving and asking directions 216
Vocabulary 220
Verb List 220
Useful Expressions 221
Asking for and Giving Directions 221
Locales 222
Grammar: passive verbal forms; impersonal constructions in the past & future; verbal nouns; present and past verbal adverbs; verb typology 224
Appendix: Verb typology 229
Exercises 230

Lesson 13: S otoka na otok i posjet Dubrovniku *Island hopping and a visit to Dubrovnik* 237
Pragmatics: Buying a ticket; booking a hotel room; clothing 238
Vocabulary 242
Verb List 242
Useful Expressions 243
Articles of Clothing 243
Accommodations 244
Grammar: conditional; preposition **s**; comparative & superlative of adjectives; comparative & superlative of adverbs; comparative constructions 244
Appendix: most frequent comparative & superlative adjective forms 252
Exercises 253

Lesson 14: Šetnja Zagrebom *A walk around Zagreb* 263
Pragmatics: Exchanging money & shopping; family members; health 264
Vocabulary 268
Verb List 268
Useful Expressions 268
Family Members 269
Parts of the Body 270
Medical Expressions 271
Grammar: imperative; modal verbs; adjectival prefix **pre-**; collective nouns; verbs of body position and movement; neuter **-en** and **-et** nouns 272
Exercises 279

Lesson 15: Marijana se vraća u Ameriku *Marijana returns to America* 285
Pragmatics: Travel terminology; saying goodbye 286
Vocabulary 292
Verb List 292
Useful Expressions 293
Grammar: future II; *if* clauses; expression **jedan drugi** *one another*; compound conjunctions; pluperfect; past conditional 294
Appendix: The pluperfect & past conditional tenses 299
Exercises 300

Key to Exercises 307

Appendix I: Declension Table—Endings 327
Appendix II: Declension Table—Examples 329
Appendix III: Personal Pronoun Declension Table 332
Appendix IV: Prepositions 333

Croatian-English Glossary with Verb List 334
English-Croatian Glossary with Verb List 351

Index of Grammatical and Pragmatic Categories 367

Audio Track List 369

Audio files available for download at:
http://www.hippocrenebooks.com/beginners-online-audio.html

Foreword

This volume is created with a multifunctional purpose. It is meant to be a handy companion for travelers to Croatia who wish to master the basic expressions of everyday communication, and also to fulfill the needs of students who would like to gain a greater familiarity with the grammatical patterns. It is designed for individuals studying Croatian and for structured class instruction.

The audio materials provide guidance through the sound and pronunciation system, while a variety of exercises (along with keys) allow for an easy measurement of progress. Some chapters have appendices containing slightly more challenging grammatical topics. While these segments are typically a part of any complete grammatical coverage of Croatian, they are not essential to the first encounter with the language. This is in line with the general approach of the book, intended to give all types of students a chance to learn as much as they need. For those who want more, the grammar sections provide both a general outline of all the relevant topics and also many details and examples. For those who are oriented towards the elementary level, a system of charts in appendices in the back of the book allows for at-a-glance consultation.

While the story line of the dialogues is meant to be amusing and offers a colloquial form of the language, it is also pragmatic in dealing with situations in which a traveler to Croatia may easily find him/herself (ordering food in a restaurant, buying tickets, booking a room in a hotel, etc.). The vocabulary included has been selected for frequency in terms of its use and is organized in clusters according to the topic or situation. The list of useful expressions in each lesson is designed to contribute to the colloquial feel of the dialogues and to supply those "ready-made" formulas that may be needed for everyday interaction. The charts in the appendices at the end of the book should prove helpful both as an easy grammar reference tool and for systematizing and reinforcing the most important grammatical material. The dual glossary (Croatian-English and English-Croatian) will supply the most indispensable vocabulary, while the brief introduction to Croatian history will answer the basic questions about how this country—at the same time very old and very young—came to be. Aida Vidan is the author of the fifteen story segments and the grammar lessons, while Robert Niebuhr wrote the historical introduction, provided English translations for the dialogues, and ran the technical aspect of the project. Both authors contributed to the exercises.

It is the authors' hope that all those readers who decide to explore the Croatian language will enjoy it as much as they are likely to enjoy the country itself, a newly discovered gem on both the tourist and economic maps.

Finally, we would like to offer our gratitude to our colleagues and friends who invested their time and energy in helping us create this volume. Very special thanks to Marijan Despalatović who commented extensively on the manuscript and contributed to its improvement in countless ways, to Vjeran Pavlaković for his detailed observations regarding the historical introduction, to Ellen Elias Bursać for productive discussions on numerous theoretical and practical issues, to Ronelle Alexander from whose knowledge and experience in writing textbooks we benefited tremendously, to Wayles Browne for sharing his linguistic expertise, to Tom Butler for suggestions in the early phase of the project, and to Nives Opačić for her native insights. Robert Niebuhr would like to extend his thanks to Stephen Batalden who, along with Danko Šipka, served as a wonderful and inspiring instructor and sparked his interest in the Balkans. Our students' very helpful questions improved the overall organization and clarity of the book, and we thank them for that. It was a pleasure to work with Lynn Visson and Mary Tahan whose editorial suggestions proved most useful. Last but not the least, we are indebted to Antonio Bilić, Diana Lasić, Pavao Planinić, and Ante D. Zubac, the native speakers who brought the dialogues in this volume to life on the audio. Needless to say, the authors are responsible for any mistakes or oversights.

Aida Vidan and Robert Niebuhr

CROATIAN HISTORY 101

Croatia's natural beauty and richness has attracted human settlement for thousands of years, and the territory that is now Croatia has served as a vital crossroads for numerous European peoples.

From the Ancient World to the Medieval

It is widely believed that in the time before recorded history, nomadic tribes of hunters and gatherers roamed the area of modern-day Croatia. These prehistoric peoples established temporary accommodations in scattered enclaves across the country, including the mountainous border region between Croatia and Slovenia and along the coast of the Adriatic Sea.

In the few centuries prior to Christ, various tribes of Illyrians, Celts, and Greeks arrived in the region. The Illyrian settlement grew to become the most significant over time and penetrated all parts of the country. The question of where the Illyrians came from is still hotly debated by scholars because the history of this people remains unclear—including the question of who their descendents are today. Not only did Napoleon Bonaparte name

Croatian Political Map (COURTESY OF THE UNIVERSITY OF TEXAS LIBRARIES, THE UNIVERSITY OF TEXAS AT AUSTIN.)

the French-occupied territories on the Eastern Adriatic the "Illyrian Provinces," but even contemporary myths concerning the roots of the Albanian people trace the ancestry of Albanians to the Illyrians of old.

East met West when the Illyrians succumbed to the power of the Roman Empire in 168 BC. Traces of Roman influence clearly predated this time of conquest, as can be seen from some of the architecture, especially along the coastal regions. The impact of Roman civilization, though, remains debatable, since Rome had a difficult time maintaining control of its Adriatic possessions due to troublesome warfare and an overburdened bureaucracy. Rome's lack of profound influence is also partly due to the fact that its conquest of the Balkans coincided with a general period of instability. During the latter half of the first millennium, tribes from the East—Slavs included—would move in and wear down the Roman authorities through never-ending wars.

Until roughly the seventh century, Slavic peoples were largely unknown to the region, but once migration began, Slavs overwhelmed the other tribes and came to dominate the entire Balkan Peninsula, including Croatia. Over the next two hundred years, the Croats organized into two groups: one centered on the fertile Pannonian Plain in the north, the other along the rocky, coastal region of the south.

This period of Slavic migration and settlement also coincided with the drive toward Christianization that rose out of the ashes of a fallen Rome and would forevermore associate Croatia with Roman Catholicism. The first Christian converts were of course Croatia's ruling elite, with a more complete wave of conversion reaching the populace in the following decades. No united Croatian kingdom existed for quite some time following Slavic migration; instead a series of competing duchies vied for control over the country. The most influential duchy at this time was controlled by the founder of the famous Trpimirović dynasty, Trpimir I (845–864). His state extended from the beautiful coastal city of Zadar to the River Drava, which today lies at the border between Croatia and Hungary. In 879, fifteen years after the end of Trpimir's rule, Pope John VIII became the first pope to recognize a ruler of the land of Croats—Duke Branimir.

For several generations following Branimir's rule, Croatia remained divided into different duchies. But Tomislav (910–928), a member of the Trpimirović dynasty, united the duchies and allegedly became the first King of Croatia. A little more than a hundred years later, in the eleventh century, this Croatian kingdom reached its peak under King Petar Krešimir IV (1058–1074).

Although this period is significant in that it established the foundations of Croatian culture in this territory, the next two hundred years following Krešimir saw a relative decline in Croatian power. The death of King Stjepan II in 1090 left the Trpimirović dynasty without any heirs, and various power struggles resulted in a descent into anarchy. The death of Petar Svačić, a pretendant to the throne and effectively the last Croatian king, at the Battle of Gvozd Mountain in 1097 resulted in a power vacuum that was not filled until 1102. That year Croatian rulers recognized Koloman of the Hungarian Arpadović dynasty as king of Croatia and Dalmatia, even though it took Koloman several more years of campaigning before pacifying all of the towns on the Dalmatian coast. The unification of the Croatian and Hungarian kingdoms lasted until the twentieth century, having endured innumerable political and ideological changes.

A Multipolar World

Within the new kingdom, Hungarians dominated the cultural, economic, and political life. During this entire medieval era, Hungary stood out as a force with lasting influence in the region; as opposed to its respective neighbors in the Balkans, who rose in power but lacked the ability to maintain any expansion. In addition, the overwhelming might of the Ottoman Empire emerged by the fourteenth century and its northward drive into the heart of Europe made the situation of independent kingdoms in the Balkans increasingly precarious. Finally, it must be noted that part of Croatia—principally the Dalmatian coast and the Istrian Peninsula—was, until the late eighteenth century, controlled by Venice, which took advantage of Hungary's inability to exert political power to the coast. The Hungarian Kingdom, the Ottoman Empire, and Venice would remain the dominant forces in Croatia until the dawn of the modern era.

The expansion of the Ottoman Empire into the Balkan Peninsula from the fourteenth century onward represented the predominant political dilemma for the whole region. Although the conquest was slow and not without setbacks, for three hundred years the armies of the sultans gradually extended the Ottoman territory northward. The Balkan kingdoms rarely united, had fewer resources to draw from, and suffered from poor lines of communication. Nor did the rivalries between the various defenders help matters, and the Croats soon found themselves on the front line of what seemed an unstoppable military machine emanating from Constantinople. As the Ottoman forces pushed towards Hungary, and eventually Vienna (the seat of Habsburg power), they conquered Bosnia, Serbia, and most of Croatia.

At the Battle of Mohács in 1526, the Hungarian King Louis II (Lajos II) was killed fighting a much stronger Ottoman army. The power vacuum in the wake of his death caused the most serious realignment in Central and Southeastern Europe following the Ottoman conquests. The famous Habsburg family, then a successful dynasty with primarily German holdings, recognized the opportunity unfolding in front of them. When calls for help came from the Hungarian nobility, Habsburg Emperor Ferdinand I (1503–1564) responded by virtually taking over much of Hungary—including parts of Croatia. Croatia was thus incorporated into the Empire and remained under Habsburg rule, with varying degrees of autonomy, until its collapse in 1918.

Though Ferdinand gained impressive amounts of land in 1527, he was forced to defend his capital city of Vienna from besieging Ottoman forces. Ferdinand won, and by 1534, his forces were pushing back the Ottomans. With his throne and lands now secure, Ferdinand's attention was directed at slowly forcing the Ottomans to retreat from Europe. As a result, the Croatian lands were the site of constant warfare until the end of the 1590s, which subsequently limited the economic development of the region and contributed to the depopulation of the border areas.

Vojna Krajina

The *Vojna Krajina*—or Military Frontier as it is known in English—grew into the primary line of defense of the Habsburg lands against further Ottoman conquests. This border covered a large defensible region, stretching from the mountains near the Adriatic Sea up to the plains of Eastern Croatia. Thanks to almost a hundred years of prior conflict, this entire area was largely deserted and to fill the void, the Austrian authorities (since the Habsburg lands became associated with Austria) encouraged settlement by various groups from across the region. Vlachs, Serbs, Croats, and others came to this military frontier and lived as free men in return for occasional military service against the Ottomans. What this meant in practice was that these groups of settlers were left largely to their own devices, and, while free from certain financial responsibilities, they were forced to plunder villages and towns inside the Ottoman Empire for survival. In response, the Ottomans erected a similar system of relying on their inhabitants to pillage the areas under Austrian control, thus creating a system of normalized banditry.

By the 1700s, much of Croatia remained safe from the series of Ottoman incursions, but the Croats themselves still participated in the fighting. Over the years, Austria utilized Croatian soldiers in many of its wars and, as a result, Croats saw action all across the continent.

The Modern Era

The most stunning series of wars, engulfing the entire continent of Europe and realigning the European order, came as a result of Napoleon Bonaparte's success in Revolutionary France. While Croats had fought alongside Austria in each of the wars waged against Napoleon, war finally reached Croatian territory when Napoleon's victory over the Austrians in 1804 resulted in his decision to annex some Austrian territory. Much of modern-day Croatia and Slovenia became incorporated into the Illyrian Provinces and became legally incorporated into France. Though French power never really manifested itself completely in the provinces, French rule persisted until 1813. The most significant inroads made by the French occurred with respect to the legal system and to cultural policy. The French authorities recognized what they called *Slavonian* as an official language (a cluster of Slovenian and Croatian dialects) in the provinces and expressed overtures to more fully develop and standardize this language. When the Austrians finally regained the territory during the chaos of Napoleon's downfall beginning in 1813, they reversed many Napoleonic policies. While it was easy to abolish French as an official language of the provinces, other issues, such as freedom for Jews and the recognition of a Slavic language, persisted after the defeat of France.

The post-Napoleonic era was a period of growing national consciousness in Europe, culminating in the Revolutions of 1848, known as the "Springtime of the Peoples." During this time the Croatian people experienced a national renaissance, which was expressed through art, literature, and political movements. They had been under foreign rule for centuries, and therefore influenced by the cultures of Venice, Budapest, and Vienna (which can still be seen today in various parts of Croatia), but the nineteenth century was notable for the consolidation of Croatian identity and the accompanying political demands within the multi-ethnic Habsburg Empire. Two political tendencies developed during this period which were to have a profound impact on Croatia up through the twentieth century. One was Yugoslavism, the idea that Croatian interests would best be served by uniting with other "South Slavic" peoples (Serbs, Slovenes, Montenegrins, etc.) in order to challenge the domination of the Austrians and Hungarians in the Empire. The second political option was one of complete independence and the creation of a Croatian nation-state. The supporters of both options also sought the unification of Croatian lands which were under separate administration in the Habsburg Empire; the Habsburgs recognized Hungary's historic claims to the Croatian throne and the right to administer most of Croatia from Budapest, while the coastal territories were ruled directly from Vienna after they were wrested from Venetian control during the Napoleonic Wars.

The Habsburgs were faced not only with increasing demands from their multi-ethnic subjects, but also problems of contested authority and administration within the Empire. They had crushed the Hungarian revolutionary movement of 1848 (with help from Croatian Ban Josip Jelačić), but eventually had to negotiate a restructuring of the Empire, which from then on was known as the Austro-Hungarian Empire, or the Dual Monarchy. Howerver, the Croats and other Slavic peoples remained dissatisfied with the compromise between Vienna and Budapest, which left them in a subjugated position under the political formula of Dualism. While the Croatian ruling elite honed their tactics of political struggle within the framework of the Austro-Hungarian parliamentary system, Budapest provoked divisions between Croats and Serbs in the Croatian lands as a way to strengthen Hungarian control. Meanwhile, in neighboring Serbia, the nineteenth century was notable for an ongoing liberation war against the increasingly weak Ottoman Empire. This resulted in a growing Serbian nation-state, which aspired to even greater territorial gains, to be carved from the multi-ethnic empires in the region.

Decades of political conflict centered on who would control the land within Austria-Hungary, leaving open the possibility of reform and more sovereignty for Croats. When a Serbian nationalist assassinated the heir to the throne, Archduke Franz Ferdinand, during a visit to Sarajevo in 1914, Croats lost a major advocate for far-reaching internal reforms. Europe's complex system of alliances forced the Habsburg lands into a global war on the side of the Central Powers (along with Germany, the Ottoman Empire, and initally Italy) against the Entente or Allied Powers (England, France, Russia, Serbia, and eventually the United States). Many had hoped that war would unite the various peoples of the Austro-Hungarian Empire through a common struggle; instead, the outbreak of World War I exacerbated the situation and led to total devastation. By 1918, defeat in war and internal revolutions destroyed the great multi-ethnic Austro-Hungarian, Russian, and Ottoman Empires, transforming the geopolitical landscape of Europe.

The total power vacuum that existed in 1918–19 left the victorious Allies with a host of problems. The realignment of Europe in the wake of the war led to the creation of many small states in place of the former empires. Croatia, threatened by Italian territorial ambitions and optimistic about South Slavic unity, entered into a common state with Serbia on 1 December 1918—first called the Kingdom of Serbs, Croats, and Slovenes, but renamed the Kingdom of Yugoslavia in 1929.

Time would show the dangers inherent in Croatia's inclusion into this multi-national state of Yugoslavia, and how this would increase political tensions to a breaking point. Competing views of what a Yugoslav state should look like gave Yugoslavia few opportunities to prosper during the interwar period (1919–1941). The Croats' Habsburg heritage inspired them to envision a loose confederation as the most desirable form of statehood, while the Serbs thought that a centralized, unitary system was best. Racked by internal tensions, the country ultimately remained unable to properly function by the end of this time period. When the Nazis finally invaded Yugoslavia on 6 April 1941, they found a country weakened by almost twenty years of internal strife. Not surprisingly, in less than a week, Hitler's armies rolled over the Yugoslav forces and achieved total victory. The face of wartime Yugoslavia grew increasingly ugly as Hitler manipulated the local elites for his own purposes and escalated hostilities among the inhabitants of Yugoslavia, which descended into a multi-sided civil war.

Nazi Germany and Fascist Italy established the notorious wartime Ustaša state, run by Ante Pavelić, which proceeded with a campaign of brutality and genocide against all ethnic and political opponents, allegedly in the name of the Croatian people. As World War II progressed, the Ustaša regime alienated many Croats—let alone the Serbs, Roma, and Jews targeted by the Ustaše—and allowed one of the most famous of all Croats, Josip Broz Tito, to emerge from the wartime chaos as the foremost contender for power in Yugoslavia. Combining the rhetoric of a national liberation war with cunning political skills and Western support, Tito's communist-led Partisan movement fought for a multi-ethnic Yugoslavia, and was able to defeat all of the other extreme nationalist and collaborationist forces by 1945. However, the victorious Partisans carried out bloody reprisals against all collaborators, both real and alleged, and mercilessly presecuted all potential political opponents of the new communist regime.

The Communist Yugoslav Era

The renewed Yugoslavia was a federal state of six republics (Slovenia, Croatia, Serbia, Montenegro, Bosnia-Herzegovina, and Macedonia) and two autonomous provinces (Kosovo and Vojvodina) based on the ideological principles of communism. Workers had a prominent role in Tito's state, and Croatia's relatively advanced industrial base finally seemed to provide a chance for prosperity. Although Croatia remained the second most developed Yugoslav republic after Slovenia, political struggles with the central authority in Belgrade hindered Croatians' desire for significant cultural, political, and economic autonomy. Furthermore, thousands of people from Yugoslavia, including a large number of Croats, emigrated because of political repression under the new communist authorities, while thousands of others became seasonal guest workers (*Gastarbeiter*) in neighboring European countries.

In Tito's Yugoslavia, the most decisive event for Croatia came about in 1971, during the so-called Croatian Spring. That year a series of cultural issues came to a head, building from the prior publication of the *Declaration on the Name and Position of the Croatian Literary Language* in 1967, which requested the affirmation of Croatian culture within the state's legal framework. Some of the Croatian intellectual elite protested the impossibility of using the Croatian language as a literary standard in Croatia owing to a politically motivated imposition of the Serbian-permeated official language called Serbo-Croatian. Tito eventually threatened to use armed force in Croatia to calm the situation and then followed up with a widespread purge of the Croatian Communist Party and other organizations which had advocated greater liberalization and democracy in addition to Croatian rights. In

1974, however, Tito approved a new, decentralized constitution that gave the republics greater control over their own affairs. The situation in Croatia then remained calm until the late 1980s.

War Again

Tito's death in 1980 signalled the beginning of the end for the second Yugoslavia, which had, to a large degree, been held together by an amalgam of Marxist ideology and the communist leader's cult of personality. The collapse of communism throughout Eastern and Central Europe a decade later left a political vacuum which in Yugoslavia was filled by nationalist politicians.

The country's catastrophic economic crisis in the 1980s, a result of flawed communist economic policies, narrow republican interests, and mismanaged projects in Yugoslavia's less-developed regions, fueled the nationalist agendas. Once again the internal structure of the state became an issue of utmost importance. Whereas Serbia, under former communist bureaucrat Slobodan Milošević, pushed for greater centralization, the westernmost republics (Croatia and Slovenia) advocated a looser confederal system. Serbs in Croatia, manipulated by Milošević and bombarded by propaganda warning of a return to the violence of World War II, rebelled against control from Zagreb in the summer of 1990. Acts of violence escalated, and by the time Croatia and Slovenia declared independence on 25 June 1991, a full-scale war had essentially broken out. Some Croatian Serbs, backed by the Yugoslav People's Army and various volunteer units from Serbia, carved out their own parastate in the early months of the fighting. War took a particularly ugly turn when each side sought to control ethnically homogeneous territory, that is, an "ethnically clean" area. The dramatic and unsettling war in Croatia eventually moved east to neighboring Bosnia-Herzegovina. The horrors and the human losses brought about by the conflict in Bosnia spurred the international community into action. By 1995, greater U.S. involvement and a series of successful Croatian Army offensives (coordinated with Muslim and Croat forces in Bosnia) changed the balance of power on the battlefield and forced the various sides to agree to a political solution to end the war, known as the Dayton Agreement. In 1998, Croatia peacefully reintegrated the remaining territories occupied by Serb forces. Since that time, Croatia has been able to fruitfully exploit its independence and to seek greater Euro-Atlantic integration. Despite a long history of political and military struggles, and the challenges of overcoming the legacies of the war in the 1990s, Croatia has made considerable strides in creating a stable democracy and taking advantage of its natural and human resources in the twenty-first century.

List of Abbreviations

acc.	accusative case
adj.	adjective
adv.	adverb
aux.	auxiliary form of verb
dat.	dative case
f.	feminine
gen.	genitive case
irr.	irregular
I	imperfective aspect
instru.	instrumental case
lit.	literally
loc.	locative case
m.	masculine
m. anim.	masculine animate
m. inan.	masculine inanimate
n.	noun
neg.	negative
neu.	neuter
nom.	nominative case
P	perfective aspect
pers.	person
pl.	plural
reg.	regular
s.o.	someone
s.th.	something
subj.	subject
sg.	singular
voc.	vocative case

The stressed syllable in polysyllabic words is marked by underlining in all reading sections and vocabulary lists.

Alphabet and Pronunciation Guide

The Alphabet

There are thirty letters in the Croatian alphabet:

Letter	As in	Croatian examples	Meaning
A, a	*a* as in father	antena	antenna
B, b	*b* as in being	brat	brother
C, c	*ts* as in spots	crven	red
Č, č	*ch* as in cheese	četka	brush
Ć, ć	*tch* as in gotcha	ćup	jar
D, d	*d* as in dad	dobar	good
Dž, dž	*j* as in enjoy	džem	jam
Đ, đ	*j* as in jeep	đak	pupil
E, e	*e* as in pen	ekonomija	economy
F, f	*f* as in fission	frula	pipes
G, g	*g* as in grab	gladan	hungry
H, h	*h* as in hope	hrana	food
I, i	*i* as in ski	ići	to go
J, j	*y* as in yesterday	jezero	lake
K, k	*k* as in break	krava	cow
L, l	*l* as in love	led	ice
LJ, lj	*l* as in value	ljuljati	to swing
M, m	*m* as in mother	majmun	monkey
N, n	*n* as in no	nebo	sky
NJ, nj	*ny* as in canyon	njuška	snout
O, o	*o* as in orange	otac	father
P, p	*p* as in opera	pisati	to write
R, r	*r* as in round	ruka	hand
S, s	*s* as in simple	soba	room
Š, š	*sh* as in sheet	šešir	hat
T, t	*t* as in start	trava	grass
U, u	*oo* as in food	ulica	street
V, v	*v* as in view	vlak	train
Z, z	*z* as in zip	zid	wall
Ž, ž	*su* as in measure	žaba	frog

Script

The Croatian alphabet uses Latin script but with several distinctive characters:

č š ć ž đ

There are also several compound letters which are, however, pronounced as single sounds:

dž lj nj

You will encounter these letters frequently when using Croatian. Note also that the letters **p**, **t**, and **k** are not aspirated (followed by a rush of air) as is the case when they appear in the stressed position in a word in English.

One thing that makes learning to pronounce, read, and write Croatian simple is that each letter signifies a single sound. Spelling words in Croatian is easier than in English, because you pronounce each written letter.

Stress

Each word has one accent with the exception of some small words which share an accent with a longer neighboring word. In longer words a secondary accent is sometimes present. The accent may fall on any syllable but the last one (only a few words are exceptions to this rule). Therefore, in a two-syllable word the accent is on the first syllable.

In some words the length of the accented syllable may affect the meaning. Note that **r** has a dual purpose as both a consonant and as a vowel and can thus occasionally carry the accent.

There are four different types of accents in Croatian but for practical purposes it's enough to simply learn on which syllable the accent falls. The stressed syllable is marked by underlining in the reading sections and vocabulary lists. Normally, accents are omitted in writing. In this chapter and Lesson 1, underlining in *all* polysyllabic words marks the syllable where the stress falls, but in subsequent lessons only the words that have *more than two syllables* will be marked because in a two-syllable word, the first syllable is almost always the accented one.

Vježba 1.1/Exercise 1.1

Practice pronouncing the following words:

čamac boat
đurđica lily of the valley
džungla jungle
jesen fall, autumn
kino movie theater

kuća house
ljubav love
mlijeko milk
prozor window
računalo computer

šapat whisper
slobodan free
vrt garden
zadatak task
žut yellow

Lekcija 1
Tko je Marijana?

Lesson 1
Who is Marijana?

Lekcija 1: Tko je Marijana?

Mjesto: Zračna luka, Zagreb.

Darko: Dobar dan! Jeste li Vi Marijana?

Marijana: Da, ja sam Marijana Tomich. A Vi, tko ste Vi?

Darko: Ja sam Darko Tomić, Vaš hrvatski rođak.

Marijana: Konačno da se upoznamo! Drago mi je.

Darko: I meni! Kako ste?

Marijana: Hvala, odlično.

Darko: Govorite li hrvatski?

Marijana: Ne baš dobro. A kako se Vi zovete?

Ivan: Zovem se Ivan Dvornik.

Darko: Ivan je moj prijatelj. On je student kao i ja.

Marijana: Drago mi je. Svi smo mladi. Molim Vas, možemo li prijeći „na ti"?

Ivan: Naravno! Znam da si Amerikanka, ali ne znam jesi li i ti studentica?

Marijana: Ne, nisam studentica. Ja već radim. Ja sam ekonomistica.

Ivan: Zanimljivo! Jesi li tu kao ekonomist ili kao turist?

Marijana: I jedno i drugo!

Lesson 1: Who is Marijana?

Place: Airport, Zagreb.

Darko:	Good afternoon! Are you Marijana?
Marijana:	Yes, I am Marijana Tomich. And you, who are you?
Darko:	I am Darko Tomić, your Croatian cousin.
Marijana:	Finally we've become acquainted! Pleased to meet you.
Darko:	So am I. How are you?
Marijana:	Great, thank you.
Darko:	Do you speak Croatian?
Marijana:	Not so well. And what is your name?
Ivan:	My name is Ivan Dvornik.
Darko:	Ivan is my friend. He is also a student like me.
Marijana:	Pleased to meet you. We are all young. Please, can we call each other by [our] names [use the informal address]?
Ivan:	Of course! I know that you are American, but I don't know whether you are also a student.
Marijana:	No, I am not a student. I already work. I am an economist.
Ivan:	Interesting! Are you here as an economist or a tourist?
Marijana:	Both!

Vocabulary

All nouns have gender in Croatian. In these glossaries, *m.* stands for masculine gender, *f.* for feminine, and *n.* for neuter. In multisyllabic words, underlining indicates where the stress falls in a word.

a and, but
Amerikanka *f.*/**Amerikanac** *m.* American
baš really, exactly, quite
da yes
dan *m.* day
dobar good
dobro well
drago mi je I am pleased [to meet you]
ekonomist *m.*/**ekonomistica** *f.* economist
hrvatski Croatian
hvala thank you
i and
ili or
jedno i drugo both
kako how
kako ste how are you
kao like
konačno finally
meni to me; **i meni** me too
mjesto *neu.* place
mladi *pl.* young
moj my
molim vas please
„na ti" [to use] informal address
naravno of course
ne no, not
odlično excellent
prijatelj *m.* friend
rođak *m.* cousin
student *m.*/ **studentica** *f.* student
tko who
tu here
turist *m.* tourist
već already
zanimljivo interesting
zračna luka *f.* airport

Verb List

For all verbs, the present tense forms for the first person singular and third person plural will be supplied in parentheses. In the case of irregular verbs, the third person singular will also be supplied. All other forms can be derived according to the explanations found in the section on verbs in the Grammar. (Again, underlining indicates where the stress falls in multisyllabic words.)

biti to be *(see charts in Grammar section below)*
govoriti (govorim, govore) to speak
moći (*irr.*: **mogu**, **može**, **mogu**) to be able to, can
prijeći (prijeđem, prijeđu) to cross, to switch
raditi (radim, rade) to work
upoznati se (upoznam se, upoznaju se) to get acquainted
znati (znam, znaju) to know

zvati (**zovem**, **zovu**) to call
zvati se (**zovem se**, **zovu se**) to be called

Greetings

Dobar dan! Good day! *(used from approximately 10 a.m. until evening hours)*
Dobro jutro! Good morning!
Dobra večer! Good evening! *(used after approximately 7 p.m.)*
Laku noć! Good night!
Doviđenja! Good-bye!
Bok! Hi! *(informal)*
Vidimo se! See you! *(informal)*

Grammar

1. Noun gender

In Croatian even inanimate objects have gender. Masculine nouns typically end in a consonant (with several exceptions, one of which is the commonly used word **auto** for *car*), feminine nouns mostly end in a vowel (a smaller group of feminine nouns ending in a consonant is discussed later in the book), and neuter nouns end in **-o** or **-e**.

luk*a* *f.* port **telefo*n*** *m.* telephone **sel*o*** *neu.* village

2. Personal pronouns

As you noticed in the dialogue, Croatian distinguishes between formal (**Vi**) and informal (**ti**) address. The formal address is always capitalized in writing. It agrees with the second person plural. Furthermore, the third person plural has three pronouns which indicate gender. Croatian thus has a total of ten personal pronouns:

person	singular	plural
1st	**ja** I	**mi** we
2nd	**ti** you	**vi** (**Vi**) you
3rd *m.*	**on** he	**oni** they
3rd *f.*	**ona** she	**one** they
3rd *neu.*	**ono** it	**ona** they

When referring to a group of females or objects that are feminine in gender, the pronoun **one** *they* should be used. Similarly, if one is referring to a group of objects that are neuter in gender or to a group of children, the pronoun

ona *they* (which looks exactly like third person singular feminine) should be used. Use **oni** *they* if the group is masculine or mixed in gender.

You will notice later that Croatian often omits personal pronouns in the subject position because necessary information such as number and gender is conveyed by the verb ending.

3. Possessive pronouns

Possessive pronouns behave like adjectives in terms of their form. Like other types of adjectives in Croatian, the possessive pronouns refer to the noun they modify and agree with it in gender and number. They can be placed right before the noun or they can be a part of the predicate, i.e., they can follow the verb **biti** *to be*:

Tu je *moja* knjiga. Here is *my* book.
Knjiga je *moja*. The book is *mine*.

If you address a person with **Vi**, you will also have to use the *formal* possessive forms **Vaš**, **Vaša**, etc. Just like feminine nouns, feminine forms of possessive pronouns end in **-a**, while neuter ones end in **-o**, or **-e**. If the last consonant is **-j** or **-š**, the neuter possessives end in **-e**, otherwise they end in **-o**. Note that *her* has two possible forms.

Singular Possesive Pronouns

	masculine	feminine	neuter
my	**moj**	**moja**	**moje**
your	**tvoj**	**tvoja**	**tvoje**
his	**njegov**	**njegova**	**njegovo**
her	**njezin/njen**	**njezina/njena**	**njezino/njeno**
its	**njegov**	**njegova**	**njegovo**
our	**naš**	**naša**	**naše**
your	**vaš (Vaš)**	**vaša (Vaša)**	**vaše (Vaše)**
their	**njihov**	**njihova**	**njihovo**

4. Verbs

While English has several ways of expressing the present tense (*you are reading*; *you read*), Croatian has only one present tense. This tense, however, has six forms. There are several verb conjugation types in Croatian, to be discussed later.

The following are present-tense conjugation patterns of some verbs from this lesson.

raditi (to work)

singular	plural
rad**im** I work	rad**imo** we work
rad**iš** you work	rad**ite** you work
rad**i** he works	rad**e** they work

znati (to know)

singular	plural
zna**m** I know	zna**mo** we know
zna**š** you know	zna**te** you know
zn**a** he knows	zn**aju** they know

zvati (to call)

singular	plural
zove**m** I call	zove**mo** we call
zove**š** you call	zove**te** you call
zov**e** he calls	zov**u** they call

If we take the third person singular (here: **radi** *he works*, **zna** *he knows*, **zove** *he calls*) as the base form, we add the endings **-m** and **-š** to form the first and second person singular respectively and **-mo** and **-te** to form the first and second person plural. To form the third person plural, we drop the endings for the third person singular and replace them as follows:

replace:	**3rd *pers. sg.* endings**	**with:**	**3rd *pers. pl.* endings**
	-i	→	**-e**
	-a	→	**-aju**
	-e	→	**-u**

As is clear from the verb **zvati** *to call*, other changes can occur during conjugation, but at the initial stage it is best to memorize these stem-changing verbs individually.

5. Irregular verbs *biti* (to be) and *moći* (to be able to)

Because the verbs **biti** *to be* and **moći** *to be able to* are irregular, they will be listed separately.

moći (to be able to)

singular	plural
ja mogu I am able to	**mi možemo** we are able to
ti možeš you are able to	**vi možete** you are able to
on može he is able to	**oni mogu** they are

Biti *to be* has two forms: long and short.

biti (to be)

long form		short form	
singular	**plural**	**singular**	**plural**
ja jesam I am	**mi jesmo** we are	**ja sam** I am	**mi smo** we are
ti jesi you are	**vi jeste** you are	**ti si** you are	**vi ste** you are
on jest he is	**oni jesu** they are	**on je** he is	**oni su** they are

The long forms of **biti** are used in the initial position in a sentence for emphasis or in one-word responses and can be used without a pronoun.

Long:

Jesmo turisti.	We ARE tourists *(as opposed to something else).*
Jesam.	I am./[I] have done it.
Jesu dobro.	They ARE well *(as opposed to not well).*

The short forms of **biti** are normally not accented. They can appear at the beginning of a sentence only if they are preceded by a noun, a pronoun, or some other accented word such as a question word or an adverb.

Short:

Tko ste Vi?	Who are you?
Mi smo turisti.	We are tourists.
Student sam.	I am a student.
Dobro su.	They are well.

In order to form a question with the verb *to be*, insert the interrogative particle **li** right after the long form of the verb and place the pronoun after **li**.

Forming questions with biti (to be)

biti + interrogative **li**

singular	plural
jesam li am I?	**jesmo li** are we?
jesi li are you?	**jeste li** are you?
je li is he/she/it?	**jesu li** are they?

The third person singular is an exception: it uses **je li** (the short form) in the interrogative form and not ***jest li.** (For more on interrogative forms see **7. Interrogative forms** below.)

Jeste li Vi turist?	Are you a tourist?
Jesu li oni turisti?	Are they tourists?
Jesi li ti student?	Are you a student?
Je li on Amerikanac?	Is he an American?

6. Negation of Verbs

Negation is done by inserting the word **ne** immediately before the verb.

Ja *ne* radim.	I *don't* work.
Oni *ne* znaju.	They *don't* know.

While normally negation is written separately from the verb, in the case of **biti**, it is joined together with the verb.

negation of biti (to be)

singular	plural
ja nisam I am not	**mi nismo** we are not
ti nisi you are not	**vi niste** you are not
on nije he is not	**oni nisu** they are not

The following are sample affirmative and negative sentences using the verb **biti** *to be*:

***Je li on* Amerikanac?**	*Is he* an American?
Ne, *on nije* Amerikanac.	No, he *is not* an American.
***On je* Hrvat.**	*He is* a Croat.

***Jesi li ti* student?**	*Are you* a student?
***Jesam. Ja sam* student.**	Yes, *I am. I am* a student.
***Ja nisam* ekonomist.**	*I am not* an economist.

7. Interrogative forms

Questions can be formed in several ways.

- Use a rising intonation in voice (the simplest way to form a question):
  Vi ste turist? ↑ You are a tourist? ↑
- Use a question word:
  ***Tko* ste Vi?** *Who* are you?
  ***Kako* se zovete?** *What* is your name? [*lit:* How are you called?]
- **Verb + li**: To ask a *yes-no question*, insert the interrogative particle **li** immediately after the verb which is placed as the initial word in the sentence:

Jeste li Vi turist?	Are you a tourist?
Radi li on?	Does he work? Is he working?
Znate li?	Do you know?
Govore li hrvatski?	Do they speak Croatian?
Je li on radi?	Does he/she/it work? Is he/she/it working?
Je li radi?	Does he/she/it work? Is he/she/it working?

Note that the use of the pronoun is optional (especially with verbs other than **biti** *to be*). When used, the pronoun is placed after the particle **li**. The particle **li** never carries an accent, unlike some other one-syllable words including pronouns.

- Use the phrase **da li**, which serves as a universal question marker to ask a *yes*-no question and replaces the English words *are, is, do, does, was, were,* etc. **Da li** never changes its form.

Da li ste Vi ekonomist?	Are you an economist?
Da li on radi?	Does he work?/Is he working?
Da li radi?	Does he/she/it work?/Is he/she/it working?

The word order with **da li** in combination with the verb **biti** *to be* is slightly different. It requires the short form of **biti** to be placed right after **da li** as in the first example sentence above:

Da li	+	form of **biti**	+	pron.	+	rest of question
Da li	+	**ste**	+	**Vi**	+	**ekonomist?**

Are you an economist?

Although **da li** is encountered frequently enough in colloquial speech, standard Croatian shows a clear preference for the **verb + li** format.

Exercises

Vježba 1.2

A. Fill in the most logical answers in the blanks provided.
Example: **Dobar dan. Tko ste Vi? Ja sam Marko**.

1. _______ dan. Jeste li Vi Marijana? _______, ja sam Marijana.
2. Radim kao ekonomist. Jesi li ti ekonomist? _______________.
3. ____ ste Vi?
4. Ja sam ________ prijatelj.
5. Kako se Vi _________?
6. ___________se Mladen. A kako se on___________?

B. Fill in the blanks in the following dialogue using this lesson's dialogue as an example.

Mislav: Dobar dan. Ja sam Mislav. Tko ste _______?
Maja: Dobar _______. Ja sam Maja. Drago_______je.

Mislav: Tko je on?
Maja: On je _______hrvatski rođak.
Drago: Dobar dan. _______ se zovete?
Mislav: Zovem _______Mislav.
Drago: Jeste li student ili radite?
Mislav: Ja već radim. _______student.

Vježba 1.3 Mark the correct gender for the noun provided and translate into English.

Example: **priča** *f.* **story**

1. zračna luka __ ___________
2. prijatelj __ ___________
3. Amerikanka __ ___________
4. rođak __ ___________
5. mjesto __ ___________

Vježba 1.4 Fill in the correct forms of the verb **biti** *to be* or personal pronouns below.

1. Ja ___
2. Mi ___
3. __ je
4. __ si
5. Oni __
6. Vi __
7. On __
8. __ nisam
9. __ nije
10. Ti ____ (*negative*)
11. __ smo
12. Vi _____ (*negative*)

Vježba 1.5 Translate into Croatian:

A.

1. What is your name?

____

2. Are you a student or a tourist?

____

3. He is my friend.

____

4. Are you American?

____

5. He doesn't know whether I am a student.

____

6. They know that you work.

____

7. I am pleased (to meet you).

____

8. We are all young. I am your Croatian cousin.

____

B. My name is Petra. I am young. I am not American. I speak Croatian. I am a student and I don't work. John is my friend. He is a student like myself. He speaks English [engleski].

____

____

____

____

____

____

Vježba 1.6 Determine whether the italicized word is an adjective, noun, or verb.

1. Znam da si *Amerikanka*. ______________
2. Ja sam *dobar* student. ______________
3. Ja već *radim* kao ekonomist. ______________
4. *Knjiga* je moja. ______________
5. *Radi* li on kao ekonomist? ______________

Vježba 1.7 Practice Croatian by answering the following questions.
Example: **Tko ste Vi? Ja sam Darko**.

1. Jeste li Vi turist? ____________________________
2. Govorite li engleski? ____________________________
3. Radite li već? ____________________________
4. Kako se zovete? ____________________________
5. Kako ste? ____________________________

Lekcija 2
Marijana, Darko i Ivan razgovaraju

Lesson 2
Marijana, Darko and Ivan talk

Lekcija 2: Marijana, Darko i Ivan razgovaraju

Mjesto: zračna luka, Zagreb. Nastavak.

Prvi dio

Darko: Marijana, kako si?

Marijana: Dobro, ali stalno žurim i uvijek radim. Amerika je takva.

Darko: Hrvatska je odlična zemlja za odmor.

Marijana: Odlična zemlja za ... što? Ne razumijem. Molim te, možeš li ponoviti?

Darko: Za odmor. A možeš i raditi – ako baš hoćeš.

Marijana: Darko, ti se šališ!

Ivan: Darko se voli šaliti. To je njegova dobra osobina.

Marijana: Slažem se!

Ivan: Ti odlično govoriš hrvatski jezik.

Marijana: Ne govorim baš dobro i pišem loše. Moji roditelji su Hrvati, ali ja sam i Hrvatica i Amerikanka. Zapravo Bostonka.

Ivan: Boston! To je moj omiljeni grad!

Marijana: Da, oduvijek živim tamo. A gdje ti živiš?

Ivan: Ja sam Dalmatinac i vrlo sam sretan što je tako. Naša obala je lijepa. Sada sam student i, otkako živim ovdje, pomalo sam i Zagrepčanin.

Drugi dio

Marijana: Govoriš li engleski?

Ivan: Nažalost, vrlo loše. Hrvatska je sigurno zemlja kamo često putuješ?

Marijana: Ne, nećeš vjerovati, ali ovo je prvi put da sam ovdje.

Darko: Marijana je umorna i pospana, a sigurno i gladna.

Marijana: Zaista! Vrlo sam žedna i gladna, ali nekako nisam pospana. Baš lijepo što ste ovdje. Sada je sve lako!

Ivan: Ono je moj auto. Onaj veliki plavi. Ali gdje su moji ključevi?

Darko: Strašno!

Lesson 2: Marijana, Darko and Ivan talk

Place: Airport, Zagreb. Continuation.

Part 1

Darko:	Marijana, how are you?
Marijana:	Fine, but I am constantly rushing and always working. America is that way.
Darko:	Croatia is an excellent country for a vacation.
Marijana:	A great country for ... what? I don't understand, can you repeat, please?
Darko:	For a vacation. And you can work too—if you really want to.
Marijana:	Darko, you are joking!
Ivan:	Darko likes to joke. That is his good trait.
Marijana:	I agree!
Ivan:	You speak Croatian excellently.
Marijana:	I don't speak so well and I write badly. My parents are Croatian, but I am both Croatian and American. In fact, a Bostonian.
Ivan:	Boston! That is my favorite city!
Marijana:	Yes, I've always lived there. And where do you live?
Ivan:	I'm a Dalmatian and I am very happy that is so. Our coast is beautiful. I am a student now and since I started living here I've become a bit of a Zagreb dweller too.

Part II

Marijana:	Do you speak English?
Ivan:	Unfortunately, quite poorly. Croatia is probably a country to which you travel often?
Marijana:	No, you won't believe it, but this is my first time here.
Darko:	Marijana is tired and sleepy, and probably hungry too.
Marijana:	True! I'm very thirsty and hungry, but somehow I'm not sleepy. So nice that you're here. Now everything is easy!
Ivan:	That is my car. That big blue one. But where are my keys?
Darko:	[This is] terrible!

Marijana: **Što sada?**

Ivan: **Oprostite! Nije moguće! Darko, hoćemo li zvati taksi?**

Darko: **Ključevi su tu. Nešto si danas zbunjen, pogotovo popodne. Pitam se zašto! Mislim da počinje jedna lijepa priča.**

Ivan: **Marijana, slažem se, on se uvijek šali.**

Darko: **Šala i istina često idu zajedno!**

Marijana:	What now?
Ivan:	I'm sorry! This is not possible! Darko, shall we call a cab?
Darko:	The keys are here. You seem to be confused today, especially this afternoon. I wonder why! I think a lovely story is beginning.
Ivan:	Marijana, I agree, he is always joking.
Darko:	Joke[s] and truth often go together!

Vocabulary

ako if
ali but
Amerika America
auto car
Bostonka *f.* Bostonian
često often
Dalmatinac *m.*/**Dalmatinka** *f.*/ **Dalmatinci** *pl.* person from Dalmatia
danas today
dobar *m.*/**dobra** *f.*/**dobro** *neu.* good
dobro well
gdje where
gladan *m.*/ **gladna** *f.*/**gladno** *neu.* hungry
grad city
Hrvatska Croatia
Hrvat *m.*/**Hrvati** *pl.* Croat
Hrvatica *f.*/**Hrvatice** *pl.* Croat
istina true, truth
jezik language
kamo where to (also **kuda**; both with verbs of motion)
ključ key
lako easy
lijep *m.*/**lijepa** *f.*/**lijepo** *neu.* beautiful, lovely
lijepo nicely, beautifully
loše badly
moguće possible
nastavak continuation
nažalost regrettably, unfortunately
nešto something, somehow
njegov *m.*/**njegova** *f.*/**njegovo** *neu.* his
odličan *m.*/**odlična** *f.*/**odlično** *neu.* excellent
odlično excellently
odmor vacation, rest, break
oduvijek always, since long ago
omiljen *m.*/**omiljena** *f.*/**omiljeno** *neu.* favorite
osobina trait
ovaj *m.* this
ovdje here
plav *m.*/**plava** *f.*/**plavo** *neu.* blue
početak beginning
pogotovo especially
pomalo a little bit
popodne afternoon
pospan *m.*/**pospana** *f.*/**pospano** *neu.* sleepy
priča story
prvi put first time
roditelj parent
sada now
sigurno definitely, surely
sretan *m.*/**sretna** *f.*/**sretno** *neu.* happy
stalno constantly
strašno terrible
svi, sve all
šala joke
što what, that
tako that way, so
taksi cab
takav *m.*/**takva** *f.*/**takvo** *neu.* such
tamo (also **ondje**) there
tek only, barely
umoran *m.*/**umorna** *f.*/**umorno** *neu.* tired
uvijek always
velik *m.*/**velika** *f.*/**veliko** *neu.* big
vrlo very
za for
Zagrepčanin *m.*/**Zagrepčanka** *f.*/**Zagrepčani** *pl.* inhabitant of Zagreb
zaista indeed, really
zajedno together
zapravo actually, as a matter of fact

zašto why
zbunjen *m.*/**zbunjena** *f.*/**zbunjeno** *neu.* confused
zemlja country
žedan *m.*/**žedna** *f.*/**žedno** *neu.* thirsty

Verb List

From this lesson on, all verbs will be marked with *I* for imperfective and *P* for perfective; two verb aspects are explained in detail in Lesson 11. To avoid mistakes, for the time being remember only that verbs marked with *I* indicate a true present action. Every time you want to express something happening now, use verbs from this group. Verbs marked with *P* have to be used in conjunction with some other verb and refer to the future or the past. Thus, you can't say ***Oprostim ti** (in the sense *I forgive you),* but you can say **Mogu ti oprostiti** *I can forgive you*, regardless of whether the actual act takes place two minutes or two months from the point when the statement was made.

htjeti (*irr.*: **hoću**, **hoće**, **hoće**; *neg.*: **neću**, **neće**, **neće**) to wish, to want
ići (*I* **idem**, **idu**) to go
misliti (*I* **mislim**, **misle**) to think
oprostiti (*P* **oprostim**, **oproste**) to forgive, to excuse
pisati (*I* **pišem**, **pišu**) to write
pitati se (*I* **pitam se**, **pitaju se**) to ask oneself, to wonder
pitati (*I* **pitam**, **pitaju**) to ask
počinjati (*I* **počinjem**, **počinju**) to begin
ponoviti (*P* **ponovim**, **ponove**) to repeat
putovati (*I* **putujem**, **putuju**) to travel
razgovarati (*I* **razgovaram**, **razgovaraju**) to talk
razumjeti (*I* **razumijem**, **razumiju**) to understand
slagati se (*I* **slažem se**, **slažu se**) to agree
šaliti se (*I* **šalim se**, **šale se**) to joke
vjerovati (*I* **vjerujem**, **vjeruju**) to believe
voljeti (*I* **volim**, **vole**) to love, to like
živjeti (*I* **živim**, **žive**) to live
žuriti (se) (*I* **žurim**, **žure**) to rush

Useful Expressions

Ne razumijem. I don't understand.
Molim te/Molim Vas. Please.
Molim te/Vas možeš/možete li ponoviti? Can you please repeat?
Oprosti(te)! Excuse me!
Nije moguće! It's not possible!
Slažem se! I agree!
Baš lijepo što ste ovdje. It's so nice you're here.
Kako si/ste? How are you?
Dobro! [I'm] Well!
Odlično! Excellent!
Tako-tako! So-so!
Loše! Bad. *(Not great.)*
A ti/Vi? And what about you?
Govoriš li/govorite li engleski? Do you speak English?

Grammar

1. Cases: Nominative

Instead of using word order and prepositions as English does to indicate how one noun relates to another in a sentence, Croatian uses case endings. There are seven cases in Croatian: nominative, genitive, accusative, dative, locative, vocative, and instrumental. They change the endings of nouns, adjectives, pronouns, and some numbers. Dictionaries always provide entries in the nominative, the "basic" case that expresses the subject in the sentence. Almost all the nouns, adjectives, and pronouns we have encountered thus far have been in the nominative case.

2. Nominative plural of nouns

For nouns ending in a consonant, the nominative plural ending is **-i**. This category contains predominantly *masculine* nouns and a handful of feminine nouns that end in a consonant (called *zero-ending feminine*), which need to be memorized individually. Zero-ending feminine nouns take feminine adjectival forms.

singular	plural	translation
roditelj *m.*	**roditelji**	parents
student *m.*	**studenti**	students
noć *f.*	**noći**	nights

For nouns ending in **-a**, the plural ending is **-e**. This category contains most of the *feminine* nouns, but also a few masculine ones (such as terms of endearment and a few others). Masculine nouns ending in **-a** take adjectives with masculine endings.

singular	plural	translation
kuća *f.*	**kuće**	houses
knjiga *f.*	**knjige**	books
tata *m.*	**tate**	dads

Neuter nouns all end in **-a** in the nominative plural:

singular	plural	translation
pitanje *neu.*	**pitanja**	questions
pismo *neu.*	**pisma**	letters

There is a very small subgroup of neuter nouns which add **-en** in the plural, and the two most important and frequently used examples from this group are:

singular	plural	translation
vrijeme *neu.*	**vremena**	times
ime *neu.*	**imena**	names

Additional rules for forming the plural of masculine nouns.
There are, however, a few other changes that need to be discussed in relation to masculine nouns.

One of these changes affects masculine nouns ending in **-k, -g,** or **-h**. When the nominative plural **-i** is added, these consonants change into **-c**, **-z**, **-s,** respectively. Thus:

singular	plural	translation
pjesni*k* *m.*	**pjesni*c*i**	poets
etnolo*g* *m.*	**etnolo*z*i**	ethnologists
ora*h* *m.*	**ora*s*i**	walnuts

If the last consonant is **-c** or **-k** and is preceded by **-a**, this vowel, the so called *fleeting -a*, will disappear when the plural ending is added. There are also a few other nouns in which *fleeting -a* appears in endings other than **-ac** and **-ak**.

singular	plural	translation
Amerikan*ac* *m.*	**Amerikanci**	Americans
star*ac* *m.*	**starci**	old men
p*a*s *m.*	**psi**	dogs

Masculine nouns ending in **-ak** are subject to the first and second of these rules and also to the third rule which requires dropping of **-t** in the **-tc** combination:[1]

Forming the Plural of Masculine Nouns Ending in –ak and -ac

m. sg.	add -i	drop fleeting-a	k → c before -i	drop –t in -tc combo	
zadat*ak*	**zadat*a*ki**	**zadatki**	**zada*tc*i**	**zadaci**	tasks
stav*ak*	**stav*a*ki**	**stavki**	**stav*c*i** entries *(as in a chart)*		
prav*ac*	**prav*a*ci**	**pravci** directions			

The next group of masculine nouns in plural comprises *monosyllabic words* which add **-ov** or **-ev** before the plural ending **-i**. With very few exceptions that will have to be memorized individually (most notably **dan**, **dani** meaning *day, days*), one-syllable masculine nouns add one of the following two syllables, while multisyllabic nouns do not:

-ov is inserted when the noun ends in a *hard consonant*
-ev is inserted when the noun ends in a *soft consonant.*

soft consonants
–č, –ć, –dž, –đ, –š, –ž, –lj, –nj, –j, –c

singular	plural	translation
muž *m.*	**muževi**	husbands
grad *m.*	**gradovi**	cities
vlak *m.*	**vlakovi**	trains
ključ *m.*	**ključevi**	keys

1. Owing to historical circumstances, Croatian orthography and lexicography are still coming to terms with certain aspects of the language. As this volume goes to print, the Council for Standardization of the Croatian language has made a recommendation to discontinue implementation of this rule. However, a vast majority of native speakers and publications continue to apply it.

Masculine nouns ending in **-lac** discard the **-lac** in nominative plural and add **–oci**.

nom. sg.	***nom. pl.***
spasi*lac* *m.* rescuer	**spasi*oci*** recuers
roni*lac* *m.* diver	**roni*oci*** divers

The last group of masculine nouns concerns *words for certain nationalities and ethnic groups* and *inhabitants of certain cities*. Nouns that have the ending **-in** in the singular will lose the final **-in** when they add endings for the plural:

singular	**plural**	**translation**
Zagrepčanin	**Zagrepčani**	inhabitants of Zagreb
Splićanin	**Splićani**	inhabitants of Split
Srbin*	**Srbi**	Serbs

*Some of the nouns indicating nationality (such as **Srbin/Srbi**) do not conform to the rule mentioned above which requires that monosyllabic masculine nouns in the plural add **-ov** or **–ev**. Here are a few examples:

Čeh/Česi	**Grk/Grci**	**Rus/Rusi**
Czech/Czechs	Greek/Greeks	Russian/Russians

3. Verbs

In this lesson we have encountered one irregular verb, **htjeti** *to want*, that has the same form for both third person singular and plural. We have also encountered verbs such as **pisati** *to write* and **slagati se** *to agree* that have changes in the verb stem as well as in the endings. They essentially belong to the same *e-group* of verbs (according to the third person singular ending). Note also that **slagati se** is used here as a reflexive verb (see **3.2** below) and that the particle **se** is the same for all persons.

htjeti (to want)

singular	**plural**
hoću I want	**hoćemo** we want
hoćeš you want	**hoćete** you want
hoće he wants	**hoće** they want

pisati (to write)		**slagati se** (to agree)	
singular	**plural**	**singular**	**plural**
pišem I write	**pišemo** we write	**slažem se** I agree	**slažemo se** we agree
pišeš you write	**pišete** you write	**slažeš se** you agree	**slažete se** you agree
piše he writes	**pišu** they write	**slaže se** he agrees	**slažu se** they agree

3.1. Verb Negation

As explained in Lesson 1, verbs are negated by simply inserting the negative particle **ne** right before the verb. It is spelled as a separate word except for a few cases, such as the verb **biti** *to be* (see Lesson 1), **imati** *to have* (see Lesson 4) and **htjeti** *to wish*:[2]

Affirmative: htjeti (to want)		**Negative: ne htjeti** (to not want)	
singular	**plural**	**singular**	**plural**
hoću I want	**hoćemo** we want	**neću** I don't want	**nećemo** we don't want
hoćeš you want	**hoćete** you want	**nećeš** you don't want	**nećete** you don't want
hoće he wants	**hoće** they want	**neće** he doesn't want	**neće** they don't want

Oni *ne govore* engleski. They *don't speak* English.
Ti *ne radiš* kao ekonomist. You *don't work* as an economist.

BUT

Ja *nisam* student. I *am not* a student.
Oni *nisu* ekonomisti. They *are not* economists.
***Nećeš* vjerovati!** You *won't* believe it! [*lit.*: You *don't want to* believe it!]
***Neću* žuriti.** I *won't* rush. [*lit.:* I *don't wish* to rush.]

Unlike English, Croatian verbs can be negated more than once by using *two or more negative words (double negation)* in a sentence. In English multiple negation is considered substandard, but in Croatian it is obligatory. Thus a sentence like **On ništa ne razumije** translates literally as **He doesn't understand nothing*. The standard English translation would be *He doesn't understand anything.*

Here are the most common negative pronouns:

Positive Pronouns		**Negative Pronouns**	
netko	somebody	**nitko**	nobody
nešto	something	**ništa**	nothing
negdje	somewhere	**nigdje**	nowhere

2. The recommendation of the the Council for Standardization of the Croatian language is to spell **neću** and other forms of **ne htjeti** separately (i.e., **ne ću**, **ne ćeš**, etc.), as was done in the period before Croatian adopted certain aspects of Serbian orthography owing to political circumstances. The vast majority of the population, however, still adheres to the spelling indicated above, which became prevalent in the course of the twentieth century.

Positive Pronouns		Negative Pronouns	
nekamo, nekuda *(with verbs of motion)*	somewhere	**nikamo, nikuda** *(with verbs of motion)*	nowhere
nekada	at some time, once	**nikada**	never
nekako	somehow, in some way	**nikako**	in no way

Ključevi su tu negdje.	The keys are somewhere here.
Mi ne možemo ništa.	We can't do anything.
Nitko nije tu.	Nobody is here.
On nikada nikamo ne putuje.	He never travels anywhere.
Ovdje nitko nikada ništa ne zna.	Nobody ever knows anything here.

3.2. Reflexive verbs

Reflexive verbs can have several functions. As the word *reflexive* suggests, quite often the action of these verbs refers back to the subject. Such are most of the verbs having to deal with personal hygiene, e.g., to wash *oneself.* The reflexive particle **se** is the same for all persons.

prati se (to wash oneself)

singular	plural
perem se I wash myself	**peremo se** we wash ourselves
pereš se you wash yourself	**perete se** you wash yourselves
pere se he washes himself	**peru se** they wash themselves

While some verbs are always reflexive (e.g., **šaliti se**, *to joke*: **Mi se ne šalimo.** *We are not joking.*), others can be both reflexive and regular. For instance, the verb **pitati** *to ask (somebody)* can also be reflexive **pitati se** *to ask oneself, to wonder.*

Reflexive verbs can involve another participant and then express *reciprocal* activity:

Mi se slažemo.	We agree. *(implying: with you or with each other)*
Volimo se.	We love one another.

Word order and *se*: Se can never appear in the initial position in the sentence. It either follows a noun or a pronoun or, if there is no noun or pronoun, it is placed after the verb or adverb. In questions, it follows the question word or the particle **li**.

Se is only one of many Croatian short words known as *clitics.*

On se ne šali.	He is not joking.
Sada se ne šali.	He is not joking now.

Zovem se Goran.	My name is Goran.
Je li se oni vole?	Do they love one another?
Kako se ona zove?	What is her name?

If a verb does not have **se**, you can add **se** and put the verb in the third person singular. This meaning is similar to English *one*: somebody does the action but you're not saying who. This is often used to express a *general condition or situation.*

Ne može se tako raditi.	One can't work that way.
Nikada se ne zna.	One never knows.

Exercises

Vježba 2.1 Fill in the blanks with the most logical words and then answer the questions. First do the exercise using informal address, then again using formal address.

1. Dobar dan. _____ si?
2. Je li Hrvatska zemlja _____ često putuje_?
3. Moji _______ su Hrvati, ali ja sam i Hrvatica i ___________. Jesi li ti ___________ ili Amerikanac?
4. Razumije__ hrvatski. A _________ li hrvatski?
5. Oprosti, ________ li ponov__?

Vježba 2.2 Translate the following *negative* sentences from English into Croatian.

1. Nobody understands anything.

   ____

2. Nothing is good here.

   ____

3. I don't see my car anywhere.

   ____

4. I don't work as an economist.

   ____

Vježba 2.3 Translate the following words found in the vocabulary lists of Lessons 1 and 2.

beginning	________	Croatia	________	now	________
žedna	________	pomalo	________	well	________
or	________	very	________	zbunjen	________
like	________	excellently	________	language	________
life	________	loše	________	moguće	________
velik	________	to love	________	place	________
turist	________	odmor	________	what	________
day	________	often	________	key	________
happy	________	regrettably	________	there	________
mladi	________	sigurno	________	gdje	________
zajedno	________	nastavak	________		

*Once you finish inserting the answers, drill yourself by repeating each of the words three times.

Vježba 2.4 Insert the first person singular, third person singular, and third person plural forms of the following verbs:

1. govoriti ____________ ____________ ____________
2. ići ____________ ____________ ____________
3. šaliti se ____________ ____________ ____________
4. živjeti ____________ ____________ ____________
5. znati ____________ ____________ ____________
6. moći ____________ ____________ ____________
7. zvati ____________ ____________ ____________
8. putovati ____________ ____________ ____________
9. pisati ____________ ____________ ____________
10. oprostiti ____________ ____________ ____________

Vježba 2.5
A. Translate into Croatian:

1. That is my favorite city.

____

2. That is my car.

____

3. I think a lovely story is beginning.

____

4. How are you? (*informal*)

____

5. Where are my keys?

____

B. Translate from Croatian into English:

1. Priča je dobra.

____

2. A gdje ti živiš?

____

3. Govoriš li engleski?

____

4. Vrlo sam žedan i gladan.

____

5. Stalno žurim i uvijek radim.

____

Vježba 2.6 Write the plural for each word. Remember that some of the plural constructions are irregular!

1. vrijeme ______________
2. majka ______________
3. auto ______________
4. grad ______________
5. turist ______________
6. muž ______________
7. student ______________
8. žena ______________
9. knjiga ______________
10. vlak ______________
11. Splićanin ______________
12. početak ______________
13. starac ______________
14. pjesnik ______________
15. Amerikanac ______________

Vježba 2.7 Part of doing well in any language is being able to respond and understand basic, common expressions. Supply the context for the expressions given below.

1. Baš lijepo što ste ovdje.

   ____

2. Dobar dan, kako ste?

   ____

3. Tako-tako.

   ____

4. Oprostite.

   ____

5. Dobro, a Vi?

   ____

6. Kako si?

   ____

7. Loše!

   ____

8. Hvala, dobro.

   ____

Lekcija 3
Vožnja

Lesson 3
Driving

Lekcija 3: Vožnja

Prvi dio

Marijana: Dobar auto! Je li nov?

Ivan: Ne, prilično je star, ali dobro vozi.

Marijana: Kakva lijepa boja! Plava je moja omiljena boja.

Ivan: I moja! Ali model i povoljna cijena također su važni.

Marijana: Točno! Ipak je zgodno da je plav, a ne crven ili žut.

Darko: Marijana, ti sigurno voziš svaki dan?

Marijana: Naravno, Amerika je zemlja gdje svi nekamo voze. Javni prijevoz uglavnom nije dobar. A ovdje?

Ivan: Ljudi ovdje više upotrebljavaju javni prijevoz jer benzin nije jeftin. To je i inače europski problem.

Drugi dio

Marijana: Darko, i ti voziš?

Darko: Vozim kada moram, ali radije hodam. Zagreb je zelen i lijep grad. Kada je vrijeme sunčano, uživam šetati.

Ivan: Marijana, radiš li već dugo kao ekonomistica?

Marijana: Zapravo prilično kratko. Posao je zanimljiv i mnogo putujem, a to volim. Kako ide vaš studij?

Darko: Odlično! Pogotovo sada kada su ispiti gotovi.

Ivan: Zadnja godina. Konačno!

Darko: Ivane, zašto voziš tako polako? Ovo je autocesta! Mislim da se ovdje smije voziti brzo.

Ivan: Tko vozi, ti ili ja? Ja sam izvrstan vozač! Možeš se opustiti i uživati!

Marijana: Slažem se, nikamo se ne žurimo!

Lesson 3: Driving

Part I

Marijana:	Nice car! Is it new?
Ivan:	No, it's quite old, but it drives well.
Marijana:	Such a lovely color! Blue is my favorite color.
Ivan:	Mine too! But the model and a suitable price are also important.
Marijana:	Correct! Still it is nice that it's blue and not red or yellow.
Darko:	Marijana, you probably drive everyday?
Marijana:	Of course, America is a country in which everyone drives everywhere. Public transportation is generally not good. And here?
Ivan:	People here use public transportation more because gas is not cheap. That is a general European problem.

Part II

Marijana:	Darko, do you drive as well?
Darko:	I drive when I have to, but I prefer to walk. Zagreb is a green and beautiful city. When the weather is sunny, I enjoy walking.
Ivan:	Marijana, have you been working long as an economist?
Marijana:	In fact, quite a short time. The job is interesting and I travel a lot, and I like that. How is your studying going?
Darko:	Excellently! Especially now that the exams are over.
Ivan:	The last year. Finally!
Darko:	Ivan, why are you driving so slowly? This is a highway! I think that one can drive fast here.
Ivan:	Who is driving, you or me? I am an excellent driver! You can relax and enjoy!
Marijana:	I agree, we are not in a hurry!

Vocabulary

autocesta highway
benzin gasoline
brzo quickly
boja color
cijena price
crven red
dosta quite, enough
dugo long
europski European
godina year
gotov over, finished
inače otherwise, generally
ipak nonetheless, still
ispit exam
Ivane *voc.* Ivan *(addressing form of Ivan)*
izvrstan *m.*/**izvrsna** *f.*/**izvrsno** *neu.* extraordinary
javni public
jeftin cheap, inexpensive
jer because
kada when
kakav what kind of, such
kratko shortly
ljudi people
mnogo a lot
naravno of course
nekamo somewhere *(with verbs of motion)*
nikamo nowhere *(with verbs of motion)*
ništa nothing
nov new
polako slowly
posao *nom.*/ **poslovi** *pl.*/**posla** *gen. sg.* job
povoljan suitable, cost-effective
prijevoz transportation
prilično quite
radije preferably
star old
studij coursework *(at college)*
sunčano sunny
svaki each, every
također also
točno correct
uglavnom mostly
važan important
više more
vozač driver
vrijeme/**vremena** *pl.* weather, time
zadnji last
zanimljiv interesting
zelen green
zgodno lovely, nice
žut yellow

Verb List

hodati (*I* **hodam**, **hodaju**) to walk
morati (*I* **moram**, **moraju**) to have to, must
opustiti se (*P* **opustim se**, **opuste se**) to relax
smjeti (*I* **smijem**, **smiju**) to be allowed to
šetati (*I* **šetam**, **šetaju**) to stroll
upotrebljavati (*I* **upotrebljavam**, **upotrebljavaju**) to use
uživati (*I* **uživam**, **uživaju**) to enjoy
voziti (*I* **vozim**, **voze**) to drive

Useful Expressions

zapravo actually, as a matter of fact
točno correct
sigurno surely
radije + *verb* prefer ***(ja radije hodam** I prefer to walk)*
kako ide? how is it going?
konačno finally
Voziš li/vozite li? Can you drive?
mislim da I think that
Nikamo se ne žurimo. We are not in a hurry.

Useful adjective pairs*

brz	**spor**	fast	slow
bogat	**siromaš*a*n**	rich	poor
čist	**prljav**	clean	dirty
debeo	**mršav**	fat, thick	slim, skinny
dob*a*r	***za*o/loš**	good	evil, bad
dug	**krat*a*k**	long	short
glup	**pamet*a*n**	stupid	clever
hlad*a*n	**top*a*o**	cold	warm
jak	**slab**	strong	weak
jeftin	**skup**	cheap	expensive
lagan, lak	**tež*a*k**	easy, light	difficult, heavy
lijep	**ruž*a*n**	beautiful	ugly
malen/mali	**velik**	small	big
mlad/nov	**star**	young, new	old
niz*a*k	**visok**	low, short	tall, high
rijed*a*k	**čest**	rare	frequent
slad*a*k	**gor*a*k**	sweet	bitter
sret*a*n	**tuž*a*n**	happy	sad
širok	**uz*a*k**	wide	narrow
tih	**buč*a*n**	quiet	noisy

*In the next lesson you will learn more about the *fleeting -a* in adjectives. For future reference *the fleeting -a* is marked with *italics* in this list of adjective pairs as well as in subsequent vocabulary lists.

Grammar

1. Adjectives

As we know from English, adjectives modify nouns. In Croatian they can immediately precede that noun (*attributive position*) or they can be placed after the verb (*predicative position*). They always reflect the gender, number, and case of the noun.

Attributive

Veliki auto je moj, a mali je tvoj.
The big car is mine and the little one is yours.
Velika knjiga je moja, a mala je tvoja.
The big book is mine and the little one is yours.

Predicative

Auto je mali.	The car is small.
Knjiga je velika.	The book is big.

The dictionary always lists the masculine singular form because the other forms are derived from it. *Most masculine adjectives end in a consonant*, but there is a small group that ends in a vowel:

zao evil **topao** warm **debeo** fat, thick **okrugao** round

The *feminine form* ends in **-a**, and the *neuter* in **-o/-e** (**-e** follows a soft consonant). These forms are derived from the masculine adjective. If the masculine adjective has an **-a** preceding the final consonant, in many cases that vowel will disappear in the feminine and neuter forms as well as in cases other than the nominative, and the appropriate vowels (**-a** for feminine, **-o/-e** for neuter) will be added in the final position.

dobar auto *m.*	good car
dobra priča *f.*	good story
dobro pitanje *neu.*	good question

With the masculine adjectives ending in **-ao** and **-eo** (such as **zao** *evil*, **topao** *warm*, **debeo** *fat, thick*), these final two vowels are discarded, an **-l** is inserted, and then the appropriate vowels for neuter and feminine are added:

topao dan *m.* warm day	**debeo rječnik** *m.* thick dictionary
topla soba *f.* warm room	**debela knjiga** *f.* thick book
toplo jelo *neu.* warm dish *(food)*	**debelo pismo** *neu.* thick letter

Certain changes that occur in the derivation of forms are the result of language-specific speech processes that ease pronunciation. One such process is *voicing assimilation.* Consonants in all languages can be either voiced or voiceless (vowels are typically voiced).

Voiced consonants are pronounced with vibrating vocal cords, while voiceless consonants are pronounced with no vibration.When two consonants next to each other are not *both voiced* or *both voiceless*, the first consonant will adapt to the voicing of the second one. The following is a chart of the relevant voiced and voiceless consonants in Croatian:

voiced	b	d	g	dž	đ	ž	z
voiceless	p	t	k	č	ć	š	s

Here are some examples of these changes due to voicing assimilation:

masculine	feminine	neuter	translation	change
težak	**te*šk*a**	**te*šk*o**	heavy	**ž→ š**
sladak	**sla*tk*a**	**sla*tk*o**	sweet	**d→ t**
uzak	**u*sk*a**	**u*sk*o**	narrow	**z→ s**
blizak	**bli*sk*a**	**bli*sk*o**	close	**z→ s**

Masculine adjectives have another distinctive feature: most of them can be *short and long.* Though feminine and neuter adjectives in fact share this feature, it is reflected only in a slightly longer quality of the final vowel in the long forms. The masculine adjectives, however, do differ in the long and short forms since the long form has an extra **-i** at the end. Masculine adjectives ending in **-ao** discard **-ao**, insert **-l**, and then add **-i** in the long form).

Short & Long Masculine Adjectives

short	long	translation
dobar čovjek	**dobri čovjek**	good man
topao dan	**topli dan**	warm day
težak ispit	**teški ispit**	difficult exam

All of the changes made in deriving the feminine and neuter forms from the short masculine adjectival form also apply to the process of deriving the long masculine form from the short one.

When do you use the long vs. short form? Generally, when an item is first introduced the short form is used (**dobar čovjek** could be translated as *a good man*), and when the topic has already been introduced the long form is used (**dobri čovjek** could be translated as *the good man*). It is best to memorize the short form, since that is the one that appears in the dictionary.

Marko, je li taj auto *star*?	Marko, is that car *old*?
Da, ali taj *stari* auto dobro vozi.	Yes, but that *old* car drives well.
Ovo je *lijep* stan.	This is a *beautiful* apartment.
Da, ali ovaj *lijepi* stan je skup.	Yes, but this *beautiful* apartment is expensive.

Plural adjectival endings in the nominative are: **-i** for masculine plural (corresponding to the long adjectival form for masculine nouns), **-e** for feminine plural, **-a** for neuter plural.

	singular	plural	translation
m.	**pametan student**	**pametni studenti**	clever students
neu.	**dugo pismo**	**duga pisma**	long letters
f.	**dobra knjiga**	**dobre knjige**	good books
f.	**lijepa stvar**	**lijepe stvari**	beautiful things

	Nominative Singular			Nominative Plural		
	adj.	noun		*adj.*	noun	
m.	-i	various	**pametan student**	-i	-i	**pametni studenti**
neu.	-o/-e	-o/-e	**dugo pismo**	-a	-a	**duga pisma**
f.	-a	-a	**dobra knjiga**	-e	-e	**dobre knjige**
f.Ø	-a	Ø	**lijepa stvar**	-e	-i	**lijepe stvari**

NB: *f.Ø* stands for feminine zero ending nouns

Interrogative question words are also adjectival in form and agree with the noun. Several forms are used to inquire *what kind*, *which*, or *whose*:

kakav (what kind)

	singular	plural
m.	**kakav**	**kakvi**
f.	**kakva**	**kakve**
neu.	**kakvo**	**kakva**

Kakva knjiga? What kind of book?
Kakva je to knjiga? What kind of book is that?
Kakav film? What kind of film?
Kakav je to film? What kind of film is that?
Kakvi studenti? What kind of students?
Kakvi studenti žive tamo? What kind of students live there?

koji (which)

	singular	**plural**
m.	**koji**	**koji**
f.	**koja**	**koje**
neu.	**koje**	**koja**

Koja žena?	Which woman?
Koja je to žena?	Which woman is that?
Koji film?	Which film?
Koji film gledaš?	Which film are you watching?
Koje studentice?	Which *(female)* students?
Koje studentice vidiš?	Which *(female)* students do you see?

Question words requiring the use of possessive pronouns are also in this category:

čiji (whose)

	singular	**plural**
m.	**čiji**	**čiji**
f.	**čija**	**čije**
neu.	**čije**	**čija**

Čiji auto?	Whose car?
Čiji je to auto?	Whose car is that? [*lit.:* Whose is that car?]
Čije mjesto?	Whose place?
Čije je to mjesto?	Whose place is that? [*lit.:* Whose is that place?]
Čija knjiga?	Whose book?
Čija je to knjiga?	Whose book is that? [*lit.:* Whose is that book?]

2. Adverbs

While adjectives provide information answering the questions *what kind* and *which*, adverbs answer the question *how*. Adjectives change their form to reflect the noun they modify, but adverbs remain unchanged. Adverbial forms in Croatian correspond to those of the *neuter singular adjective*:

dobro well **loše** badly **lijepo** nicely **teško** difficultly

On je *dobar* čovjek.	He is a *good* man. (*adj.*)
On *dobro* govori hrvatski.	He speaks Croatian *well*. (*adv.*)
On je *dobro*!	He feels *well*! (*adv.*)
Kako si? *Loše*!	How are you? *Bad*! (*adv.*)
On vozi *brzo*.	He drives *fast*. (*adv.*)
To je *brz* auto.	That is a *fast* car. (*adj.*)

3. Plural of possessive pronouns

The endings of possessive pronouns behave like those of other adjectives. You have already learned the singular forms in Lesson 1. Here are the plural forms:

Plural Possessive Pronouns

	masculine	**feminine**	**neuter**
my	**moji**	**moje**	**moja**
your	**tvoji**	**tvoje**	**tvoja**
his	**njegovi**	**njegove**	**njegova**
her	**njezini**	**njezine**	**njezina**
its	**njegovi**	**njegove**	**njegova**
our	**naši**	**naše**	**naša**
your	**vaši (Vaši)**	**vaše (Vaše)**	**vaša (Vaša)**
their	**njihovi**	**njihove**	**njihova**

4. Demonstrative pronouns—*this/these* and *that/those*

There are two basic types of demonstrative pronouns, depending on their position in the sentence. One type refers to objects, people, and situations and is typically found at the beginning of the sentence. It is followed by **biti** *to be* and never changes in form:

***Ovo* je moj muž.**	*This* is my husband.
***Ovo* je moja žena.**	*This* is my wife.
***Ovo* su moje knjige.**	*These* are my books.

The second type of demonstrative pronoun behaves like an adjective and precedes the noun it modifies. This group of demonstratives reflects the gender, number, and case of the noun they modify.

***Ovaj* visoki gospodin je moj muž.**	*This* tall gentleman is my husband.
***Ova* visoka gospođa je moja žena.**	*This* tall lady is my wife.
***Ovo* slatko dijete je moje.**	*This* sweet child is mine.
***Ovi* studenti su Zagrepčani.**	*These* students are from Zagreb.
***Ove* knjige su dosadne.**	*These* books are boring.
***Ova* pitanja su odlična.**	*These* questions are excellent.

Depending on the *distance* between the speaker and the object to which he or she is pointing, three different demonstrative pronouns can be used. If the object is right next to the speaker, **ovaj** (or other pronouns from this group reflecting the appropriate gender, number, and case) will be used.

ovaj/ovi (this/these): **when object is right next to speaker**

	***nom.* singular**		***nom.* plural**	
m.	**ovaj Amerikanac**	this American	**ovi Amerikanci**	these Americans
f.	**ova stvar**	this thing	**ove stvari**	these things
neu.	**ovo slovo**	this letter	**ova slova**	these letters

If the object is relatively close, the following demonstratives will be used:

taj/ti (this/these): **when object is relatively close to speaker**

	***nom.* singular**		***nom.* plural**	
m.	**taj Amerikanac**	this American	**ti Amerikanci**	these Americans
f.	**ta stvar**	this thing	**te stvari**	these things
neu.	**to slovo**	this letter	**ta slova**	these letters

Alternatively, when the object is quite far the pronoun **onaj** will be used. **Onaj** behaves just like **ovaj** and has all the accompanying forms.

onaj/oni (that/those): **when object is quite far from speaker**

	***nom.* singular**		***nom.* plural**	
m.	**onaj Amerikanac**	that American	**oni Amerikanci**	those Americans
f.	**ona stvar**	that thing	**one stvari**	those things
neu.	**ono slovo**	that letter	**ona slova**	those letters

Exercises

Vježba 3.1 Translate the following words.

također	________________	žut	________________
friend	________________	dugo	________________
or	________________	zelen	________________
highway	________________	new	________________
grad	________________	naravno	________________
radije	________________	extraordinary	________________
place	________________	blue	________________
quite	________________	već	________________
price	________________	nigdje	________________
kada	________________	jeftin	________________
dan	________________	exam	________________

easy	________	sunčano	________
driver	________	posao	________
beginning	________	osobina	________
interesting	________	prijevoz	________
nešto	________	godina	________

Vježba 3.2

A. Determine the gender of the following nouns and create a sentence with one of the question words (**kakav** *what kind*, **koji** *which*, or **čiji** *whose*).

Example: **auto** *m.* **Kakav je to auto?**

film ____ ________________
knjiga ____ ________________
noć ____ ________________
student ____ ________________
ispit ____ ________________
boja ____ ________________

B. Fill in the blank with an appropriate *question* word: **kakav**, **koji**, or **čiji** (remember the correct ending).

1. _______ je ovo pitanje?
2. _______ jezik govoriš?
3. _______ auto je tamo?
4. _______ student piše e-mail?
5. _______ auto voziš?

Vježba 3.3 Translate into Croatian:

1. Those economists are clever.

   ____
2. Who is that thin student?

   ____
3. This is an interesting place.

   ____
4. What is your tall cousin called?

   ____
5. He is a new driver.

   ____
6. That is a difficult exam.

   ____
7. Today is a cold day.

   ____

8. Croatian is not an easy language.

____

9. The small key is mine and the big one is his.

____

10. This is a happy story.

____

Vježba 3.4 Fill in the following sentences with either an adverb or adjective.

1. On je __________ profesor.
2. Taj auto je _________.
3. Ona ________ govori engleski.
4. Ovaj film je _________.
5. Moja _________ knjiga je tamo.

Vježba 3.5

A. Give the plural form of the following nouns:

1. pismo	_______________	6. grad	_______________
2. dan	_______________	7. vrijeme	_______________
3. vozač	_______________	8. ispit	_______________
4. posao	_______________	9. cijena	_______________
5. problem	_______________	10. Zagrepčanin	_______________

B. Now, using the above 10 nouns, create simple sentences using an adjective or an adverb. Try to use all of the vocabulary from the prior lessons.

Example: **Je li to pismo dugo?**

1. ____
2. ____
3. ____
4. ____
5. ____
6. ____
7. ____
8. ____
9. ____
10. ____

Vježba 3.6

A. Translate the following adjectives from Croatian into English.
Example: **jak strong**

1. lijep ____________
2. star ____________
3. velik ____________
4. bogat ____________
5. odličan ____________
6. zanimljiv ____________
7. mlad ____________
8. loš ____________
9. sladak ____________
10. dobar ____________

B. Now, take those same adjectives and pair them with an appropriate noun.
Example: **jak čovjek**

1. ______________________
2. ______________________
3. ______________________
4. ______________________
5. ______________________
6. ______________________
7. ______________________
8. ______________________
9. ______________________
10. ______________________

Vježba 3.7 Determine whether the **boldfaced** word is an adverb or an adjective.

1. Taj student je **dobro**. _______
2. On je **dobar** čovjek. _______
3. Auto **dobro** vozi. _______
4. Tamo je **dobra** knjiga. _______
5. Govoriš hrvatski **dobro**. _______
6. **Dobro** pitanje. _______

Lekcija 4
Marijana posjećuje zagrebački restoran

Lesson 4
Marijana visits a Zagreb restaurant

Lekcija 4: Marijana posjećuje zagrebački restoran

Prvi dio

Darko: Marijana, jesi li sigurna da nisi pospana? Ako hoćeš, ja mogu pripremiti nešto za jelo. Ne moramo ići u restoran.

Marijana: Vrlo sam radosna što sam ovdje. Budući da zaista nisam umorna, idemo nekamo van. Ja častim!

Darko: Ivane, imaš li kakav prijedlog kamo da idemo?

Ivan : (*smije se*) Darko, ti barem znaš da sam ja siromašan student i da nisam stručnjak za restorane. No kada me već pitaš, znam jedno skromno, a dobro mjesto. Tu je blizu. Zove se Purger.

Darko: Odlična ideja! Što ti kažeš, Marijana?

Marijana: Zvuči dobro. Idemo tamo.

Ivan: Već smo tu! Da sjednemo ovdje? Molim Vas, jelovnik!

Konobar: Izvolite.

Ivan: Hvala lijepa.

Marijana: Vi, čini se, dobro poznajete ovaj restoran. Jedete li ovdje često?

Darko: Prilično često. Hrana je ukusna i nije preskupo.

Marijana: Što preporučujete za ručak?

Ivan: Svakako preporučujem juhu, ali ni druge stvari nisu loše. Vruće je. Ja mislim uzeti nešto lagano.

Drugi dio

Darko: Konobar, možemo li naručiti?

Marijana: Za mene riblju juhu i rižoto.

Konobar: Želite li još nešto?

Marijana: I desert, molim Vas, čokoladni kolač. Hvala.

Ivan: Za mene juhu od povrća, miješanu salatu i prženu ribu, molim Vas.

Darko: Ti si pravi Dalmatinac. Uvijek riba! Za mene, molim, zelenu salatu, meso na žaru i palačinke za desert. Hvala.

Konobar: Što želite piti?

Marijana: Mineralnu vodu za mene.

Lesson 4: Marijana visits a Zagreb restaurant

Part 1

Darko:	Marijana, are you sure you're not sleepy? If you wish, I can prepare something to eat. We don't have to go to a restaurant.
Marijana:	I am very happy that I'm here. Since I am really not tired let's go out somewhere. It's on me!
Darko:	Ivan, do you have a suggestion where to go?
Ivan : (*laughing*)	Darko, you of all people know that I am a poor student and that I am not an expert on restaurants. But since you ask, I know a modest but good place. It is nearby. It's called *Purger*.
Darko:	A great idea! What do you say, Marijana?
Marijana:	Sounds good. Let's go there.
Ivan:	We are already there! Shall we sit here? Could we have the menu please?
Waiter:	Here you are.
Ivan:	Thank you very much.
Marijana:	It seems that you know this restaurant well. Do you eat here often?
Darko:	Quite often. The food is tasty and it is not that expensive.
Marijana:	What do you recommend for lunch?
Ivan:	Definitely try the soup, but other things are not bad either. It's hot. I plan to take something light.

Part II

Darko:	Waiter, can we order?
Marijana:	For me, fish soup and risotto.
Waiter:	Would you like anything else?
Marijana:	And dessert too, please, chocolate cake. Thank you.
Ivan:	For me vegetable soup, mixed salad, and fried fish, please.
Darko:	You are a real Dalmatian. Always fish! For me, please, a green salad, grilled meat and crepes for dessert. Thank you.
Waiter:	What would you like to drink?
Marijana:	Mineral water for me.

Ivan: Bijelo vino za mene i jedno pivo za mladog gospodina, molim Vas.

Marijana: Što znači Purger?

Darko: To je staro ime za Zagrepčanina.

Marijana: Ovaj restoran baš je lijep, a ima i vrt.

Darko: Da, dobro mjesto. Nije bučno.

Marijana: Možemo li ovamo doći opet u utorak?

Darko: Svakako! Mi se ovdje često srećemo.

Konobar nosi hranu.

Konobar: Izvolite! Dobar tek!

Marijana: Hvala. Mmm, odličan miris!

Ivan: Živjela i dobro došla, Marijana!

Marijana: Hvala! Živjeli!

Ivan:	White wine for me, and one beer for the young gentleman, please.
Marijana:	What does Purger mean?
Darko:	That is an old name for an inhabitant of Zagreb.
Marijana:	This restaurant is quite lovely and it has a garden.
Darko:	Yes, a good place. It is not noisy.
Marijana:	Can we come here again on Tuesday?
Darko:	By all means! We often meet here.

The waiter brings the food.

Waiter:	Here you are! Bon appetit!
Marijana:	Thank you. Mmm, [what a] great smell!
Ivan:	Cheers and welcome, Marijana.
Marijana:	Thank you! Cheers!

Vocabulary

All instances of *fleeting -a* in nouns and adjectives are marked with italics.

barem at least
bijel white
blizu close, nearby
budući da since
bučno *adv.* noisy
čaša glass
čokoladni kolač chocolate cake
dobro došao *m.*/**dobro došla** *f.*/**dobro došli** *pl.* welcome
drugi other, second
gospodin Mr., gentleman
hrana food
ideja idea
ime/**imena** *pl.* name
jed*a*n one
jelo food, dish
jelovnik menu
još more, another, still, in addition
juha soup
juha od povrća vegetable soup
konobar waiter
lagan light
loš bad
meso meat
meso na žaru grilled meat
mineralna voda mineral water
miris smell
miješan mixed
mlad young
negdje somewhere
no but
opet again
ovamo over here *(with verbs of motion)*
palačinke crepes
pivo beer
pravi real
preskup too expensive
prijedlog suggestion
pržen fried
radost*a*n delighted, happy, joyful
riba fish
riblja juha fish soup
rižoto risotto
ruč*a*k lunch
salata salad
siromaš*a*n poor
skrom*a*n modest
skupo expensive
stručnjak expert
stvar thing
svakako definitely, by all means
također also, too
ukus*a*n tasty
utor*a*k Tuesday
van out *(as a destination,* **vani** *as a location)*
vino wine
voda water
vrt garden
vruće hot
živjeli cheers *(also* **nazdravlje***)*

Verb List

častiti (*I* **častim**, **časte**) to treat
činiti (*I* **činim**, **čine**) to do
činiti se (*I* **činim se**, **čine se**) to seem, to give an impression

doći (*P* **dođem, dođu**) to come
imati (*I* **imam, imaju**; *neg.*: **nemam, nemaju**) to have
jesti (*I* **jedem, jedu**) to eat
kazati (*I* **kažem, kažu**) to say
moliti (*I* **molim, mole**) to beg, to ask for
naručiti (*P* **naručim, naruče**) to order
nositi (*I* **nosim, nose**) to carry, to wear
otići (*P* **otiđem, otiđu**) to go to, to leave
piti (*I* **pijem, piju**) to drink
posjećivati (*I* **posjećujem, posjećuju**) to visit
poznavati (*I* **poznajem, poznaju**) to be acquainted with
preporučivati (*I* **preporučujem, preporučuju**) to recommend
pripremiti (*P* **pripremim, pripreme**) to prepare
sjesti (*P* **sjednem, sjednu)** to sit down
smijati se (*I*, **smijem se, smiju se**) to laugh
sretati (se) (*I*, **srećem se, sreću se**) to meet
uzeti (*P* **uzmem, uzmu**) to take
vidjeti se (*I* **vidim se, vide se**) to see oneself, to see each other, to meet
vidjeti (*I, P* **vidim, vide**) to see *(the ability) I*, to spot *P*
značiti (*I* **značim, znače**) to mean
zvučati (*I* **zvučim, zvuče**) to sound
željeti (*I* **želim, žele**) to wish, to want

Useful Expressions

Molim Vas please
Izvoli(te). Please, help yourself.
Hvala lijepa. Thank you very much.
Želimo naručiti. We would like to order.
Molim Vas, jelovnik! Could we have the menu? [*lit.:* The menu, please.]
Molim Vas, račun! The bill, please!
Možemo li platiti? Can we pay?
Jeftino je. It's inexpensive/cheap.
Skupo je. It's expensive.
Zadržite sitniš. Keep the change.
Dobar tek! Bon appetit!
Što znači ***xxx*****?** What does *xxx* mean?
Dobro došao *m.*/**Dobro došla** *f.*/**Dobro došli** *pl.* Welcome!
Živio *m.*/**Živjela** *f.*/**Živjeli!** *pl.* Cheers! *(A common toast. [lit.: To your health!])*

Sample menu

Restoran "Hippocrene"

Istarska ulica 12
10000 Zagreb

Jelovnik

Salate

Miješana salata	10
Salata od plodova mora	10
Salata od cikle	11
Zelena salata	11
Salata Adria	9
Krumpir salata	13

Juhe

Riblja juha	12
Pileća juha	13

Meso

Miješani roštilj	85
Teletina	65
Janjetina	55
Pljeskavica	45
Biftek	70
Pariški odrezak	65

Riba

Orada	45
Trlje	45
Lignje	65
Srdele	35

Prilozi

Kruh	4
Pomfrit	9
Ajvar	5
Pohane gljive	5
Kajmak	6
Masline	9

Pivo	14
Mineralna voda	11
Orangina	16
Coca Cola	15
Fanta	15
Schwepps	15
Capuccino	7
Espresso	6
Bijelo vino	22
Crno vino	23
Žestoka pića	19
Sok	18

Grammar

1. Verb *imati* (to have)

As you may remember, the verb *to have* is one of the few verbs in Croatian which, in the negative form, requires that the particle **ne** be combined with the verb into one word. This verb requires the use of the *accusative case* discussed below.

Affirmative: imati (to have) | **Negative: nemati** (to not have)

singular	plural	singular	plural
imam	**imamo**	**nemam**	**nemamo**
I have	we have	I don't have	we don't have
imaš	**imate**	**nemaš**	**nemate**
you have	you have	you don't have	you don't have
ima	**imaju**	**nema**	**nemaju**
he has	they have	he doesn't have	they don't have

2. Cases: The Accusative

2.1. Nouns, adjectives, possessive pronouns

The direct object in a sentence is always in the accusative case. The direct object in English is usually placed after the verb and answers the questions *what* or *whom*. For example: I have [*what?*] *a good book.* I see [*whom*?] *a clever student*. While in English these grammatical relations are governed by sentence structure, in Croatian they are defined by *case endings*.

nominative singular	accusative singular
tvoja dobra knjiga *f.* your good book	**Imam *tvoju dobru knjigu.*** I have *your good book*
naša lijepa stvar *f.* our beautiful thing	**Želi *našu lijepu stvar.*** S/he wants *our beautiful thing.*
moje dugo pismo *neu.* my long letter	**Vološ *moje dugo pismo.*** You like *my long letter*.
njegov veliki brod *m.* his big ship	**Vidim *njegov veliki brod.*** I see *his big ship.*
Vaš pametan student *m.* your clever student	**Poznaju Vašeg pametnog studenta.** They know your clever student.

nominative plural	accusative plural
tvoje dobre knjige *f.* your good books	**Imam tvoje dobre knjige.** I have your good books.
naše lijepe stvari *f.* our beautiful things	**Želi *naše lijepe stvari.*** S/he wants *our beautiful things.*
moja duga pisma *neu.* my long letters	**Voliš *moja duga pisma.*** You like my long letters.
njegovi veliki brodovi *m.* his big ships	**Vidim *njegove velike brodove.*** I see *his big ships.*
Vaši pametni studenti *m.* your clever students	**Poznaju *Vaše pametne studente.*** They know *your clever students.*

In the nominative case the question words for *who* and *what* are **tko** and **što**, respectively. In the accusative, **tko** changes into **koga** and **što** remains the same. Therefore, to ask *Whom do you see?* one doesn't say **Tko vidiš?* but rather **Koga vidiš?**

Here is the accusative chart of endings for adjectives and nouns:

	Accusative Singular		
	adj.	**noun**	
m. anim.	-og/eg	-a	**pametnog studenta**
m. inan.	same as *nom.*		**veliki brod**
neu.	same as *nom.*		**dugo pismo**
f.	-u	-u	**dobru knjigu**
f.Ø	-u	Ø	**lijepu stvar**
	Accusative Plural		
	adj.	**noun**	
m. anim.	-e	-e	**pametne studente**
m. inan.	-e	-e	**velike brodove**
neu.	-a	-a	**duga pisma**
f.	-e	-e	**dobre knjige**
f.Ø	-e	-i	**lijepe stvari**

NB *m. inan.* stands for masculine inanimate, while *m. anim.* stands for masculine animate.

Here is how possessive pronouns look in the accusative. Remember, they behave exactly like any other adjective and thus have the same endings as adjectives in all cases.

	Accusative Singular Possessives		**Accusative Plural Possessives**	
	my		**our**	
m.anim.	**-og/eg**	**mojeg**	**-e**	**moje**
m.inan.	same as nom.	**moj**	**-e**	**moje**
neu.	same as nom.	**moje**	**-a**	**moja**
f.	**-u**	**moju**	**-e**	**moje**

Colloquial Croatian also allows short forms **mog** *my* and **tvog** *your*.

For both feminine and masculine nouns there are two types of endings. Most feminine nouns end in **-a** in the nominative and take the ending **-u** in the accusative singular:

nom. sg. f.: **knjig*a*** book → ***acc. sg. f.***: **knjig*u***

Adjectives as well as both possessive and demonstrative pronouns have that same **-u** ending:

acc. sg.**: moj*u*/ov*u* lij<u>e</u>p*u* knjig*u*** my/this beautiful book

In the accusative plural, feminine nouns take the ending **-e.**

Zero-ending feminine nouns constitute a small group of feminine nouns that end in a consonant. For example, abstract nouns ending in **-ost/-est** are all feminine:

mladost *f.* youth **bud<u>u</u>ćnost** *f.* future **radost** *f.* joy

These nouns have a different pattern of declension from the rest of the feminine nouns and in the accusative have the same endings as in the nominative. The accompanying adjectives, possessives, or demonstratives, however, follow the *feminine* adjectival declension. Thus:

acc. sg. f.: **lij<u>e</u>p*u* noć** beautiful night **moj*u* mladost** my youth

Neuter nouns in the accusative singular are the same as the nominative singular; the accusative plural is the same as the nominative plural.

In the accusative singular, *masculine nouns* behave differently depending on whether they belong to the category of *animate* or *inanimate* nouns. While animate masculine nouns add **-a** in the accusative singular (**st<u>u</u>dent-a** *student*), inanimate nouns maintain the same form as in the nominative singular (**brod** *ship*).

Adjectives that modify animate nouns add **-og** (**dobr-og** *good*) except when they end in a soft consonant (see Lesson 2). In that case they add **-eg** (**loš-eg** *bad*). This same rule applies to possessives.

***acc. m. anim. sg.* possessives**
njegov*og* his **vaš*eg*** your **moj*eg*** my

Adjectives and possessives referring to inanimate nouns remain the same as in the nominative.

In the *accusative plural* both masculine animate and inanimate nouns have the ending **-e** for nouns as well as for any accompanying modifier:

***acc. m. pl.* nouns** (*anim.* & *inan.*):
naš*e* pametn*e* student*e* our clever students
tvoj*e* velik*e* brodov*e* your (*pl.*) big ships

Masculine nouns ending in **-lac** have **-oce** in the accusative plural:

spasilac rescuer **spasioce** rescuers

In many cases masculine adjectives in the short-form nominative have the so-called *fleeting -a*, which disappears in the long form as well as in other cases or genders.

dobar (good)

	nominative	accusative
m. short form	**dobar**	**dobrog**
m. long form	**dobri**	**dobrog**
f.	**dobra**	**dobru**
neu.	**dobro**	**dobro**

The vast majority of masculine adjectives that in the short form end in **-ak** or **-an** lose the vowel in other forms, while the consonant undergoes a change due to voicing assimilation (see Lesson 3). For instance, **uzak** *narrow* will become **uskog** in the accusative singular. Similarly, masculine adjectives ending in **-ao** (e.g., **zao** *evil*) lose the final two vowels and insert an **-l** plus the proper ending (see Lesson 3).

	nominative	accusative	meaning
m. sg. adj.	zao	zlog	evil

Demonstrative pronouns (*this/that/these/those*) behave exactly like possessives and take the same endings. Thus **ovaj**, **onaj**, **taj** become **ov*og***, **on*og***, **t*og*** respectively in the singular, masculine animate accusative; **ova**, **ona**, **ta**, become **ov*u***, **on*u***, **t*u*** in the singular, feminine accusative respectively, etc.

2.2. Personal pronouns in the accusative case

Just as nouns and adjectives change in different cases, so do personal pronouns. In Croatian they have a short and a long form. The long form is used for emphasis, after a preposition, and in the initial position in a sentence. The short form, though, is far more prevalent in everyday speech.

short form:	I see *him. (most common form)*	**Vidim *ga.***
long form:	I see *HIM (as opposed to s.o. else)*	***Njega* vidim.**
long form:	That is good for *him. (after prep.)*	**To je dobro za *njega.***

Personal Pronouns in Nominative & Accusative

	nom. sg.	***acc. sg.* long**	***acc. sg.* short**	***nom. pl.***	***acc. pl.* long**	***acc. pl.* short**
1st	**ja** I	**mene** me	**me** me	**mi** we	**nas** us	**nas** us
2nd	**ti** you	**tebe** you	**te** you	**vi** you	**vas** you	**vas** you
3rd *m.*	**on** he	**njega** him	**ga** him	**oni** they	**njih** them	**ih** them
3rd *f.*	**ona** she	**nju** her	**ju/je*** her	**one** they	**njih** them	**ih** them
3rd *neu.*	**ono** it	**njega** it	**ga** it	**ona** they	**njih** them	**ih** them

*The accusative singular feminine has two acceptable short forms.

2.3. Prepositions that take the accusative

You may have noticed in the above examples that certain verbs require the use of the accusative. The same goes for certain prepositions. Some of the most common ones appear below. The personal pronouns can only be in the *long form* after a preposition.

za *for* + noun/pronoun in *acc.*

To je *za mene.*	That is *for me.*
Knjiga je *za pametnog studenta.*	The book is *for the clever student.*

kroz *through* + noun/pronoun in *acc.*

Vozimo *kroz Zagreb.*	We are driving *through Zagreb.*
Putujemo *kroz lijepu zemlju.*	We are traveling *through a beautiful country.*

na *on, about* (esp. in conjunction with motion) + noun/pronoun in *acc.*

Vozimo *na otok Krk.*	We are driving *to the island of Krk.*
Ona ne misli *na mene.*	She is not thinking *about me.*

u *in* (in conjunction with motion)

Putujem *u Split.*	I'm traveling *to Split.*
Ide *u grad.*	S/he is going *to the city.*

u *on* + day of the week

Vidimo se *u srijedu.*	We'll see one another *on Wednesday.*
Putujem *u utorak.*	I'm traveling *on Tuesday.*

Days of the week

Sunday	**nedjelja**
Monday	**ponedjelj*ak***
Tuesday	**utor*ak***
Wednesday	**srijeda**
Thursday	**četvrt*ak***
Friday	**pet*ak***
Saturday	**subota**

Days of the week are not capitalized in Croatian.

3. Cases: The Vocative

The vocative is the case used for addressing or calling people. It is therefore mostly found with names although not all names (especially foreign ones) have this form. Even with local names its use is often optional.

Masculine names that end in a consonant add **-e**:

nominative	vocative
Ivan	**Ivan*e***
Damir	**Damir*e***

Masculine names ending in a vowel remain unchanged. If the masculine noun ends in **k**, **g**, or **h**, these consonants will be changed into **č**, **ž**, **š** respectively and **-e** will be added after them.

nominative	vocative
-k	**-če**
-g	**-že**
-h	**-še**

For example, **čovjek** *man* becomes **čovje*če*** in the vocative case.

Some *short feminine names* (but not all!) replace the final **-a** with **-o**, as do common nouns.

nominative	vocative
majk*a* mother	**majk*o***
sestr*a* sister	**sestr*o***
Lad*a*	**Lad*o***
Nad*a*	**Nad*o***
Ljilj*a*	**Ljilj*o***

Feminine names and nouns ending in **-ica** have the ending **-ice** in the vocative.

nominative	vocative
Dan*ica*	**Dan*ice***
koleg*ica* colleague	**koleg*ice***
prijatelj*ica* friend	**prijatelj*ice***

Forms of address frequently used in addressing someone are:

	nominative	vocative
Mr.	**gospodin**	**gospodine**
Mrs.	**gospođa**	**gospođo**
Miss	**gospođica**	**gospođice**

4. The Conjunction *da* (that)

The conjunction **da** is typically used to connect main and subordinate clauses. It is translated as *that* but, unlike English usage, it cannot be left out.

Jesi li sigurna *da* nisi pospana?
Are you sure (*that*) you're not sleepy?

Ti barem znaš *da* sam ja siromašan student.
You of all people know *that* I am a poor student.

Similarly **da** can be used to connect the *embedded yes-no question* with the main sentence; the **verb + li** formulation can also be used this way.

Rade li?	Are they working?
Želimo znati *da li rade*.	We wish to know *whether they are working.*
Želimo znati *rade li*.	We wish to know *whether they are working.*
Je li umorna?	Is she tired?
Darko pita Marijanu *da li je umorna*.	Darko is asking Marijana *whether she is tired.*
Darko pita Marijanu *je li umorna*.	Darko is asking Marijana *whether she is tired.*

Da also appears in statements or questions that express desire and include another subject. When used with verbs expressing desire, **da** is translated as *to*:

Želim *da* ona dođe.	I want her *to* come.
Hoću *da* mi se javiš.	I want you *to* call me.

In this lesson it has been used to suggest an activity:

Da sjednemo ovdje?	Shall we sit here?
Da kupimo benzin?	Should we buy [some] gas?

The conjunction **da** can express purpose or intention and in this instance is best translated with *in order to*:

Idemo tamo *da* vidimo prijatelje.	We're going there *in order to* see friends.
Jedemo *da* nismo gladni.	We eat *in order* not *to* be hungry.

This conjunction is also found in the phrase **budući da**, which means *since*:

***Budući da* sam gladan, idem u restoran.**
Since I'm hungry, I'm going to a restaurant.

***Budući da* nisam umorna, idemo nekamo van.**
Since I am not tired, let's go out somewhere.

Finally, **da** is used in questions:

Kada da dođem?	When should I come?
Kako da nađem glavni trg?	How can I find the main square?
Gdje da kupi karte?	Where should s/he buy tickets?

Interrogative pronouns such as **kada** *when,* **gdje** *where,* **kamo** *where to,* **kako** *how,* **što** *what*, etc. can also serve as conjunctions.

Znaš li *kada* on ide tamo?	Do you know *when* he is going there?
Pitam se *što* on govori!	I wonder *what* he is talking about!

Exercises

Vježba 4.1 Fill in either the English or Croatian forms for the following useful expressions:

1. Please ____________________________
2. Zadržite sitniš ____________________________
3. It's cheap ____________________________
4. Hvala lijepa ____________________________
5. The bill please ____________________________
6. So-so ____________________________

7. Baš lijepo što ste tu ________________________
8. Excuse me ________________________
9. Good morning ________________________
10. Želim naručiti ________________________

Vježba 4.2 From the following nouns and adjectives construct a sentence using both the nominative AND accusative cases.

Example: *nom.:* **Ta knjiga je lijepa.** *acc.*: **Imam lijepu knjigu**.

1. lijepi novi auto

   ____

2. bijelo vino

   ____

3. sretni studenti

   ____

4. dobra skupa hrana

   ____

5. spori tužni konobar

   ____

Vježba 4.3 Translate and then conjugate the following verbs in every form.

Example: **znati** to know **znam, znaš, zna, znamo, znate, znaju**

1. ići ________

   ____

2. piti ________

   ____

3. moći ________

   ____

4. željeti ________

   ____

5. vidjeti ________

   ____

6. pitati ________

   ____

7. imati ________

   ____

8. doći ________

   ____

9. hodati _________
____

10. žuriti _________
____

Vježba 4.4

A. Use the following accusative prepositions in a sentence.
Example: **Ova knjiga je za mene**.

1. na ____________________________
2. u (with days of the week) ____________________________
3. za ____________________________
4. u ____________________________
5. kroz ____________________________

B. Translate the following sentences.

1. The book is for you.
____
2. I see them.
____
3. She knows him.
____
4. We visit her often.
____
5. My friends are thinking about me.
____
6. Is there anything for us?
____
7. I have it.
____

Vježba 4.5 Complete the following dialogues.

1. Dobar dan. ______ se Darko. A kako se ti ___________?
2. Drago __ je. Ja se ______ Stjepan. Ja sam pravi Dalmatinac. Uvijek jedem _________.
3. Zanimljivo. Pijem pivo, ali ne _____ kada vozim _____. Zašto? Nije ______ piti pivo kada voziš.

4. Gdje ____________ u srijedu? U srijedu ______________u
   ______________.
5. Idemo sada. Imam odličnu hranu. Imam _________ i _______ za nas.
6. Volim _________________. A zašto ____________________ voliš?
   Zato jer je/su ___________________.
7. Hoću da Sanja _______________________. Kada?
   U______________________.
8. Što želite jesti? ____________________________________. A što želite
   piti? ___________________________________.
9. Danas idem u kupovinu. Što kupuješ? Kupujem___________________
   ________. Za koga? Za__________________________.
10. Što imaš, a što____________________?
    Imam_____________________, ali nemam_______________________.
11. Voliš li više ____________________ ili ____________________?
    Više volim ______________________.
12. Nitko ovdje ___________________ zna. Nije istina! Svi ovdje sve
    _________________ .

Vježba 4.6

A. Match the antonyms from the two columns below.

1.	brz	a.	ružan
2.	bučan	b.	tužan
3.	nizak	c.	visok
4.	lijep	d.	spor
5.	sretan	e.	tih
6.	jak	f.	glup
7.	pametan	g.	slab

B. Circle the word that best completes each sentence.

1. Konobar, možemo li *naručiti / učiti*.
2. Vidimo se *na / u* četvrtak.
3. Živjela i *dobro došao / dobro došla* Marijana!
4. Što ti *kažete / kažeš* Darko?
5. Knjiga je za *glupu / pametnog* studenta.

Vježba 4.7

A. Translate into Croatian:

1. You (*formal*) don't have a hot soup?
2. They have a new menu.
3. You (*informal*) don't have a fast car.
4. I have an excellent friend.
5. The professor has clever students.
6. We have good highways.
7. Which city has inexpensive public transportation?

B. Translate these sentences into Croatian using the conjunction **da**:

1. Are you sure that you are not tired?
2. We wonder whether they understand history [povijest].
3. I want him to drive.
4. Shall we eat grilled meat?
5. I'm going to Šibenik in order to see friends.
6. Since I speak Croatian, I want to see that country.
7. When should I come?

Lekcija 5
Kako naći stan?

Lesson 5
How to find an apartment?

Lekcija 5: Kako naći stan?

Prvi dio

Darko: **Marijana, ti danas sigurno želiš potražiti stan.**

Marijana: **Svakako. Bojim se tog zadatka, ali tvoj je stan studentski i kod tebe je tijesno. Ostajem nekoliko tjedana i moram imati vlastiti stan.**

Darko: **Šteta što te ne mogu bolje ugostiti. Evo novina! Danas ima mnogo oglasa. Kakav stan želiš? Jednosoban ili dvosoban?**

Marijana: **Jednosoban stan negdje blizu centra. Predgrađa su daleko, a ja nemam auto. I, naravno, da ne košta puno!**

Darko (*čita*): **Evo jednog koji možda odgovara.**

Marijana: **Koja je adresa?**

Darko: **Palmotićeva ulica.**

Marijana: **Idemo ga vidjeti! A nakon toga idemo na ručak.**

Darko: **Dobri stanovi blizu centra iznajme se brzo, pa moramo požuriti. Imam Ivanov auto. On je trenutačno zauzet.**

Marijana: **Baš lijepo od njega što želi pomoći. Palmotićeva je prometna ulica. Jesu li stanovi tamo bučni?**

Darko: **Ne vjerujem. Ako stan gleda na dvorište, sigurno je tih. Tamo ima lijepih, prostranih stanova.**

Marijana: **Tu smo! Stan se nalazi točno između željezničkog kolodvora i glavnog trga. Kakva lijepa zgrada! Mislim da uopće ne trebam ni autobus ni tramvaj jer svuda mogu ići pješke.**

Darko: **Treći kat. Nema dizala.**

Marijana: **Nema problema! Ovo je dobra vježba.**

Lesson 5: How to find an apartment?

Part I

Darko: Marijana, you probably want to look for an apartment today.

Marijana: Definitely. I'm afraid of that task, but your apartment is a student one and it is overcrowded. I am staying for a few weeks and there is a need for me to have my own apartment.

Darko: Pity I can't be a better host! Here's the newspaper. There are many ads today. What kind of apartment do you like? A studio or a one-bedroom?

Marijana: Studio, somewhere close to the center. The suburbs are far and I don't have a car. And, of course, I don't want it to cost much!

Darko (*reading*): Here's one that may be suitable.

Marijana: What is the address?

Darko: Palmotić Street.

Marijana: Let's go see it! And after that let's have lunch.

Darko: Good apartments near the center get rented quickly, so we should hurry. I have Ivan's car. He is busy right now.

Marijana: So nice of him to help. Palmotić is a busy street. Are the apartments there noisy?

Darko: I don't believe so. If the apartment looks out on the courtyard, it is definitely quiet. There are nice, spacious apartments there.

Marijana: Here we are! The apartment is located exactly between the railway station and the main square. Such a nice building! I think that I don't need either the bus or streetcar at all since I can walk everywhere.

Darko: The third floor. There is no elevator.

Marijana: No problem. This is good exercise.

Drugi dio

Darko:	Dobar dan! Je li ponuda za stan još vrijedi?
Gospodin Horvat:	Da, da. Dobar dan! Uđite! Ovo je stan moje sestre. Ona više ne živi ovdje. Kuhinja i kupaonica su ovdje, a soba je tamo.
Marijana:	Nije loše! Tu su krevet, ormar, stol, stolice i televizor. Stan je namješten. Jedna briga manje! Koliko ima odavde do Trga bana Jelačića?
Gospodin Horvat:	Pet minuta pješke. Nije daleko.
Marijana:	Kolika je stanarina?
Gospodin Horvat:	Dvije tisuće kuna.
Marijana:	To je dobra cijena za ovu lokaciju. Je li grijanje na plin ili struju i jesu li režije uključene?
Gospodin Horvat:	Nisu. Grijanje je na plin.
Marijana:	Ako se slažete, uzimam ga.
Gospodin Horvat:	Na koliko vremena?
Marijana:	Na godinu dana. Sada ostajem samo jedan mjesec, ali zbog posla moram često putovati ovamo. Zato želim imati svoj stan. Radim za jednu veliku međunarodnu tvrtku.
Gospodin Horvat:	Odlično! Evo ključeva!
Marijana:	Hvala lijepa.
Darko:	Marijana, jesi li zadovoljna?
Marijana:	I više od toga! Hvala puno. Ništa bez tebe!
Darko:	Prava sitnica! Sada idemo na ručak. A čeka nas i Ivan!

Part II

Darko:	Good afternoon! Is the offer for the apartment still valid?
Mr. Horvat:	Yes, yes. Good afternoon! Come in! This is my sister's apartment. She no longer lives here. The kitchen and the bathroom are here and the bedroom is there.
Marijana:	Not bad! Here is a bed, an armoir, a table, chairs, and a TV. The apartment is furnished. One less worry! How far is it from here to Ban Jelačić's square?
Mr. Horvat:	Five minutes on foot. It is not far.
Marijana:	How much is the rent?
Mr. Horvat:	Two thousand kunas.
Marijana:	That is a good price for this location. Is the heating gas or electric and are the utilities included?
Mr. Horvat:	They are not included. It has gas heating.
Marijana:	If you agree, I'll take it.
Mr. Horvat:	For how long?
Marijana:	For a year. I am staying only for a month now, but because of work I have to travel here often. Therefore I wish to have my own place. I work for a big international company.
Mr. Horvat:	Excellent! Here are the keys!
Marijana:	Thank you very much.
Darko:	Marijana, are you satisfied?
Marijana:	More than that! Thanks so much. I couldn't do it without you!
Darko:	Don't mention it! Now let's have lunch. And Ivan is waiting for us!

Vocabulary

adresa address
bez without
bolje better
briga worry
daleko far
dvije tisuće kuna two thousand kunas
centar center
dizalo elevator (also **lift**)
dvorište courtyard
dvosoban stan one-bedroom apartment
evo here is/are
glavni main
grijanje heating
Ivanov Ivan's
između between
iznajmljivanje renting
jednosoban stan studio
kat floor
kod at someone's, near
krevet bed
kuhinja kitchen
kupaonica bathroom
lokacija location
manje less
međunarodni international
mjesec month
možda maybe
nakon after
nekoliko several
novine *pl.* newspaper
odavde from here
oglas advertisement
ormar wardrobe
pješke on foot
plin gas
ponuda offer
predgrađe suburb
prometan busy with traffic
prostran spacious
puno a lot
put path, journey, time *(as in twice)*
režije utilities
samo only
sestra sister
sitnica trifle
soba room
stan apartment
stanarina rent
stol table
stolica chair (also **stolac**)
struja electricity
studentski *adj.* student
svoj own
svuda everywhere *(with verbs of motion)*
televizor TV
tih quiet
tijesno *adv.* tight, overcrowded
tjedan week
tramvaj tram, streetcar
treći third
trenutačno right now, momentarily
trg square
tvrtka company
ulica street
uključen included, turned on
uopće in general, at all
vježba exercise
vlastit one's own
zadatak task
zadovoljan satisfied
zato therefore, hence
zauzet occupied
zbog because of
zgrada building
željeznički kolodvor railway station

Verb List

bojati se (*I* **bojim se, boje se**) to be afraid
čekati (*I* **čekam, čekaju**) to wait
čitati (*I* **čitam, čitaju**) to read
gledati (*I* **gledam, gledaju**) to look
iznajmiti (*P* **iznajmim, iznajme**) to rent to someone
koštati (*I* **koštam, koštaju**) to cost
naći (*P* **nađem, nađu**) to find
nalaziti (*I* **nalazim, nalaze**) to find, to be situated (**nalaziti se**)
odgovarati (*I* **odgovaram, odgovaraju**) to answer, to be suitable
ostajati (*I* **ostajem, ostaju**) to stay
pomoći (*P* **pomognem, pomognu**) to help
potražiti (*P* **potražim, potraže)** to look for
požuriti (se) (*P* **požurim, požure**) to hurry
trebati (*I* **trebam, trebaju**) to need
ući (*P* **uđem, uđu**) to enter
ugostiti (*P* **ugostim, ugoste**) to host
unajmiti (*P* **unajmim, unajme**) to rent from someone
uzimati (*I* **uzimam, uzimaju**) to take
vrijediti (*I* **vrijedim, vrijede**) to be valid, to be worth

Useful Expressions

Svakako! By all means!
Šteta! Pity!
Koja je adresa? What is the address?
Ne vjerujem. I don't believe so.
nema problema no problem
godina dana a year-long period
uđite come in *(formal pl.)*
lijepo od njega nice of him
nije loše not bad
koliko košta how much
grijanje na plin/na struju gas/electric heating
briga manje one less worry
uživajte enjoy

Grammar

1. Cases: Genitive

1.1. Nouns, adjectives, possessive pronouns

One of the most important functions of the genitive case is to express *possession.* In English this is expressed by the preposition *of* or by an *'s* after the noun (*the car of my brother*, *my brother's car*). In Croatian the appropriate word ending expresses this relationship between two nouns. The first noun can be in any case, while the second one expressing possession is in the genitive.

To je stan nove studentice.	This is the new student's apartment.
Čitam knjigu njihovog prijatelja.	I am reading their friend's book.

Genitive can express some other relations, and sometimes these can be translated with the English preposition *of.* For more on genitive use see below.

Bojim se ispita. I am afraid of the exam/exams.

The genitive endings for *all masculine and neuter singular nouns and adjectives* are the same as those for masculine *animate* nouns and adjectives in the accusative singular, namely **-a** for nouns and **-og/eg** for adjectives.

Feminine nouns and adjectives ending in **-a** replace the **-a** with **-e** in the genitive singular. Feminine nouns that end in a consonant add **-i** in both the genitive singular and plural, while the accompanying adjective behaves the same way as adjectives modifying other feminine nouns.

In the *genitive plural,* adjectives for all genders end in **-ih**, while nouns (with the exception of the feminine ones ending in a consonant) add **-a**. If the two letters preceding the final vowel are consonants other than **st, št, šć, šč, zd, žd,** and **žđ** or the word ends in two consonants other than these, an **-a** needs to be inserted between those two consonants.

	nom. sg.		*gen. pl.*
letter	**pismo**	→	**pi*sa*ma** [**-a** insertion]
student	**student**	→	**studen*a*ta** [**-a** insertion]
grapes	**grožđe**	→	**grožđa** [*no* **-a** insertion]
sort	**vrsta**	→	**vrsta** [*no* **-a** insertion]

Monosyllabic masculine nouns derive genitive from the nominative plural. In other words, they add the gentive ending to -ov/-ev:

ključ (*m. nom. sg.*) – **ključevi** (*m. nom. pl.*) – **ključeva** (*m. gen. pl.*)

Many feminine nouns look exactly the same in the nominative singular and genitive plural in writing, but in the spoken language the stressed syllable is pronounced slightly longer in the genitive plural. Similarly, because of the extra syllable added in the genitive, masculine nouns often shift their accent one syllable further towards the end of the word.

There is a rather large group of feminine nouns ending in **-a** which in the genitive plural take **-i** or allow either **-i** or **-a**:

Feminine Nouns Ending in -a

nom. sg.	gen. pl.	
majka	**majk*i***	mother(s)
vježba	**vježbi/vježb*a***	exercise(s)
borba	**borbi/borb*a***	fight(s)

There is no firm rule guiding this group but it tends to include nouns ending with certain types of consonant clusters + **a**. The nouns indicating nationalities and professions in this group take **-i.**

Feminine Nouns Ending in Consonant Clusters + a

nom. sg.	gen. pl.	
Bosanka	**Bosanki**	Bosnian
Amerikanka	**Amerikanki**	American
bolničarka	**bolničarki**	nurse

The most important deviations in neuter are: **dijete** *child*, which inserts **-et** in the singular in cases other than nominative and accusative; **vrijeme** *time/weather* and **ime** *name*, which insert **-en**. In the genitive singular they become **djeteta**, **vremena**, **imena**. (For more see Lesson 14).

In the genitive, the question words **tko** *who* and **što** *what* become **koga** and **čega** respectively.

	Genitive Singular			Genitive Plural		
	adj.	noun		*adj.*	noun	
m.	-og/eg	-a	**pametnog studenta**	-ih	-a	**pametnih studen*a*ta***
neu.	-og/eg	-a	**dugog pisma**	-ih	-a	**dugih pisama**
f.	-e	-e	**dobre knjige**	-ih	-a	**dobrih knjiga**
f.Ø	-e	-i	**lijepe stvari**	-ih	-i	**lijepih stvari**

*Insert **-a** if the stem ends in two consonants other than **st, št, šć, šč, zd, žd, žđ.**

Many masculine nouns ending in **-ac** and **-ak** have a *fleeting -a* in the genitive singular:

nom. sg.: **pisac** writer ***gen. sg.***: **pisca** writer's, of writer

When necessary this kind of change also triggers *voicing assimilation* (see Lesson 3):

nom. sg.: **vrabac** sparrow
gen. sg.: **vrapca** sparrow's, of sparrow
gen. pl.: **vrabaca** sparrows', of sparrows

Masculine nouns that end in **-lac** drop that ending altogether and insert **-oca** in the genitive singular. The dropped **-lac** reappears in the genitive plural:

nom. sg.	gen. sg.	gen. pl.
spasilac rescuer	**spasioca**	**spasilaca**
ronilac diver	**ronioca**	**ronilaca**

Also nouns ending in **-ao, -eo, -io** such as **posao** *job, work* will replace the final two vowels with **-la** in the genitive singular: **posla**. This is a change similar to the one that occurs with adjectives ending in **-eo** (see Lesson 3). Because the accusative and genitive singular for animate masculine nouns are identical, all the rules pertaining to masculine nouns explained above are applicable to both cases.[1]

We have already observed that **possessive pronouns** share the same endings with adjectives in all cases when there is a change in the ending, and this is also true for the genitive.

gen. singular	gen. plural
moje knjige my book	**mojih knjiga** my books
tvoje knjige your book	**tvojih knjiga** your books
mojeg pisma my letter	**mojih studenata** my students
tvojeg pisma your letter	**tvojih studenata** your students

	***gen. sg.* possessives**		***gen. pl.* possessives**	
m.	**-og/eg**	**mojeg**	**-ih**	**mojih**
neu.	**-og/eg**	**mojeg**	**-ih**	**mojih**
f.	**-e**	**moje**	**-ih**	**mojih**

In colloquial speech one can also hear possessives **mog**, **moga** *my,* and **tvog**, **tvoga** *your*, etc.

1. Masculine adjectives in the genitive and accusative as well as in several other cases can add an additional vowel (corresponding to the vowel with which the noun ends) to their long form: **lijepog studenta/lijepoga studenta**. Both mean *handsome student* and the difference is more stylistic than semantic. The latter is used more in literary than in everyday language.

1.2. The use of genitive

There are some expressions in which the use of the genitive is obligatory. These include the so called *pointer words* such as *here is* and *there is*.

evo	here's
eto	here's (*but a little bit more distant from the speaker)*
eno	there's

***Evo* novina.**	*Here's* the newspaper.
***Eto* njih.**	*There* they are.

The genitive is also required with *quantifiers* such as:

koliko how much/many
nekoliko several, some
toliko so much/many
mnogo a lot
puno a lot
malo a little, little
ima there is/are
nema there isn't/aren't.
dosta quite, enough

***Koliko* tjedana ostajete?**	How many weeks are you staying?
***Nekoliko* tjedana.**	Several weeks.
Vidim *mnogo* oglasa.	I see *many* ads.
Ima vode.	*There's* water.
***Nema* problema.**	*No* [there isn't a] problem.
Imam *malo* vremena.	I have *little* time.

Ima *there is/are* in conjunction with the genitive case is associated with the so called *partitive meaning*, which is in English usually translated as *any* or *some of*:

***Imate* li ribe?**	Do *you* have *any* fish?
***Ima* li kruha?**	Is there *any* bread?
***Imaju* li vina?**	Do *they* have *any* wine?

The most common prepositions that require the genitive case are:

blizu near
bez without
do to
ispod under
ispred in front of
iz from
iza behind
između between
iznad above
kod at someone's, in s.o.'s possession, by
nakon after
od from
oko around
pored next to, by
poslije after
preko over, across
prije before
protiv against
s from, off and down a surface

***Kod* tebe je tijesno.**
It's overcrowded *at your place.*

Stan se nalazi točno *između* željezničkog kolodvora i glavnog trga.
The apartment is located exactly *between* the railway station and the main square.

Koliko ima *od* Palmotićeve ulice *do* Trga bana Jelačića?
How far is it *from* Palmotić Street *to* Ban Jelačić's square?

Ništa *bez* tebe!
I couldn't do it *without* you! [*lit.:* Nothing without you!]

***Nakon* toga idemo na ručak.**
After that let's have lunch.

Marijana je *iz* Bostona, a Darko je *iz* Zagreba.
Marijana is *from* Boston and Darko is *from* Zagreb.

Auto je *ispred* restorana.
The car is *in front of* the restaurant.

Tko živi *iznad* tebe?
Who lives *upstairs from* [*above*] you?

There are also *verbs that require the genitive.* These will be introduced gradually. Two frequent ones are **bojati se** *to be afraid of* and **sjećati se** *to remember.*

Bojim se tog zadatka. I'm afraid of that task.
Sjećam se ovog gospodina. I remember this gentleman.

Finally, the genitive is also used to designate *color* in the expressions **plave boje** *of blue color* and **crvene boje** *of red color.* Use **boje** with all colors.

auto *plave boje* a *blue* car **knjiga *zelene boje*** a *green* book

1.3. Personal pronouns in the genitive

Most forms for the personal pronouns in the genitive are identical to the accusative:

	nom.sg.	*gen. sg.* long	*gen. sg.* short	*nom. pl.*	*gen. pl.* long	*gen. pl.* short
1st	**ja** I	**mene** me	**me** me	**mi** we	**nas** us	**nas** us
2nd	**ti** you	**tebe** you	**te** you	**vi** you	**vas** you	**vas** you
3rd *m.*	**on** he	**njega** him	**ga** him	**oni** they	**njih** them	**ih** them
3rd *f.*	**ona** she	**nje** her	**je** her	**one** they	**njih** them	**ih** them
3rd *neu.*	**ono** it	**njega** it	**ga** it	**ona** they	**njih** them	**ih** them

2. Possessive forms of names

Possession in English is expressed by adding *'s* to a personal name (e.g., *Mary's*), while in Croatian the appropriate ending is added to the noun.

For masculine and neuter nouns, the ending, depending on the softness of the final consonant, is **-ov** or **-ev**.

Ivan→Ivan*ov* Ivan's **Blaž→Blaž*ev*** Blaž's

Masculine names ending in **-a** replace the final vowel with **-in.**

Andrija→Andrij*in* Andrija's

The ending for female names is also **-in**.

Sanja→Sanj*in* Sanja's **Edita→Edit*in*** Edita's

Feminine names ending in **-ica** form the possessive by changing that ending into **-ičin**:

Anica→Anič*in* Anica's **Marica→Marič*in*** Marica's

These forms behave like adjectives, meaning that in the different cases they will take the appropriate adjectival endings.

Vidim *Ivanovu* knjigu. I see *Ivan's* book.
Bojim se *Sanjinog* rođaka. I'm afraid of *Sanja's* cousin.
To je *Aničina* mačka. That is *Anica's* cat.

3. Conjunctions *i, a, ali, pa, ili, ni, niti, jer, ako*

In the previous texts we have encountered the most frequent conjunctions. They are listed below along with their meanings and explanations of their use.

i and, too, in addition

This most common of conjunctions primarily means *and.*

Darko *i* Ivan su iz Hrvatske. Darko *and* Ivan are from Croatia.
On *i* ja putujemo u srijedu. He *and* I are departing on Wednesday.

It can also indicate inclusion. When **i** is doubled it should be translated as *both.*

Drago mi je. *I* meni! I'm glad. *So* am I. *(Me* too.*)*
Ima *i* lijepi vrt. It *also* has a beautiful garden.

***I* on *i* ja putujemo u srijedu.** He *and* I *too* are traveling on Wednesday. (Both *he and I are traveling on Wednesday.)*

a but, and

This conjunction indicates that two items have something in common but are contrasted. Depending on the context, it can be translated as *but* or *and*. It is preceded by a comma.

Kuhinja i kupaona su ovdje, *a* soba je tamo.
The kitchen and the bathroom are here, *and* the bedroom is there.
On putuje u srijedu, *a* ja u četvrtak.
He is traveling on Wednesday, *but* I'm traveling on Thursday.

It can also convey the meaning of *in addition.*

Ovo mjesto nije bučno, *a* ima i lijepi vrt.
This place is not noisy and it *also* has a beautiful garden.
Ja putujem danas, *a* ide i on.
I'm traveling today *and* he is going *too*.

ali but

Ali is employed in contrasted clauses and is closest to English *but*. It is separated by a comma.

Sada ostajem samo jedan mjesec, *ali* zbog posla moram često putovati ovamo.
I am staying only for a month now, *but* because of work I have to travel here often.
Vozim kada moram, *ali* radije hodam.
I drive when I have to, *but* I prefer to walk.
On putuje, *ali* ja ostajem.
He is traveling, *but* I'm staying.

pa so, therefore, then

Pa is used in enumerating multiple actions or objects and in order to point to a causal relation between two occurrences. It is preceded by a comma.

Dobri stanovi blizu centra se iznajme brzo, *pa* moramo požuriti.
Good apartments near the center get rented quickly *so* we should hurry.
On dugo spava ujutro, *pa* uvijek kasni.
He sleeps late in the morning *and so* [he] is always late.

ili or, either

The basic meaning of **ili** is *or*.

Jesi li tu kao ekonomist *ili* kao turist?
Are you here as an economist *or* as a tourist?
Putuješ li ti *ili* on?
Is it you *or* he who's traveling?

Its secondary meaning is *either/or*, but in this case **ili** has to be repeated in the sentence.

***Ili* znaš *ili* ne znaš.** You *either* know *or* don't know.
Putuje *ili* on *ili* ja. *Either* he *or* I is traveling.

ni either, neither

***Ni* on ne zna.** He doesn't know *either*. [lit.: *Neither* does he know.]
***Ni* mi ne putujemo.** We are not traveling *either*. [*lit.: Neither* are we traveling.]

The secondary meaning is *neither . . . nor*, but in that case **ni** has to be repeated.

***Ni* on *ni* ja ne znamo.** *Neither* he *nor* I know.
***Ni* vi *ni* mi ne putujemo.** *Neither* you *nor* we are traveling.

niti neither *(intensifier)*

***Niti* on niti ja ne znamo.** *Neither* he nor I know.
***Niti* mi niti vi ne putujemo.** *Neither* you nor we are traveling.

jer because, since

Ljudi ovdje više upotrebljavaju javni prijevoz *jer* benzin nije jeftin.
People here use public transportation more *because* gas is not cheap.
Ne trebam ni autobus ni tramvaj *jer* svuda mogu ići pješke.
I don't need either the bus or tram at all *since* I can walk everywhere.

ako if

***Ako* hoćeš, ja mogu pripremiti nešto za jelo.**
If you wish, I can prepare something to eat.
***Ako* se slažete, uzimam ga.**
If you agree, I'll take it [am taking it].

Exercises

Vježba 5.1 Fill in the blanks below with the correct word from the choices.
Example: **Jedemo ručak kod**________. a) on b) **njega** c) njezin

1. Nema ________. Dvije tisuće kuna nije puno za ovu lokaciju.
   a) problem b) problemu c) problema
2. Danas želim tražiti stan ______________tebe.
   a) s b) pored c) bez
3. Kolika je stanarina? Pet ______________ kuna.
   a) tisuću b) tisuće c) tisuća
4. Možeš li ostati kod _____________ ?
   a) me b) ja c) mene
5. Za mene mineralnu ________________ i čašu vode za gospodina.
   a) voda b) vode c) vodu
6. Vozim ____________ kad moram.
   a) autu b) auto c) auta
7. To su knjige za _____________ .
   a) oni b) njih c) ih
8. Je li _________________ ti poznaješ?
   a) nje b) ju c) nju
9. Ovo je stan ______________________ .
   a) moja sestra b) moju sestru c) moje sestre
10. Moj stan je blizu ___________________.
    a) centar b) centru c) centra

Vježba 5.2 Translate the following prepositions which take the genitive case and use them in a sentence:

1. bez __________
   ____
2. kod __________
   ____
3. poslije __________
   ____
4. iz __________
   ____
5. do __________
   ____
6. oko __________
   ____

7. nakon _________
____
8. blizu _________
____
9. između _________
____
10. od _________
____

Vježba 5.3

A. Indicate the proper genitive ending for the nouns below.

Example: **stan** *sg.* **stana** *gen.*

1. knjiga *sg.* _______
2. muž *pl.* _______
3. tramvaj *sg.* _______
4. zgrada *pl.* _______
5. student *pl.* _______
6. kat *pl.* _______
7. pismo *pl.* _______
8. stvar *sg.* _______
9. oglas *pl.* _______
10. zadatak *pl.* _______
11. prozor *sg.* _______
12. profesorica *sg.* _______

B. Use the nouns from the exercise above to form sentences that correctly use the conjunctions **i**, **a**, **ali**, **pa**, **ili**, **ni**, **niti**, **jer** or **ako**

Example: **stan** – **Stan je mali, ali zgrada je velika**.

1. ____
2. ____
3. ____
4. ____
5. ____
6. ____
7. ____
8. ____
9. ____
10. ____
11. ____
12. ____

Vježba 5.4

A. Translate into Croatian:

I have many friends. Gabriella is from Italy [Italija], but her mother is from England [Engleska]. Igor is from Russia [Rusija], but his father is from Greece [Grčka]. Andrew is from Canada [Kanada], and Soomi is from South Korea [Južna Koreja]. Ines is from Argentina [Argentina], and Nino is from Portugal [Portugal]. My Croatian friends are from Stari Grad, Pula, Vukovar, and Gospić.

B. Using the pattern "Is there any x" ask about the items listed below. Try to use an adjective of your choice as well (e.g. white wine):

wine, cakes, food, soup, fish, meat, water, salad

Vježba 5.5 Translate the following sentences:

1. Ima i lijepo dvorište.
2. Bojim se tog profesora.
3. That is a bad price for this location.
4. I wish to have a glass of water and mixed salad.
5. Vidim auto tvojeg prijatelja. Je li on student ili radi?
6. He is busy today, but it's nice of him that he wants to help.

Vježba 5.6 Genitive practice. Translate and answer the following questions:

1. Čega ima, a čega nema ovdje?
   ____
2. Gde je ____x_____? Evo ____x________!
   ____
3. Što radite prije ručka?
   ____
4. Što radite nakon ručka?
   ____
5. Kod koga su ključevi od mojeg novog auta?
   ____
6. Odakle ste?
   ____
7. Koliko ima od vaše kuće do centra?
   ____
8. Što je ispred Vas?
   ____
9. Što je iza Vas?
   ____
10. Čiju knjigu čitate?
    ____
11. Bez čega ne možete?
    ____
12. Čega/koga se bojite?
    ____

Vježba 5.7
A. Translate into Croatian:

What one can do without – Bez čega se ne može

I want to buy some bread and a few trifles. I live close to the center and I don't need a tram. I go on foot. It is a nice day. I run into Marko and we go for a beer [na pivo]. We watch a soccer match [nogometna utakmica]. We sit [sjedimo] in front of the TV for a long time. After that, when we arrive to the store [u trgovinu], there is no bread. There's nothing. This is not good because I'm hungry. What now? I say "One can live without beer, but not without bread." Marko doesn't agree: "No, one can't live without beer." He likes to joke. He laughs and says: "Let's go to my place. I'm an excellent cook." [kuhar]

____

____

____

____

____

____

____

____

____

____

____

____

B. Describe your apartment in a minimum of five sentences.

____

____

____

____

____

Lekcija 6
Kupovina

Lesson 6
Shopping

Lekcija 6: Kupovina

Prvi dio

Marijana: Danas moram kupiti namirnice i neke stvari za stan.

Darko: Samoposluživanje je blizu. Hoćemo li najprije otići tamo?
Marijana: Važi. Moj hladnjak je prazan i treba ga napuniti.
Darko: Tu vani, ispred trgovine nalazi se tržnica gdje se prodaje svježe voće i povrće.
Marijana: Idem prvo unutra kupiti mlijeko, kruh, meso i slično.

Darko: Sada su dva sata i petnaest minuta. Moramo sve završiti do četiri, jer tada imam dogovor.
Marijana: I ja imam sastanak u pet i trideset. Sreća što nema gužve.
Prodavačica: Izvolite?
Marijana: Koliko košta ovaj sir?
Prodavačica: Kilogram je četrdeset pet kuna. Nije skup i ukusan je.

Marijana: Molim Vas, dvadeset dekagrama sira i isto toliko salame. Darko, dok ja čekam, možeš li pronaći sok, molim te?
Darko: Odmah se vraćam!
Marijana: Molim Vas, još pola kilograma kruha. Znate li gdje su kolači?
Prodavačica: S druge strane one police.
Marijana: A imate li još jogurta?
Prodavačica: Nažalost, već je kasno, pa ga više nema. Ali zato su kolači na sniženju!
Marijana: Hvala. Darko, ti si nevjerojatno brz.

Drugi dio

Darko: Što još moramo kupiti?
Marijana: Dva kilograma šećera, sedam litara mineralne vode, paket kave, jedan deterdžent, jedan šampon, tri sapuna i to je sve.

Lesson 6: Shopping

Part I

Marijana:	Today I have to buy groceries and some things for the apartment.
Darko:	The grocery store is nearby. Are we going there first?
Marijana:	Fine. My refrigerator is empty and needs to be filled.
Darko:	Here outside, in front of the grocery store is an open market where fresh fruit and vegetables are sold.
Marijana:	I am going inside first to buy milk, bread, meat, and similar things.
Darko:	It's two-fifteen now. We have to finish everything by four because I have an appointment then.
Marijana:	I have a meeting at five-thirty too. Luckily the store isn't crowded.
Salesperson:	How can I help you?
Marijana:	How much is this cheese?
Salesperson:	One kilogram costs forty five kunas. It's not expensive and it's tasty.
Marijana:	Twenty decagrams of cheese and the same amount of salami please. Darko, while I'm waiting, can you please find juice?
Darko:	I'll be right back!
Marijana:	Also half a kilogram of bread please. Do you know where the sweets are?
Salesperson:	On the other side of that shelf.
Marijana:	And do you have any more yogurt?
Salesperson:	Unfortunately, it is late and there is no more yogurt. But the sweets are on sale!
Marijana:	Thank you. Darko, you are incredibly fast.

Part II

Darko:	What else do we have to buy?
Marijana:	Two kilograms of sugar, seven liters of mineral water, a package of coffee, one [container of] detergent, one shampoo, three bars of soap and that is all.

Darko: **Još malo, pa smo gotovi!**

Marijana: **Gdje je blagajna?**

Darko: **Eno je kod izlaza.**

Marijana: **Primate li kreditne kartice ili samo gotovinu?**

Blagajnica: **Primamo jedno i drugo.**

Marijana: **Sve vrste kartica?**

Blagajnica: **Da. Potpišite se ovdje, molim, i izvolite račun.**

Darko: **Hoćemo li sada kupiti malo svježeg voća?**

Marijana: **One jabuke izgledaju odlično. Da kupimo pola kilograma?**

Darko: **To je premalo. Molim Vas, kilogram jabuka i pola kilograma grožđa za gospođicu.**

Marijana: **Ali to je previše!**

Darko: **Grožđe je slatko, moraš ga probati!**

Prodavačica: **Ukupno šesnaest kuna.**

Darko: **Stvarno je jeftino. Izvolite novac.**

Marijana: **Gotovi smo! Ako imaš vremena, sutra možemo razgledati neke znamenitosti. Želim vidjeti Hrvatsko narodno kazalište i Muzej Mimara. U četvrtak imam poslovne obveze i zauzeta sam cijeli dan.**

Darko: **Važi. Vidimo se sutra!**

Marijana: **Doviđenja, Darko!**

Darko:	We're almost done!
Marijana:	Where is the cashier?
Darko:	It's over there by the exit.
Marijana:	Do you accept credit cards or cash only?
Cashier:	We accept both.
Marijana:	All types of credit cards?
Cashier:	Yes. Sign here please, and here's the receipt.
Darko:	Are we going to buy some fresh fruit now?
Marijana:	Those apples look great. Shall we buy half a kilo?
Darko:	That is too little. One kilogram of apples and half a kilogram of grapes for the young lady.
Marijana:	But that is too much!
Darko:	The grapes are sweet, you have to try them!
Salesperson:	That is sixteen kunas altogether.
Darko:	It's really inexpensive. Here's the money.
Marijana:	We are done! If you have time, tomorrow we can see some of the sights. I'd like to see the Croatian National Theater and the Mimara Museum. On Thursday I have business obligations and I am busy the entire day.
Darko:	Fine. See you tomorrow.
Marijana:	Good-bye, Darko!

Vocabulary

blagajna cash register
blagajnica female cashier
cijeli whole, entire
crkva church
dekagram decagram
deterdžent detergent
dogovor appointment
dok while
gotovina cash
grožđe grapes
gužva crowd, busy place, uproar
hladnjak refrigerator
ispred in front of
isto the same
izlaz exit
jabuka apple
jeftin inexpensive, cheap
jogurt yogurt
još more, again, still
kasno late
kava coffee
kilogram kilogram *(2.2 lbs.)*
kolač sweet, cake
kreditna kartica credit card
kruh bread
kuna Croatian monetary unit
kupovina shopping
litra liter *(.26 gallons)*
malo a little, little
minuta minute
mlijeko milk
najprije firstly, first of all
namirnice groceries
neki some
nevjerojatno incredibly
novac money[1]
obveza obligation
odmah immediately
paket package
pola half
polica shelf
povrće vegetables
prazan empty
premalo too little
previše too much
prodavačica female salesperson
pun full
račun bill, receipt
rano early
salama salami
samoposluživanje grocery store
sapun soap
sastanak meeting
sat o'clock, hour, clock, watch
sir cheese
skup expensive
slično similar
sniženje sale
sreća luck, luckily
sok juice
sutra tomorrow
strana side
stvarno really
svjež fresh
šampon shampoo
šećer sugar
tada then
toliko so much/many
trgovina shop
tržnica food market
ujutro in the morning
ukupno total

---

1. **Novca** *gen. sg*/**novaca** *gen. pl.* In quantity expressions *gen. pl.* is often used: **puno novaca** *a lot of money*, **premalo novaca** *too little money*, **nemamo novaca** *we don't have any money.*

ulaz entrance
unutra inside
vani outside
voće fruit
vrsta type, kind
znamenitost *f.* sight, point of interest

Verb List

izgledati (*I* **izgledam**, **izgledaju**) to seem, appear
kupiti (*P* **kupim**, **kupe**) to buy
napuniti (*P* **napunim**, **napune**) to fill
potpisati (se) (*P* **potpišem**, **potpišu)** to sign
primati (*I* **primam**, **primaju**) to accept
probati (*I/P* **probam**, **probaju**) to try
prodavati (*I* **prodajem**, **prodaju**) to sell
pronaći (*P* **pronađem**, **pronađu**) to locate, to find
razgledati (*P* **razgledam**, **razgledaju**) to sightsee
važiti (*I* **važim**, **važe**) to be valid
vratiti se (*P* **vratim se**, **vrate se**) to return
završiti (*P* **završim**, **završe**) to finish

Useful Expressions

treba it's necessary to
važi fine *(agreed)*
potpišite se, molim sign, please
nema gužve it is not crowded
izvolite račun/novac here's the receipt/money
na sniženju on sale
koliko košta? how much?
Odmah se vraćam! I'll be right back!
Još malo, pa smo gotovi! We're almost done!
Primate li kreditne kartice ili gotovinu? Do you take credit cards or cash?

Grammar

1. Numerals

1.1. Cardinal Numbers

The Croatian word for *number* is **broj**. In compound numbers the conjunction **i** *and* may be omitted.

nula 0
jedan, jedna, jedno 1
dva, dvije 2
tri 3
četiri 4
pet 5
šest 6
sedam 7
osam 8
devet 9
deset 10

jedanaest 11
dvanaest 12
trinaest 13
četrnaest 14
petnaest 15
šesnaest 16
sedamnaest 17
osamnaest 18
devetnaest 19
dvadeset 20

dvadeset (i) jedan 21
dvadeset (i) dva 22 ...
trideset 30
četrdeset 40
pedeset 50
šezdeset 60
sedamdeset 70
osamdeset 80
devedeset 90
sto 100

sto (i) jedan 101
sto dvadeset (i) pet 125
dvjesto 200
tristo 300
četiristo 400
tisuća/ tisuću 1,000
tisuću i jedan 1001

tisuću sto trideset (i) osam 1138
tri tisuće 3000
pet tisuća 5000
milijun 1,000 000
milijun i jedan 1,000 001
milijarda billion

Numbers in Slavic languages are rather difficult and Croatian is no exception. As with everything else, however, memorizing some basic rules and a bit of practice will make learning them easier.

As you can see from the list above, use of the conjunction **i** *and* is optional. Note also that the noun for one thousand is **tisuća**, but in counting it becomes **tisuću**. This noun (as well as the ones for million and billion) are affected by *the rule of five* discussed below and that is why they change depending on which number precedes them.

In Croatian the number *one*, **jedan**, behaves like an adjective. This means that its form changes depending on the gender of the noun it accompanies:

jedan stan *m.* one apartment
jedna jabuka *f.* one apple
jedno pismo *neu.* one letter

It also changes depending on the case:

Vidim jednog studenta.	I see one student/I see a student.
Molim Vas, jednu kavu za mene.	A coffee for me, please.

Jedan can be translated as *one* or as the indefinite article *a/an* in English, depending on the meaning and context.

Similarly, the number *two* **dva, dvije** reflects gender:

dva studenta *m.*	two *(male)* students
dvije studentice *f.*	two *(female)* students

The most important thing to memorize about numbers is the so-called *rule of 5*:

- numbers 2 to 4 and all compound numbers ENDING in 2, 3, or 4 are followed by a noun in the *genitive singular*.

dva stola *gen. sg.*	2 tables
tri stola *gen. sg.*	3 tables
četiri stola *gen. sg.*	4 tables
dvadeset dva stola *gen. sg.*	22 tables
trideset četiri studenta *gen. sg.*	34 students

- numbers from 5 through 20 and all the compound numbers that END in 5, 6, 7, 8, 9 and 0 (for example, **trideset pet** *35,* **četrdeset osam** *48,* **šezdeset** *60,* etc.), take a noun in the *genitive plural*.

pet stolova *gen. pl.*	5 tables
sedam stolova *gen. pl.*	7 tables
jedanaest stolova *gen. pl.*	11 tables
dvanaest stolova *gen. pl.*	12 tables
šezdeset stolova *gen. pl.*	60 tables
osam studenata *gen. pl.*	8 students
sedamdeset osam studenata *gen. pl.*	78 students

- *One* and numbers ENDING in *one* (such as *twenty-one*, *thirty-one*, etc. but NOT *eleven*) are followed by a noun in the *nominative singular*.

jedan stol *nom. sg.*	1 table
dvadeset i jedan student *nom. sg.*	21 students
jedanaest studenata *gen. pl.*	11 students

This rule also affects the verb. The numbers 2–4 and compound numbers ending in these digits take the verb in the plural; all other numbers starting with 5 and up use a verb in the singular.

Dva studenta *jedu* ručak.	Two students are eating lunch.
Pet studenata *jede* ručak.	Five students are eating lunch.

The *rule of 5* extends to adjectives as well. While adjectives for the numbers 5 and up take the genitive plural form just like the noun, those modifying the numbers 2–4 have a special form. The most important thing to remember is that the adjectives in the 2–4 group have the same endings as the nouns. The exception are adjectives modifying feminine nouns ending in a consonant since they have the same ending as adjectives modifying other feminine nouns.

dva pametna studenta	two clever *(male)* students
tri dobra stola	three good tables
dva duga pisma	two long letters
četiri mlade profesorice	four young *(female)* professors
dvije lijepe stvari	two beautiful things
pet pametnih studenata	five clever *(male)* students
osam dobrih stolova	eight good tables
sedamnaest dugih pisama	seventeen long letters
dvadeset šest mladih profesorica	twenty-six young *(female)* professors
četrdeset osam lijepih stvari	forty-eight beautiful things

Numbers take precedence over the verb when it comes to determining the case. While the verb **imati** *to have* takes the accusative, if we add numbers, the object will be in the case dictated by those numbers, i.e., the genitive singular or plural.

Imam tri stola.	I have three tables.
Imam pet stolova.	I have five tables.

It is equally important to distinguish between *countable* and *uncountable nouns* in the genitive. While countable nouns (even when their exact number is not mentioned) will be in the genitive plural, uncountable nouns will be in the singular. For native English speakers the questions *how many* and *how much* convey a similar distinction.

Ima puno krušaka.	There are a lot of pears.
Koliko knjiga ima ovdje?	How many books are there here?
Nema vode.	There is no water.
Koliko kave moraš kupiti?	How much coffee do you need to buy?

1.2. Ordinal Numbers

Ordinal numbers behave like adjectives in terms of their endings and they decline along with the noun they modify.

Ordinal Numbers

masculine	feminine	neuter	meaning
prvi	**prva**	**prvo**	first
drugi	**druga**	**drugo**	second
treći	**treća**	**treće**	third
četvrti	**četvrta**	**četvrto**	fourth
peti	**peta**	**peto**	fifth
šesti	**šesta**	**šesto**	sixth
sedmi	**sedma**	**sedmo**	seventh
osmi	**osma**	**osmo**	eighth
deveti	**deveta**	**deveto**	ninth
deseti	**deseta**	**deseto**	tenth
jedanaesti	**jedanaesta**	**jedanaesto**	eleventh
četrnaesti	**četrnaesta**	**četrnaesto**	fourteenth
....			
dvadeseti	**dvadeseta**	**dvadeseto**	twentieth
pedeseti	**pedeseta**	**pedeseto**	fiftieth
stoti	**stota**	**stoto**	one hundreth
tisućiti	**tisućita**	**tisućito**	one thousandth

Simply add **-i** for masculine, **-a** for feminine, and **-o** for neuter to the cardinal number. Note that numbers ending in a vowel have additional changes as noted above, thus **četiri—četvrti, sto—stoti, tisuća—tisućiti.**

Vidim našeg *prvog* profesora.	I see our *first* professor.
On čita *petu* knjigu.	He is reading the *fifth* book.
Ona pije *treću* čašu mlijeka.	She is drinking the *third* glass of milk.

2. Dates

Ordinal numbers in the genitive are used in dates. The number indicating the day is in the genitive with verbs other than the verb *to be*. This means that in expressions such as *Today is...* **Danas je...**, the day will be an ordinal number in the nominative and the month will be an ordinal noun/number in the genitive.

Danas je peti kolovoza/osmog. Today is the fifth of August.

With other verbs, both numbers will be in the genitive. In dates that include the year one says **tisuću** (not * ***tisuća***) for *one thousand* and the final digit is an ordinal number in the genitive feminine.

Kada putujete?	When are you traveling?
Putujemo trideset prvog osmog.	We are traveling on August 31st.

Koji je danas datum?	What is the date today?

Danas je trideset prvi osmog dvije tisuće i šeste godine.
Today it is August 31st, 2006.

Kada ste rođeni?	When were you born?

Rođen (rođena, *f.***) sam osamnaestog devetog tisuću devetsto sedamdeset i šeste godine.**
I was born on the eighteenth of September 1976.

The Croatian names for the months are not capitalized as in English. In a date the name of the month is in the genitive.

Months

siječanj *nom.*/**siječnja** *gen.* January
veljača *nom.*/**veljače** *gen.* February
ožujak *nom.*/**ožujka** *gen.* March
travanj *nom.*/**travnja** *gen.* April
svibanj *nom.*/**svibnja** *gen.* May
lipanj *nom.*/**lipnja** *gen.* June
srpanj *nom.*/**srpnja** *gen.* July
kolovoz *nom.*/**kolovoza** *gen.* August
rujan *nom.*/**rujna** *gen.* September
listopad *nom.*/**listopada** *gen.* October
studeni *nom.*/**studenog** *gen.* November
prosinac *nom.*/**prosinca** *gen.* December

Putujemo trideset prvog kolovoza.	We are traveling on August 31st.
Danas je trideset prvi kolovoza.	Today it is August 31st.

Below are the names of the seasons in Croatian. The colloquial way of saying *in winter* is **zimi** and *in summer* is **ljeti** (used only with these two seasons). It is also quite common to use expressions like **na zimu** *in the winter*, **na jesen** *in the fall*, etc., which can be used with all seasons.

proljeće spring **ljeto** summer **jesen** fall **zima** winter

Kamo putujete ljeti?
Where are you traveling in the summer?
Planiram biti u Dubrovniku na proljeće.
I plan to be in Dubrovnik in the spring.

3. Telling time

The basic units of time are as follows. Note the short genitive plural for **sat** *hour* and **mjesec** *month*. There is also the word **satovi** (*gen. pl.* **satova**) but it means *clock* or *watch.*

sekunda second
minuta minute
sat *nom. sg.*/**sati** *gen. pl.* hour
dan/dani *pl.* day
tjedan week
mjesec *nom. sg.*/**mjeseci** *gen. pl.* month
godina year

When **sat** *hour,* **tjedan** *week,* **mjesec** *month*, or **godina** *year* are used in the *singular* to mean *one whole period of time* (e.g., an hour, a week, a month, a year), the following genitive constructions, which are often modified by an intensifier **već** *already*, are used:

sat vremena	an hour
tjedan/mjesec/godinu dana	a week/a month/a year

Njega nema već *sat vremena.*	He's been gone already for *an hour*.
On ne piše već *godinu dana.*	It has been *a year* since he wrote.

BUT

Njega nema već *četiri sata.*	He's been gone already for *four hours*.
On ne piše već *četiri godine.*	It has been *four years* since he wrote.

Other expressions indicating a point in time also use the genitive. For example, one says: **idućeg tjedna** *next week*, **iduće godine** *next year*, **prošlog mjeseca** *last month*, **prošle godine** *last year*, **ovog tjedna** *this week*, **cijelog života** *whole life*, etc.

Idućeg tjedna idem u Pariz.	Next week I'm going to Paris.
Ovog tjedna sam vrlo umorna.	This week I'm very tired.
Cijelog života živim u Zagrebu.	My whole life I've been living in Zagreb.

It is not unusual, however, to hear the following also:

Vidimo se idući tjedan! *See you next week!*

Note that the prepositions **za** and **na** have different meanings in the expressions listed below:

> ***za* mjesec dana** – *in* a month from now, *within* a month
> ***za* tjedan dana** – *in* a week from now, *within* a week
>
> ***na* mjesec dana** – *(to go somewhere) in order to* spend a month; *for* a month
> ***na* tjedan dana** – *(to go somewhere) in order to* spend a week; *for* a week

Times of the day are:

jutro, prije podne morning
podne noon
popodne, poslije podne afternoon
večer evening
noć night
ponoć midnight

Several other frequent markers of time are:

danas today
jučer yesterday
sutra tomorrow
jutros this morning
ujutro in the morning
večeras this evening
navečer in the evening
noćas tonight
sinoć last night
preksutra day after tomorrow
prekjučer day before yesterday
rano early
kasno late
odmah immediately
uskoro soon

Koliko je sati?	What time is it?
Sada je jedan sat.	It is . . . one o'clock.
Sada su tri sata.	. . . three o'clock.
Sada je pet sati.	. . . five o'clock.
Sada je šest sati i deset minuta (šest i deset).	. . . ten past six.
Sada je osam i četvrt (osam i petnaest).	. . . quarter past eight.
Sada je deset i pol (deset i trideset).	. . . half past ten.
Sada je dvadeset do dva.	. . . twenty to two.
Sada je pet do jedanaest.	. . . five to eleven.
Sada je četvrt do dvanaest (petnaest do dvanaest).	. . . quarter to twelve.

In official announcements the hours are counted up to twenty four.

Točno je sedamnaest sati i trideset minuta. It is exactly 5:30 pm.

A slightly more colloquial expression—**pola + number**—gives the time on the half-hour:

pola pet 4:30 [*lit.:* halfway to five] **pola osam** 7:30 [*lit.:* halfway to eight]

Note that the use of **pola** in regards to time does not refer to what most English speakers refer to as *half-past the hour*; instead, think of the expression in terms of *halfway towards the hour.*

Appendix: Collective Numbers

This group of numbers is used for groups of people. Depending on the gender mix, the numbers used will differ. When referring to a group of women consisting of more than two persons, cardinal numbers should be used. Different forms are used, however, to indicate a group of men or a mixed male-female group.

mixed group	men	women	
dvoje	**dvojica**	**dvije**	two
oboje	**obojica**	**obje**	both
troje	**trojica**	**tri**	three
četvero	**četvorica**	**četiri**	four
petero	**petorica**	**pet**	five

The two of us and similar expressions (the *three of you*, the *five of them*) require the use of the genitive plural for the pronoun as well as the correct form for the number, depending on the gender.

the 2 of them	the 3 of you	the 5 of us
– **njih dvije** 2 women	– **vas tri** 3 women	– **nas pet** 5 women
– **njih dvojica** 2 men	– **vas trojica** 3 men	– **nas petorica** 5 men
– **njih dvoje** mixed pair	– **vas troje** mixed group of 3	– **nas petero** mixed group of 5

Other numeral forms

For fractions, add **-na** to the ordinal number to create the form for the denominator. The exception to this is the word for *half*, which is **polovina**. All of these forms are feminine and conform to the *rule of five*.

½ – **jedna polovina**	⅖ – **dvije šestine**
¾ – **tri četvrtine**	⅚ – **pet šestina**

The word for *percent* is **postot*a*k**, but in combination with the actual number, it is abbreviated to **posto**:

Koji postotak studenata je iz Hrvatske?
What percentage of students are from Croatia?

Osamdeset posto studenata je iz Hrvatske, a dvadeset posto iz Amerike.
Eighty percent of students are from Croatia, and twenty percent are from America.

To provide an approximate number, the ending **-ak** is added to the tens, while hundred has a slightly different form:

desetak – approximately ten	**pedesetak** – approximately fifty
dvadesetak – approximately twenty	**stotinjak** – approximately hundred

Exercises

Vježba 6.1 Write out the following cardinal numbers and use the appropriate form of the noun.

Example: **15** petnaest **knjiga** petnaest knjiga

1.	9	________	stan	________________
2.	1	________	hladnjak	________________
3.	11	________	jabuka	________________
4.	4	________	paket	________________
5.	25	________	račun	________________
6.	22	________	strana	________________
7.	34	________	tržnica	________________
8.	30	________	sok	________________
9.	51	________	dizalo	________________
10.	100	________	stol	________________

Vježba 6.2 Convert the above numbers into ORDINAL numbers in the *masculine* gender only.

Example: **15 petnaesti**

1. 9	______	6. 22	______
2. 1	______	7. 34	______
3. 11	______	8. 30	______
4. 4	______	9. 51	______
5. 25	______	10. 100	______

Vježba 6.3 Write the following sentences in Croatian. For months, try to use both the number and the name.

1. I (male) was born on the twentieth of June 1985.

   ____

2. Today it is September 12, 2006.

   ____

3. We are traveling on January 5.

   ____

4. I (female) was born on the thirtieth of May 1969.

   ____

5. Today is November 2.

   ____

Vježba 6.4 Telling Time. Fill in the blanks below.

Example: **Sada je šest sati i pet minuta.** It is five past six.

1. Sada su dva sata	______________
2. ______________	It is twelve past three.
3. Sada je pola pet	______________
4. ______________	It is quarter to ten.
5. Sada je dvadeset do dva	______________

Vježba 6.5 Practice Plurals: Give the plural form of the noun.
Example: **profesor** *gen.* **profesora**

1. krevet *acc.* ____________
2. ormar *gen.* ____________
3. stan *nom.* ____________
4. cijena *gen.* ____________
5. student *gen.* ____________
6. mjesec *acc.* ____________
7. godina *nom.* ____________
8. oglas *acc.* ____________
9. konobar *acc.* ____________
10. studentica *gen.* ____________
11. riba *nom.* ____________
12. ljudi *acc.* ____________
13. sniženje *gen.* ____________
14. vrijeme *gen.* ____________
15. ekonomist *nom.* ____________
16. Amerikanac *nom.* ____________
17. auto *gen.* ____________
18. odmor *acc.* ____________
19. osobina *gen.* ____________
20. noć *gen.* ____________

Vježba 6.6 Correctly complete the sentence using each of the different choices.

1. Molim Vas, još 300 grama *sir / kobasica / kruh.*
2. Onaj čovjek putuje u Boston u *petak / srijeda / 3 sata.*
3. Za mene, molim, *čaša vode / zelena salata / miješano meso.*
4. Ovo je stan *moj brat / moja majka / moja rođaka.*
5. On ne studira već *mjesec dan_ / 5 godina / 3 tjedan.*

Vježba 6.7 A. Answer the following questions about Marijana and Darko:

1. Što Marijana danas mora raditi?

   ____

2. Gdje je samoposluživanje?

   ____

3. Što se nalazi ispred trgovine?

   ____

4. Do kada moraju Marijana i Darko sve završiti?

   ____

5. Što Marijana kupuje?

   ____

6. Što Darko traži?

   ____

7. Čega ima, a čega nema?

   ____

8. Gdje je blagajna?

   ____

9. Što Marijana kupuje poslije toga?

   ____

10. Što Marijana želi raditi sutra?

   ____

B. Answer the following questions about yourself:

1. Što Vi obično kupujete?

   ____

2. Volite li više male ili velike trgovine?

   ____

3. Je li je hrana skupa?

   ____

4. Koji je danas datum?

   ____

5. Putujete li uskoro nekamo?

   ____

6. Kada je Vaš rođendan?

   ____

7. Što sada radite?

   ____

8. Koliko je sati?

   ____

9. Kada obično ručate?

   ____

10. Kada obično idete spavati?

   ____

Vježba 6.8 Look at the pictures below and tell what time it is.

Koliko je sati?

Lekcija 7
Na poslovnom sastanku

Lesson 7
At a business meeting

Lekcija 7: Na poslovnom sastanku

Prvi dio

Marijana: Halo! Ovdje Marijana Tomich. Trebam gospodina Darka Tomića, molim Vas.

Glas: Dobili ste pogrešan broj. Ovdje nema gospodina Tomića.

Marijana: Oprostite!

Marijana: Halo! Mogu li dobiti gospodina Tomića, molim Vas?

Tajnica: Gospodin Tomić je zauzet. U laboratoriju je kod profesora Klarića i ne može sada razgovarati. Tko ga treba?

Marijana: Ovdje Marijana Tomich.

Tajnica: Želite li ostaviti poruku?

Marijana: Možete li mu reći da imam poslovni sastanak u dva? Moram biti u uredu i ne mogu doći do njega danas popodne.

Tajnica: U redu. Koji je Vaš broj telefona? Hoćete li da Vas nazove kasnije?

Marijana: Nije potrebno. Hvala i doviđenja.

Drugi dio

Nešto kasnije.

Marijana: Dobar dan. Nadam se da ne kasnim.

Ravnateljica: Gospođice Tomich, stižete u pravi trenutak. Ako smo svi ovdje, možemo započeti sastanak. Gospođica Tomich ima prezentaciju o našem poslovanju u Hrvatskoj.

Marijana: Prezentacija je kratka i pozitivna. Imam neke materijale za vas.

Vlasnik: Mogu li dobiti jedan primjerak, molim Vas?

Marijana: Izvolite. Imamo novu tvornicu, pet novih poslovnica i sve rade uspješno, kao što se vidi iz brojeva u mojem izvješću. Također, imamo velik broj stranaka, nove ugovore i otvaramo još dvije poslovnice idućeg mjeseca. Želimo zaposliti još mladih ljudi i uložiti u turizam. Hrvatska i njezino gospodarstvo su u usponu.

Lesson 7: At a business meeting

Part I

Marijana:	Hello! This is Marijana Tomich. I am looking for Mr. Darko Tomić, please.
Voice on Phone:	You have the wrong number. There is no Mr. Tomić here.
Marijana:	Excuse me!
Marijana:	Hello! Can I speak to Mr. Tomić, please?
Secretary:	Mr. Tomić is busy. He is in the lab with Professor Klarić and he can't talk right now. Who is calling?
Marijana:	This is Marijana Tomich.
Secretary:	Do you want to leave a message?
Marijana:	Can you tell him that I have a business meeting at 2 p.m? I have to be in my office and I cannot come to see him this afternoon.
Secretary:	No problem. What is your phone number? Would you like him to call you later?
Marijana:	That is not necessary. Thanks and goodbye.

Part II

Some time later.

Marijana:	Good afternoon! I hope that I am not late.
CEO:	Miss Tomich, you have arrived just at the right moment. If we are all here, we can begin the meeting. Miss Tomich has a presentation about our business in Croatia.
Marijana:	The presentation is brief and positive. I have some materials for you.
Owner:	Can I get one copy please?
Marijana:	Here you are. We have a new factory and five new branches, and all are doing business with great success as can be seen from the numbers in my analysis. Furthermore, we have a large number of clients, new contracts, and we are opening two more branches next month. We want to employ more young people and invest in tourism. Croatia is a growing economy.

Vlasnik: Postoje li negativni pokazatelji? Moramo govoriti i o tome, zar ne?

Marijana: Za sada ne. U našoj tvrtki rade uglavnom mladi ljudi. Oni su nadareni i njihove se ideje cijene na tržištu. Po mojem mišljenju, pomaže nam i to što nemamo veliko suparništvo. Oko 65% proizvoda prodajemo na domaćem tržištu, a ostali dio ide za izvoz. U tome je dodatna sigurnost.

Ravnateljica: Vaše izvješće sadrži stanovite brojeve. Koristimo domaće materijale, pa imamo manji porez i nemamo troškova uvoza.Vrlo sam zadovoljna.

Vlasnik: I ja! Kada je u Hrvatskoj, gospođica Tomich nam redovito šalje izvješća u Ameriku. Ona nam daju jasnu sliku o svemu. Čini mi se da imamo dobre rezultate. Naši zaposlenici u Hrvatskoj također kažu da im je dobro u našoj tvrtki jer imaju odlične plaće. Gospođice Tomich, čestitam Vam na uspjehu!

Marijana: Hvala. Meni je ovaj posao vrlo zanimljiv i sviđa mi se raditi u Hrvatskoj.

Ravnateljica: Sastanak je završen. Gospođice Tomich, hvala na pomoći!

Marijana: Nema na čemu. Zadovoljstvo mi je raditi za vas.

Ravnateljica: Hvala svima i vidimo se idući tjedan.

Owner: Are there any negative indicators? We need to talk about those as well, don't we?

Marijana: For now, there aren't any. Primarily young people work in our company. They are creative and their ideas are highly appreciated on the market. In my opinion, it helps that we don't have a lot of competition. We sell about 65% of our products to the domestic market and the rest goes to export. There is additional security in this.

CEO: Your analysis includes some concrete figures. We use domestic materials, so we have lower taxes and no import expenses. I am very satisfied.

Owner: Me too! When she is in Croatia, Miss Tomich regularly sends reports to America. They give us a clear picture of everything. It seems to me that we have nice results. Our employees in Croatia also say that they feel good in our firm because they have excellent salaries. Miss Tomich, congratulations on your success!

Marijana: Thank you. For me this job has been very interesting and I really enjoy working in Croatia.

CEO: The meeting is over. Miss Tomich, thank you for your help.

Marijana: Not at all. It's a pleasure to work with you.

CEO: Thanks everyone and we will see each other next week.

Vocabulary

broj number
dodatni additional
domaći domestic
dio part
gospodarstvo economy
izvješće report
izvoz export
jasan clear
kasnije later
laboratorij laboratory
materijal material
mišljenje opinion
nadaren creative
negativan negative
oko approximately, around
ostali remaining
plaća salary
pogrešan wrong
pokazatelj indicator
porez tax
poruka message
poslovanje doing business
poslovni business
poslovnica company branch
potrebno necessary
pozitivan positive
primjerak copy
proizvod product
ravnatelj *m.*/**ravnateljica** *f.* CEO
redovito regularly
rezultat result
sastanak meeting
sigurnost *f.* safety, security
slika picture
stanovit certain
stranka client
suparništvo, konkurencija competition
tajnica secretary
trenutak moment
trošak expenditure
tržište market
tvornica factory
uglavnom mainly
ugovor contract
ured office
uspjeh success
uspješno successfully
uspon ascent
uvoz import
turizam tourism
vlasnik owner
zaposlenik, djelatnik employee
zauzet busy
završen finished

Verb List

cijeniti (*I* **cijenim, cijene**) to appreciate
čestitati (*I* **čestitam, čestitaju**) to congratulate
davati (*I* **dajem, daju**) to give
dobiti (*P* **dobijem, dobiju**) to get
kasniti (*I* **kasnim, kasne**) to be late
kazati (*I* **kažem, kažu**) to say
koristiti (*I* **koristim, koriste**) to use, to utilize
nadati se (*I* **nadam se, nadaju se**) to hope

nazvati (*P* **nazovem, nazovu**) to call
ostaviti (*P* **ostavim, ostave**) to leave
otvoriti (*P* **otvorim, otvore**) to open
pomagati (*I* **pomažem, pomažu**) to help
poslovati (*I* **poslujem, posluju**) to do business
postojati (*I* **postojim, postoje**) to exist
reći (*P* **reknem, reknu**) to say
sadržati (*I/P* **sadržim, sadrže**) to contain
slati (*I* **šaljem, šalju**) to send
stizati (*I* **stižem, stižu**) to arrive
sviđati se (*I* **sviđam se, sviđaju se**) to like
uložiti (*P* **uložim, ulože**) to invest
započeti (*P* **započnem, započnu**) to start
zaposliti (*P* **zaposlim, zaposle**) to employ

Useful Expressions

Mogu li dobiti gospodina X? Can I please speak with Mr. X?
Dobili ste pogrešan broj! You've got the wrong number!
Želite li ostaviti poruku? Do you wish to leave a message?
Nije potrebno! It is not necessary!
Koji je Vaš broj telefona? What is your phone number?
U redu. OK.
Nadam se da ne kasnim. I hope I'm not late.
Stižete u pravi trenutak. You're arriving at the right moment.
u usponu in ascent, increasing
u padu in descent, decreasing
za sada for now
na tržištu on the market
Imamo jasnu sliku o svemu. We have a clear picture of everything.
Moramo govoriti o tome. We have to speak about that.
po mojem mišljenju in my opinion
Hvala na pomoći. Thank you for your help.
Nema na čemu. Not at all. *(In response to being thanked.)*
Zadovoljstvo mi je. It is my pleasure.

Professions/zanimanja

arhitekt architect
bolničar *m.*/**bolničarka** *f.* nurse
ravnatelj *m.*/**ravnateljica** *f.* CEO
domaćica homemaker
ekonomist economist
mehaničar mechanic
konobar *m.*/**konobarica** *f.* waiter/waitress
kuhar *m.*/**kuharica** *f.* chef
liječnik *m.*/**liječnica** *f.* doctor
odvjetnik *m.*/**odvjetnica** *f.* lawyer
pisac writer
poduzetnik *m.*/**poduzetnica** *f.* contractor
prevoditelj translator
profesor *m.*/**profesorica** *f.* professor
radnik *m.*/**radnica** *f.* (also **djelatnik** *m.*/**djelatnica** *f.*) worker
student *m.*/**studentica** *f.* student
umjetnik *m.*/**umjetnica** *f.* artist
upravnik *m.*/**upraviteljica** *f.* manager
vojnik soldier
vozač *m.*/**vozačica** *f.* driver
zemljoradnik farmer
zubar *m.*/**zubarica** *f.* dentist

Grammar

1. Cases: dative and locative

The dative case is typically used to express the *indirect object* in a sentence, while the locative case is used to designate the *location of a person or object.* The questions associated with these cases are:

dative: **kome** to whom
čemu to what
locative: **na/u/o kome** on/in/about whom
na/u/o čemu on/in/about which

The endings are identical for these two cases. In the dative or locative, masculine and neuter singular nouns add **-u**, while adjectives add **-om** or if the stem is soft **-em** (e.g., **lošem** *bad*). Masculine nouns ending in **-lac** replace **-lac** with **-ocu** in the dative and locative:

nom. sg.: spasi*lac* *m.* ***dat./loc. sg.***: spasi*ocu* rescuer

Feminine singular nouns add **-i** and feminine singular adjectives add **-oj.** If the final consonant in a feminine singular noun is **k, g,** or **h,** the consonant tends to change into **c**, **z**, **s** respectively before the addition of the **-i** ending:

nom. sg.	dat./loc.sg.	
knjiga *f.* book	(**u**) **knji*zi***	in a book
banka *f.* bank	(**u**) **ban*ci***	in a bank

There is a very small group of exceptions in which the final consonant doesn't change such as:

nom. sg.	**dat./loc.sg.**	
Amerikanka *f.*	**Amerikan*ki***	American *(woman)*
baka *f.*	**ba*ki***	grandmother
igračka *f.*	**igrač*ki***	toy

In the plural, all adjectival forms add **-im**, while masculine, neuter and feminine nouns ending in a consonant add **-ima** and feminine nouns ending in a vowel add **-ama**. Masculine nouns ending in **-lac** replace it with **-ocima** in the dative and locative plural.

nom. sg.: **spasi*lac*** rescuer
dat./loc. sg.: **spasi*ocu*** rescuer
dat./loc. pl.: **spasi*ocima*** rescuers

	Dative/Locative Singular			**Dative/Locative Plural**		
	adj.	**noun**		**adj.**	**noun**	
m.	**-om/em**	**-u**	**pametnom studentu**	**-im**	**-ima**	**pametnim studentima**
neu.	**-om/em**	**-u**	**dugom pismu**	**-im**	**-ima**	**dugim pismima**
f.	**-oj**	**-i**	**dobroj knjizi**	**-im**	**-ama**	**dobrim knjigama**
f.Ø	**-oj**	**-i**	**lijepoj stvari**	**-im**	**-ima**	**lijepim stvarima**

As always, possessives behave like any other adjective.

Possessive Pronouns

	dat./loc. sg.		**dat./loc. pl.**	
	ending	**my** *sg.*	**ending**	**our** *pl.*
m.	**-om/em**	**mojem**	**-im**	**mojim**
neu.	**-om/em**	**mojem**	**-im**	**mojim**
f.	**-oj**	**mojoj**	**-im**	**mojim**

The same endings are added to all possessive pronouns to form the dative and locative cases. Croatian also allows the forms **mome**, **momu** and **mojemu**, **tvome**, **tvomu** and **tvojemu**, as well as the ending **-ima** in adjectival plural forms (e.g., **mojima** *our*).

Personal pronouns in the dative/locative cases

The personal pronouns can only have the *long form* in the locative because this case always uses a preposition. The general rule is: *in any case only a long-form pronoun can follow a preposition.*

Personal Pronouns

	nom. sg.	***dat./ loc. sg.*** **long**	***dat. sg.*** **short**	***nom. pl.***	***dat./ loc. pl.*** **long**	***dat. pl.*** **short**
1st	**ja**	**meni**	**mi**	**mi**	**nama**	**nam**
2nd	**ti**	**tebi**	**ti**	**vi**	**vama**	**vam**
3rd *m.*	**on**	**njemu**	**mu**	**oni**	**njima**	**im**
3rd *f.*	**ona**	**njoj**	**joj**	**one**	**njima**	**im**
3rd *neu.*	**ono**	**njemu**	**mu**	**ona**	**njima**	**im**

1.1. Dative usage

The primary use of the dative is to indicate *the indirect object*. The indirect object answers the question *to whom?* or *to what?* after the verb.

Kupujem *ti* knjigu.	I am buying *you* a book.
Pišem pismo *Darku*.	I am writing a letter *to Darko.*
Pomažem *svima*.	I help *everyone.*
Dajem *joj* dar.	I am giving *her* a gift.

There is a whole list of verbs that require the dative. Those used in this lesson are:

davati to give	**čestitati** to congratulate	**činiti se** to seem
pomagati to help	**sviđati se** to like	**slati** to send
govoriti to tell		

Other important verbs are **vjerovati** *to believe* and **obećavati** *to promise.*

On *mi* uvijek pomaže.	He always helps *me.*
Ona često šalje poruke *sestri*.	She often sends messages to her *sister.*
Vjerujem *ti*.	I believe *you.*
Obećavam *ti* da neću zaboraviti.	I promise you that I won't forget.
Govorimo *vam* istinu.	We are telling *you* the truth.
Dajem *Vam* časnu riječ.	I am giving *you* my word of honor.

The verb **sviđati se** *to like* also requires the dative. It can be somewhat confusing for English speakers because *what* is liked is in the *nominative*, while the person who is *doing the liking* is in the *dative*. The verb changes depending on whether the object that is liked is in the singular or in the plural.

Sviđa *mi* se ovaj restoran.	*I* like this restaurant. [*lit.:* This restaurant pleases *me*.]
Sviđaju *mi* se ove haljine.	*I* like these dresses. [*lit.:* These dresses are pleasing *to me*.]
To *mi* se ne sviđa.	*I* don't like that. [*lit.:* That doesn't please *me*.]

The verb **trebati** *to need* is somewhat special in that it can be used both with and without a dative construction. The usage in the following sentences parallels English structure:

Trebam **tvoj auto večeras.**	*I need* your car tonight.
Trebaju **naš auto večeras.**	*They need* our car tonight.

The next sentences with **trebati** *to need,* in which the person who needs something is in the dative, is completely different. This construction is more colloquial.

Treba *mi* tvoj auto večeras.	*I* need your car tonight.
Treba *im* naš auto večeras.	*They* need our car tonight.

A dative in combination with the third person singular of a verb can be used to *express a desire* to perform a certain action. All the verbs used in this type of expression have the reflexive particle **se**, regardless of whether or not they normally fall into the category of reflexive verbs. Note that only imperfective verbs are used in this construction which conveys the meaning *I feel like . . .*:

Danas mi se ne uči.	I don't feel like studying today.
Spava mi se.	I feel like sleeping. *(I'm sleepy.)*
Gleda mi se neki dobar film.	I feel like watching a good movie.
Ne da mi se.	I don't feel like doing it.

Some *impersonal expressions* also use the dative. In this case an adverb plus a dative pronoun or noun must be used.

Teško im je.	It is difficult for them.
Ivanu i Darku je teško.	It is hard for Ivan and Darko.
Hladno mi je.	I'm cold.
Marijani je hladno.	Marijana is cold.
Dobro joj je.	She is fine.
Ani je dobro.	Anna is fine.
Dosadno mu je.	He is bored.

In some instances the dative can also indicate *possession*. This is a rather colloquial use, but it is frequently used in everyday speech. The meaning of sentences using the dative in the first column is exactly the same as those using a possessive in the second column:

Dative	Possessive
Kako *ti* je *brat*? How is *your brother*? *(What's up with your brother?)*	**Kako je *tvoj brat*?**
Što *mu* radi *majka*? What is *his mother* doing?	**Što radi *njegova majka*?**
***Muž mi* je otputovao u Zagreb.** *My husband* has departed for Zagreb.	***Moj muž* je otputovao u Zagreb.**
Gdje *im* je *kuća*? Where is *their house*?	**Gdje je *njihova kuća*?**

There are many *idiomatic expressions* that use the dative, one of which you encountered already in the first lesson as a part of the conversation on getting acquainted (*Drago mi je*). Here are several more:

Čini mi se da...	It seems to me that...
Drago mi je.	I am pleased.
Svejedno mi je.	It is all the same to me.
Žao mi je.	I am sorry.
Nije mi jasno.	It is not clear to me.
Dosta mi je.	I've had enough.
Zadovoljstvo mi je.	It's my pleasure.
Blago tebi!	Lucky you!

The *prepositions* that use the dative are:

k (ka when it occurs before **-k, -g)** to/toward

Idem *k* tebi. I'm coming *to* you/I'm going *toward* you.

prema toward

Idem *prema* tebi. I'm going *toward* you.

nasuprot opposite from

Sjedim *nasuprot* njemu. I'm sitting *opposite* him.

1.2. Locative usage

The locative case indicates the *location of a person or an object* only if they are stationary. When motion is involved, a noun in the accusative will follow.

Ja sam *u Zagrebu.* *loc.* — I'm *in Zagreb.*

BUT

Idem *u Zagreb.* *acc.* — I'm going *to Zagreb.*

Knjiga je *na stolu.* *loc.* — The book is *on the table.*

BUT

Ona stavlja knjigu *na stol.* *acc.* — She is placing the book *on the table.*

The two prepositions used here, **u** and **na**, mean exactly the same thing in both cases, but depending on whether movement is involved, they will require the accusative or locative. An easy formula to remember this is:

accusative = motion   locative = location

Another frequent preposition associated with the locative is **o**, meaning *about*.

Oni govore *o meni.* — They are speaking *about me.*
***O čemu* govoriš?** — *What* are you talking *about*?

Finally, the preposition **po** means *according to*, *all over*, and *along* (especially a street).

***Po mojem mišljenju,* on ništa ne zna.**
In my opinion he doesn't know anything.
Knjige su razbacane *po podu.*
Books are scattered *all over the floor.*
Hodamo *po gradu* cijeli dan.
We've been walking *all over the city* the whole day.
Šetamo *po Jagićevoj (ulici).*
We are taking a stroll *on Jagić street.*

In the meaning *at, in,* some nouns require the preposition **na** instead of **u**. Many of these nouns denote events, some of them denote places. They, too, can be followed by either the accusative or the locative depending on whether motion is involved. Examples below are given in the *locative*:

Nouns that Follow *Na* (at, in)

na koncertu concert
na predavanju lecture
na predstavi performance
na fakultetu college, school
na ručku lunch
na večeri dinner
na brodu boat
na zrakoplovu/avionu on the plane
na ulici street
na trgu square
na sudu court
na moru seaside, at the seaside
na odmoru vacation
na poslu work

Nouns that Follow *U* (at, in)

u kinu movie theater
u školi school
u kazalištu theater
u kupovini shopping
u gradu city
u vlaku train
u restoranu restaurant
u moru sea, in the sea
u zrakoplovu/avionu inside the plane

Many *country names* are in fact adjectival forms rather than nouns, and they decline according to the adjectival pattern. These names are not difficult to identify because they invariably end in **-ska, -ška** or **-čka**.

	Nominative	**Accusative**	**Locative**
Croatia	**Hrvatska**	**u Hrvatsku**	**u Hrvatskoj**
England	**Engleska**	**u Englesku**	**u Engleskoj**
Germany	**Njemačka**	**u Njemačku**	**u Njemačkoj**
Norway	**Norveška**	**u Norvešku**	**u Norveškoj**
Spain	**Španjolska**	**u Španjolsku**	**u Španjolskoj**
France	**Francuska**	**u Francusku**	**u Francuskoj**
Greece	**Grčka**	**u Grčku**	**u Grčkoj**

2. Tag questions

Tag questions are negative questions that often express surprise or request a response from the listener. In Croatian these often appear at the end of the sentence, as **zar ne**, and unlike in English in which they change depending on the tense, in Croatian they remain the same.

Moramo govoriti i o tome, *zar ne*?
We have to talk about that as well, *don't we*?
Ideš na koncert, *zar ne*?
You are coming to the concert, *aren't you*?
On je u Zagrebu, *zar ne*?
He is in Zagreb, *isn't he*?

The word **zar** can also appear at the beginning of the sentence although in this position it invariably expresses *surprise*:

> **Zar nećeš kupiti kruh?**
> Won't you buy bread? [Aren't you going to buy bread?!]
> **Zar je u Zagrebu?**
> Is it possible that s/he is in Zagreb?

Exercises

Vježba 7.1 Translate the following prepositions.

1. k/ka ____________
2. prema ____________
3. po ____________
4. u ____________
5. nasuprot ____________

Now write a simple sentence using each of the prepositions. Remember which case (dative or locative) you are using!

1. ____
2. ____
3. ____
4. ____
5. ____

Vježba 7.2 Determine which locative preposition (**na** or **u**) should be used with the nouns below. Then write out the noun with its locative ending.

Example: **škola** **u školi**

1. kupovina ____________
2. kino ____________
3. brod ____________
4. zrakoplov ____________
5. predstava ____________
6. večera ____________
7. stadion ____________
8. kuća ____________
9. ulica ____________
10. grad ____________
11. restoran ____________
12. fakultet ____________
13. koncert ____________
14. autocesta ____________
15. posao ____________

Vježba 7.3 Location and direction practice. Write out two sentences for each of the place names provided. The first sentence should indicate the presence of motion, while the second sentence should indicate position.

Example: **U srijedu idem u Njemačku.**
Sada sam u Njemačkoj.

1. Boston ____

   ____
2. Vinkovci ____

   ____
3. Karlovac ____

   ____
4. Rijeka____

   ____
5. Dugo Selo ____

   ____
6. London ____

   ____
7. Zagreb ____

   ____
8. Washington ____

   ____
9. Split ____

   ____
10. Portland ____

    ____

Vježba 7.4

A. Circle the correct choice in the sentences below.

1. Čini *(me, mi)* se da je sve odlično.
2. To mi *(si, se)* sviđa.
3. *(Ti, tebe, tebi, te)* je tvoj posao zanimljiv.
4. Auto je *(u, na)* ulici.
5. Sastanak je završen. Hvala svima i vidimo se *(prošli, idući)* tjedan.
6. Pomaže *(im, ih, njih)* to što dobro rade.

7. Nema problema. Ja također imam poslovni *(sastanak, sigurnost)* u dva sata.
8. Zadovoljstvo *(nas, nam, mi)* jer raditi za vas.
9. Moramo govoriti i o tome, *(zar da, zar ne)*?
10. Po *(moj, mog, mojem)* mišljenju, naša tvrtka dobro posluje.

B. Translate into Croatian:

1. I feel like reading something.
   ____
2. I don't feel like eating anything.
   ____
3. I don't feel like waiting.
   ____
4. I feel like going home.
   ____
5. I don't feel like talking.
   ____

Vježba 7.5

A. Determine the proper dative /locative *singular* endings for the words given below.

Example: **dobar proizvod – dobrom proizvodu**

1. velika knjiga ______________________
2. lijepa zemlja ______________________
3. zagrebački fakultet ______________________
4. mali brod ______________________
5. staro kazalište ______________________

B. Now use the same words to form the dative – locative *plural* endings

Example: **dobar proizvod – dobrim proizvodima**

1. ______________________
2. ______________________
3. ______________________
4. ______________________
5. ______________________

Vježba 7.6 Translate the sentences below using the dative case.

1. He is always bored in school because he is very smart.
2. What is your father doing now? I need him!
3. I have had enough. I am going home.
4. Darko is walking towards us. He is there, opposite Ivan!
5. I am sorry, but I have an important business meeting.
6. That is very hard for him!
7. I don't feel like working now.
8. I am cold!
9. What is your friend doing?
10. I like that car.

Vježba 7.7 Look over the list of professions given in this lesson. Choose a profession and imagine what you would do if you were this person, where you would live, how old you would be, whether you would be married and have a family, etc. Try to truly impersonate this character and instead of saying *I would be an architect* (which you don't know how to say yet), say e.g., *I'm an architect. My name is Josip Koludrović*, etc.

a) Write a brief composition about your imaginary self using some of these elements.

b) Role-play your profession with another person studying Croatian pretending the two of you have just met and don't know anything about each other. If you're studying the language by yourself, write out a dialogue in which two people get to know one another.

Lekcija 8
Marijana ide na zabavu

Lesson 8
Marijana goes to a party

Lekcija 8: Marijana ide na zabavu

Prvi dio

Darko: Bok, Marijana, imam dobre vijesti!

Marijana: Bok, Darko, otkud ti ovdje?

Darko: Danas je petak, pa smo gotovi s laboratorijem malo ranije. Ovog vikenda Ivan priređuje veliku zabavu i poziva nas da dođemo. Što misliš o tome? Dolazi mnogo mladih ljudi.

Marijana: Nisam sigurna, još ne govorim hrvatski tako dobro.

Darko: Marijana, moraš sa mnom! Kako možeš naučiti jezik ako ni s kim ne govoriš?

Marijana: Imaš pravo. Kada je zabava?

Darko: Počinje u deset navečer, a završava kada svi otiđu kući. Hoćeš li da najprije dođem k tebi, pa možemo zajedno tramvajem ili taksijem?

Marijana: Važi. Ali imam jedan problem. Nemam sa sobom prikladnu odjeću za zabavu.

Darko: Bez brige! Svi idemo u trapericama.

Drugi dio

Petak navečer, kod Ivana.

Ivan: Dobra večer, Marijana, lijepo što si tu. Jesi li sama?

Marijana: Dobra večer, Ivane. Darko je sa mnom, ali mislim da još razgovara s nekim u ... Kako se kaže "courtyard" na hrvatskom?

Ivan: Dvorište. Aha, Darko je u dvorištu. Izvoli, uđi! Da te upoznam sa svojim prijateljima. Ovo su Sanja, Mario, Željko, Petra. Evo i Darka!

Darko: Dobra večer, Ivane! Izvrsna glazba! S tobom nikada nije dosadno.

Ivan: Dobro se zabavite. Ima mnogo hrane i pića, a i društvo je zanimljivo. Pred nama je lijepa večer. Čime vas mogu ponuditi?

Darko: Čašu crnog vina, molim te.

Ivan: A što ćeš ti, Marijana?

Lesson 8: Marijana goes to a party

Part I

Darko: Hi, Marijana, I have good news!

Marijana: Hi, Darko, how come you're here?

Darko: Today is Friday and we are done with lab a little early. This weekend Ivan is giving a big party and is inviting us to come along. What do you think? A lot of young people will be there.

Marijana: I am not sure because I still do not speak Croatian that well.

Darko: Marijana, you have to [come] with me! How can you learn Croatian if you don't talk with anybody?

Marijana: You're right. When is the party?

Darko: It will begin at 10 p.m. and finish when everyone has gone home. Do you want me to come to your place first so we can go together by tram or taxi?

Marijana: Okay, but I have one problem. I don't have appropriate clothes for the party.

Darko: Don't worry. Everyone goes wearing jeans!

Part II

Friday evening, at Ivan's.

Ivan: Good evening, Marijana it's nice that you are here. Are you here alone?

Marijana: Good evening, Ivan. Darko is with me, but I think that he's still talking with someone in the ... how does one say *courtyard* in Croatian?

Ivan: Courtyard. Aha, Darko is in the courtyard. Come in! Let me introduce you to my friends. This is Sanja, Mario, Željko, and Petra. And here is Darko!

Darko: Good evening Ivan! Excellent music! With you things are never boring.

Ivan: I hope everyone has fun. There is a lot of food and things to drink, and the company is interesting. A nice evening awaits us. What can I offer you?

Darko: A glass of red wine, please.

Ivan: What would you like Marijana?

Marijana: **Za mene isto. Hvala, Ivane.**

Darko: **Ovo je već tradicija! Ivan obično petkom organizira zabavu. Pleše se noću, a spava danju.**

Marijana: **Kada se uči?**

Ivan: **Sve se stigne. Nemamo zabavu svakog vikenda, samo nakon položenih ispita. Dolaze blagdani i moramo to nekako proslaviti. Ali razlog ovoj zabavi nešto je drugo: sretan rođendan, Marijana!**

Marijana: **Kakvo iznenađenje! Kako znate da je moj rođendan ovog vikenda?**

Darko: **Moja majka, a tvoja tetka, nikada ne zaboravlja takve stvari. Zabava u tvoju čast Ivanova je ideja. Živjela, Marijana! Ovo je za tebe. To je zajednički dar.**

Marijana: **Zabava, dar, društvo! Uopće mi ne nedostaje Amerika.**

Ivan: **Želiš li ga otvoriti? Tražili smo ti dar prilično dugo. Sviđa li ti se?**

Marijana: **Divno! Ovo će mi stvarno dobro doći, veliki rječnik hrvatskog jezika s gramatikom i CD s glazbom hrvatskih pop-grupa. Hvala vam na svemu! Pravi ste prijatelji!**

Marijana:	The same for me. Thank you, Ivan.
Darko:	This is already a tradition! Ivan usually organizes parties on Fridays. Dancing at night and sleeping in the daytime.
Marijana:	And when does one study?
Ivan:	There's time for everything. We don't have parties every weekend, only after passing exams. Holidays are coming, and we must do something to celebrate. But there is another reason for this party: Happy birthday Marijana!
Marijana:	What a surprise! How did you know that it is my birthday this weekend?
Darko:	My mother, your aunt, never forgets these things. The party in your honor is Ivan's idea. To your health, Marijana. This is for you. It is a gift from both of us.
Marijana:	A party, gift, company! I don't miss America at all.
Ivan:	Do you want to open the present? We searched a long time for it. Do you like it?
Marijana:	Great! This will really come in handy, a big dictionary of the Croatian language with grammar and a CD featuring Croatian pop bands. Thank you very much for everything! You're true friends!

Vocabulary

blagdan holiday
čast *f.* honor
dar present
dosadno *adv.* boring
društvo company, society
glazba (also **muzika**) music
gramatika grammar
iznenađenje surprise
nekako somehow
nikada never
obično usually
odjeća clothes
otkud from where
piće drink, beverage
položen passed
pravo right, law
pred in front of
predavanje lecture
prikladan suitable, appropriate
ranije earlier
razlog reason
rječnik dictionary
rođendan birthday
sam *m.*/**sama** *f.* alone
siguran sure
tetka aunt
tradicija tradition
traperice jeans
vijesti *f. pl.* news
vikend weekend
zabava party *(social event)*
zajednički common

Verb List

brinuti (se) (*I* **brinem**, **brinu**) to worry, to take care of
dolaziti (*I* **dolazim**, **dolaze**) to come
naučiti (*P* **naučim**, **nauče**) to learn, to master a subject
nedostajati (*I* **nedostajem**, **nedostaju**) to miss
organizirati (*I/P* **organiziram**, **organiziraju**) to organize
otvoriti (*P* **otvorim**, **otvore**) to open
plesati (*I* **plešem**, **plešu**) to dance
ponuditi (*P* **ponudim**, **ponude**) to offer
pozivati (*I* **pozivam**, **pozivaju**) to invite
priređivati (*I* **priređujem**, **priređuju**) to prepare
proslaviti (*P* **proslavim**, **proslave**) to celebrate
spavati (*I* **spavam**, **spavaju**) to sleep
stići (*P* **stignem**, **stignu**) to arrive
učiti (*I* **učim**, **uče**) to learn
zabaviti se (*P* **zabavim se**, **zabave se**) to entertain oneself, to have fun
zaboravljati (*I* **zaboravljam**, **zaboravljaju**) to forget
završavati (*I* **završavam**, **završavaju**) to finish

Useful Expressions

Imaš pravo! You're right!
Nisam siguran/sigurna! I am not sure!
Bez brige! Don't worry!
Kako se kaže *x* **na hrvatskom?** How does one say *x* in Croatian?
Da te upoznam... Let me introduce you...
Čime vas mogu ponuditi? What can I offer you?
Sretan rođendan! Happy birthday!
Sve se stigne. There's time for everything.
Kakvo iznenađenje! What a surprise!
U tvoju čast! In your honor!
Ovo će mi stvarno dobro doći! This will really come in handy!
Hvala vam na svemu! Thank you for everything!
Pravi ste prijatelji! You're true friends!

Grammar

1. The Instrumental Case

As the name of this case indicates, in many situations nouns in the instrumental case point to the *instrument* with which or through which an action is accomplished; for animate nouns it in fact indicates an accompaniment to the action.

The noun ending for all genders in the singular is **-om**, (**-em** after soft consonants, see Lesson 2); for feminine nouns ending in a consonant the ending is **-i**.[1]

Masculine nouns ending in **-lac** end in **-ocem** in the instrumental.

nom. sg. spasi*lac m.* ***instru. sg.*** spasi*ocem* rescuer

The adjectival endings in the instrumental are **-im** for the masculine and neuter and **-om** for the feminine.

The plural endings for nouns and adjectives are the same as those in the locative and dative: for masculine and neuter nouns, and for feminine nouns ending in a consonant it is **-ima**, for other feminine nouns **-ama**, and for all adjectives **-im**.

The question words for the instrumental are:

(s) kim? *(with)* whom? **(s) čim?** *(with)* what?

---

1. Feminine nouns ending in **-ost/-est** or a soft stem can take either **-i** (**mladosti** *youth*, **riječi** *word*) or **-u** (**mladošću, riječju**) in the instrumental. The latter is accompanied by softening.

These words also have a longer form: **(s) kime?** and **(s) čime?**

	Instrumental Singular			Instrumental Plural		
	adj.	noun		*adj.*	noun	
m.	-im	-om/em	**pametnim studentom**	-im	-ima	**pametnim studentima**
neu.	-im	-om/em	**dugim pismom**	-im	-ima	**dugim pismima**
f.	-om	-om	**dobrom knjigom**	-im	-ama	**dobrim knjigama**
f.Ø	-om	-i	**lijepom stvari**	-im	-ima	**lijepim stvarima**

Possessive Pronouns

	instrumental singular ending	(my)	instrumental plural ending	(my *pl.*)
m.	-im	**mojim**	-im	**mojim**
neu.	-im	**mojim**	-im	**mojim**
f.	-om	**mojom**	-im	**mojim**

All the other possessive pronouns take the same endings.

1.1. Personal Pronouns in the instrumental case

Personal pronouns in the instrumental have only the long form.

	nom. sg.	*instr. sg.*	*nom. pl.*	*instr. pl.*
1st	**ja** I	**mnom*** me	**mi** we	**nama** us
2nd	**ti** you	**tobom** you	**vi** you	**vama** you
3rd *m.*	**on** he	**njim** him	**oni** they	**njima** them
3rd *f.*	**ona** she	**njom** her	**one** they	**njima** them
3rd *neu.*	**ono** it	**njim** it	**ona** they	**njima** them

*Note that **-a** has to be added to the preposition **s** *with* (**sa**) when it precedes the pronoun **mnom** *me*: **sa mnom** *with me*

1.2. Use of the instrumental

The most common *preposition* used with the instrumental is **s** or **sa** meaning *with.* The longer form, **sa**, is used only before words that start with **s, š, z, ž,** and also before the first person singular personal pronoun in the instrumental, **mnom** *me* (see chart of personal pronouns above).

***S kim* ideš u kino?**	*Who* are you going to the movies *with*?
Idem *s bratom.*	I'm going *with [my] brother.*
Idem *sa sestrom.*	I'm going *with [my] sister.*
Nitko ne ide *sa mnom* u kino.	Nobody is going to the movies *with me.*

Several other prepositions are also used with the instrumental case:

pred in front of
nad above
pod under
za behind, but also at
među between

You have already encountered a set of prepositions with other cases that express the same spatial relations, most notably the following, which take the *genitive*:

ispred in front of
ispod under
iza behind
između between
iznad above

Though some of the prepositions taking the instrumental listed above seem like truncated versions of the prepositions taking the genitive and their meanings are the same, the ones introduced here take the instrumental. (Again, note that for the sake of easier pronunciation prepositions ending in a consonant add **-a** before the pronoun **mnom**.)

Instrumental	**Genitive**
***Preda mnom* je stol.** The table is *in front of me.*	***Ispred mene* je stol.**
On je *pod stolom.* He is *under the table.*	**On je *ispod stola.***
On je *za kućom.* He is *behind the house.*	**On je *iza kuće.***
On je za stolom. He is *at the table.*[2]	*No genitive equivalent*
Nebo je *nad nama.* The sky is *above us.*	**Nebo je *iznad nas.***

The instrumental is used to designate a specific means of *transportation.* Note that no preposition is needed:

Idem na posao *autom.*	I go to work *by car.*
Često putujem zrakoplovom.	I frequently fly *by plane.*
Vozite li se *autobusom* svaki dan?	Do you ride *(take) the bus* every day?

2. Literally, **za stolom** means *behind the table*, but it actually means *to be seated at the table.*

In addition, the instrumental case is used for any *instrument* with which an action is performed. In such instances no preposition is used:

Pišem *olovkom.* I write *with a pencil.*
Piše *rukom.* S/he writes *by hand.*
Jedem *žlicom.* I eat *with a spoon.*
Komuniciramo *telefonom.* We communicate *by telephone.*
Plaćam *kreditnom karticom.* I am paying *with a credit card.*

The instrumental is also used to refer to the *spatial framework* of movement:

Vozim se *gradom.* I'm driving *around the city.*
Putuje *Amerikom.* S/he is traveling *around America.*
Idu *ulicom.* They are walking *down the street.*

And the instrumental case also serves as a *temporal marker* for actions occurring regularly (the first three examples below) or lasting for long periods of time (the last two examples below).

Ivan organizira zabave *petkom.*
Ivan organizes parties *every Friday.*
Ja *utorkom* putujem u New York.
On Tuesdays I travel to New York.
Ona radi *subotom.*
She works *on Saturdays.*
On već *godinama* piše tu knjigu.
He has been writing that book *for years.*
Ja već *tjednima* putujem.
I've been traveling *for weeks.*

2. Interrogative, affirmative, neutral, and negative pronouns

Most question words, such as **tko** *who,* **gdje** *where,* **kada** *when*, etc. have affirmative, neutral, and negative counterparts. The English equivalents are, for instance:

where *(interrogative)* anywhere *(neutral)*
somewhere *(affirmative)* nowhere *(negative)*

In the category of neutral pronouns, there is more stress on the indefinite quality of the situation than in English and the meaning is thus closer to *anywhere at all*, *anybody at all*, *anything at all*, etc.

Interrogative	Affirmative	Neutral	Negative
tko	**netko**	**itko**	**nitko**
who	somebody	anybody	nobody
što	**nešto**	**išta**	**ništa**
what	something	anything	nothing
gdje	**negdje**	**igdje**	**nigdje**
where	somewhere	anywhere	nowhere
kamo/kuda	**nekamo/ nekuda**	**ikamo/ ikuda**	**nikamo/ nikuda**
where to	somewhere	anywhere	nowhere
kada	**nekada**	**ikada**	**nikada**
when	once, at some time	ever	never
kako	**nekako**	**ikako**	**nikako**
how	in some way	in any way	in no way
kakav	**nekakav**	**ikakav**	**nikakav**
what kind	some kind	any kind	not any kind
čiji	**nečiji**	**ičiji**	**ničiji**
whose	somebody's	anybody's	nobody's

The word **ponekad** means *sometimes.*

As we saw earlier when we discussed verb negation (see Lesson 3), Croatian requires multiple negation (negatives):

Tko ovdje *nešto* zna?	Who knows *something* here?
Zna li ovdje *itko išta*?	Does *anybody* here know *anything*?
Ovdje *nitko nikada ništa* ne zna.	Here *nobody* ever knows anything.
Je li je ovo *ičiji* stol?	Is this *anybody's* table?
Je li je ovo *nečiji* stol?	Is this *somebody's* table?
Ne, ovo *nije ničiji* stol.	No, this is *nobody's* table.

To form the Croatian equivalent of the English phrases *whoever, whatever,* etc. the word **bilo** is inserted before the interrogative form. A few examples are:

bilo tko whoever **bilo što** whatever **bilo gdje** wherever

3. Prepositional objects

We already know that the locative and instrumental cases in most situations take a preposition. To use these cases in a negative context, the verb is negated and a negative particle is inserted before the preposition. In these constructions the negative adverb is split, and the preposition is inserted between the negative particle and the rest of the negative word. For example, **tko** *who* in instrumental becomes **kim** *whom*, and when negated it becomes **ni s kim** *with no one* (rather than **s nikim*).

***S kim* ideš u šetnju?**	*Who* do you go for a walk *with*?
***Ni s kim ne* idem u šetnju.**	*I don't go* for a walk with anybody.
O čemu govoriš?	What are you talking about?
***Ne govorim ni* o čemu.**	*I'm not talking* about anything.
O kome pišeš?	Who are writing about?
***Ne pišem ni* o kome.**	*I'm not writing* about anyone.

4. Impersonal *se* constructions

To avoid stating the subject of an action, an impersonal construction is used. It is easy to form impersonal sentences by simply putting the verb in the *third person singular* and adding the reflexive particle **se**.

If the sentence has an object, the verb will agree with the object, as in the last example below. If the verb is reflexive, only one **se** is necessary. The particle **se** is placed in second position in the sentence or after the interrogative particle **li**. These constructions are often translated into English using *one* as the subject:

Kako se kaže *courtyard*?
How does one say *courtyard*?
Kaže li se *dvorište*?
Does one say *dvorište*?
Pleše se noću, a spava danju.
One dances during the night and sleeps during the day.
Kada se uči?
When does one study?
Sve se stigne.
There's time for everything.
Kako se ide do centra?
How does one go to the center?
Gdje se prodaju karte?
Where can one buy tickets? [*lit.*: Where are tickets being sold?]

Impersonal constructions are possible both in past and future tenses, see Lesson 12.

5. Reflexive pronouns

5.1. The reflexive personal pronouns *sebe/sebi/sobom*

The personal pronouns **sebe** *of oneself*, **sebi** *to/about oneself*, and **sobom** *with oneself* are used to refer to the *subject* of the sentence. They decline like the second person singular pronoun:

case	pronoun	meaning
acc	**sebe**	oneself (object)
gen.	**sebe**	of oneself
dat.	**sebi**	to oneself
loc.	**sebi**	about oneself
instru.	**sobom**	with oneself

In English, such reflexive pronouns change depending on the subject of the sentence (*myself, herself, themselves*, etc.). In Croatian they are the same for all persons, though their endings change depending on the *case*.

Ne želim govoriti *o sebi.*
I don't want to talk *about myself.*
Oni su nosili *sa sobom* mnogo stvari.
They carried [*with/on themselves*] many things.
Ja se ne bojim tebe nego *sebe.*
I am not afraid of you but *of myself.*
Nemam *sa sobom* prikladnu odjeću za zabavu.
I don't have *with me* suitable clothes for the party.

5.2. Reflexive possessive pronoun *svoj*
Like the personal pronoun **sebe**, the reflexive possessive **svoj** refers to the subject of the sentence. It corresponds to the English reflexive pronoun *own*, as in *my own, your own* etc.

Svoj is declined like any other possessive pronoun: **svog** or **svojeg** in the genitive and accusative masculine animate, **svoje** in the genitive singular feminine, etc.

The simple rule for its use is as follows: replace any possessive with the reflexive possessive **svoj** (in the appropriate case) if the subject = possessor. This pronoun is obligatory in the third person singular and plural because its presence or absence carries different meanings.

On čita *svoju* knjigu.
He is reading *his (own)* book.
Oni se boje *svog* psa.
They are afraid of *their (own)* dog.
Ona kupuje dar za *svoje* roditelje.
She is buying a present for *her (own)* parents.
Dolazim sa *svojim* kolegom.
I'm coming with *my* colleague.

Note how ambiguity may arise if the pronoun **svoj** is not used in the third person singular or plural:

> **On čita *njegovu* knjigu.**
> He is reading his [some other man's] book.
> **Oni se boje *njihovog* psa.**
> They are afraid of their [other people's] dog.

In some cases, the two pronouns are interchangeable, although the first example below is commonly preferred:

> **Volim *svoju* majku.** I love my *(own)* mother.
> **Volim *moju* majku.** I love my mother.

Exercises

Vježba 8.1
A. Use the following vocabulary words from this lesson to create sentences. Try to incorporate some of the useful expressions provided in the lessons. Be creative!

1. dar ______________________________
2. glazba ______________________________
3. blagdan ______________________________
4. dosadno ______________________________
5. piće ______________________________

B. Use the instrumental case with the words provided below.

1. rječnik, gramatika ______________________________
2. autobus, Zagreb ______________________________
3. tetka, ja ______________________________
4. vikend, zabava ______________________________
5. kava, šećer ______________________________

Vježba 8.2 Write out all of the different verb forms for the verbs below.
Example: **kuhati – kuham, kuhaš, kuha, kuhamo, kuhate, kuhaju**

1. zaboravljati ______________________________
2. spavati ______________________________
3. učiti ______________________________

4. stići ____
5. brinuti ____

Vježba 8.3 Use each of the following words *once* to complete each sentence. Make sure to conjugate/decline the listed words when necessary.

A. vikend, ići, obično, Boston, pisati

1. Ideš li u ________ zrakoplovom?
2. Kako znate da mi je rođendan ovog ________?
3. Ivan ________ subotom spava jer ima puno posla od ponedjeljka do petka.
4. Sada ________ olovkom.
5. Ja uvijek _______ u kupovinu sa sestrom.

B. svoj, ja, on, Vi, ti

1. Tko ide s(a)_____________ u Dubrovnik?
2. Ide li na koncert s(a)___________ prijateljem?
3. Mogu li doći s(a)___________?
4. Zadovoljstvo mi je raditi s(a)_____________.
5. Obično se vidim s(a) _________ srijedom.

Vježba 8.4

A. Determine which *instrumental* preposition belongs in the following sentences.

Example: **On je ____ stablom. pod**

1. On je ____ stolom
2. Ona je ____ njima.
3. Ivan je _____ vratima.
4. Tepih je _____ mnom.
5. Sunce je _____ gradom.

B. Using the same sentences, try to use a genitive preposition to say the same thing. Change the noun (when possible) accordingly.

1. ____
2. ____
3. ____
4. ____
5. ____

Vježba 8.5 Translate the following:

1. Does anyone have a pencil?
2. I never see you.
3. Can you find any kind of car?
4. This is nobody's house.
5. I am not going to the movies with anyone.
6. I am not thinking about anything.
7. Nobody sees him.
8. Do you ever travel to Croatia in summer?
9. She never travels anywhere.
10. They are not talking about anybody.

Vježba 8.6 Answer the following questions and try to elaborate on your answer.

1. Što radite ponedjeljkom?
2. Kako obično idete na posao?
3. Čime obično pišete?
4. S kim idete na večeru sutra?
5. S kim idete u kino preko vikenda?
6. Kako plaćate u samoposluživanju, novcem ili kreditnom karticom?
7. Kakvu kavu volite?
8. Kako putujete u Europu?

9. Šetate li ikada parkom?

___

10. Ima li nešto što već godinama planirate?

___

Vježba 8.7

A. Translate into Croatian:

Time for holidays – Vrijeme za odmor

I often travel to Croatia by plane. I have lots of friends and business partners [suradnik] there. On Mondays we usually talk by phone. This time I will travel there with my wife. I've been promising her for years that we are going there for holidays. Finally we have time for that. We are going to Zagreb and to Zadar. She likes the idea. We are traveling on June 18th. We talk of nothing else but [nego] the trip. It seems to me that this is such a nice present for our anniversary [godišnjica].

___

___

___

___

___

___

___

B. Write out a short text based on the dialogue. Try to incorporate as much new vocabulary as possible, and make it interesting. **Hajde!** *Let's go!*

___

___

___

___

___

___

___

___

___

Lekcija 9
Vrlo važna poruka

Lesson 9
A very important message

Lekcija 9: Vrlo važna poruka

Prvi dio

Draga Marijana,

Već je prošlo nekoliko tjedana otkako si otputovala u Hrvatsku. Nadam se da si dobro i da već imaš mnogo prijatelja. Vjerujem da i na poslu sve ide uspješno. Kod mene je ovih dana stalno gužva, a imam i novosti. Kao što znaš, ja sam ti planirao doći u posjet za tjedan dana, ali došlo je do nekih promjena. Upravo sam saznao da sam primljen na doktorat na Stanfordu. Ovo je jedinstvena prilika za mene. Umjesto da putujem u Hrvatsku, selim se u Kaliforniju.

Rekao sam ti prije tvojeg odlaska da postoji mogućnost da se ovo dogodi. Već sam našao novi stan u Kaliforniji, završio sve poslove u Bostonu i spakirao stvari.

Žao mi je što ne mogu doći u Hrvatsku, ali vjerujem da razumiješ situaciju. Čini mi se da oboje moramo razmisliti što želimo raditi, gdje želimo živjeti i vidimo li budućnost zajedno. Sada je prilika da to napravimo.

Srdačno te pozdravlja
Andrew

Drugi dio

Darko: Marijana, već dugo sjediš pred računalom. Ništa ne pišeš i ništa ne govoriš. Što se dogodilo? Je li sve u redu?

Marijana: Nažalost, imam loše vijesti. Dobila sam poruku od svog dečka Andrewa. Primljen je na doktorat i seli se u Kaliforniju. Piše da ne može doći u Hrvatsku, a obećao je doći. Baš sam razočarana. Takvo čudno ponašanje! Znala sam za tu mogućnost, ali nisam očekivala da me uopće neće posjetiti.

Darko: Siguran sam da sve ima svoj razlog. On vjerojatno sada ne želi brak nego studij. Koliko ste dugo već zajedno?

Lesson 9: A very important message

Part I

Dear Marijana,

It has already been several weeks since you left for Croatia. I hope that you are well and that you already have many friends. I also hope all is going well at work.

It has been constant chaos at my end these days, but I have some news. As you know, I was planning to visit you in a week, but there have been some changes. I just found out that I have been accepted for doctoral studies at Stanford. This is a unique chance for me. Instead of traveling to Croatia, I am moving to California.

I told you before you left that there was a possibility that this could happen. I have already found a new apartment in California, have finished all business in Boston, and packed my things. I am sorry that I cannot come to Croatia, but I believe that you understand the situation. It seems to me that both of us must decide what we want to do for a living, where we want to live, and if there is a future for us together. Now is the chance for us to do it.

Best regards,
Andrew

Part II

Darko: Marijana, you have been sitting at the computer for a long time. You have not written or said anything. What happened? Is everything OK?

Marijana: Unfortunately, I have bad news. I received a message from my boyfriend, Andrew. He was admitted to a doctoral program and is moving to California. He writes that he can't come to Croatia, but he had promised that he would come. I am so disappointed. Such strange behavior! I knew that this was a possibility, but I did not expect that he would not visit me here at all.

Darko: I am sure that everything has its reason. He probably doesn't want marriage now but instead [wants to] study. How long have you two been together?

Marijana: Dvije godine. Pitam se što ovo znači? Predomislio se u posljednji trenutak. Ne znam što mu je. Probala sam ga zvati telefonom prošlog tjedna, ali je telefon bio isključen. Dosta mi je! Ne mogu više ovako!

Darko: Ljutiš se, a to ti neće pomoći. Možda pretjeruješ, možda je stvarno zauzet i ima namjeru doći poslije. Zašto ne porazgovarate?

Marijana: Ne dolazi u obzir! Ne želim se svađati.

Darko: Je li Andrew želio da ti dođeš živjeti u Hrvatsku neko vrijeme?

Marijana: Mislim da mu nije bilo drago kada sam to odlučila. Ali imam dojam da mu je sada svejedno. Glupost! Ništa više nema smisla.

Darko: Što je—tu je. Meni se čini da se nešto promijenilo, ali teško je znati što. Kako se ti osjećaš?

Marijana: Ne znam ni sama. Zbunjena sam. Moram razmisliti o svemu.

Darko: A ja te moram razveseliti. Jesi li večerala?

Marijana: Nisam.

Darko: Predlažem da idemo van. Jesi li raspoložena za večeru i kino?

Marijana: Hvala, Darko. Ti uvijek sve razumiješ!

Marijana: Two years. I wonder what this means? He has changed his mind at the last moment. I don't know what's with him. I tried to call him on the phone last week, but it was off. I've had enough. I can't take it any more!

Darko: You are getting angry and that is not going to help you. Maybe you're exaggerating, maybe he is really busy and intends to come later. Why don't you talk?

Marijana: It's out of question! I don't want to argue.

Darko: Did Andrew want you to come live in Croatia for some time?

Marijana: I think that he was not that pleased when I decided to come. But I have an impression that it's all the same to him now. How stupid! There's no point any more!

Darko: What happened, happened! It seems to me that something has changed and it is hard to know what. How do you feel?

Marijana: I myself don't know. I am confused. I have to think about everything.

Darko: And I have to cheer you up. Have you had dinner?

Marijana: I haven't.

Darko: I suggest we go out. Are you in the mood for dinner and a movie?

Marijana: Thanks Darko. You always understand everything!

Vocabulary

brak marriage
budućnost *f.* future
čud*a*n strange
dečko boyfriend, boy
doj*a*m impression
doktorat doctorate
glupost *f.* stupidity
isključen turned off
jedinstven unique
kino movie theater
mogućnost *f.* opportunity
namjera intention
novosti *f. pl.* news
obzir consideration
oboje both *(male and female)*
odlaz*a*k departure
otkako since
ovako this way
ponašanje behavior
poruka message
posljednji last
prilika chance
primljen accepted
promjena change
posjet visit
računalo computer
raspoložen za + *acc.* to be in the mood for
razočaran disappointed
smisao *nom.*/**smisla** *gen. sg.* sense
svejedno all the same
umjesto instead
upravo just
večera dinner
vjerojatno likely

Verb List

dogoditi se (*P* **dogodim se**, **dogode se**) to happen, to occur
ljutiti (se) (*I* **ljutim**, **ljute**) to anger, to get angry
napraviti (*P* **napravim**, **naprave**) to do, get done
obećati (*P* **obećam**, **obećaju**) to promise
očekivati (*I* **očekujem**, **očekuju**) to expect
odlučiti (*P* **odlučim**, **odluče**) to decide
osjećati (*I* **osjećam**, **osjećaju**) to feel
otputovati (*P* **otputujem**, **otputuju**) to set off
planirati (*I* **planiram**, **planiraju**) to plan
porazgovarati (*P* **porazgovaram**, **porazgovaraju**) to talk briefly, to chat
posjetiti (*P* **posjetim**, **posjete**) to visit
predlagati (*I* **predlažem**, **predlažu**) to suggest
predomisliti se (*P* **predomislim se**, **predomisle se**) to change one's mind
pretjerivati (*I* **pretjerujem**, **pretjeruju**) to exaggerate
proći (*P* **prođem**, **prođu**) to pass
promijeniti (*P* **promijenim**, **promijene**) to change
razmisliti (*P* **razmislim**, **razmisle**) to think through

razveseliti (se) (*P* **razveselim, razvesele**) to make happy
saznati (*P* **saznam, saznaju**) to learn, find out
seliti se (*I* **selim se, sele se**) to move house
spakirati (se) (*P* **spakiram, spakiraju**) to pack
svađati se (*I* **svađam se, svađaju se**) to argue
večerati (*P/I* **večeram, večeraju**) to dine

Useful Expressions

Nadam se da si dobro. I hope you're well.
Došlo je do nekih promjena. There have been some changes.
Kao što znaš... As you know...
postoji mogućnost there is a possibility
Čini mi se da... It seems to me that...
Žao mi je! I'm sorry!
Ovo je jedinstvena prilika. This is a unique chance.
Srdačno te/Vas pozdravlja Best regards...
Što se dogodilo? What happened?
Je li sve u redu? Is everything OK?
Imam dobre/loše vijesti. I have good/bad news.
Što mu je? What's with him?
Dosta mi je! I've had enough.
Ne mogu više ovako! I can't take it any more!
imati namjeru to have an intention
Ne dolazi u obzir! It's out of question!
Imam dojam da....I have an impression that...
Nema smisla! There's no point!
Što je – tu je. What happened, happened!
Ne znam ni sam/sama. I myself don't know.
Jesi li raspoložen/a za... ? Are you in the mood for... ?

Grammar

1. The past tense

Croatian has several past tenses, but only one is commonly used in everyday speech. It consists of the short form of the verb **biti** *to be* and the past participle of the given verb, which agrees with the subject in gender and number.

In most of its forms the participle has an **l** and behaves like adjectives ending in the masculine **-o** form, such as **zao** *evil,* **debeo** *fat, thick*. Adjectives in other forms add an **-l**: **debela** *f.*, **debelo** *neu.*, **debeli** *pl.*, etc.

Similarly, all verbs ending in **-iti** or **-ati** discard the final **-ti** and add these same endings to form the past participle:

Past Participles

čitati (to read)

	singular	plural
m.	**čitao**	**čitali** *m., m. & f.*
f.	**čitala**	**čitale**
neu.	**čitalo**	**čitala**

biti (to be)

	singular	plural
m.	**bio**	**bili** *m., m. & f.*
f.	**bila**	**bile**
neu.	**bilo**	**bila**

Ja ***sam čitala*** **knjigu jučer.** I *read* a book yesterday.
Oni ***su bili*** **kod mene.** They *were* at my place.

For the group of verbs that end in **-jeti**—such as **htjeti** *to want*, **vidjeti** *to see*, **razumjeti** *to understand*, **željeti** *to wish*—in the masculine form of the participle in the past tense **-jeti** is discarded and replaced by **-io**. The other forms of the participle, however, discard only the final **-ti** and replace it by the usual past tense markers, **-la**, **-li**, **-lo**, etc. The past tense pattern for this group is:

Past Participles

	htjeti (to want)			**vidjeti** (to see)	
	sg.	***pl.***		***sg.***	***pl.***
m.	**htio**	**htjeli** *m., m. & f.*	*m.*	**vidio**	**vidjeli** *m., m. & f.*
f.	**htjela**	**htjele**	*f.*	**vidjela**	**vidjele**
neu.	**htjelo**	**htjela**	*neu.*	**vidjelo**	**vidjela**

Htio sam **doći, ali** ***nisam mogao.***
I wanted to come, but I *couldn't.*
Vidjeli smo **ga jučer.**
We saw him yesterday.

There are a few frequently occurring verbs that are somewhat irregular and should therefore be memorized. Most important here is the verb **ići** *to go* and all the verbs derived from it, such as:

doći to come
otići to leave, depart
stići to arrive
izaći to exit
naći to find
proći to pass
ući to enter

The final **-ći** is discarded and the past tense endings are added according to the scheme below:

Past Participles

	ići (to go)			**naći** (to find)	
	sg.	*pl.*		*sg.*	*pl.*
m.	**išao**	**išli** *m., m. & f.*	*m.*	**našao**	**našli** *m., m. & f.*
f.	**išla**	**išle**	*f.*	**našla**	**našle**
neu.	**išlo**	**išla**	*neu.*	**našlo**	**našla**

There are several other verbs ending in **-ći and -sti** whose past tense forms should also be memorized. These include **moći** *be able to*, **reći** *to say*, **jesti** *to eat*, and **sjesti** *to sit down.*

Past Participles

	moći (to be able to)			**reći** (to say)	
	sg.	*pl.*		*sg.*	*pl.*
m.	**mogao**	**mogli** *m., m. & f.*	*m.*	**rekao**	**rekli** *m., m. & f.*
f.	**mogla**	**mogle**	*f.*	**rekla**	**rekle**
neu.	**moglo**	**mogla**	*neu.*	**reklo**	**rekla**

	jesti (to eat)			**sjesti** (to sit down)	
	sg.	*pl.*		*sg.*	*pl.*
m.	**jeo**	**jeli** *m., m. & f.*	*m.*	**sjeo**	**sjeli** *m., m. & f.*
f.	**jela**	**jele**	*f.*	**sjela**	**sjele**
neu.	**jelo**	**jela**	*neu.*	**sjelo**	**sjela**

In the past tense, reflexive verbs do not take the auxiliary verb **je** *is* in the third person singular:

On *se bojao.*
He *was afraid. (no auxiliary verb)*

BUT

Oni *su se bojali.*
They *were afraid. (auxiliary verb* ***su****)*

The formal address form of **Vi** always requires plural masculine agreement, including in the past tense, regardless of whether the individuals addressed are male or female. For instance, one *cannot* say ***Vi ste išla**; the form must be **Vi ste išli** *you (pl./formal) went* regardless of whether **Vi** refers to a male or a female subject.

This same rule applies to adjectives. Thus one would *never* say ***Vi ste vrlo ljubazan** or ***Vi ste vrlo ljubazna**, but rather **Vi ste vrlo ljubazni** *You're very kind.* (Of course, in the adjective/noun combination, it is possible to say **Vi ste *ljubazan čovjek*** *You're a very kind man* and **Vi ste *ljubazna žena*** *You're a very kind woman.*)

1.1. Negative and interrogative statements in the past tense

In the past tense, negation is rendered by the negative form of the verb **biti** *to be* (**nisam**, **nisi**, **nije**, etc.) plus the past participle.

Jučer *nisam bio* u školi.	*I was not* in school yesterday.
Ona *nije htjela* kupiti tu knjigu.	She *didn't want* to buy that book.

Since a sentence cannot begin with the short form of **biti** *to be*, the long form must be used in questions concerning the past:

***Jesi* li jučer *bio* u školi?**	*Were you* in school yesterday?
***Je* li *htjela* kupiti tu knjigu?**	*Did she want* to buy that book?

A one-word answer to questions concerning the past requires the long form of **biti** *to be.*

Jesi li jučer bio u školi?	Were you in school yesterday?
Jesam.	I was.
Nisam.	I wasn't.

1.2. Impersonal sentences in the past tense

All impersonal constructions in the past tense utilize the *neuter singular participle* of the verb **biti**. These constructions in English typically begin with *it's* and *there is/are,* although some Croatian dative constructions may require a somewhat different translation:

Present	Past
Hladno je. It's cold.	**Bilo je hladno.** It was cold.
Hladno mi je. I'm cold. [*lit.:* It's cold to me.]	**Bilo mi je hladno.** I was cold. [*lit.:* It was cold to me.]

Ovdje ima mnogo filmova. There are many films here.	**Ovdje je bilo mnogo filmova.** There were many films here.
Nema vode. There isn't any water.	**Nije bilo vode.** There wasn't any water.

1.3. Past time markers

Some of the typical time markers that appear with past tense are:

prošle godine last year	**ranije** earlier
prošlog mjeseca last month	**prije** before
prošlog tjedna last week	**dok** while
jučer yesterday	

Note that **dok** by itself means *while*, but in combination with the negative particle **dok ne** it means *until.*

***Dok je ona čitala*, on je kuhao ručak.**
While she was reading, he cooked lunch.
***Dok ne dođeš*, ne možemo ništa.**
Until you arrive, we can't do anything.

1.4. Numbers in the past tense

While the past tense is rather straightforward, the use of numbers slightly complicates the picture. The old *rule of five* becomes decisive for the use of the plural as opposed to the singular form of the auxiliary verb **biti** and of the participle. Here are a few examples:

Student *je došao* u Boston.	A student *arrived* in Boston.
Studenti *su došli* u Boston.	Students *arrived* in Boston.
Dva studenta *su došla* u Boston.	Two students (*m.) arrived* in Boston.
Dvije studentice *su došle* u Boston.	Two students (*f.) arrived* in Boston.
Pet studenata *je došlo* u Boston.	Five students *arrived* in Boston.
Pet studentica *je došlo* u Boston.	Five students *(f.) arrived* in Boston.

The first two sentences above are clear. The third and fourth, however, conform to the rule that the numbers 2–4 and all compound numbers ending in these digits are followed by a noun in the genitive singular. Like the adjectival form, the participle also agrees in its ending with the noun. The plural form of the auxiliary verb is required.

For sentences five and six, in the past tense, quantities of five and up require a genitive plural noun, but the verb is in the neuter singular because the items or individuals are regarded as a group.

2. Reported speech

Unlike in English, where it is necessary in reported speech to "push" all the tenses one step back in the subordinate clause, in Croatian the tense remains unchanged. Compare these examples and note how the same meaning is expressed by different tenses in English and Croatian:

On je *rekao* da *dolazi*. *past* *present*	He *said* that he *was coming*. *past* *past*
On je *rekao* da *je došao*. *past* *past*	He *said* that he *had come*. *past* *past perfect*

3. Word order

While the word order in Croatian is not as strict as in English, there are some rules especially when it comes to the "little words" or *clitics*. We have already discussed that the short forms of **biti** *to be* are not accented (see Lesson 1), and that they cannot appear as the first word in a sentence. This is particularly important with the past tense since the clitics are essential to its formation. Thus one cannot say ***Sam kupio računalo**, but one can say:

Kupio sam računalo.	I bought a computer.
Ja sam kupio računalo.	I bought a computer.
Danas sam kupio računalo.	Today I bought a computer.
Zašto sam kupio računalo?	Why did I buy a computer?

The rule of thumb is that in questions the particle **li** (**je li**) has to come before all other short forms. In statements, the first accented word is followed by the short form of the verb **biti** *to be*, with the exception of the third person singular **je** *is*, which always comes last. The short forms of pronouns in the dative or genitive/accusative come next in the sentence.

Finally, the last two clitics are the reflexive particle **se**, and the third person singular of **biti**, **je** *is*. This formula can be shown as follows:

word order:

li – short form of **biti** (except **je**) – pronoun in *dat.*or *gen./acc.* – **se** – **je**

The following examples demonstrate this scheme:

Kupila mu je kaput.	She bought him a coat.
Je li joj on pisao?	Did he write to her?
Oni su nam je vratili.	They returned it to us.
Mi smo se upoznali.	We got acquainted.
Jesmo li im ga dali?	Did we give it to them?

4. The expressions **sve** ***all/everything*****, svi** ***all/everybody*****, takav** ***such*****, ovakav** ***this kind*** **and onakav** ***that kind***

The expressions **sve** *all/everything*, **svi** *all/everybody* and **takav** *such,* **ova-kav** *this kind,* and **onakav** *that kind* are pronominal adjectival forms, which means that they decline similarly to all other adjectives.

The pattern for **takav** *such,* **ovakav** *this kind,* and **onakav** *that kind* corresponds precisely to the pattern for **kakav** *what kind of.* (See p.52, 329–331 for chart of forms of **kakav**.)

Since the pattern for **sav** *all* differs from this model, the forms are given below. Note that **svi** (*m. pl.*) also means *everybody*, and **sve** (*neu. sg.*) means *everything.*

svi (everybody) and **sve** (everything)

	m. sg.	*neu. sg.*	*f. sg.*	*m. pl.*	*neu. pl.*	*f. pl.*
nom.	sav	SVE	sva	SVI	sva	sve
acc.	sav/svega	sve	svu	sve	sva	sve
gen.	sveg(a)	sveg(a)	sve	svih	svih	svih
dat./loc.	svem(u)	svem(u)	svoj	svim(a)	svim(a)	svim(a)
instru.	svim	svim	svom	svim(a)	svim(a)	svim(a)

Note: In some instances both the shorter and the longer forms are acceptable. The longer form is made by adding to the short form, where indicated, the additional vowels in parentheses.

Je li je *sve* u redu?
Is *everything* OK?

Siguran sam da *sve* ima svoj razlog.
I'm sure that *everything* has its reason.

***Sve* u *svemu*, rezultati nisu loši.**
All in *all*, the results are not bad.

***Svi* idemo u trapericama!**
We are *all* going in jeans.

Vidim *sve*.
I can see *everyone/everything*.

Ona je prijateljica sa *svima*.
She is a friend with [to] *everybody*.

***Takvo* čudno ponašanje!**
Such strange behavior!

Ona nikada ne zaboravlja *takve* stvari.
She never forgets *such* things!

***Takav* lijep dan!**
Such a nice day!

Imamo *ovakve* proizvode, ako želite pogledati.
We have *these kinds* of products, if you wish to have a look.

***Onakav* koncert teško je zaboraviti.**
That kind of concert is difficult to forget.

Exercises

Vježba 9.1 Write out the past tense of the following verbs using the short form of the verb **biti** *to be* as provided. Gender is indicated in italics.

Example: **ići – sam** *m.*, **ste** *f.* – **išao sam, išle ste**

1. misliti – je *m.*, su *m.*

   ____

2. jesti – si *m.*, su *f.*

   ____

3. proći – je *neu.*, ste *f.*

   ____

4. planirati – si *f.*, su *m.*

   ____

5. čekati – sam *f.* , ste *m.*

   ____

6. obećati – smo *f.*, ste *m.*

   ____

7. napraviti – si *m.*, sam *f.*

   ____

8. posjetiti – je *m.*, sam *f.*

   ____

9. plesati – smo *m.*, ste *m.*

   ____

10. reći – sam *f.*, su *m.*

    ____

11. vidjeti – si *m.*, je *f.*

    ____

12. moći – sam *f.*, je *m.*

    ____

Vježba 9.2 In the sentences below, change the verb from present to past tense and negate the past tense. Be creative and, when appropriate, choose whichever gender and number you wish!

Example: **Idem u Boston zrakoplovom. Jučer nisam išao u Boston zrakoplovom.**

1. Studiram na fakultetu u Kaliforniji.

   ____

   ____

2. Planiram ti doći u Ameriku.

   ____

   ____

3. Pišeš joj poruku o novom filmu.

   ____

   ____

4. Predlažem ručak, pa muzički centar.

   ____

   ____

5. Imam auto, ali je pokvaren.

   ____

   ____

6. Čekam da on dođe.

   ____

   ____

7. Ove godine putujem u Australiju.

   ____

   ____

Vježba 9.3 Translate the sentences below.

1. She was afraid, but I was not.

   ____

2. Yesterday, I arrived in New York and went to the movies.

   ____

3. There were no books in this library.

   ____

4. They said that they would go to the seashore in August.

   ____

5. Five students were accepted to the doctoral program at Harvard. Fifty-two students expected to visit Harvard in September.

____

____

6. Last week I watched four good films.

____

7. My five cousins arrived in Texas.

____

Vježba 9.4

A. Fill in the blank to complete the sentence.

1. Mi smo se upoznali __ Budimpešti.
2. Oni su mi _____ da imam pravo.
3. Jučer ____ kupio šešir.
4. Čekao ____ je u stanu.
5. Išla sam ____ stadion u Zagrebu.

B. Negate each sentence from above.

1. ____
2. ____
3. ____
4. ____
5. ____

Vježba 9.5

Construct sentences using the past tense forms of the following verbs.

1. promijeniti _______________________________________
2. saznati ____
3. spavati ____
4. vratiti se ____
5. voziti ____
6. htjeti ____
7. biti ____

Vježba 9.6

A. Complete the sentences below by filling in the most appropriate preposition(s).

1. Kupujem nekoliko knjiga ___ svog oca. Želim knjige ___ slikama.
2. Idućeg tjedna idem ___ Šibenik, a nakon nekoliko dana putujem ___ neki otok ___ blizini.
3. Pišem pismo ___ olovkom zato što nemam računalo ___ kuće.
4. Mačka je ___ stolice, a pas ___ zgrade.
5. Imam poslovni sastanak danas ___ pet sati, pa ne mogu doći ___ njega ___ sutra.

B. Practice the pronoun "ja" in different cases. When you are finished, substitute "ja" with other pronouns.

1. On______piše svaki dan.
2. Želiš li putovati sa______u Indiju?
3. Ti______dobro znaš.
4. Vidiš li_____?
5. Možeš sjesti do_____.
6. Je li_____vjeruješ?
7. Ti se uvijek smiješ kada si sa_____.
8. Ona_____je preporučila odmor u Italiji.
9. Morate u grad bez_____.
10. Što_____želiš reći?
11. Tko govori takve stvari o_____?
12. Sviđa_____se ta ideja.
13. To je dar za_____?
14. Ne želim da_____se bojiš.
15. Dali su_____odličnu plaću.

Vježba 9.7
A. Translate into Croatian:

<u>Love dilemmas—Ljubavne dileme</u>

My name is Krešimir and I had a big uproar [gužva] last week. First at work, and then [onda] with my girlfriend. What happened at work is less important than what happened with my girlfriend. It was a cold evening and we were strolling along the Zrinjevac. She was bored. She is not interested in romance [romantika]. She wanted us to go to a concert and then to some party. But there were no more tickets [karta] for the concert. I suggested we go somewhere for dinner, but that wasn't good either. We walked like that and did not talk about anything. She was angry and said that I could have remembered something better [bolje]. Ah, what an evening! The next day she apologized, but now I don't know what to think about her at all.

____

____

____

____

____

____

____

____

____

____

B. Write an email in Croatian to a friend telling him or her what you have been doing for the last two months. Include both positive and negative news and be sure to use plenty of past tenses.

____

____

____

____

____

____

____

____

____

____

Lekcija 10
Put na jug

Lesson 10
A journey to the South

Lekcija 10: Put na jug

Prvi dio

Marijana: Darko, idućeg tjedna otputovat ću na more. Mislim da mi treba odmor, a imat ću i priliku razmisliti o svemu. Mnogo se toga dogodilo u prošlih nekoliko tjedana.

Darko: Bit će ti dosadno samoj. Nikog ne poznaješ u Dalmaciji. Što ćeš raditi? Ivan je rekao da će možda posjetiti obitelj za blagdane. Možemo otići svi zajedno na jug.

Marijana: Ne misliš li da moramo pitati Ivana slaže li se?

Darko: Naravno, ali Ivan će se složiti, to znam. Evo, sada ću ga odmah nazvati na mobitel. Ivane, halo, Darko ovdje. Gdje si? U kojoj knjižari? Aha, ti si u knjižari „Miroslav Krleža" u kojoj smo bili prije nekoliko dana. Da se nađemo tamo? Bit ćemo tamo za pet minuta.

Marijana: Idemo razgovarati s Ivanom?

Darko: Da, on je slučajno tu blizu. Tako ćemo se moći o svemu zajedno dogovoriti.

Drugi dio

Malo kasnije.

Ivan: Baš ste brzi! Drago mi je što ste došli jer u nedjelju putujem u Split.

Darko: Možda nećeš putovati sam. Što misliš o tome da ti se ja i Marijana pridružimo? Marijani treba odmor, a ni meni neće škoditi.

Ivan: Izvrsna ideja! Imat ću društvo za put, i to kakvo društvo! Planirao sam ići vlakom, ali ako idemo svi, možemo i mojim autom.

Marijana: Možda nam možeš preporučiti kakav dobar hotel u Splitu?

Ivan: Neće vam trebati hotel jer moji roditelji imaju veliku kuću na moru. Ima mjesta za sve!

Marijana: Vrlo lijepo od tebe što nas pozivaš. Jesi li siguran da naš posjet neće biti problem?

Ivan: Siguran sam. Mojim roditeljima će biti drago kada čuju da dolazite.

Lesoon 10: A journey to the South

Part I

Marijana: Darko, next week I am going to go to the coast. I think that I need a vacation, and I will also have a chance to think everything over. There has been a lot going on these last few weeks.

Darko: It will be boring all alone. You don't know anyone in Dalmatia. What are you going to do there? Ivan said that he might visit his family for the holidays. We can all go to the south together.

Marijana: You don't think that we need to ask Ivan to make sure it's ok?

Darko: Naturally, but Ivan will agree; I know that. Look, I will call him right away on his cell phone. Ivan, hello, Darko here. Where are you? Which bookstore? Aha, you are in the *Miroslav Krleža* bookstore in which we were a few days ago. Shall we meet there? We'll be there in five minutes.

Marijana: We're going to talk to Ivan?

Darko: Yes, by chance he is close by. Then we'll be able to sort out everything together.

Part II

A short time later.

Ivan: You guys are really fast. I'm glad that you came because on Sunday I'll be traveling to Split.

Darko: Maybe you will not be going alone. What do you think about me and Marijana joining you? Marijana needs a vacation, and it wouldn't hurt me either.

Ivan: An excellent idea! I'll have company on the trip and what company! I had planned to go by train, but if we're all going, we can go in my car.

Marijana: Maybe you can recommend a good hotel in Split?

Ivan: You won't need a hotel because my parents have a big house on the seashore. There is room for everybody!

Marijana: That's very nice of you to invite us. Are you sure that our visit won't be a problem?

Ivan: I'm sure. My parents will be happy when they hear that you're coming.

Darko: Ivan već ima plan što ćemo sve raditi u Splitu.

Ivan: Domaćin koji sve organizira mora imati plan. Razgledat ćemo Split, navečer ćemo ići van, a otići ćemo i na izlet. Ako se Marijana slaže, možemo otići na otok Brač koji nije daleko.

Marijana: Neće nam biti dosadno, to već sada znam.

Ivan: Moja majka će sigurno kuhati dobra jela. Ona uvijek kuha nešto posebno kada ja dođem.

Darko: Bit će kolača, u to ne sumnjam.

Ivan: Ne žali se, bit će upravo kako Marijana želi. Ona je naš zajednički gost.

Marijana: Radujem se putu i društvu. Kada krećemo?

Ivan: Krećemo u 9 ujutro, a u Split ćemo doći u 1 popodne.

Darko: Dogovoreno!

Darko:	Ivan already has a plan about what to do in Split.
Ivan:	The host who organizes everything must have a plan. We will go sightseeing in Split, in the evening we will go out, and we will also go on a trip. If Marijana agrees, we can go to the island of Brač, which is not far away.
Marijana:	We will not be bored, that I already know.
Ivan:	My mother will certainly cook good food. She always cooks something special when I come home.
Darko:	There will be plenty of cakes, I don't doubt that!
Ivan:	Don't complain, everything will be the way Marijana wants. She is our joint guest.
Marijana:	I look forward to both the trip and to the company. When are we leaving?
Ivan:	We're leaving at 9 in the morning and will arrive in Split at 1 in the afternoon.
Darko:	Fine!

Vocabulary

dogovoreno fine (*lit.* agreed)
domaćin host
gost guest
izlet trip
jug south
knjižara bookstore
kuća house
mobitel cell phone
more sea
obitelj *f.* family
otok island
poseb*a*n special
slučajno by chance
vlak train

Verb List

čuti (*I/P* **čujem, čuju**) to hear
dogovoriti se (*P* **dogovorim se, dogovore se**) to agree upon
kretati (*I* **krećem, kreću**) to set off
kuhati (*I* **kuham, kuhaju**)to cook
otputovati (*P* **otputujem, otputuju**) to depart, to leave
pozivati (*I* **pozivam, pozivaju**) to invite
pridružiti se (*P* **pridružim se, pridruže se**) to join
radovati se (*I* **radujem se, raduju se**) to look forward to
razgledati (*P* **razgledam, razgledaju)** to sightsee
skuhati (*P* **skuham, skuhaju**) to cook
složiti se (*P* **složim se, slože se**) to agree
sumnjati (*I* **sumnjam, sumnjaju**) to doubt
škoditi (*I* **škodim, škode**) to harm, to hurt
trebati (*I* **trebam, trebaju**) to need
žaliti se (*I* **žalim se, žale se**) to complain

Useful Expressions

Što ćeš raditi? What are you going to do?
za blagdane for holidays
neće škoditi it won't harm; it won't hurt
Da se nađemo tamo? Shall we meet there?
Ima mjesta za sve! There's room for everyone!
U to ne sumnjam! I don't doubt it!
Treba mi odmor. I need a vacation.
Kada krećemo? When are we leaving?

Compass directions

sjever north **jug** south **istok** east **zapad** west

The preposition typically used with directions is **na**. If movement is involved, the accusative case is required; if a stationary event is described, the locative is used.

Putujemo *na jug*.	We are traveling *to the South.*
***Na jugu* je lijepo.**	It is beautiful *in the South.*

Grammar

1. The future tense

In Croatian the future tense is formed using **htjeti** *to wish, to want* as an auxiliary verb with the infinitive of the given verb. While most commonly used in its short form in the future tense, the full form of the verb **htjeti** can also be used, especially in questions, in one-word responses, and in the negative.

Here is the conjugation chart for the verb **htjeti**:

	htjeti (to want) *reg.*		**htjeti** (to want) *aux.*	
	sg.	***pl.***	***sg.***	***pl.***
1st	**hoću**	**hoćemo**	**ću**	**ćemo**
2nd	**hoćeš**	**hoćete**	**ćeš**	**ćete**
3rd	**hoće**	**hoće**	**će**	**će**

When used as an auxiliary, **htjeti** cannot be the initial word in a sentence; it is always in second place, just like **biti** when used as an auxiliary in the past tense. When there is no pronoun or other stressed word at the beginning of the sentence, the main verb comes before this auxiliary verb and the infinitive loses the final **-i**. (Verbs ending in **-ći** are exceptions to this rule).

With a pronoun	**Without a pronoun**	
Ja *ću pisati* pismo.	***Pisat ću* pismo.**	*I will write* a letter.
Ti *ćeš pisati* pismo.	***Pisat ćeš* pismo.**	*You will write* a letter.
***On će pisati* pismo.**	***Pisat će* pismo.**	*He will write* a letter.
***Mi ćemo pisati* pismo.**	***Pisat ćemo* pismo.**	*We will write* a letter.
***Vi ćete pisati* pismo.**	***Pisat ćete* pismo.**	*You will write* a letter.
***Oni će pisati* pismo.**	***Pisat će* pismo.**	*They will write* a letter.

1.1. Negative and interrogative statements in the future tense

Questions are formed by inserting the particle **li** between the long form of **htjeti** and the infinitive form of the verb:

Hoću *li* pisati pismo?	Will I write the letter?
Hoćeš *li* mi doći u posjet?	Will you visit me?

Negation is indicated by adding **ne** to the auxiliary verb.

ne + aux. form of **htjeti** = will not

	singular	plural
1st	**neću**	**nećemo**
2nd	**nećeš**	**nećete**
3rd	**neće**	**neće**

***Neću pisati* pismo.**	*I will not write* the letter.
***Nećemo ići* na predavanje.**	*We will not go* to the lecture.

Negative questions are formed by using the negative auxiliary of **htjeti** and the particle **li** or by the question word **zar**:

***Nećemo li ići* na predavanje?**	*Won't we go* to the lecture?
***Zar mi nećeš* doći u posjet?**	*Won't you* visit me?

1.2. Impersonal sentences in the future tense

The future is rendered in impersonal sentences through the use of the infinitive form of the verb **biti** *to be* and the third person singular auxiliary of **htjeti** *to want.*

Present	Future
Hladno je. It's cold.	***Bit će* hladno.** *It will be* cold.
Hladno mi je. I'm cold.	***Bit će* mi hladno.** I *will be* cold.
Ovdje ima mnogo filmova. There are many films here.	**Ovdje *će biti* mnogo filmova.** There *will be* many films here.
Nema vode. There isn't any water.	***Neće biti* vode.** There *won't be* any water.

1.3. Future time expressions

sutra tomorrow	**za sat vremena** in an hour
idućeg tjedna next week	**za tri sata** in three hours

idućeg mjeseca next month
iduće godine next year
u buduće in the future
poslije, kasnije later

za mjesec dana in a month
za godinu dana in a year
na godinu dana for a year
na tjedan dana for a week

The preposition **za** and **na** have completely different meanings in similar time expressions:

Doći ću *za* mjesec dana. I will come *in* a month.
Doći ću *na* mjesec dana. I will come *for* a month.

2. Relative pronouns

The words **koji (koja**, **koje)**, **čiji (čija**, **čije)** and **kakav (kakva**, **kakvo**, **kakvi)** have been seen already (see declension charts on pp. 329–331) as question words meaning *which*, *whose*, and *what kind of*, respectively.

They can also serve to introduce a subordinate clause and then are translated as *who*, *which*, or *that*. Unlike *that* in English, these words cannot be omitted. The relative pronoun **koji** *who/which* comes after both the nouns for humans (and therefore corresponds to English *who*) and the nouns for non-human items (thus it also corresponds to English *which*). Relative pronouns are also sometimes referred to as relative adjectives because they take adjectival endings.

Ti si u knjižari *Miroslav Krleža u kojoj* smo bili prije nekoliko dana.
You are in the *Miroslav Krleža* bookstore *in which* we were a few days ago.

Možemo otići na otok Brač *koji* nije daleko.
We can go to the island of Brač, *which* is not far away.

Domaćin *koji* sve organizira mora imati plan.
The host *who* organizes everything must have a plan.

In determining which relative pronoun to use, it is important to remember the following:

a) Find the noun in the main clause to which the relative pronoun is referring, because the relative pronoun will have the same gender and number as the noun it refers to.

b) Locate the verb in the subordinate clause to determine the case of the relative pronoun.

Let's analyze the following sentence:

Spavat ćemo u hotelu koji je vrlo skup.
We will sleep in a hotel that is very expensive.

The above sentence consists of two clauses:

Spavat ćemo u hotelu. Hotel je vrlo skup.
We will sleep in a hotel. The hotel is very expensive.

In the second clause **Hotel je vrlo skup** *The hotel is very expensive* (which is in fact the *subordinate clause* in the first sentence above), we have the verb **je** *is* and the noun **hotel** *hotel* in the nominative. Since **hotel** is masculine and singular, the relative pronoun will be masculine singular nominative—**koji**.

Let's analyze another sentence:

Jesi li kupio knjigu *koju* si tražio?
Have you bought the book *that* you looked for?

The above sentence consists of two clauses:

Jesi li kupio knjigu? Tražio si knjigu.
Have you bought the book? You looked for the book.

In the first sentence above, the relative pronoun **koju** *that* refers to *the book*, and the book is a direct object in the subordinate clause [*You looked for the book*] and for this reason, **koju** is in the accusative.

Here are a few more examples of relative pronouns in different cases:

To je pismo *koje* mi je napisala majka.
That is the letter *that* my mother wrote to me.

Broken into its two consituent clauses:

To je pismo. Pismo mi je napisala majka.
This is the letter. Mother wrote me the letter.

To je student *kojem* sam pisala pismo.
This is the student *to whom* I wrote a letter.

Broken into its two consituent clauses:

To je student. Studentu sam pisala pismo.
This is the student. I wrote a letter to the student.

Profesor o *kojem* je govorila Ana je odličan.
The professor about whom Anna spoke is excellent.

Broken into its two consituent clauses:

Profesor je odličan. Ana je govorila o njemu.
The professor is excellent. Anna talked about him.

The same rules apply to the use of **čiji**, **čija**, **čije** *whose*:

Gdje je čovjek *čija* je to kuća?
Where is the man *whose* house this is?

Susjed, *čijeg* psa se bojimo, nije ovdje.
The neighbor, *of whose* dog we are afraid, is not here.

Kolegica, *čiju* majku sam jučer vidjela u gradu, sjedi tamo preko puta.
The colleague, *whose* mother I saw in the city yesterday, is sitting over there.

The same thing is true for **kakav**, **kakva**, **kakvo**, **kakvi** *what kind*:

Auto *kakav* on vozi više nitko nema.
Nobody any longer has *the kind* of car *that* he drives.

Naočale *kakve* ona ima su vrlo skupe.
The *kind of* glasses [*that*] she has are very expensive.

On piše knjigu *kakvu* nitko još nije napisao.
He is writing *the kind* of book *that* nobody has yet written.

Što *what, that* and **tko** *who* can sometimes also be used as relative pronouns but must be preceded by:

- a demonstrative pronoun
  to što **ovo što** **ono što**
  taj tko **ovaj tko** **onaj tko**
- the word **sve**
  sve što (**što** has to be in the appropriate case dictated by the verb; thus **sve o čemu, sve čega**, etc.)
- or an indefinite pronoun.
  nešto što **netko tko** **ništa što** **nitko tko**

***To što* on kaže nije istina.**
What [*that which*] he is saying is not true.

***Sve* o čemu on razmišlja je put u Ameriku.**
All that he thinks about is the trip to America.

***Onaj tko* je bio u Splitu zna da je taj grad na moru.**
Everyone who was in Split knows that that city is on the coast.

***Sve* čega se bojiš je laž.**
All that you are afraid of is a lie.

Jedino *onaj tko* ga nije vidio mogao je misliti da je on zdrav.
Only *someone who* hasn't seen him could have thought that he was healthy.

Exercises

Vježba 10.1 Translate the following sentences from English into Croatian. Try to use both the long and short forms for the future tense when possible!

Example: I will travel to Zagreb by car.
Ja ću putovati u Zagreb autom.
Putovat ću u Zagreb autom.

1. I will go to the store to buy a sandwich and a kilo of bread.

____

____

2. I am going to read 5 books this month.

____

____

3. I won't write a letter to my mother but I will call her on the phone.

____

____

4. Will you come with me to the seashore for the weekend?

____

____

5. How long will you be living in Boston?

____

____

6. I know that you will agree.

____

____

7. Where will we travel in Croatia?

____

____

Vježba 10.2

A. Which sentence in the pairs below is correct? Circle your answer.

Example: Hladno mi je – Hladno me je. **Hladno mi je.**

1.	Bit će toplo danas.	Bit ćemo toplo danas.
2.	Nema bilo vode.	Nije bilo vode.
3.	Ovdje ima puno problema.	Ovdje će ima puno problema.
4.	Ovdje nema ništa.	Ovdje neće imati ništa.
5.	Mi je dosadno.	Dosadno mi je.

B. Practice using negatives. Make the following sentences negative and then write a sentence in response.

Example: **Ja ću pisati pismo sutra na fakultetu**
Ja neću pisati pismo sutra na fakultetu.
Pisat ću pismo danas.

1. Ja sam bio u Splitu s Ivanom.

____

____

2. Idem na kavu, a onda ću čitati novine.

____

____

3. Dobio sam novca prošle godine.

____

____

4. Ja ću spavati u hotelu koji je vrlo jeftin.

____

____

5. Ovaj čovjek je kupio kuću u Splitu. Ja ću biti tamo idućeg tjedna.

____

____

Vježba 10.3 Create sentences with the vocabulary words provided.

Example: tjedan; ići; more; odmor –
Prošlog tjedna išao sam na more, ali treba mi drugi odmor.

1. Dalmacija; riba; restoran

____

____

2. izlet; kuća; vikend

___

___

3. gost; vrijeme; obitelj

___

___

4. čuti; na miru; kavana

___

___

5. pridružiti se; dobar; plan

___

___

Vježba 10.4
Translate into Croatian:

<u>Life without stress – Život bez stresa</u>

My name is Tomislav and I'm a CEO of a large company. Next month I will have many business meetings. The economy is growing [in ascent] one moment and decreasing [in descent] the next. This will bring [donijeti] many problems, I don't doubt it. It is difficult to say whether it will be bad or good. We thought that we would open five new branches and two factories. As it stands now [kako sada stvari stoje], we will have to wait. To tell you the truth [da vam pravo kažem], I will not worry about it any more. I will not read the newspapers any more. I will not watch the news. I will not read business reports. I have decided that I will be happy and live without stress [stres], come what may [pa kako bude].

___

___

___

___

___

___

___

___

___

___

Vježba 10.5 Relative Pronouns. Choose the correct relative pronoun for the sentences provided.

Example: Profesor o _____ je govorio Branimir je odličan – **kojem**

1. Jesi li kupio auto ________ si tražio?
2. Gdje je čovjek __________ je to knjiga?
3. Ti si bio u trgovini u _____ smo bili prije nekoliko dana.
4. Ovo je moj prijatelj s _____ sutra putujem na more.
5. Sve o _____ on razmišlja je odmor u Splitu.
6. Je li ovo trgovina ___________si kupio te naočale?
7. Ljudi _______________ ste upoznali su moji prijatelji.
8. Gdje je stol ______________sam jučer vidio ovdje.
9. Dao si mi knjigu _____________ je dosadna.
10. Znate li gdje je zgrada ____________ živi Ivan?

Vježba 10.6 Create a dialogue using all of the following words and phrases.

jedinstven, iznenađenje, morati, čime Vas mogu ponuditi?, probati, doći, dodatni, nadati se, dobili ste pogrešan broj, domaćin, ima mjesta za sve, veliki problem, složiti se, moći.

____

____

____

____

____

____

____

____

____

____

Vježba 10.7 Sažetak/Summary

A. Read and translate:

Marijana želi otputovati na more. Treba joj odmor. Želi o svemu razmisliti jer se mnogo toga dogodilo u prošlih nekoliko tjedana. Darko misli da će joj biti dosadno samoj u Dalmaciji. On zna da Ivan ide posjetiti obitelj za blagdane. Predlaže da svi putuju zajedno. Zovu Ivana na telefon jer se žele dogovoriti s njim. Ivan se slaže. Kaže da će imati lijepo društvo za put. On predlaže da idu njegovim autom. Svi mogu biti kod njegovih roditelja jer oni imaju veliku kuću na moru. Ivanova majka voli kuhati i uvijek kuha nešto posebno kada Ivan dođe. Ivan ima plan jer je on domaćin. Kaže da mogu razgledati Split i otići na izlet. Marijana se raduje putu. Oni kreću u 9 ujutro, a u Split će doći u 1 popodne.

B. Answer the following questions:

1. Kamo Marijana želi otputovati?
2. Zašto?
3. O čemu ona mora razmisliti?
4. Što Darko misli o Marijaninom planu?
5. Što Darko zna o Ivanovim planovima?
6. Gdje živi Ivanova obitelj?

7. Što Darko predlaže?

____

8. Koga on i Marijana zovu?

____

9. Što kaže Ivan?

____

10. Kako će oni putovati u Dalmaciju?

____

11. Hoće li Marijana i Darko biti u hotelu?

____

12. Što radi Ivanova majka kada Ivan dođe?

____

13. Što će Marijana, Darko i Ivan raditi u Splitu?

____

14. Kada oni kreću iz Zagreba, a kada će doći u Split?

____

Lekcija 11
Izgubljene isprave

Lesson 11
Lost documents

Lekcija 11: Izgubljene isprave

Prvi dio

Marijana: Darko, već tri sata vozimo bez odmora. Možemo li stati na nekoliko minuta?

Darko: Planirao sam uskoro stati jer moram kupiti benzin.

Ivan: A ja želim kupiti novine i sendvič.

Na odmorištu.

Marijana: Ne volim kupovati hranu na ovakvim mjestima, ali ovi topli sendviči izgledaju dobro, pa ću ipak kupiti jedan.

Darko: Ja idem popiti kavu. Želite li i vi kavu, sok ili nešto drugo?

Ivan: Sok za mene, molim te! Idem po novine i odmah se vraćam.

Marijana: I za mene. Jutros prije polaska nije bilo vremena za doručak.

Ivan: Nema gužve na autocesti. Mislim da ćemo doći do Splita za jedan sat.

Marijana: Izvrsno, možda još stignem i na plažu. Hvala vam na ovom lijepom putovanju. Dopustite da vas barem počastim kavom. Ali joj, gdje je moj novčanik? U njemu su sve moje isprave, putovnica, novac, kreditne kartice, vozačka dozvola! Strašno! Kako sam ga mogla izgubiti?

Drugi dio

Darko: Marijana, smiri se. Ti nikada ne gubiš stvari. Maloprije ti je novčanik bio u ruci kada si plaćala sendvič.

Marijana: Istina, platila sam i mislim da sam ga stavila u torbu.

Ivan: Jesi li sigurna da ga nisi stavljala nigdje drugdje?

Marijana: Potpuno.

Darko: Tu je policajac, idemo pitati njega. Oprostite, možete li nam pomoći? Gospođica je izgubila novčanik crne boje s ispravama. Znate li je li ga možda tko pronašao?

Policajac: Ne, ništa ne znam o tome. Što je točno bilo u novčaniku?

Lesson 11: Lost documents

Part I

Marijana: Darko, we've already been driving for three hours without a break. Do you think that we should stop for a few minutes?

Darko: I was planning on us stopping shortly because I have to buy gas.

Ivan: And I want to buy a newspaper and a sandwich.

At the rest area.

Marijana: I don't like to buy food in these places but these hot sandwiches look good so I will buy one nonetheless.

Darko: I am going to drink some coffee. Would you also like a coffee, juice or something else?

Ivan: Juice for me, please. I'm going for a newspaper and will be right back.

Marijana: And for me, too. This morning before we left, there was no time for breakfast.

Ivan: There are no traffic jams on the highway. I think that we will arrive in Split in an hour.

Marijana: Excellent, maybe I will even make it to the beach. Thank you for this nice trip. At least allow me to treat you to coffee. But oooh, where is my wallet? Inside were all my documents, my passport, money, credit cards, driver's license! This is terrible! How could I have lost it?

Part II

Darko: Marijana, calm down. You never lose things. A little while ago you had the wallet in your hands when you paid for the sandwich.

Marijana: That's right, I paid and I think that I put it back in my bag.

Ivan: Are you sure that you did not put it somewhere else?

Marijana: Entirely.

Darko: Here is a policeman, let's go ask him. Excuse me, can you help us? The lady has lost a black wallet with all her documents. Do you know if someone has turned it in?

Policeman: No, I don't know anything about it. What exactly was in your wallet?

Marijana: **Bilo je 750 kuna, moja američka putovnica, 100 dolara, vozačka dozvola, i moje kreditne kartice.**

Policajac: **Ako ga ne nađemo, morat ćete ispuniti formular. Tako Vas možemo obavijestiti ako ga tko vrati. Gdje ste ga posljednji put imali?**

Marijana: **Kada sam kupovala sendvič, tamo u trgovini.**

Ivan: **Ja sam ga tamo već tražio, ali ga nisam našao. To ništa ne znači, možda ga ipak nađemo.**

Policajac: **Da vidimo! Pa niste pogledali ispod pulta. Evo ga! Je li ovo Vaš novčanik?**

Marijana: **Da, moj je. Valjda mi je ispao iz torbe kada sam kupovala sendvič.**

Policajac: **Izgleda da ga je netko nehotice gurnuo ispod pulta.**

Marijana: **Ne znam kako da Vam zahvalim!**

Policajac: **Nema na čemu. Sretan put!**

Darko: **E, sada mi stvarno treba kava!**

Marijana:	There were 750 kuna, my American passport, 100 dollars, a driver's license, and my credit cards.
Policeman:	If it does not turn up, you must fill out a form. That way we can inform you in case someone returns it. Where was the last place you had it?
Marijana:	When I bought a sandwich over there in the store.
Ivan:	I already looked there, but I did not find it. It doesn't matter, maybe we'll still find it.
Policeman:	Let's see! Aha, you did not look underneath the counter. Here it is. Is this your wallet?
Marijana:	Yes, it is mine. It must have fallen from my bag when I bought the sandwich.
Policeman:	It looks like someone accidentally pushed it underneath the counter.
Marijana:	I don't know how to thank you!
Policeman:	Not at all. Have a good trip!
Darko:	And now I really need a coffee!

Vocabulary

benzin gasoline
isprava document
doruč*a*k breakfast
drugdje elsewhere
formular form
izgubljen lost
maloprije a little bit ago
nehotice by chance
novčanik wallet
odmorište rest area
plaža beach
polaz*a*k departure, leaving
polic*a*j*a*c policeman
potpuno entirely
pult counter
putovnica passport
sendvič sandwich
sok juice
slučaj case
top*a*o warm
torba bag
uskoro soon
valjda possibly, perhaps
vozačka dozvola driver's license

Verb List

dopustiti (*P* **dopustim, dopuste**) to allow
gubiti (*I* **gubim, gube**) to lose
gurnuti (*P* **gurnem, gurnu**) to push
ispasti (*P* **ispadnem, ispadnu**) to fall out
ispuniti (*P* **ispunim, ispune**) to fill
izgubiti (*P* **izgubim, izgube**) to lose
kupiti (*P* **kupim, kupe**) to buy
kupovati (*I* **kupujem, kupuju**) to buy
obavijestiti (*P* **obavijestim, obavijeste**) to inform
plaćati (*I* **plaćam, plaćaju**) to pay
platiti (*P* **platim, plate**) to pay
počastiti (*P* **počastim, počaste**) to treat
popiti (*P* **popijem, popiju**) to drink
smiriti se (*P* **smirim se, smire se**) to calm down
stati (*P* **stanem, stanu**) to stop
staviti (*P* **stavim, stave**) to put
stavljati (*I* **stavljam, stavljaju**) to put
stići (*P* **stignem, stignu**) to arrive
vraćati (se) (*I* **vraćam, vraćaju**) to return
vratiti (se) (*P* **vratim, vrate**) to return

Useful Expressions

na nekoliko minuta for a few minutes
Idem po novine i mlijeko. (object in *acc.*) I'm going for a newspaper and milk.
Dopustite da vas počastim. Allow me to treat you.
smiri se calm down
Oprostite, možete li nam pomoći? Excuse me, can you help us?
Morat ćete ispuniti formular. You must fill out a form.
to ništa ne znači It doesn't matter [*lit.*: that doesn't mean anything]
Da vidimo! Let's see!
Ne znam kako da Vam zahvalim! I don't know how to thank you!
Nema na čemu. Not at all.
Sretan put! Have a good trip!

Grammar

1. The preposition *po* and the particle *po*

We first encountered the preposition **po** when we discussed the dative and locative cases (see Lesson 7). The preposition **po** can also take the accusative. It means *to go get/fetch something* or *to go and pick somebody up.*

Idem po novine.
I'm going for a newspaper. [to get a newspaper].
Ideš li danas po knjige?
Are you going to get the books today?
Tko će doći po tebe?
Who will meet you?
Idemo po njih.
We are going to pick them up.

In addition there is a particle **po** that expresses the meaning *so and so many for each person.* When used in this sense, it has no influence on the case in the sentence. Rather, it is the verb and the number that dictate the case.

Svima dajem po jedan komad.	I'm giving everyone one piece each.
Došli su s po dva kofera.	They arrived with two suitcases each.
Kupili su po pet knjiga.	They each bought five books.

2. Verb aspect

2.1. Practical use of aspect

For a native speaker of English, verb aspect is possibly one of the most complex grammatical categories to master in Croatian.

What is aspect, and why do we need it? Unlike tenses which tell us when something happened, aspect designates *how it happened*, i.e., whether a certain activity expressed by the verb is completed and permanent (*perfective*), or whether it is in progress or repeated at regular intervals (*imperfective*). The meaning to be conveyed determines the choice of verb aspect.

Croatian has two verb aspects, *perfective and imperfective*. Most verbs have an *aspectual partner*; some have more than one, and some have none.

While English uses the *same* verb in different tenses, Croatian uses paired verbs. The *continuous* and the *simple* tenses in English express duration or repetition, but the manner in which these concepts are expressed is organized differently. For example, *I am going to school now* is the *present continuous* tense in English, while *I go to school every day* is the *present simple*. The English continuous tense is usually translated by imperfective verbs in Croatian, but verbs in the simple tense can go either way.

In Croatian the perfective aspect is used to convey the notion that something has been done or has occurred (i.e., the activity is completed), while the imperfective is used for activities that are continuous or repeated (i.e., they have no sense of closure). Consider the following examples:

Imperfective	Perfective
Kuham ručak. I'm cooking lunch.	**Dođi kada skuham ručak.** Come when I have cooked lunch. (i.e., when I shall have finished cooking it)
Kada putuješ na more? When are you traveling to the shore?	**Prvo moram završiti posao, pa ću onda otputovati na more.** First I have to finish work, and then I will travel to the shore. (i.e., I will get one thing done, and then the other)
Čitam knjigu. I'm reading a book.	**Kada pročitam knjigu otići ću u kino.** When I have read the book, I will go to the movie theater. (i.e., when I finish reading it)
On piše roman. He is writing a novel.	**Ako napiše dobar roman, on će biti poznat.** If he writes a good novel, he will be famous.
Što kupuješ? What are you buying?	**Ništa. Već sam sve kupila.** Nothing. I have already bought everything. (i.e., I am done buying)

The examples show that the *imperfective* is generally used in reference to activities occuring in the present, as well as in generalizations, while the *perfective* is used to refer to actions that are planned for the future or that have been completed in the past.

If an action is definitely planned for the future, the perfective referring to the future is used in a subordinate clause, while the future tense is used in the main clause. Once the present action is completed, the speaker will undertake the next, subsequent action. For this reason, the perfective is often found in **kada/ako** *when/if* type of sentences: *when/if x, then y*. These kinds of statements typically describe a string of completed actions.

Kada kupi kruh, doći će kući.
When she buys (i.e., has bought) bread, she will come home.

Kada stignem, nazvat ću te.
When I arrive, I will call you.

Ako položiš ispit, idemo na zabavu.
If you pass the exam, we will go to the party.

Because the two actions are related, it is not possible to use a perfective verb in these future constructions if it is the sole verb in the sentence. In other words, one *cannot* say: **Kupim cipele*. One can, however, say:

Kupujem cipele.
I am buying shoes.
Kada kupim cipele, idem na ručak.
When I buy shoes [shall have bought], I'm going to lunch.

The perfective is also used in *the past tense* to indicate one or a series of completed actions:

Kupila sam hranu, skuhala sam ručak i napisala pismo.
I bought food, cooked lunch, and wrote a letter.

To convey the idea that each of these actions continued over a long period of time or may have remained unfinished, the *imperfective* should be used in the past tense:

Cijelo jutro sam kupovala hranu, kuhala ručak i pisala pismo (ali ništa nisam završila).
All morning I've been buying food, cooking lunch, and writing the letter (but I haven't finished anything).

A similar logic guides the use of perfective and imperfective in the future tense. Perfective verbs are used in the future tense to indicate something that will be completed.

Sutra ću kupiti hranu, skuhati ručak i napisati pismo.
Tomorrow I will buy food, cook lunch, and write a letter.

When the imperfective aspect is used in the future tense, the focus is on the process rather than the completion of the action:

Sutra ću cijelo jutro kupovati hranu, kuhati ručak i pisati pismo.
Tomorrow all morning I will be buying food, cooking lunch, and writing a letter.

The imperfective indicates *repetition of action on a regular basis*:

On uvijek dolazi kasno. He always comes late.
On je svaki dan kupovao novine. He used to buy newspapers every day.

The perfective and imperfective can both be used in a single sentence to show that a completed action interrupted or occurred during a longer-term action.

On je stigao dok sam čitala. He arrived while I was reading.

Dok je ona spavala, Davor je kupio hranu i spremio doručak.
While she was sleeping, Davor bought food and prepared breakfast.

In some instances *only the imperfective* can be used, e.g., after the verbs **početi/počinjati** *to begin*, **prestati/prestajati** *to stop*, and **nastaviti/nastavljati** *to continue*. In the following examples, perfective is marked by *P* above the verb, and imperfective by *I*.

I I
Danas *počinjem čitati* roman Miroslava Krleže.
I am *beginning to read* a novel by Miroslav Krleža today.
[I start reading a novel by Miroslav Krleža today.]

P I
Kada ćeš *prestati pušiti*? When will you *stop smoking*?

P I
Hoćeš li *nastaviti pisati* to pismo? Will you *continue writing* that letter?

The word **dok** *while* clearly indicates duration and therefore requires the imperfective. The perfective, however, is mandatory after the phrase **dok ne** *until.*

> **Dok vozim, ne volim razgovarati.**
> I don't like to talk while I'm driving.
> **Ne idemo nikamo dok ne pojedeš sve.**
> We won't go anywhere until you eat up everything.

2.2. Formation: How to recognize perfective and imperfective verbs

2.2.1 Vowel/consonant changes

A large group of aspectual pairs share the same stem (root) but differ in the final vowel preceding the infinitive ending **-ti**. The first person singular and third person plural are provided in addition to the infinitive form.

Perfective	Imperfective	
prim*i*ti (**primim, prime**)	**prim*a*ti** (**primam, primaju**)	to receive
bac*i*ti (**bacim, bace**)	**bac*a*ti** (**bacam, bacaju**)	to throw
odgovo*ri*ti (**odgovorim, odgovore**)	**odgova*ra*ti** (**odgovaram, odgovaraju**)	to reply, to answer

There are variations and exceptions to these rules, but verbs from the **-iti** group tend to be perfective, and those belonging to the **-ati** group tend to be imperfective. Sometimes the vowel change triggers a consonant change/ addition as well; the vowel/consonant changes may also occur in the stem:

Perfective	Imperfective	
pla*ti*ti (**platim, plate**)	**pla*ća*ti** (**plaćam, plaćaju**)	to pay
zabora*vi*ti (**zaboravim, zaborave**)	**zabora*vlja*ti** (**zaboravljam, zaboravljaju**)	to forget
sta*vi*ti (**stavim, stave**)	**sta*vlj*ati** (**stavljam, stavljaju**)	to place, to put
dogo*di*ti se (**dogodim, dogode**)	**doga*đa*ti se** (**događam, događaju**)	to happen
opro*sti*ti (**oprostim, oproste**)	**opra*šta*ti** (**opraštam, opraštaju**)	to forgive

2.2.2 Forming the imperfective through infixes

A large group of verbs inserts a whole syllable (**-iva, -ova**, **-ava**) right after the stem to form the imperfective.

Perfective	Imperfective	
završiti (**završim, završe**)	**završ*av*ati** (**završavam, završavaju**)	to finish
potpisati (**potpišem, potpišu**)	**potpis*iv*ati** (**potpisujem, potpisuju**)	to sign
dati (**dam, daju**)	**da*vati*** (**dajem, daju**)	to give
prodati (**prodam, prodaju**)	**prod*av*ati** (**prodajem, prodaju**)	to sell
kupiti (**kupim, kupe**)	**kup*ov*ati** (**kupujem, kupuju**)	to buy

Although there are several other infixes, the group above is by far the largest.

Perfective	Imperfective	
sresti (**sretnem, sretnu**)	**sre*ta*ti** (**srećem, sreću**)	to meet, to run into
stati (**stanem, stanu**)	**sta*ja*ti** (**stajem, staju**)	to stop
pomoći (**pomognem, pomognu**)	**poma*ga*ti** (**pomažem, pomažu**)	to help

The infix **-nu** usually indicates a momentary one-time action and is therefore associated with the perfective*:

Perfective	Imperfective	
kre*nu*ti (**krenem, krenu**)	**kretati** (**krećem, kreću**)	to set off
maknuti (**maknem, maknu**)	**micati** (**mičem, miču**)	to move

*There are a few exceptions, such as **brinuti** *to worry,* which are imperfective.

2.2.3 Forming the perfective through prefixes

The group of verbs that is easiest to identify is the one that forms the perfective through a prefix. The most common prefixes are listed below. Prefixes ending in a consonant have two variants, depending on whether the following consonant is voiced or voiceless. Many of these prefixes have the same meaning as the preposition whose meaning they share.

do up to, as far as
iz/is from, out of, all over
na bringing an action to completion
nad/nat above
o/ob around, all over
od/ot away from, reversed action
po comprehensive completion of an action
pod/pot under
pre over
pred/pret before
pri to join to
pro through, past
raz/ras in various directions
s put together
u into
za to start the action

Imperfective	Perfective	
žuriti (se) (**žurim, žure**)	***po*žuriti (se)** (**požurim, požure**)	to hurry
čitati (**čitam, čitaju**)	***pro*čitati** (**pročitam, pročitaju**)	to read
kuhati (**kuham, kuhaju**)	***s*kuhati** (**skuham, skuhaju**)	to cook
kasniti (**kasnim, kasne**)	***za*kasniti** (**zakasnim, zakasne**)	to be late
puniti (**punim, pune**)	***na*puniti** (**napunim, napune**)	to fill
učiti (**učim, uče**)	***na*učiti** (**naučim, nauče**)	to study
veseliti (se) (**veselim, vesele**)	***raz*veseliti (se)** (**razveselim, razvesele**)	to rejoice
putovati (**putujem, putuju**)	***ot*putovati** (**otputujem, otputuju**)	to travel

Most verbs take only one prefix, but some may take several. Since each prefix has a specific meaning, the meaning of the verb itself also changes. The basic pair of verbs **pisati—napisati** meaning *to write* can be expanded to cover a whole range of meanings through the use of other prefixes.

However, the imperfective **pisati** does not form an aspectual pair with **potpisati** or **prepisati**, since these verbs mean *to sign* and *to copy*, respectively. These prefixed verbs therefore have their own *derived imperfectives*, typically formed by inserting **-iva**, **-ova**, **-ava** infixes.

Imperfective	Imperfective	Perfective	
pisati (pišem)	—	**_na_pisati (napišem)**	to write
	potpis_iva_ti (potpisujem)	**_pot_pisati (potpišem)**	to sign
	zapis_iva_ti	**_za_pisati**	to note down
	upis_iva_ti	**_u_pisati**	to enroll, to enter data
	popis_iva_ti	**_po_pisati**	to make a list
	dopis_iva_ti se	—	to correspond
	dopis_iva_ti	**_do_pisati**	to add to the written text
	otpis_iva_ti	**_ot_pisati**	to write off
	ispis_iva_ti	**_is_pisati**	to write all over
	prepis_iva_ti	**_pre_pisati**	to copy
	pripis_iva_ti	**_pri_pisati**	to attribute
	raspis_iva_ti	**_ras_pisati**	to announce a competition
	opis_iva_ti	**_o_pisati**	to describe
	propis_iva_ti	**_pro_pisati**	to regulate

Prefixes are thus a rather simple way to dramatically expand vocabulary.

Verbs of Motion

A particularly important group in this category is the one formed around the verb **ići** *to go*, encompassing the majority of the so called *motion verbs*. You will notice that the second group of imperfectives listed below all have **laz**, which follows the prefix to form a new verb. This is characteristic only of this group of verbs.

Imperfective	Imperfective	Perfective	
ići (idem; to go)	**dolaziti (dolazim)**	**doći (dođem)**	to come, to arrive
	ulaziti	**ući**	to enter
	izlaziti	**izaći**	to exit
	odlaziti	**otići**	to leave
	prilaziti	**prići**	to approach
	obilaziti	**obići**	to circle
	prolaziti	**proći**	to pass
	polaziti	**poći**	to set off, to come along
	prelaziti	**prijeći**	to cross
	silaziti	**sići**	to step down
	nalaziti	**naći**	to find

Verbs of Transportation

Verbs of transportation form a separate group since they also have two imperfectives, one of which is more general in meaning. In the following table, there are three groups of transportation verbs formed around the imperfective verbs **nositi** *to carry*, **voditi** *to lead*, and **voziti** *to drive.*

The perfective infinitives in the **voditi** *to lead* and **voziti** *to drive* groups overlap, but when conjugated the former have **-d** (which is present also in the imperfective forms), and the latter have **-z**. The verbs that have **-z** as a part of their stem always include transportation.

nositi (*I* nosim, nose) to carry:

Imperfective	Perfective	Meaning
donositi (**donosim, donose**)	**donijeti** (**donesem, donesu**)	to bring
prenositi	**prenijeti**	to carry over, to transmit

voditi (*I* vodim, vode) to lead:

Imperfective	Perfective	Meaning
prevoditi (**prevodim, prevode**)	**prevesti** (**prevedem, prevedu**)	to translate, to lead over
dovoditi	**dovesti**	to bring someone
odvoditi	**odvesti**	to take someone somewhere
provoditi	**provesti**	to lead through, to spend time, to implement

voziti (se) (*I* vozim, voze) to drive, transport:

Imperfective	Perfective	Meaning
prevoziti (**prevozim, prevoze**)	**prevesti** (**prevezem, prevezu**)	to drive/transport over
dovoziti	**dovesti**	to drive/transport to
odvoziti	**odvesti**	to drive/transport away

On nosi istu torbu svaki dan.
He carries the same bag every day.
Ako donese torbu, neće morati sve nositi u rukama.
If he brings a bag, he won't have to carry everything in his hands.

Ona vozi Darka svaki dan na posao.
Everyday she drives Darko to work.

Hoće li te on dovesti ili ćeš doći pješke?
Will he drive you or will you come on foot?

2.3. Verbs of perception and expression
Several frequently used verbs have two pairs: one pair in which both verbs have the same stem, and a second pair with a verb that differs from the stem.

Imperfective	Perfective
govoriti (**govorim**) to say	**progovoriti** to begin to speak *(same stem)* **reći** (**reknem**) to tell *(different stem)* **kazati** (**kažem**) to tell *(different stem)*
slušati (**slušam**) to listen	**poslušati** to listen for a while *(same stem)* **čuti (čujem)** to hear *(different stem)*
gledati (**gledam**) to look	**pogledati** to have a look, to see *(same stem)* **vidjeti** (**vidim**) to see *(different stem)*

2.4. Bi-aspectual verbs
In some contexts the two verbs from the group above (**čuti** *to hear* and **vidjeti** *to see*) may be *bi-aspectual*, that is, they may play the role of either the perfective or the imperfective verb. Some other verbs that fall in this category are **moći** *can*, **razumjeti** *to understand*, **ručati** *to eat lunch*, and **večerati** *to dine*.

Vidiš li me? *I*
Do you see me? [i.e., now]
Kada ga vidim, reći ću mu. *P*
When I see him, I'll tell him. [projecting into the future]
Gledaš, a ništa ne vidiš. *I*
You are looking but you don't see anything.

Čujem ptice kako pjevaju. *I*
I hear the birds singing.
Ako čuješ to predavanje, promijenit ćeš mišljenje. *P*
If you hear that lecture, you'll change your mind.
Slušala si tu pjesmu sto puta, a kažeš da je nikada nisi čula. *P*
You've listened to that song a hundred times and you say that you have never heard it before.

Exercises

Vježba 11.1

A. Choose the appropriate verb(s) and in cases where more than one option is possible, explain how the meaning differs.

Example: **Idem piti / popiti kavu** – *both*
(**piti** = stress on the process of drinking a cup of coffee; **popiti** = stress on the accomplishment of the action)

1. Ja sam pisao / napisao knjigu prošle godine.
____
2. Jeste li sigurni da ga niste nigdje drugdje stavile / stavljale?
____
3. Pogledao / Gledao / Vidio sam film jučer i mislim da izvrstan.
____
4. Kupila / Kupovala sam kruh jutros, ali opet ću ići u trgovinu.
____
5. Hoćeš li nastaviti / nastavljati voziti moj auto?
____

B. Translate the following sentences.

Example: I had 100 dollars and my credit cards inside my wallet.
U novčaniku sam imao 100 dolara i kreditne kartice.

1. I am going to drink a [cup of] coffee. Can you please buy me a newspaper and join me in the café?
____
____
2. I saw a terrible film last week in that new theater.
____
____
3. The police will inform me if someone finds my wallet.
____
____
4. I cannot believe that I lost my passport. I never lose anything.
____
____
5. I don't like to drink alchohol while eating dinner in an expensive restaurant.
____
____

Vježba 11.2

A. Define the verb given below, determine whether it is perfective or imperfective, and provide the other verb form in the verbal pair. Remember, there might be more than one correct answer!

Example: **obilaziti** (*I*) – **obići** (*P*) to circle around

1. čekati ______
2. putovati ______
3. ući ______
4. voziti ______
5. platiti ______
6. naći ______
7. gubiti ______

B. Now write two sentences for each verb pair, one for imperfective and one for perfective.

1. ______
1a. ______
2. ______
2a. ______
3. ______
3a. ______
4. ______
4a. ______
5. ______
5a. ______
6. ______
6a. ______
7. ______
7a. ______

Vježba 11.3 Create sentences with the words provided below.
Example: student; pismo; napisati
Ovaj student je napisao odlično pismo.

1. policajac; izgubljen; sendvič

____

2. profesor; pročitati; knjiga

____

3. Marijana; kupovati; kava; trgovina

____

4. Nema na čemu; pronaći; isprave

____

5. doći; Dubrovnik; sat vremena

____

Vježba 11.4 Correctly match the sentences in the columns below.

1.	Koliko košta?	a.	Puno ti hvala! Ovo će mi stvarno dobro doći.
2.	Hvala Vam na pomoći.	b.	I meni!
3.	Kupio sam ti dar.	c.	Pedeset kuna.
4.	Moram ići. Kasnim.	d.	Nema na čemu.
5.	Treba mi odmor!	e.	Bez brige! Stići ćeš.

Vježba 11.5 Translate the following text into Croatian:

A desperate student—Očajni student

I have been writing a paper [referat] for eight days already, but I still haven't written it. I am preparing [spremati] a big exam in economics, but I still haven't prepared for it. I'm studying Croatian verbs, but I haven't learned them well either. I am reading a big history book [povijest], but I'll read it to the end [do kraja] only on Wednesday, and the exam is on Monday. I also have a chemistry experiment [pokus iz kemije], which I've been finishing for five weeks, and I still haven't finished it. I work a lot, but there is so much to be done. Every day I say: "I'll finish everything today," but there is more and more work. It seems to me that I will never be done!

Vježba 11.6 Write a short dialogue using the past, present, and future tenses. Incorporate as much of the new vocabulary as you can.

Vježba 11.7 Sažet*a*k/Summary

A. Read and translate:

Darko, Ivan i Marijana se voze već tri sata bez odmora. Marijana želi stati. Darko kaže da će stati uskoro jer mora kupiti benzin. Ivan je gladan. Želi sendvič i novine. Marijana obično ne kupuje hranu na autocesti, ali sendviči ne izgledaju loše. Ona je gladna i ona isto kupuje sendvič. Nakon što je kupio benzin, Darko želi popiti kavu. Marijana i Ivan naručuju sok. Oni nisu imali vremena za doručak prije puta.

Marijana želi svih počastiti, ali je izgubila novčanik. Ona nikada ne gubi stvari. Marijana je ljuta i tužna. Darko joj kaže da se smiri jer je imala novčanik kada je kupovala sendvič. Ona misli da ga je stavila u torbu. Darko predlaže da pitaju policajca da im pomogne. On kaže policajcu što je bilo u novčaniku: 750 kuna, američka putovnica, 100 dolara, vozačka dozvola i kreditne kartice. Ako ne pronađu novčanik, Marijana će morati ispuniti formular, kaže policajac. Tako će policija moći obavijestiti Marijanu ako se novčanik pronađe.

Policajac ide s Marijanom u trgovinu gdje je ona kupila sendvič. On nalazi novčanik ispod pulta. Marijana je vrlo sretna.

B. Answer the following questions:

1. Koliko dugo se voze Marijana, Darko i Ivan?
____
2. Zašto moraju stati?
____
3. Što oni kupuju?
____
4. Tko je pojeo doručak prije puta?
____
5. Što Marijana želi napraviti?
____
6. Zašto Marijana ne može ništa kupiti u kavani?
____
7. Gubi li Marijana obično stvari?
____
8. Što joj kaže Darko?
____
9. Što Marijana misli, kamo je stavila novčanik?
____
10. Što predlaže Darko?
____
11. Što je bilo u novčaniku?
____
12. Zašto će Marijana morati ispuniti formular?
____
13. Kamo idu policajac i Marijana?
____
14. Jesu li pronašli novčanik?
____

Lekcija 12
Marijana u gradu cara Dioklecijana

Lesson 12
Marijana in Emperor Diocletian's city

Lekcija 12: Marijana u gradu cara Dioklecijana

Prvi dio

Darko: Ivan će biti naš vodič kroz Split, zar ne, Ivane?

Ivan: Naravno, grad mi je dobro poznat. Idemo u centar, gdje ćemo razgledati palaču cara Dioklecijana.

Marijana: Kako se ide do centra?

Ivan: Ravno, a onda kod prvog semafora lijevo. Potom trebamo proći još dvije ulice i onda skrenuti desno. Parkirat ćemo auto i nastaviti pješke. U centru je zabranjeno voziti.

Marijana: Znači, dan počinjemo razgledavanjem. Ja sam čitala u turističkom vodiču nešto o Splitu. Piše da je to vrlo star grad. Tko je bio car Dioklecijan?

Ivan: Dioklecijan je bio rimski car koji je vladao krajem trećeg i početkom četvrtog stoljeća naše ere. Njegova palača izgrađena je u to vrijeme. Palača je poslije postala centar grada Splita.

Marijana: Je li palača sada pretvorena u muzej?

Ivan: Da i ne. Palača je zaštićena kao spomenik svjetske kulturne baštine, ali ona je i dalje nastanjena. U njoj su, na primjer, ne samo stanovi nego i trgovine, kavane, galerije.

Drugi dio

Marijana: Ovo je divno, pravi mali grad u gradu. Kamo vode ove stube?

Darko: Odgovor na to pitanje znam čak i ja! Njima se ide s glavnog trga palače, Peristila, u podrume cara Dioklecijana. Kada prođemo kroz podrume, doći ćemo na obalu.

Marijana: Što se nalazi na obali?

Ivan: Svaki primorski grad ima šetnicu. Tamo obično ima mnogo kavana u kojima ljudi vole sjediti, pričati i gledati more i otoke.

Marijana: Moramo otići na neki otok! Svi kažu da je tamo lijepo!

Lesson 12: Marijana in Emperor Diocletian's city

Part I

Darko: Ivan will be our tour guide through Split, isn't that right Ivan?

Ivan: Of course, I know the city very well. We will go to the center where we will take a look at the Emperor Diocletian's Palace.

Marijana: How does one get to the center?

Ivan: Straight and then a left at the first traffic light. Afterwards, we need to pass another two streets and then turn to the right. We will park the car and continue on foot. It is forbidden to drive in the center.

Marijana: That means that the day begins with sightseeing. I read in the travel guide something about Split. It says that this is a very old city. Who was Emperor Diocletian?

Ivan: Diocletian was a Roman Emperor who reigned at the end of the third and beginning of the fourth centuries after Christ. His palace was built during this time. The palace later became the center of the city of Split.

Marijana: Is the palace now transformed into a museum?

Ivan: Yes and no. The palace is protected as a monument of world culture but it is still inhabited. Inside, for example, there are not only apartments, but also shops, cafés, and galleries.

Part II

Marijana: This is splendid, a real small city within a city. Where do these steps lead?

Darko: The answer to that question even I know! On these steps one goes from the main square of the palace, Peristil, into the cellars of Emperor Diocletian. When we have gone through the cellars, we will be by the sea.

Marijana: What is located by the sea?

Ivan: Every coastal city has a promenade. Usually there are many cafés in which people love to sit, talk, and look at the sea and the islands.

Marijana: We must go to some island! Everyone says that it is pretty there!

Ivan: Svakako, a moramo otići i do Trogira. Trogir je poznat po vrlo staroj katedrali čiji je portal napravio majstor Radovan u 13. stoljeću. U katedrali je i zbirka starih rukopisa. Možemo na Brač ili Hvar već sutra, što ti misliš Darko?

Darko: Vremenska prognoza kaže da će biti toplo i sunčano. Ljeti rijetko pada kiša. Cijela obala je lijepa. Hvar ili Brač, meni je svejedno.

Ivan: I meni. S ovako zanimljivim i lijepim društvom mogu i na put oko svijeta!

Darko: Ja mislim da ću sjesti, a vi, ako hoćete, nastavite šetati.

Marijana: Mene bole noge od hodanja.

Ivan: A mene boli grlo od pričanja.

Darko: Dobro, možemo na piće zajedno, ali ja sam mislio da ste htjeli prošetati sami.

Ivan: Ah, da, imaš pravo, Darko. Pridružit ćemo ti se poslije. Marijana, zaboravio sam ti nešto pokazati!

Ivan: Certainly, and we also must go to Trogir. Trogir is famous for a very old cathedral whose portal was built by master Radovan in the thirteenth centruy. In the cathedral there is a collection of old manuscripts. We can go to Brač or Hvar as soon as tomorrow, what do you think Darko?

Darko: The weather forecast says that there will be warm and sunny weather. It rarely rains in summer. The entire coast is beautiful. Hvar or Brač, it's all the same to me.

Ivan: Me too. With this kind of interesting and nice company I can travel around the world!

Darko: I think that I will sit somewhere, and if you like, you can continue walking.

Marijana: My legs hurt from walking!

Ivan: And my throat hurts from talking!

Darko: Fine, we can have a drink together, but I thought that you guys would like to walk around alone!

Ivan: Ah yes, you are right Darko. We will join you later. Marijana, I forgot to show you something!

Vocabulary

car emperor
čak even
dalje continuously, further
divno *adv.* wonderful
era era
hodanje walking
izgrađen built
katedrala cathedral
kiša rain
kraj end
krajem at the end
kulturna baština cultural heritage
majstor master
nastanjen inhabited
obala coast
odgovor answer
onda then
palača palace
pitanje question
počet*a*k beginning
početkom at the beginning
podrum cellar
portal portal
potom after that
poznat known
pretvoren transformed
pričanje talking
primjer example
primorski coastal
prognoza forecast
razgledavanje sightseeing
rimski Roman
rijetko rarely
rukopis manuscript, handwriting
semafor traffic light
spomenik monument
stoljeće century
stube stairs
sunčano sunny
svakako by all means
sveti holy, saint
svijet world
svjetski *adj.* world
šetnica promenade
zabranjeno forbidden
zaštićen protected
zbirka collection
življenje living

Verb List

boljeti (*I* **bolim**, **bole**) to hurt
najavljivati (*I* **najavljujem**, **najavljuju**) to announce
nastaviti (*P* **nastavim**, **nastave**) to continue
padati (*I* **padam**, **padaju**) to fall
pokazati (*P* **pokažem**, **pokažu**) to show
postati (*P* **postanem**, **postanu**) to become
pretvoriti (*P* **pretvorim**, **pretvore**) to transform, to turn into
pričati (*I* **pričam**, **pričaju**) to talk, to narrate
prošetati (*P* **prošetam**, **prošetaju**) to take a walk
skrenuti (*P* **skrenem**, **skrenu**) to turn
vladati (*I* **vladam**, **vladaju**) to reign
voditi (*I* **vodim**, **vode**) to lead
zaboraviti (*P* **zaboravim**, **zaborave**) to forget

Useful Expressions

turistički vodič travel guide
krajem trećeg i početkom četvrtog stoljeća at the end of the third and beginning of the fourth centuries
ne samo ..., nego i ... not only..., but also...
na primjer for example
vremenska prognoza weather forecast
Svi kažu da je tamo lijepo! Everyone says that it is pretty there!
meni je svejedno it's all the same to me
imaš pravo you're right
mene bole noge my legs are hurting (*verb is pl. to agree with pl. subj.* **noge** *legs*)
mene boli grlo my throat is hurting

Asking for and giving directions

Directions

Kako se ide do centra? How does one get to the center?
Gdje se nalazi glavni trg? Where is the main square?
Koji autobus ide do centra? Which bus goes to the center?

idite go (*formal*)
ravno straight
lijevo to the left
desno to the right
skrenite desno take a right
skrenite kod prvog semafora lijevo turn left at the first traffic light
prođite još dvije ulice go by two more streets
prijeđite ulicu cross the street
iza ugla round the corner
na uglu at the corner
kod semafora at the traffic light
na križanju at the crossing
idite Splitskom ulicom do glavnog trga take Split Street to the main square
idite autobusom broj 3 take bus number 3
siđite na četvrtoj stanici get off at the fourth stop

Locales

autobusni kolodvor bus station
autobusna stanica bus stop
banka bank
bolnica hospital
fakultet college
galerija gallery
hitna pomoć ambulance
hotel hotel
kavana (also **kafić**) café
kazalište theater
knjižnica library
križanje crossing
ljekarna pharmacy
luka/trajektna luka port/ferry port
muzej museum
policija police
pošta post office
prodavaonica (also **trgovina**) shop
samoposluživanje grocery store
stanica stop, station
tramvajska stanica streetcar/tram stop
trg/glavni trg square/main square
trgovina (also **prodavaonica**) shop
željeznički kolodvor railway station
zračna luka (also **aerodrom**) airport

City map

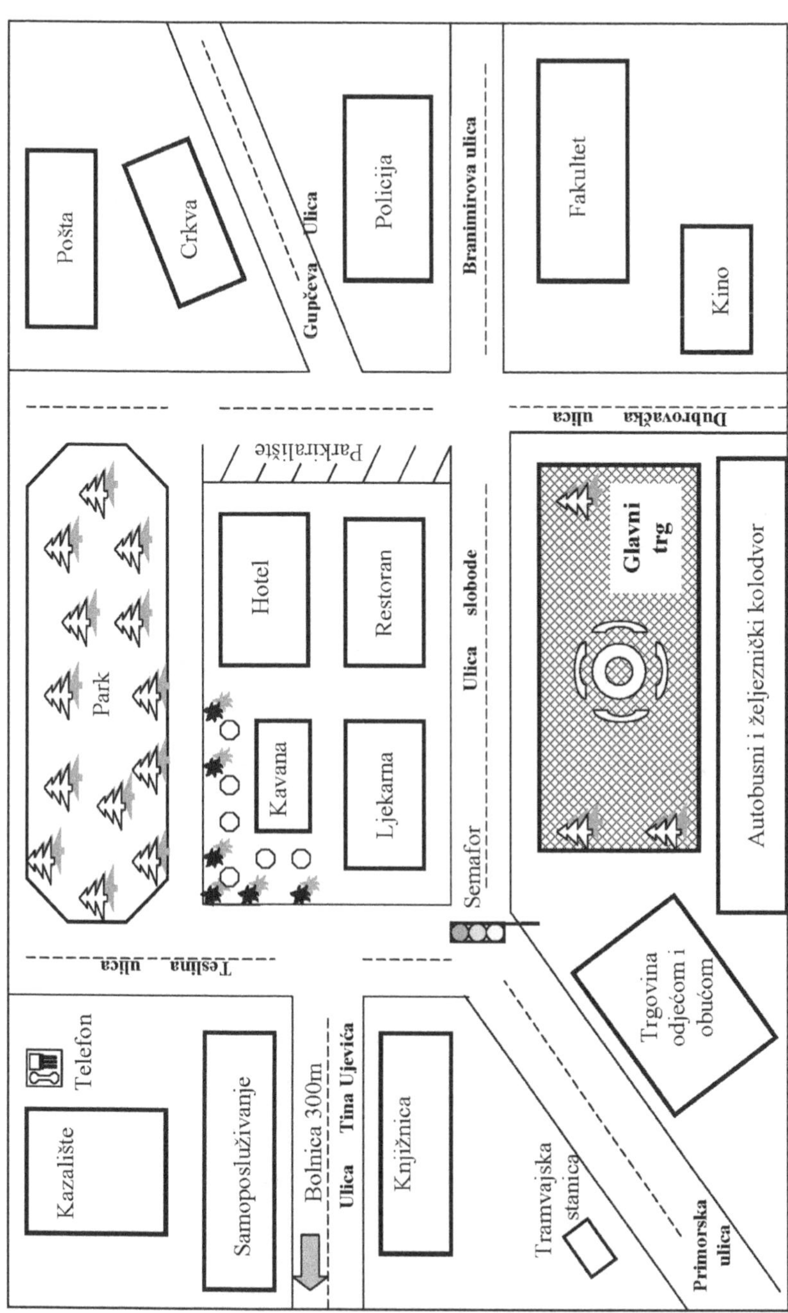
Pošta
Crkva
Gupčeva Ulica
Policija
Branimirova ulica
Fakultet
Kino
Dubrovačka ulica
Parkiralište
Park
Hotel
Restoran
Kavana
Ljekarna
Ulica slobode
Semafor
Glavni trg
Autobusni i željeznički kolodvor
Teslina ulica
Kazalište
Telefon
Samoposluživanje
Bolnica 300m
Ulica Tina Ujevića
Knjižnica
Tramvajska stanica
Trgovina odjećom i obućom
Primorska ulica

Grammar

1. Passive verbal forms

Actions in a sentence can be expressed through both active and passive forms. The object of the verb in an active sentence becomes the subject in the passive sentence. Only transitive verbs (those that take objects) have passive forms.

I drove the car. (*active*)
The car was driven by me. (*passive*)

In Croatian, passive verbal forms can be derived from both perfective and imperfective verbs. They behave like adjectives and take adjectival endings:

Čitana knjiga je bila zanimljiva.
The book that was being read was interesting.
Pročitano pismo je bilo na stolu.
The letter that was read was on the table.
U centru je zabranjeno voziti.
It is forbidden to drive in the center.

There are several ways of forming the passive forms, depending on the verb type. For verbs ending in **-ati**, discard the final **-ati** and add **-an**. The form you get will be masculine. Like other masculine adjectival forms, the passive can be short and long.

Just as with adjectives, for the feminine add **-a**, neuter **-o**, plural masculine and mixed gender, **-i**, plural feminine **-e**, plural neuter **-a**. Note that unlike regular adjectives, these forms do not have a *fleeting -a*.

regular adjective with *fleeting -a*:

krat*a*k dan *nom.*
kratkog dana *gen.* short day

passive form with no *fleeting -a*:

pis*a*ni komentar *nom.*
pis*a*nog komentara *gen.* written commentary

Passive Forms of *Pisani* (written)

m. sg.	*f. sg.*	*neu. sg.*	*m. pl.*	*f. pl.*	*neu. pl.*
pisan(i)	**pisana**	**pisano**	**pisani**	**pisane**	**pisana**

active	passive
parkirati	**parkiran** parked
osnovati	**osnovan** established
očekivati	**očekivan** expected

Since some verbs allow for two forms, there are a few exceptions to this rule. As we saw in the dialogue above, the verb **znati** (**znan**) *to know*, has the perfective passive **poznat** *known*. So too, the verb **dati** *to give* can have both forms, **dan** and **dat**.

Verbs ending in **-iti** and many ending in **-eti** (such as **voljeti (voli)** *to love*, **vidjeti (vidi)** *to see*) form the passive by discarding the final **-iti/-eti** and adding **-en**. Note that the consonant immediately before **-en** is softened (palatalized).

active	passive	meaning
pretvoriti	**pretvoren**	changed, transformed
učiti	**učen**	learned
kupiti	**kupljen**	bought
izgraditi	**izgrađen**	built
zaštititi	**zaštićen**	protected
vidjeti	**viđen**	seen
voljeti	**voljen**	loved
zabraniti	**zabranjen**	forbidden
posuditi	**posuđen**	borrowed, lent

To form the passive verbal form from verbs ending in **-uti** and a few ending in **-eti**, drop **-uti**/**-eti**, and add **-ut**/**-et**.

active	passive	
maknuti	**maknut**	moved
zauzeti	**zauzet**	occupied

To summarize: verb – **ati** + **an**
verb – **eti/iti** + final consonant softening + **en**
verb – **uti/-eti** + **ut/-et**

2. Impersonal constructions in the past and future tenses

In passive sentences the "actor"—the person who performs the action—is often omitted and the subject is not stated. Similarly, impersonal constructions do not state who performs the action. You will recall that these kinds of sentences are formed by putting the verb in the third person singular and adding the reflexive particle **se**. In this lesson we will see how they are formed in the past and future tenses.

In the past tense, the auxiliary form of the verb *to be* is not used; instead the particle **se** is combined with the **l participle** (the past tense participle) in the neuter singular.

In the future tense, the auxiliary form of **htjeti** is retained in the third person singular and is followed by **se**. Each example below is given in the present, past, and future tenses.

Vidi se da je on odličan profesor.
One can see that he is an excellent professor.
Vidjelo se da je on odličan profesor.
One could see that he was an excellent professor.
Vidjet će se da je on odličan profesor.
One will [be able to] see that he is an excellent professor.

Ovdje se ne može proći.
One cannot pass here.
Ovdje se nije moglo proći.
One couldn't pass here.
Ovdje se neće moći proći.
One will not be able to pass here.

Govori se da je ovo dobra knjiga.
They say that this is a good book.
Govorilo se da je ovo dobra knjiga.
They said that this was a good book.
Govorit će se da je ovo dobra knjiga.
They will say that this is a good book.

3. Verbal nouns

Verbal nouns are formed from verbs and mean an action or activity. We have encountered several in the lesson above: **razgledavanje** *sightseeing* (from **razgledavati**), **pričanje** *talking* (from **pričati**). They are formed from imperfective verbs although several come from perfective verbs (e.g., **ograničiti** *to limit*; **ograničenje** *limitation*).

Reflexive verbs drop **se**, for example, the verbal noun **nadanje** *hoping* is derived from **nadati se** *to hope*. Softening takes place before **-enje** in the same way as in the passive form: **viđen** – **viđenje** *seeing*.

Verbal nouns are rather frequent and fairly easy to form:

- drop **-ati** from verbs ending in that syllable and add **-anje**
- drop **-iti** or **-eti** from verbs ending in those syllables and add **-enje.**

Verb	Verbal noun	Meaning
čitati	**čitanje**	reading
nadati	**nadanje**	hoping
hodati	**hodanje**	walking
pisati	**pisanje**	writing
učiti	**učenje**	studying
misliti	**mišljenje**	thinking, opinion

4. Present and past verbal adverbs

Present verbal adverbs describe an action taking place concurrently with the main action, while *past verbal adverbs* indicate an action that took place before the main action. Therefore, present verbal adverbs are formed from imperfective verbs, and past verbal adverbs are formed from perfective verbs. Like other types of adverbs, verbal adverbs never change. They are more often encountered in written texts than in conversation.

The present verbal adverb is formed by adding **-ći** to the third person plural of the imperfective verb. In English these constructions are usually translated by *while*, followed by an *-ing* verb form.

Verb	3rd *pers. pl.* imperfective	Pres. verbal adverb	Meaning
hodati	**hodaju**	**hodajući**	while walking
čitati	**čitaju**	**čitajući**	while reading
učiti	**uče**	**učeći**	while studying
kupovati	**kupuju**	**kupujući**	while buying

Čitajući knjigu, on je čekao da Marijana dođe.
While reading a book, he waited for Marijana to come.

Učeći o Americi, ona je naučila mnogo toga o Indijancima.
While studying about America, she learned a lot about Indians.

Several present verbal adverbs are used idiomatically with an "acquired" meaning and in such instances they function as adjectives:

budući future — **To je naš budući predsjednik.**
This is our future president.

idući next — **Idući put nemoj zakasniti.**
Don't be late next time.

mogući possible — **Moguće posljedice su strašne.**
The possible consequences are horrible.

vodeći leading — **On je naš vodeći tenisač.**
He is our leading tennis player.

sljedeći next — **Tko je sljedeći?**
Who's next?

Not all English *-ing* constructions are translated into Croatian using present verbal adverbs. For example, in the following case the English *-ing* form is translated with **kako**:

Vidjela sam ga kako prelazi ulicu.
I saw him as he was crossing the street.

Past verbal adverbs are formed by dropping the infinitive ending (**-ti** or **-sti**) and adding **-vši**. They are usually translated into English as *having* plus a participle .

Infinitive	Past verbal *adv.*	Meaning
napisa-ti	**napisavši**	having written
nauči-ti	**naučivši**	having learned
razmisli-ti	**razmislivši**	having thought
kupi-ti	**kupivši**	having bought
vidje-ti	**vidjevši**	having seen
poje-sti	**pojevši**	having eaten

Verbs that end in **-ći** form the past verbal adverb somewhat differently. The simplest way to produce the correct form is to drop the final **-o** of the masculine participle and add **-vši.**

Infinitive	Masculine participle	Past verbal adverb	Meaning
pomoći	**pomogao**	**pomogavši**	having helped
reći	**rekao**	**rekavši**	having said
otići	**otišao**	**otišavši**	having left

Razmislivši **o svemu, odlučila je otputovati u Englesku.**
Having thought about everything, she decided to travel to England.

Kupivši **hranu, otišli su kući i skuhali večeru.**
Having bought food, they went home and cooked dinner.

Rekavši **što je mislio, krenuo je prema vratima.**
Having said what he thought, he moved towards the door.

Appendix: Verb Typology

In Lesson 1 we discussed three basic verb groups that exist in Croatian, those ending in **-i**, **-a**, and **-e** in the 3rd person singular. In the previous lesson (Lesson 12) we analyzed various verb types in terms of aspect. The division into three groups, though, is in fact much more complex and each group can be further divided into smaller subgroups. There are so many of these, however, that it may be easier to memorize the verbs that deviate from the patterns individually.

Not all Croatian verb infinitives end in **-ti**; some end in **-ći** (**ići** *to go*; **pomoći** *to help*), and others in **-sti** (**jesti** *to eat*; **pasti** *to fall*).

1.1 Infinitives in -ti. Within the group that ends in **-ti**, as we know, there are several subgroups (**čitati**: **čita** *3rd sg.*; **pisati**: **piše** *3rd sg.*; **govoriti**: **govori** *3rd sg.*). In some groups the infinitive differs from the present tense base.

If **-a** is the vowel preceding the final **-ti**, these verbs tend to belong to the **-a** conjugation, i.e., to have **-a** in the 3rd person singular. The infinitive and the present-tense stem forms are identical. Exceptions occur in two categories:

- verbs with roots ending in **č, ž, j** may belong to the **-i** conjugation (the *3rd sg.* ends in **-i** such as **držati**, **drži** *to hold* and **brojiti**, **broji** *to count*) or the **-a** conjugation (the *3rd sg.* ends in **-a** such as **pričati**, **priča** *to tell*)
- if the root ends in **lj, nj** or **j**, these verbs occasionally belong to the **-e** conjugation (**počinjati**, **počinje** *to start*; **spominjati**, **spominje** *to mention*)
- if the infinitive base ends in **s, z, t, c, k,** or **ks,** changes in the base segment are possible in the present tense and the verb may belong to the **-e** conjugation (**pisati**, **piše** *to write*; **kazati**, **kaže** *to say*; **plakati**, **plače** *to cry*).

If **-i** is the vowel preceding the final **-ti**, the verb belongs to the **-i** conjugation (**govoriti**, **govori** *to write*; **misliti**, **misli** *to think*).

If **-u** is the vowel preceding the final **-ti,** the verb belongs to **-e** conjugation (**krenuti**, **krene** *to set off*; **maknuti**, **makne** *to move*). With a few exceptions (such as **brinuti** *to worry* and **čeznuti** *to yearn*), the vast majority of verbs from this group indicate a one-time action and are, as a result, perfective.

If **-e** is the vowel preceding the final **-ti,** the verb may belong to either the **-i** or the **-e** conjugation. Since the infinitive of these verbs does not provide any clue to the conjugation to which the verb may belong, they need to be learned individually. Some of the verbs, in particular those that belong to the **-e** conjugation, may have additional changes in the stem (**uzeti**, **uzme** *to take*). If they belong to the **-i** conjugation the infinitive and the present tense base correspond (**voljeti**, **voli** *to love*; **vidjeti**, **vidi** *to see*).

1.2. Infinitives ending in -ivati/-ovati/-avati. Verbs from this category belong to the **-e** conjugation, however, they have some specific changes. All verbs ending in **-ovati** and some ending in **-ivati** replace **-ov** and **-iv** with **-uj** (**kupovati**, **kupuje** *to buy*; **dopisivati**, **dopisuje** *to correspond*). Most verbs ending in **-avati** have the present tense in **-avam**. These verbs actually belong to the **-ti** group since **-av** is part of a suffix and, as a result, is kept in the present tense (**rješavati**, **rješava** *to solve*). A few verbs in **-avati** replace **-av** with **-aj** (**davati**, **daje** *to give*; **poznavati**, **poznaje** *to be acquainted with*; **predavati**, **predaje** *to lecture*).

1.3. Infinitives ending in -ći. Verbs from this group need to be memorized individually since their infinitive and the present tense base are never the same. They belong to the **-e** conjugation. The most common verb from this group is **ići**, **ide** *to go*. Some others are **pomoći**, **pomogne** *to help* and **moći**, **može** *can*.

1.4. Infinitives in -sti. In this group, too, there are differences between the infinitive and the present tense base, and these verbs have to be memorized individually. This is a fairly small group and the verbs in it belong to the **-e** conjugation. The most frequent ones are: **jesti, jede** *to eat*; **krasti**, **krade** *to steal*; **rasti**, **raste** *to grow*.

Exercises

Vježba 12.1 Put the following nouns into nominative plural forms and then into the genitive singular.

Example: **semafor – semafori / semafora**

1. zbirka ____________ ____________
2. pitanje ____________ ____________
3. ostanak ____________ ____________
4. odgovor ____________ ____________
5. crkva ____________ ____________
6. prognoza ____________ ____________
7. obala ____________ ____________
8. mogućnost ____________ ____________
9. centar ____________ ____________
10. stoljeće ____________ ____________

Vježba 12.2 Look at the map in the lesson and use it to write out directions from one point to the other.

Example: **pošta – trgovina :**
Prvo ravno, pa druga ulica desno i onda kod semafora lijevo.

1. trgovina – crkva
____
2. hotel – kino
____
3. kavana – bolnica
____
4. pošta – knjižnica
____
5. policija – samoposluživanje
____
6. park – željeznički kolodvor
____
7. tramvajska stanica – kino
____
8. Teslina ulica – Dubrovačka ulica
____
9. pošta – kazalište
____
10. knjižnica – telefon
____

Vježba 12.3

A. Using the verbs below write out the 3rd person singular and 3rd person plural forms.

Example: **ići – ide, idu**

1. moći ____________ ____________
2. uzeti ____________ ____________
3. hodati ____________ ____________
4. boljeti ____________ ____________
5. pušiti ____________ ____________
6. zaboraviti ____________ ____________
7. skrenuti ____________ ____________
8. postojati ____________ ____________
9. stati ____________ ____________
10. jesti ____________ ____________

B. Form verbal nouns using the verbs provided. Then try to form a sentence using the verbal noun.

Example: **govoriti – govorenje**

Čitanje je lako, a govorenje na stranom jeziku je teško.

1. čekati ___________ ___________________
2. kupovati ___________ ___________________
3. voljeti ___________ ___________________
4. pisati ___________ ___________________
5. vidjeti ___________ ___________________

Vježba 12.4

Translate into Croatian:

<u>More than a house – Više od kuće</u>

My house was built a long time ago. It is forbidden to drive around it. It is protected as a monument. One can see that this is an old building. It is located in the center of the city. While reading the history of Zadar, I realized how important this building is. They say [use "se" construction] that it costs a lot, but my opinion is that it is worth more than any money. Having seen how much it means to me, my wife decided that we are not going to move from Zadar.

____

____

____

____

____

____

____

____

____

____

____

____

____

Vježba 12.5

A. Decide whether the verbs below are imperfective or perfective; then form their present or past tense verbal adverbs.

Example: **pročitati – perfective – pročitavši**

1. piti __________ __________
2. šetati __________ __________
3. kupiti __________ __________
4. napraviti __________ __________
5. pronaći __________ __________
6. tražiti __________ __________
7. studirati __________ __________
8. razmisliti __________ __________
9. gledati __________ __________
10. dolaziti __________ __________

B. Write ten sentences using the present and past tense verbal adverbs above:

Example: **Pročitavši cijeli roman Miljenka Jergovića, Ana je požurila u knjižaru kupiti novu knjigu istog pisca.**

1. ____
2. ____
3. ____
4. ____
5. ____
6. ____
7. ____
8. ____
9. ____
10. ____

Vježba 12.6 Insert the necessary passive forms using either a perfective or imperfective verb provided below and then translate the sentences.

1. Dugo ________ autobus nije došao. (čekati/dočekati)

   ____

2. __________ auto je dobro vozio. (posuđivati/posuditi)

   ____

3. __________ hladnjak je bolji od praznog. (puniti/napuniti)

   ____

4. Ona je __________ jučer u centru grada. (viđati/vidjeti)

   ____

5. __________ pismo je bilo dugo. (pisati/napisati)

   ____

6. __________ novčanik je bio plave boje. (gubiti/izgubiti)

   ____

7. Ovo mjesto je __________. (zauzimati/zauzeti)

   ____

8. __________ stan im je donio mnogo novca. (prodati/prodavati)

   ____

9. Tko zna gdje je __________ parkirati? (zabranjivati/zabraniti)

   ____

10. Marijanin ____________stan u Zagrebu nije bio skup. (unajmljivati/ unajmiti)

    ____

Vježba 12.7 Saže*t*a*k*/Summary
A. Read and translate:

Ivan će biti vodič kroz Split jer je njemu grad dobro poznat. Marijana, Darko i Ivan prvo idu u centar razgledati palaču cara Dioklecijana. Do tamo se ide ravno, a onda kod prvog semafora lijevo. Potom trebaju proći još dvije ulice i skrenuti desno. Oni će parkirati auto i nastaviti pješke. U centru je zabranjeno voziti.

Split je vrlo stari grad. Njegov centar je izgradio car Dioklecijan krajem trećeg i početkom četvrtog stoljeća naše ere. Palača je sada spomenik svjetske kulturne baštine. U njoj ljudi i dalje žive. Tamo ima mnogo trgovina, kavana i galerija. Stube vode s glavnog trga palače, koji se zove Peristil, do obale. Na obali je šetnica s mnogo kavana. Ljudi tu obično sjede, pričaju i gledaju u more i otoke.

Marijana želi otići na neki otok. Ivan kaže da moraju otići i u Trogir. Trogir je poznat po staroj katedrali s portalom majstora Radovana. Vremenska prognoza kaže da će vrijeme biti lijepo i sunčano. Marijana, Darko i Ivan će otići na otok Hvar ili otok Brač. Ivanu je svejedno kamo će ići jer s takvim društvom može i na put oko svijeta. Svi su umorni od razgledavanja. Darko je sjeo u kavanu na obali. Ivan i Marijana će još malo šetati jer je Ivan zaboravio nešto pokazati Marijani.

B. Answer the following questions:

1. Gdje se nalaze Marijana, Darko i Ivan?

____

2. Zašto Ivan poznaje Split tako dobro?

____

3. Kamo oni prvo idu?

____

4. Kako se ide do centra?

____

5. Može li se voziti u centru?

____

6. Kažite nešto o Splitu!

____

7. Tko je bio car Dioklecijan?

____

8. Što se nalazi na obali?

____

9. Kamo još Marijana želi putovati?

____

10. Po čemu je poznat Trogir?

____

11. Kakvo je vrijeme ljeti na jugu Hrvatske?

____

12. Kamo želi Ivan ići na izlet?

____

13. Tko je umoran od razgledavanja, a tko nije?

____

14. Što mislite, je li Ivan stvarno zaboravio nešto reći Marijani?

____

Lekcija 13
S otoka na otok i posjet Dubrovniku

—∞—

Lesson 13
Island hopping and a visit to Dubrovnik

Lekcija 13: S otoka na otok i posjet Dubrovniku

Prvi dio

Darko: Marijana, jesi li spremna? Moramo požuriti da ne zakasnimo na trajekt.

Marijana: Samo trenutak. U torbu sam već stavila hlače, majice, kupaći kostim, rublje, čarape, džemper, košulje i cipele. Što misliš, hoće li mi trebati još nešto? Možda neka lijepa haljina?

Darko: To je dovoljno! Već imaš najveću torbu. Idemo, Ivan nas čeka u autu. Sve ti dobro stoji. Siguran sam da će se njemu sve svidjeti.

Marijana: Bi li mi objasnio malo bolje što znače te riječi, Darko?

Darko: Ništa, nema veze. Sada nema vremena. Ali kada već pitaš, evo ukratko: ja bih rekao da se ti sviđaš Ivanu.

Marijana: Stvarno? Primijetila sam nešto, ali nisam bila sigurna...

Kasnije u trajektnoj luci.

Ivan: Molim Vas, tri putničke karte za Hvar i jednu za osobno vozilo.

Blagajnica: Trebate li povratne karte?

Ivan: Ne, samo u jednom smjeru. Je li cijena ista kao prošle godine ili je sada skuplje?

Blagajnica: Malo je skuplje nego prošle godine. Ukupno 354 kune, molim.

Ivan: Izvolite. Koji trajekt ide za Hvar?

Blagajnica: Evo, izvolite karte. Imate sreće. „Tin Ujević" ide uskoro, točno u 2 sata s veza broj 5. Samo požurite!

Ivan: Hvala.

Drugi dio

Istog dana na Hvaru.

Darko: Molim Vas, jednu dvokrevetnu i jednu jednokrevetnu sobu.

Recepcioner: Nema slobodnih soba, osim uz rezervaciju. Jeste li rezervirali sobe?

Lesson 13: Island hopping and a visit to Dubrovnik

Part I

Darko:	Marijana, are you ready? We have to hurry so [that] we are not late for the ferry!
Marijana:	Just a minute. Into my bag I have already put pants, T-shirts, a swim suit, underwear, socks, a sweater, shirts and shoes. What do you think, will I need anything else? Maybe a nice dress?
Darko:	That is enough! You already have the biggest bag! Let's go, Ivan is waiting for us in the car. It all fits you well. I'm sure that he will like everything.
Marijana:	Would you explain these words a little better, Darko?
Darko:	Nothing, it doesn't matter. There's no time now. But since you're already asking, briefly: I would say that Ivan likes you.
Marijana:	Really? I've noticed something, but I wasn't sure...

Later at the ferry port.

Ivan:	Three passenger tickets for Hvar please, and one for a personal vehicle.
Cashier:	Do you need return tickets?
Ivan:	No, just one-way. Is the price the same as it was last year or is it more expensive now?
Cashier:	It is a little more expensive than last year. The total is 354 kunas please.
Ivan:	Here you are. Which ferry goes to Hvar?
Cashier:	Here are your tickets. You're lucky. "Tin Ujević" leaves soon, at exactly 2 o'clock from berth number 5. But hurry!
Ivan:	Thanks.

Part II

The same day on Hvar.

Darko:	One double and one single room please.
Receptionist:	There are no free rooms except with a reservation. Have you booked the rooms?

Darko: Da, rezervacija je na ime Tomić.

Recepcioner: Molim vaše isprave. Sobe su spremne. Lift je lijevo. Izvolite ključeve i ugodan boravak!

Ivan: Marijana, ima li ovakvih plaža i otoka u Americi?

Marijana: Ima, ali meni su otoci i plaže ovdje najljepši. U Zagrebu je bilo lijepo, ali ovdje je još ljepše. Manja mjesta su bolja za odmor.

Ivan: Da, sve je drugačije. Mnogo je tiše i mirnije nego u velikom gradu.

Marijana: Veliki gradovi su zanimljiviji za posao i zabavu, ali ovdje ćemo se najbolje odmoriti.

Darko: Poslije ćemo razgledati centar grada Hvara sa starim kazalištem, a sada vas ostavljam i idem plivati.

Marijana: Nedostajat će mi sve ovo kada se vratim u Ameriku, a najviše prijatelji koje sam ovdje stekla.

Ivan: Pa ... ja sam se nekako nadao da se ti nećeš vratiti u Ameriku. Rekla si da ćeš ostati u Hrvatskoj duže.

Marijana: Da, to je točno, ali ovo je ipak poslovni put. Moram se najprije vratiti u Ameriku na nekoliko tjedana da sredim neke poslovne i privatne stvari. Nadam se da ću poslije toga provesti punu godinu dana u Hrvatskoj.

Ivan: Jedva čekam.

Marijana: I ja!

Za nekoliko dana u Dubrovniku.

Marijana: Vožnja brodom bila je pravi užitak! Ne bih mogla reći koji mi je otok draži: Hvar, Korčula ili Mljet.

Darko: Ipak, od svih mjesta u Hrvatskoj Dubrovnik je najpoznatiji.

Marijana: Htjela bih razgledati Palaču Sponza i Franjevački samostan.

Darko: Dogovoreno! Poslije toga ti i Ivan idete prošetati po starim zidinama. Odande se pruža prekrasan pogled i vrlo je romantično.

Marijana: Darko, tiše, Ivan bi te mogao čuti.

Darko: Pa ja i želim da me on čuje!

Darko:	Yes, the reservation is under the name Tomić.
Receptionist:	Your documents, please. The rooms are ready. The elevator is to your left. Here are the keys and have a pleasant stay!
Ivan:	Marijana, are there beaches and islands like these in America?
Marijana:	There are, but for me these islands and beaches here are the most beautiful. In Zagreb it was so nice, but here it is even nicer. Smaller places are better for vacation.
Ivan:	Yes, everything here is different. It's much quieter and more peaceful than in a big city.
Marijana:	Big cities are more interesting for work and fun, but here we can relax best.
Darko:	Later we will have a look at the city center of Hvar including the old theater, but now I'm leaving you and going for a swim.
Marijana:	I will miss all of this once I return to America, and most of all the friends whom I have met here.
Ivan:	Well … I had hoped somehow that you would not return to America. You said that you would stay in Croatia for a longer time.
Marijana:	Yes, that is correct, but this is, after all, a business trip. I must first return to America for a few weeks to sort out some work and personal things. I hope that after that I will spend a whole year in Croatia.
Ivan:	I look forward to that.
Marijana:	Me too!

A few days later in Dubrovnik.

Marijana:	Traveling by ship has been a real pleasure! I could not say which island I like better, Hvar, Korčula or Mljet.
Darko:	Nevertheless, of all the places in Croatia Dubrovnik is the most famous.
Marijana:	I would like to see the Sponza Palace and Franciscan monastery.
Darko:	Fine! After that you and Ivan can go walking along the old city walls. From there one has an excellent view and it is very romantic.
Marijana:	Darko, be a little quieter, Ivan might hear you!
Darko:	Well, I hope that he does hear me!

Vocabulary

brod ship
dovoljno enough, sufficient
drag dear, favorite
drugačije *adv*. differently
karta ticket
mirno *adv*. peacefully
nego than
odande from there
osob*an* personal
pogled view, glance
poslov*an* business
povratni return, round-trip
prekras*an* magnificent, very beautiful
privat*an* private
putnički *adj*. passenger
rezervacija reservation
riječ *f*. word
romantično *adv*. romantic
samo only
samostan monastery
slobod*an* free
smjer direction, way
sprem*an* ready
tiho quiet
trajekt ferry
trajektna luka ferry port
ukratko briefly
užit*a*k pleasure
veoma very
vez berth
vozilo vehicle, car
zidine walls, esp. city walls

Verb List

nedostajati (*I* **nedostajem**, **nedostaju**) to miss
objasniti (*P* **objasnim**, **objasne**) to explain
odmoriti se (*P* **odmorim**, **odmore**) to rest
ostati (*P* **ostanem**, **ostanu**) to stay
ostavljati (*I* **ostavljam**, **ostavljaju**) to leave
plivati (*I* **plivam**, **plivaju**) to swim
primijetiti (*P* **primijetim**, **primijete**) to notice
provesti (*P* **provedem**, **provedu**) to spend
pružati (*I* **pružam**, **pružaju**) to stretch, to extend, to offer
rezervirati (*I/P* **rezerviram**, **rezerviraju**) to book
srediti (*P* **sredim**, **srede**) to sort out
steći (*P* **steknem**, **steknu**) to obtain, to acquire
vratiti (se)(*P* **vratim (se)**, **vrate (se)**) to return

Useful Expressions

Jesi li spreman/spremna? Are you ready?
Samo trenutak. Just a minute.
Hoće li mi trebati još nešto? Will I need anything else?
To je dovoljno! That is enough!
Dobro ti stoji! It fits you well.
Nema veze. It doesn't matter.
Ja bih rekao/rekla... I'd say…
Molim Vas, tri putničke karte za Hvar. Three passenger tickets for Hvar, please.
Jednu kartu za osobno vozilo. One ticket for a personal vehicle.
Trebam povratne karte. I need round-trip tickets.
U jednom smjeru. One way.
Koji trajekt ide za Hvar? Which ferry goes to Hvar?
Imate sreće! You're lucky!
Samo požurite! But hurry!
Imate li slobodnih soba? Do you have any free rooms?
Molim Vas, jednu dvokrevetnu i jednu jednokrevetnu sobu. One double and one single room please.
Rezervacija je na ime Tomić. The reservation is under the name Tomić.
Ugodan boravak! Have a pleasant stay!
Nedostajat će mi sve ovo. I'll miss all of this.
To je točno. That is correct.
Jedva čekam. I can hardly wait.
I ja isto! Me too!
Htjela bih/htio bih... I'd like...
Dogovoreno! Fine! [*lit.*: agreed]

Articles of clothing/odjeća

bluza blouse
čarape socks
cipele shoes
čizme boots
džemper sweater
haljina dress
hlače pants
kapa cap
kaput coat
kostim suit *(woman's)*
košulja shirt
kravata tie
kupaće (gaće) man's swimming trunks
kupaći kostim woman's swimsuit
majica kratkih/dugih rukava T shirt with short/long sleeves
odijelo suit
rublje underwear, laundry
traperice jeans
šešir hat
šorc shorts

Accommodations/smještaj

apartman vacation condo, hotel suite
jednokrevetna soba single bedroom
dvokrevetna soba double bedroom
soba s kupaonom room with a bathroom
pomoćni ležaj additional bed
noćenje s doručkom overnight stay with breakfast
puni pansion full board *(accommodation with three meals)*
polupansion half board *(accommodation with breakfast and one meal)*
cijena po osobi po danu price per person per day
balkon s pogledom na more balcony with a view of the sea
plaža beach
bazen swimming pool
tenisko igralište tennis court
restoran restaurant
bar bar
telefon phone
rezervacija reservation

Grammar

1. Conditional

The conditional mood is formed by adding the past participle of a verb to an auxiliary form of the verb **biti** *to be*:

Conditional

aux. form of **biti** (to be) + past participle of **kupiti** (to buy)

	singular	plural
1st	**ja bih kupio/kupila** I would buy	**mi bismo kupili/kupile** we would buy
2nd	**ti bi kupio/kupila** you would buy	**vi biste kupili/kupile** you would buy
3rd *m.*	**on bi kupio** he would buy	**oni bi kupili** they would buy
3rd *f.*	**ona bi kupila** she would buy	**one bi kupile** they would buy
3rd *neu.*	**ono bi kupilo** it would buy	**ona bi kupila** they would buy

The *negative conditional* is formed by inserting the negative particle **ne** right before the auxiliary verb.

Ja *ne* bih kupila I would *not* buy

The *interrogative conditional* is formed with the interrogative particle **li** and inversion.

Bih li ja kupila? Would I buy?

In contrast to what you have previously learned, the auxiliary here can begin a sentence.

Bih li ja kupila Would I buy?

BUT NOT

**Sam kupila.* *I bought.*

An example of this is found in the dialogue in this lesson:

Bi li mi objasnio što znače te riječi?
Would you explain these words a little better?

The interrogative form can also be formed by using question words such as **kada** *when*, **gdje** *where*, **kako** *how*, etc. Note that some Croatian conditional forms may be translated by *could* rather than *would*:

Kada biste mogli doći k nama na večeru?
When could you come over for dinner?

The most frequent uses of the conditional are in:

a) polite requests. Note that the verbs **htjeti** *to want* or **željeti** *to want* can be omitted from this construction.

Ja bih malo vode, molim Vas.
I'd like a little water, please.
Ja bih htio/želio malo vode, molim Vas.
I'd like a little water, please.
Biste li išli u kino sa mnom?
Would you like to go to the movies with me?
Bi li mi mogla donijeti knjigu?
Could you bring me the book?

b) a polite way of expressing a preference or opinion.

Ja ne bih išla u kino, nego u kazalište.
I would rather go to the movies than to the theater.
On bi u nedjelju igrao tenis.
He would like to play tennis on Sunday.
Ja bih rekao da se ti sviđaš Ivanu.
I would say that Ivan likes you.
Nikada ne bih otišao na odmor tamo.
I would never go there for holidays.

c) repeated actions in the past (this meaning is very close to that of past tense imperfective verbs).

conditional:
Obično *bi odlazio* u knjižnicu svaki dan.
He *would* usually *go* to the library every day.

imperfective verb in the past tense:
Obično *je odlazio* je u knjižnicu svaki dan.
He usually *went* to the library every day.

d) statements expressing intention or purpose and including the conjunction **da**.

On je dugo štedio da bi kupio auto.
He was saving for a long time (in order) to buy a car.
Skuhala je ručak da ne bi bili gladni.
She cooked lunch so they would not be hungry.

e) with the verb **trebati** *should, to need, have to* indicating mild obligation.

Trebalo bi da učimo za ispit.
We *should* study for the exam.
Trebao bih popraviti auto.
I *should* fix the car.

f) with *if* clauses (for more on this function, see Lesson 15)

Bila bih vrlo sretna ako biste došli.
I would be very happy if you came.
Ako bi popravio auto, mogli bismo sutra otići u New York.
If you fixed the car, we could go to New York tomorrow.

2. The preposition *s* (down from, off, away from)

In this lesson the preposition **s** is used with a different meaning indicating movement *down from*, *off*, and *away from* something.

It is important to remember that when **s** is used in this sense the noun must be in the *genitive* as opposed to situations in which **s** means *with*, when the noun is in the *instrumental*. You will recall that the longer form, **sa**, is used before words that start with **s, š, z, ž**.

s planine na planinu	from one mountain to another
s otoka na otok	from one island to another
s kontinenta na kontinent	from one continent to another

Uzeo je knjigu s police.	He took a book off the shelf.
Tanjur je pao sa stola.	The plate fell off the table.

In Lesson 7 we discussed a group of nouns that in the locative and accusative take the preposition **na**. For example:

na koncertu/na koncert at a concert
na večeri/na večeru at dinner
na poslu/na posao at work
na fakultetu/na fakultet in college
na ulici/na ulicu in a street

All the nouns from this group take **s** with the meaning *from*. Thus one doesn't say **iz fakulteta*, **iz trga*, etc. but **s fakulteta** *from school* and **s trga** *from the square*.

Kada dolaziš s fakulteta?	When are you coming back from school?
Vratio se s posla.	He has come back from work.

3. Comparison of adjectives

3.1. Comparative adjectives: *-iji* group

A large group of comparatives (e.g., happier, cheaper) is formed by adding **-iji** for the masculine, **-ija** for the feminine, and **-ije** for the neuter to the short form of the adjective (i.e., the dictionary form).

The superlative (the happiest, the cheapest, etc.) adds the prefix **naj-**.

Comparative and superlative forms agree with the noun in gender, number, and case in exactly the same way as regular adjectives. A *fleeting -a* in the positive form will be lost in the comparative and superlative forms.

	positive	**comparative**	**superlative**
interesting	**zanimljiv**	**zanimljiviji**	**najzanimljiviji**
well-known	**poznat**	**poznatiji**	**najpoznatiji**
strange	**čudan**	**čudniji**	**najčudniji**

In the same way as in all cases except the nominative, adjectives ending in **-o** insert **-l** in the comparative and superlative forms:

	positive	**comparative**	**superlative**
joyful	**veseo**	**veseliji**	**najveseliji**
stale	**ustajao**	**ustaliji**	**najustaliji**

3.2. Comparative adjectives: *-ji* group

The next large group of comparatives is formed by adding **-ji** in the masculine, **-ja** in the feminine, and **-je** in the neuter to the short (dictionary) form of the adjective. As is often the case, here too **-j** can have a softening effect on the consonant endings of adjectives, causing **k, g, h, z, s, t** and **d** to change when **-ji** is added. Note that the **j** drops out of the comparative endings (see chart below).

An **-l** must be inserted when the adjective stem ends in **-p**, **-b**, **-v**, or **-m**; **-st** becomes **-šć** for the sake of pronunciation.

	positive			**comparative**
strong	**jak**	**ja*k* + ji**	→	**ja*č*i** stronger
stupid	**glup**	**glu*p* + l + ji**	→	**glu*pl*ji** stupider
dear	**drag**	**dra*g* + ji**	→	**dra*ž*i** dearer
quiet	**tih**	**ti*h* + ji**	→	**ti*š*i** quieter
expensive	**skup**	**sku*p* +l + ji**	→	**sku*pl*ji** more expensive
firm	**čvrst**	**čvr*st* + ji**	→	**čvr*šć*i** firmer

How can you tell which adjective belongs to which group? If an adjective is monosyllabic (i.e., consists of only one syllable) and ends in a consonant listed in the first row of the table below, it most likely belongs to the **-ji** group. It is a good idea to memorize the following chart and then the forms will fall into place.

-*ji* Group of Comparative Adjectives

pos. *adj.* ending	k	g	h	z	s	t	d	p	b	v	m	n	l	st
changes to	↓	↓	↓	↓	↓	↓	↓	↓	↓	↓	↓	↓	↓	↓
comparative	**č**	**ž**	**š**	**ž**	**š**	**ć**	**đ**	**plj**	**blj**	**vlj**	**mlj**	**nj**	**lj**	**šć**

3. 3. Comparative adjectives: *-ak/ek/ok* group

The group of adjectives that end in **-ak, -ek**, and **-ok** in the masculine drop this ending and add **-ji** to form the comparative. Softening of the remaining consonants follows the rules above.

	positive			comparative
short	**kratak**	**krat + ji**	→	**kraći** shorter
tall	**visok**	**vis + ji**	→	**viši** taller
low	**nizak**	**niz + ji**	→	**niži** lower
deep	**dubok**	**dub + ji**	→	**dublji** deeper
far	**dalek**	**dal + ji**	→	**dalji** farther

3.4. Comparative adjectives: important exceptions

Only three adjectives create the comparative by adding **-š**:

lijep→ljepši more beautiful
lak→lakši lighter in weight, easier
mek→mekši softer

Several comparatives and superlatives are completely irregular. As they happen to be some of the most frequent ones, you will have to memorize them separately.

positive	comparative	superlative
dobar good	**bolji** better	**najbolji** the best
loš/zao bad/evil	**gori** worse	**najgori** the worst
velik big	**veći** bigger	**najveći** the biggest
malen small	**manji** smaller	**najmanji** the smallest

3.5. Adjectives ending in *-čki, -ski, -ški*

Adjectives ending in **-čki**, **-ski**, **-ški** form the comparative and superlative by adding **više** *more* and **najviše** *the most.*

prijateljski friendly **više prijateljski** more friendly

On se ponašao *više prijateljski* nego prošli put.
He behaved in a *more friendly* way than the last time.

4. Comparison of adverbs

You may recall that the adverb is identical in form to that of *neuter singular adjectives*. The same is true for the comparative and superlative forms of adverbs, as in these examples from the dialogue in this lesson.

Mnogo je *tiše* i *mirnije* nego u velikom gradu.
It's much *quieter* and *more peaceful* than in a big city.

Je li sada *skuplje*?
Is it *more expensive* now?
Ovdje ćemo se *najbolje* odmoriti.
Here we can relax *best*.

Irregular adverbs are:

dobro well	**bolje** more well	**najbolje** most well
loše badly	**gore** more badly	**najgore** most badly
mnogo a lot	**više** more	**najviše** most
malo few	**manje** less	**najmanje** least

5. Comparative constructions

While English has one conjunction that is used in comparative constructions (*than*), Croatian has two: **nego** and **od.** They require the use of different cases: **od** requires the genitive, while **nego** requires the same form before it as after it. There is no difference in meaning between the two and they can be used interchangeably.

Tvoja torba je veća *od* moje torbe.
Your bag is bigger *than* my bag.
Tvoja torba je veća *nego* moja torba.
Your bag is bigger *than* my bag.

Ja sam spavala duže *od* tebe.
I slept longer *than* you.
Ja sam spavala duže *nego* ti.
I slept longer *than* you.

Volim Mariju više *od* njezine sestre.
I like Marija more *than* her sister.
Volim Mariju više *nego* njezinu sestru.
I like Marija more *than* her sister.

For a negative comparison, **manji/manja/manje** is used.

Moja torba je *manja* od tvoje.
My bag is *smaller* than yours.
Moja torba je *manja* nego tvoja.
My bag is *smaller* than yours.

Oni imaju *manje* novca od nas.
They have *less* money than us.
Oni imaju *manje* novca nego mi.
They have *less* money than us.

Before all adjectives and adverbs **manje** *less* and **najmanje** *least* can be used for a negative comparison. This is not connected with **manja/manji** *smaller*. **Manje** *less* and **najmanje** *least* are quantity words and can be thought of as the comparative and superlative of **malo** *few*.

malo studenata few students
manje studenata fewer students
najmanje studenata the fewest students

Danas je bilo *manje* sunčano nego jučer.
It has been *less* sunny today than yesterday.

For *comparison of two actions*, **nego što** is used. In this context one uses the adverbial form (identical to the neuter form).

On piše *bolje nego što* ona piše. He writes *better than* she does.

The same meaning can be expressed in a more succinct form.

On piše *bolje nego* ona. He writes *better than* she does.
Ja živim bliže centru *nego* on. I live closer to the center *than* he does.

For two linked comparatives (English *the more the merrier*), use **što…to**:

Što više znaš, to manje moraš učiti.
The more you know, the less you need to study.
Što jeftinije, to bolje.
The cheaper, the better.

To show a gradual increase or decrease, the word **sve**, translated as *more and more* or *increasingly*, plus the comparative must be used. By contrast, **sve manje** is translated as *less and less*.

Padao je mrak i ona se *sve* više bojala.
Darkness was falling and she was *more and more* afraid.
Ona mu je *sve* rjeđe pisala.
She wrote to him *more and more* infrequently.
On je imao *sve manje* novca.
He had *less and less* money.

The English construction *as...as possible* requires the use of **što** plus a comparative form:

On su došli što su brže mogli. They arrived as soon as they could.
Vrati se što prije! Come back as soon as possible!

Use **još + a comparative form** to intensify the meaning of an adjective:

Još bolje!	Even better!
Još više!	Even more!
Još bliže!	Even closer!

Appendix: Most Frequent Comparative & Superlative Adjective Forms

positive	comparative	positive superlative	meaning
bliz*a*k	**bliži**	**najbliži**	close, near
brz	**brži**	**najbrži**	fast
čest	**češći**	**najčešći**	frequent
čist	**čistiji, čišći**	**najčistiji, najčišći**	clean
čud*a*n	**čudniji**	**najčudniji**	strange
čvrst	**čvršći**	**najčvršći**	firm
dalek	**dalji**	**najdalji**	far, distant
debeo	**deblji**	**najdeblji**	fat, thick
dob*a*r	**bolji**	**najbolji**	good
drag	**draži**	**najdraži**	dear
dubok	**dublji**	**najdublji**	deep
dug	**duži**	**najduži**	long
glad*a*n	**gladniji**	**najgladniji**	hungry
glup	**gluplji**	**najgluplji**	stupid
grub	**grublji**	**najgrublji**	rough, coarse
gust	**gušći**	**najgušći**	thick, dense
jak	**jači**	**najjači**	strong
jeftin	**jeftiniji**	**najjeftiniji**	cheap
krat*a*k	**kraći**	**najkraći**	short
kriv	**krivlji**	**najkrivlji**	crooked, guilty
krut	**krući**	**najkrući**	stiff
lak, lagan	**lakši**	**najlakši**	easy, light
lijep	**ljepši**	**najljepši**	beautiful
lijen	**ljenji**	**najljenji**	lazy
loš	**lošiji, gori**	**najlošiji, najgori**	bad
lud	**luđi**	**najluđi**	crazy
ljut	**ljući**	**najljući**	angry
mali, malen	**manji**	**najmanji**	small
mek, mekan	**mekši**	**najmekši**	soft
mlad	**mlađi**	**najmlađi**	young
mršav	**mršaviji**	**najmršaviji**	slim, skinny

niz*a*k	**niži**	**najniži**	low
nov	**noviji**	**najnoviji**	new
pamet*a*n	**pametniji**	**najpametniji**	clever
plit*a*k	**plići**	**najplići**	shallow
prljav	**prljaviji**	**najprljaviji**	dirty
rijed*a*k	**rjeđi**	**najrjeđi**	rare, sparse
ruž*a*n	**ružniji**	**najružniji**	ugly
skup	**skuplji**	**najskuplji**	expensive
slab	**slabiji**	**najslabiji**	weak
slad*a*k	**slađi**	**najslađi**	sweet
sret*a*n	**sretniji**	**najsretniji**	happy
star	**stariji**	**najstariji**	old
straš*a*n	**strašniji**	**najstrašniji**	terrible
strog	**stroži**	**najstroži**	strict
suh	**suši**	**najsuši**	dry
širok	**širi**	**najširi**	wide, loose
tan*a*k	**tanji**	**najtanji**	thin, not thick
tež*a*k	**teži**	**najteži**	heavy, difficult
tih	**tiši**	**najtiši**	quiet
tijes*a*n	**tješnji**	**najtješnji**	tight
tuž*a*n	**tužniji**	**najtužniji**	sad
tvrd	**tvrđi**	**najtvrđi**	hard
uz*a*k	**uži**	**najuži**	narrow
velik	**veći**	**najveći**	big
veseo	**veseliji**	**najveseliji**	merry
visok	**viši**	**najviši**	tall, high
zao, loš	**gori**	**najgori**	bad
žed*a*n	**žedniji**	**najžedniji**	thirsty

Exercises

Vježba 13.1 Create a dialogue using at least **15** of the words below.

galerija	sunčano	poznat	karta
romantičan	džemper	lijep	od
torba	sigurno	jedinstven	nekoliko
kreditna kartica	sutra	ipak	zanimljiv
promet	naravno	za/brinuti se	baš
turistički vodič	izvrstan	nastaviti	ostati

Vježba 13.2 Translate into Croatian:

A matter of choice – Stvar izbora

My name is Katarina. I love beautiful clothes. I would like to buy a new coat and shoes. If I could choose between theater and shopping, I would choose shopping. I would be very happy if my husband would realize that beautiful clothes are not a luxury [luksuz], but a necessity. Women are happier and more beautiful when they have fashionable [moder*a*n] clothes. My husband and I would like to spend more time together, but every weekend I go shopping and he plays tennis [tenis] with his friends. I tell him that tennis is more expensive than shoes. He laughs and asks me if I would like to go to the movies. He forgives me my shoes, and I forgive him tennis. How would it be if it weren't [da nije] this way! We are a great couple!

Vježba 13.3 A. Translate from English into Croatian.

Example: Give me the tickets please. I do not know at what time we leave.
Daj mi karte, molim te. Ne znam kada odlazimo.

1. I would like a coffee please. Darko, is the weather on Hvar always so nice?

___

___

2. How much does a ticket to Mljet cost? Last year, one ticket cost only 50 kuna.

___

___

3. I need to return to America for a few weeks, but after that I will come to Croatia to live with you.

___

___

4. If you could help me study for the test, we could go dancing tonight.

___

___

5. I think that it is nicer here and I have better friends than in America.

___

___

B. Answer the following questions about yourself and then ask the same questions of someone else:

1. Što biste htjeli raditi idućeg vikenda?

___

___

2. Kamo biste htjeli otputovati?

___

___

3. Kakav biste auto kupili da imate mnogo novca?

___

___

4. Što biste danas htjeli jesti za ručak?

___

___

5. Koji biste film htjeli pogledati?

____

____

6. Koju biste knjigu htjeli pročitati?

____

____

7. Koju poznatu osobu biste htjeli upoznati i zašto?

____

____

Vježba 13.4 A. Write out the comparative and superlative forms of the adjectives/adverbs below in Croatian and then translate the adjectives into English.

Example: **suh – suši – najsuši** dry – drier – driest

1. mnogo __________ __________ __________
2. drag __________ __________ __________
3. lijep __________ __________ __________
4. blizak __________ __________ __________
5. zao __________ __________ __________
6. velik __________ __________ __________
7. žedan __________ __________ __________
8. star __________ __________ __________
9. tiho __________ __________ __________
10. dobar __________ __________ __________

B. Now create sentences using either the comparatives or superlatives from the exercise above.

Example **suh – suši – najsuši** dry – drier – driest
Zrak u primorskim gradovima nije suši nego u gradovima na planini.

1. mnogo

____

2. drag

____

3. lijep

____

4. blizak

____

5. zao

____

6. velik

____

7. žedan

____

8. star

____

9. tih

____

10. dobar

____

Vježba 13.5
A. Fill in the missing adjectives or adverbs.

1. Moj stan je __________(*tight, overcrowded*), ali tvoj je još __________ (*tighter, more overcrowded*).
2. Koji je __________(*the longest*) dan u godini?
3. Njihov auto je __________(*fast*), ali naš je još __________(*faster*).
4. Ovo je __________(*sad*) film, ali taj koji sam gledala jučer bio je još __________(*sadder*).
5. Hrvatski nije __________(*the most difficult*) jezik na svijetu.
6. Neću kupiti ni jedan krevet. Oba su __________(*hard*). Ne znam koji je __________(*harder*).
7. Nisam čula __________(*more stupid*) razlog od njegovog.
8. Tko je __________(*younger*), Vaš __________(*the best*) prijatelj ili Vaša __________(*the best*) prijateljica?
9. To je bila __________(*the craziest*) zabava na kojoj smo ikada bili.
10. Imate li neki __________(*cheaper*) džemper?
11. Koji je __________(*the most famous*) grad u Hrvatskoj?
12. Što mislite, je li Marijana __________(*happier*) u lekciji broj 9 ili u lekciji broj 13?
13. Ovaj restoran je __________(*expensive*), ali restorani u centru su još__________(*more expensive*).
14. Koji je __________(*the shortest*) put do hotela „Imperial"?
15. Što __________(*the most*) volite raditi nedjeljom? Što Vam je __________(*most interesting*): čitati knjige, gledati TV, ići u kupovinu, igrati tenis, piti pivo ili raditi nešto drugo?

B. Fill in the blanks with an/the appropriate word(s).

Example: **Jesi li spremna? Moramo ____ da ne zakasnimo na _______.**
ići / požuriti – trajekt / vlak / brod

1. Ja bih rekao da to nije dovoljno. Što ti _______?
2. Dobar dan, ____ si? ____ li ići sa mnom na piće?
3. Čitala sam ovu knjigu, ali nisam ___________ ništa.
4. ____ kažu da je tamo nevjerojatno!
5. I ____ isto. Meni se _________ Dubrovnik i otoci, ali ne bih mogla ______ koji mi je otok _______, Hvar, Korčula ili Mljet.

Vježba 13.6 Insert the conditional forms below and then change the subject and the verb form at least once.

Example: **Ja *bih* htjela otići u kino.**
Mi *bismo* htjeli otići u kino.

1. _______ li još malo kave?
2. Ona je mnogo učila da ___________ sve znala na ispitu.
3. __________ li mi mogli pomoći?
4. Mi ne ____________ jeli sada nego poslije.
5. Što ___________ htjeli sada raditi?
6. Nikada ne __________ to pomislila.
7. __________ li mi mogli dati Vaš broj telefona?
8. Oni ___________ obično išli u kino nedjeljom.
9. ___________ li on mogao to kupiti za mene?
10. Možda __________ oni mogli doći s nama.

Vježba 13.7 Sažetak/Summary

A. Read and translate:

Marijana se pakirala jer su ona, Darko i Ivan putovali na otok Hvar i u Dubrovnik. Stavila je u torbu hlače, majice, kupaći kostim, rublje, čarape, džemper, košulje i cipele. Nije bila sigurna treba li joj još i neka lijepa haljina. Darko je rekao da joj ništa više ne treba jer već ima najveću torbu. On je bio siguran da će se sva njezina odjeća svidjeti Ivanu. Marijana nije razumjela što joj je Darko želio reći. Ali nije bilo vremena za detalje. Darku se čini da se Ivan zaljubio u Marijanu. Ona je i sama primijetila nešto.

U trajektnoj luci Ivan je kupio tri putničke karte u jednom smjeru i jednu kartu za auto. Karte su bile malo skuplje nego prošle godine. Blagajnica mu je rekla da trajekt „Tin Ujević" ide točno u 2 sata. Kada su došli na Hvar, otišli su u hotel. Tamo su imali rezervirane dvije sobe. Marijana je rekla Ivanu da ima lijepih plaža i u Americi, ali su njoj plaže u Hrvatskoj draže. Njoj se sviđa i Zagreb, ali misli da su manja mjesta bolja za odmor jer su tiša. Dok je Darko plivao, Marijana i Ivan su razgovarali. Ivan joj je rekao da bi on htio da ona ostane u Hrvatskoj. Marijana mu je objasnila da je ona ipak na poslovnom putu. Mora se vratiti u Ameriku da sredi neke poslovne i privatne stvari. Poslije toga će provesti punu godinu dana u Hrvatskoj.

Nakon Hvara, Marijana, Ivan i Darko su otputovali u Dubrovnik brodom. Vidjeli su otoke Korčulu i Mljet. Vožnja brodom je bila pravi užitak. U Dubrovniku su razgledali Palaču Sponza, Franjevački samostan i šetali po gradskim zidinama.

B. Translate the following questions and then answer them:

1. Why was Marijana packing?

2. What did she put in the bag?

3. What did Darko say about her bag?

4. What did he say about Ivan?

5. How many tickets did Ivan buy in the ferry port?

6. Were the tickets more or less expensive than last year?

7. Where did Marijana, Darko and Ivan go when they arrived to Hvar?

8. What kinds of places does Marijana like for holidays?

9. Which beaches does she like best?

10. What did Marijana and Ivan talk about while Darko swam?

11. Why does Marijana have to go back to America?

12. Where did Marijana, Darko and Ivan go after Hvar?

13. How did they go to Dubrovnik?

____

____

14. Which islands did they see?

____

____

15. What did they do in Dubrovnik?

____

____

Lekcija 14
Šetnja Zagrebom

Lesson 14
A walk around Zagreb

Lekcija 14: Šetnja Zagrebom

Prvi dio

Ivan: Marijana, zašto si tužna?

Marijana: Ne mogu vjerovati da je vrijeme tako brzo prošlo i da se bliži kraj mojeg putovanja.

Ivan: Ali ti ćeš se brzo vratiti natrag.

Marijana: Istina! S jedne strane čekaju me teški zadaci u Americi, ali s druge boravak ovdje omogućio mi je da dođem do nekih zaključaka. Osim toga, sada odlično razumijem hrvatski, a i govorim ga mnogo bolje.

Ivan: Govoriš bolje nego što ja govorim engleski! Što kažeš na to da prošetamo po Tkalčićevoj ulici do Gornjeg grada i crkve svetog Marka? Tamo se nalazi i Hrvatski sabor.

Marijana: Poslije toga možemo svratiti k Darku. On stanuje na Gornjem gradu, a ja usput mogu kupiti i nekoliko darova za svoju obitelj i prijatelje u Americi. Ali prvo bih trebala promijeniti novac. Gdje to mogu napraviti?

Ivan: Mjenjačnica je u banci na Trgu bana Jelačića.

U mjenjačnici.

Marijana: Oprostite, kakav je danas tečaj dolara?

Blagajnik: Jedan dolar je 4,7 kuna.

Marijana: Promijenila bih 200 dolara, molim Vas.

Blagajnik: Nema problema. Potpišite se ovdje. Izvolite novac!

Marijana: Hvala i doviđenja. Ivane, tu na uglu je prodavaonica suvenira. Idemo do nje. Nadam se da nije već zatvorena.

Ivan: Ne, čini se da je još otvorena.

U prodavaonici.

Prodavačica: Izvolite, što biste htjeli pogledati?

Marijana: Htjela bih kupiti knjigu o Zagrebu i CD s hrvatskom narodnom glazbom.

Prodavačica: Knjige o Hrvatskoj su tamo, a CD-i su ovdje. Pogledajte i ove suvenire! To su tradicionalne nošnje iz raznih krajeva Hrvatske.

Lesson 14: A walk around Zagreb

Part I

Ivan: Marijana, why are you sad?

Marijana: I can't believe that the time has gone so fast and that the end of my trip is approaching.

Ivan: But you will be back soon.

Marijana: That's true! On the one hand a lot of hard work is waiting for me in America, but, on the other, my stay here made it possible for me to reach some conclusions. Besides that, I now understand Croatian excellently, and I speak it much better.

Ivan: You speak Croatian better than I speak English! What do you say about a walk along Tkalčićeva Street to the upper city and Saint Mark's Church? The Croatian parliament is there as well.

Marijana: After that we can drop by Darko's place. He lives in the upper city, and on the way I can buy a few presents for my family and friends in America. But first I need to change money. Where can I do that?

Ivan: There is an exchange office in a bank on Ban Jelečić Square.

In the exchange office.

Marijana: Excuse me, what is the exchange rate for the dollar today?

Cashier: One dollar equals 4.7 kunas.

Marijana: I would like to change 200 dollars please.

Cashier: No problem. Sign here please. Your money.

Marijana: Thanks and goodbye. Ivan, here on the corner is a souvenir shop. Let's go there. I hope it's not already closed.

Ivan: No, it seems to be open still.

In the shop.

Saleslady: Hello, what would you like to see?

Marijana: I would like to buy a book about Zagreb and a CD with Croatian folk music.

Saleslady: Books about Croatia are there, and CDs are here. Take a look at these souvenirs. These are traditional costumes from the different regions of Croatia.

Marijana: Sviđa mi se ova bluza, ali je prevelika. Imate li manji broj?

Prodavačica: Samo trenutak. Imamo. Imamo istu bluzu i u plavoj boji.

Marijana: Ne, hvala, ova mi se više sviđa. Kupit ću ove četiri stvari. Koliko je sve zajedno?

Prodavačica: 575 kuna.

Marijana: Evo, izvolite!

Prodavačica: Hvala i doviđenja!

Drugi dio

Poslije, šetajući gradom.

Marijana: Mislim da će se bluza svidjeti mojoj majci, a kapa mojem ocu. CD je za brata. On skuplja glazbu iz cijelog svijeta. Knjiga je za moju najbolju prijateljicu koja bi htjela posjetiti Hrvatsku.

Ivan: Dobar izbor. Nisam znao da imaš brata. Koliko mu je godina?

Marijana: Trideset tri. A koliko je godina tvojoj sestri Katiji?

Ivan: Njoj je dvadeset i jedna godina. Studira pravo. Je li tvoj brat oženjen?

Marijana: Da, njegova žena je Amerikanka. Prošle godine dobili su dijete, pa sam postala tetka. On radi kao programer. Tvoja sestra sigurno još nije udana.

Ivan: Ne, ona je još premlada i najprije mora završiti studij. Jesi li umorna?

Marijana: Pomalo. Bole me noge. Molim te, nazovi Darka i reci mu da stižemo za nekoliko minuta.

Ivan: Evo sjedni! Ovo je vrlo ugodno mjesto za predah. Darka ćemo nazvati kasnije, ako se slažeš. Htio bih razgovarati s tobom o nečemu vrlo važnom.

Marijana: I ja sam se nadala da ćemo imati priliku razgovarati nasamo prije mojeg odlaska.

Marijana: I like this blouse but it is too big. Do you have a smaller size?

Saleslady: Just a moment. We do. We also have the same blouse in blue.

Marijana: No, thank you, I like this one better. I will buy these four things. How much is everything together?

Saleslady: 575 kunas.

Marijana: Here you go.

Saleslady: Thanks and goodbye!

Part II

Later, walking through the city.

Marijana: I think that my mother would like this blouse, and my father that cap. The CD is for my brother. He collects music from around the whole world. The book is for my best friend, who would like to visit Croatia.

Ivan: Good choice. I did not know that you had a brother! How old is he?

Marijana: Thirty-three. And how old is your sister Katija?

Ivan: She is twenty-one. She studies law. Is your brother married?

Marijana: Yes, his wife is American. Last year they had a baby so I became an aunt. He works as a computer programmer. Your sister is surely not yet married.

Ivan: No, she is still too young and first must finish her studies. Are you tired?

Marijana: A little bit. My feet hurt. Please, call Darko and tell him that we'll arrive in a few minutes.

Ivan: Here, have a seat here. This is a very pleasant spot for a rest. We will call Darko later if you agree! I would like to talk with you about something very important.

Marijana: I too hoped that we would have an opportunity to talk in private before my departure.

Vocabulary

borav*a*k stay
izbor choice
kraj region, end
mjenjačnica exchange office
narodni folk
nasamo *adv.* alone, in private
natrag back
osim beside, in addition to, except for
otvoren open
oženjen *m.* married *(for a man)*
predah break
premlad too young
prevelik too big
razni various
Sabor the name for the Croatian Parliament
suvenir souvenir
tečaj exchange rate
tradicional*a*n traditional
udana *f.* married *(for a woman)*
ugodno pleasant
usput along/by the way
zaključ*a*k conclusion
zatvoren closed

Verb List

bližiti (*I* **bližim, bliže**) to approach
omogućiti (*P* **omogućim, omoguće**) to make possible
pogledati (*P* **pogledam, pogledaju**) to look
povjerovati (*P* **povjerujem, povjeruju**) to believe
promijeniti (*P* **promijenim, promijene**) to change
skupljati (*I* **skupljam, skupljaju**) to collect
stanovati (*I* **stanujem, stanuju**) to reside
studirati (*I* **studiram, studiraju**) to study
svratiti (*P* **svratim, svrate**) to drop by

Useful Expressions

Ne mogu vjerovati da ... I can't believe that...
S jedne strane...s druge strane On the one hand ... on the other hand
doći do zaključka to reach a conclusion
osim toga besides that, except for that
Odlično razumijem hrvatski. I understand Croatian excellently.
Što kažeš na to da prošetamo? What do you say about taking a walk?
Trebala/trebao bih promijeniti novac. I would need to change money.
Imate li manji/veći broj? Do you have a smaller/bigger size?
Koliko je sve zajedno? How much is everything together?
iz cijelog svijeta from around the whole world
Stižemo za nekoliko minuta! We'll arrive in a few minutes!

Family members

Like other Slavic languages, Croatian has an elaborate system of names for family relations, as well as dialectal/slang expressions, especially when referring to parents. Below is the list of the essential standard forms:

obitelj family
majka mother
ot*a*c/oca *gen. sg.*/**očevi** *nom. pl.* father
roditelj parent
muž husband
žena wife
brat/braća *pl.* brother
sestra sister
djed grandfather
baka grandmother
tet*a*k uncle *(general term)*
ujak/ujaci *pl.* maternal uncle
stric/stričevi *pl.* paternal uncle
tetka aunt *(general term)*
ujna aunt *(wife of maternal uncle)*
snaha daughter-in-law
strina aunt *(wife of paternal uncle)*
zet son-in-law
dijete/djeteta *gen.*/**djeca** *pl.* child
sin son
kćer daughter
unuk *m.*/**unuka** *f.* grandchild
nećak nephew
nećakinja niece
rođak *m.*/**rođaka** *f.* cousin

Parts of the Body

Here are pictures of the most important parts of the body.

Tijelo - Body

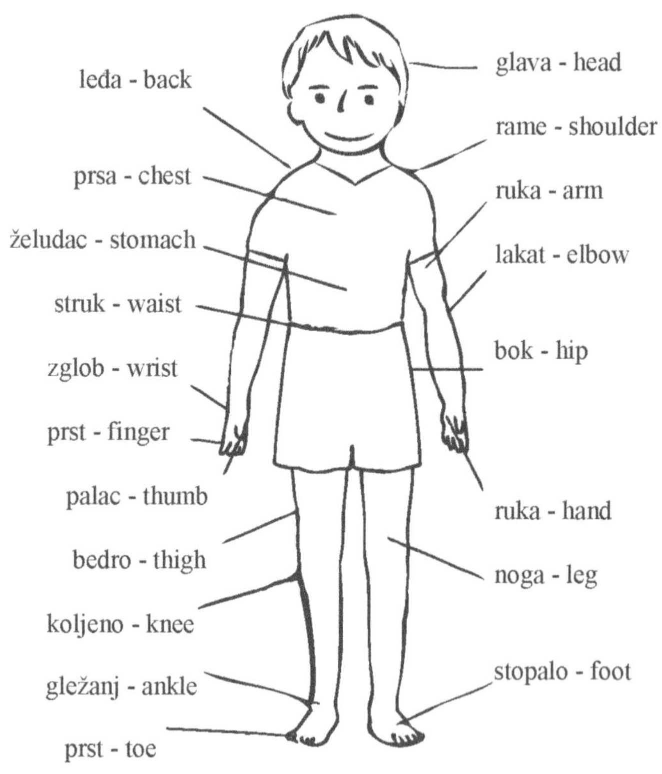

Lice - Face

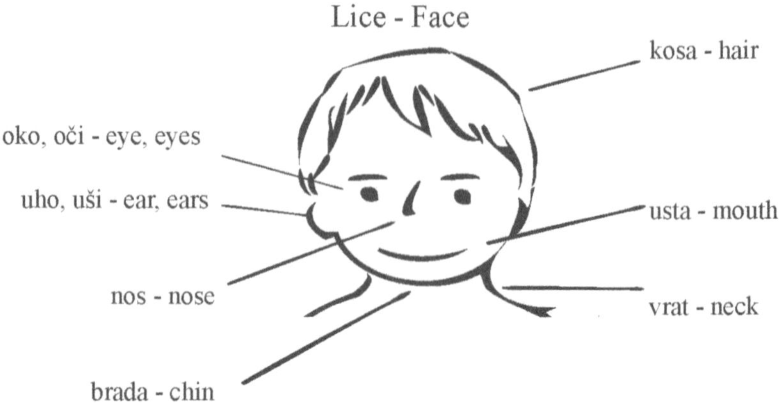

Some of the names of body parts are irregular in the plural and in cases other than the nominative. For example, **oko** *eye* and **uho** *ear*, which are neuter in the singular, become feminine in the plural—**oči** *eyes* and **uši** *ears*; **usta** *mouth* has only the plural form, and **prst** *finger* is irregular in most cases in the plural. **Rame** *shoulder* inserts **-en** in most cases in both the singular and plural (similar to **ime** *name* and **vrijeme** *time/weather*). **Ruka** *arm/hand* and **noga** *leg/foot* have an irregular genitive plural.

Parts of the Body

body part	*nom. sg.*	*acc sg.*	*gen. sg.*	*dat./ loc. sg.*	*instru. sg.*	*nom./ acc. pl.*	*gen. pl.*	*dat./loc./ instru. pl.*
eye	**oko**	**oko**	**oka**	**oku**	**okom**	**oči**	**očiju**	**očima**
ear	**uho**	**uho**	**uha**	**uhu**	**uhom**	**uši**	**ušiju**	**ušima**
mouth	—	—	—	—	—	**usta**	**usta**	**ustima**
finger	**prst**	**prst**	**prsta**	**prstu**	**prstom**	**prsti** *nom.* **prste** *acc.*	**prstiju**	**prstima**
shoulder	**rame**	**rame**	**ramena**	**ramenu**	**ramenom**	**ramena**	**ramena**	**ramenima**
arm/hand	**ruka**	**ruku**	**ruke**	**ruci**	**rukom**	**ruke**	**ruku**	**rukama**
leg/foot	**noga**	**nogu**	**noge**	**nozi**	**nogom**	**noge**	**nogu**	**nogama**

Medical Expressions

We have already encountered the verb **boljeti** *to hurt*. Just as in English, the body part that is painful is the subject of the sentence. Accordingly, if it is one body part that is hurting, the verb will be in the third person singular, and if more than one part is involved, the verb will be in the third person plural. Croatian differs from English in that the person experiencing the pain is referred to in the *accusative* case:

Bole me noge.
My feet are hurting. [*lit.:* My feet/legs are hurting me.]
Boli me glava.
My head is hurting.
Boli me zub.
My tooth is hurting.

biti bolest*a*n/bolesna
to be sick

Bolest*a*n/bolesna sam.
I am sick.

visoka temperatura
high fever

Imam visoku temperaturu.
I have a high fever.

upala grla
throat infection

Imam upalu grla.
I have a throat infection.

glavobolja headache	**Imam glavobolju.** I have a headache.
posjekotina cut	**Imam posjekotinu na nozi.** I have a cut on my leg.
opekotina burn	**Imam opekotinu na ruci.** I have a burn on my hand/arm.
sunčanica sunstroke	**Imam sunčanicu.** I have sunstroke.
prehlada cold	**Imam prehladu.** I have a cold.
gripa flu	**Imam gripu.** I have the flu.
kašljati to cough	**Mnogo kašljem.** I am coughing a lot.
pokvariti želudac to have an upset stomach	**Pokvario/pokvarila sam želudac.** I have an upset stomach.
lijek medication	**Trebam lijek.** I need medication.
bol pain	**Trebam lijek protiv bolova.** I need medication for pain.
recept prescription	**Mogu li dobiti recept?** Could I get a prescription?

Grammar

1. Imperative

The imperative is a verbal form used for expressing commands and requests. To form the imperative, drop the final vowel from the third person plural form of the verb in the present tense. If what is left ends in **-j**, that is the second person singular imperative.

Verb	Imperative
piti to drink	**pij** Drink!
dati to give	**daj** Give!

A few verbs from this group may add **-i**, producing an imperative ending in **-ji**.

brojati to count **broj** and **broji** Count!

All other verbs ending in any consonant other than **-j** will drop the final vowel and add **-i.**

To form the second person plural imperative **-te** is added to this basic imperative form, and **-mo** is added to form the first person plural.

Verb forms in the *indirect imperative*—commands and requests addressed to the first person singular/plural and the third person singular/plural such as *let him read*, and *let me go*—remain the same as in the present tense. The imperative meaning is conveyed through of the word **neka**, corresponding to the English *let* for the third person singular and plural.

First person requests are formed similarly by using the expression (**do**) **pusti da** (informal address) or (**do**) **pustite da** (formal address and plural) from the verb **dopustiti** (P), **pustiti** (I) *to let*. This expression can be abbreviated into simply **da**. Thus **pusti da/pustite da** corresponds to the English *let me*. The first person plural imperative in English is also translated as *let us*.

čitati (to read)

	singular imperative	**plural imperative**
1st	**pusti/pustite da čitam** Let me read!	**čitaj*mo*** Let us read!
2nd	**čita*j*** Read!	**čitaj*te*** Read!
3rd	**neka čita** Let him/her read!	**neka čitaju** Let them read!

pisati (to write)

	singular imperative	**plural imperative**
1st	**da pišem** let me write!	**piš*imo*** let us write!
2nd	**piš*i*** write!	**piš*ite*** write!
3rd	**neka piše** let him/her write!	**neka pišu** let them write!

Pustite me da čitam!	Let me read!
Dopustite mi da kažem!	Allow me to say!
Pusti me na miru!	Leave me alone!
Piši referat!	Write [your] paper!
Neka on skuha ručak!	Let him cook lunch!
Dođite nam često!	Visit us often!

Verbs ending in **-ći** in the infinitive take **-k** or **-g** in the third person plural present, often in combination with **-n**. To form the imperative, drop **-n** and change **-k** and **-g** to **-c** and **-z**, respectively. The most frequently occurring verbs in this small group are listed below:

Infinitive	Present 3rd person plural	Imperative 2nd person singular
reći to say	**reknu** they say	**Reci!** say!
peći to bake	**peku** they bake	**Peci!** bake!
obući to put on	**obuku** they put on	**Obuci!** put on!
pomoći to help	**pomognu** they help	**Pomozi!** help!
leći to lie down	**legnu** they lie down	**Lezi!** lie down!

Reci mi istinu! Tell me the truth!
Obuci ovu košulju! Put on this shirt!
Pomozite mi, molim Vas! Please help me!

The imperative of the verb **biti** *to be* is as follows:

budi 2nd *sg.* ***Budi* pristojan!** *Be* polite!
budimo 1st *pl.* ***Budimo* razumni!** *Let's be* sensible!
budite 2nd *pl.* ***Budite* ljubazni, gdje je pošta?** *Be* so kind [and tell me], where is the post office?

In colloquial speech the word **hajde** can be used in combination with the verb to indicate a form of persuasion.

Hajde, dođi! Do come! **Hajde, čitajmo** Let's read!

Sometimes the imperative forms of the verb **ići (idi, idemo)** *to go* are replaced with **hajde**, **hajdemo** *let's go.*

The *negative imperative* is formed by inserting the negative particle **ne** right before the imperative or by inserting the word **nemoj** (second person singular), **nemojmo** (first person plural), or **nemojte** (second person plural) before the infinitive of the verb:

Ne čitaj tu knjigu! Don't read that book!
Nemoj čitati tu knjigu! Don't read that book!

Although there is no real difference in meaning, the **nemoj** construction softens the tone of the command. While constructions with **nemoj** can take either verbal aspect, those with **ne** require an *imperfective* verb. In a very limited number of cases, the **ne** construction allows for the use of the perfective verb, but the meaning is that of a suggestion or warning rather than of a command:

Ne zaboravi napisati referat!	Don't forget to write the paper!
Nikada ne reci nikada!	Never say never!

2. Modal verbs

The English modal verbs *can/could, should, may/might, must, ought, have to, be able to, dare* have Croatian equivalents, expressing the likelihood or obligation involved in realizing an action. Most of these verbs have already been introduced, and a series of relevant examples are provided below. The only new verbs in the list below are;

smjeti (smijem, smijete) may, be allowed to, dare
valjati (valjam, valjaju; typically used in 3rd *sg.*: **valja, valjalo je, valjalo bi**) should

can **moći**

Ja mogu doći danas u 2 sata.	I can come today at 2 o'clock.
Možeš li otići u trgovinu?	Can you go to the store?

could conditional form of **moći** (**mogao bih**, etc.)

Mogla bih donijeti knjigu sa sobom.	I could bring the book with me.
Oni bi nam mogli pomoći.	They could help us.

should **morati** (obligation), **trebati** (necessity), **valjati** (recommendation)

Morate završiti referate za sutra.	You should finish the papers for tomorrow.
Trebam kupiti još mlijeka.	I should buy more milk.
Ne valja tako raditi.	One shouldn't do that.

may **moći, smjeti** (in the sense of prohibition)

Mogu li otvoriti prozor?	May I open the window?
Ovdje ne smijete pušiti.	You may not smoke here.

might conditional form of **moći** (**mogao bih**, etc.)

Mogli bismo biti gotovi sa svim prije puta.
We might be done with everything before the trip.
On bi mogao upravo to napraviti.
He might do just that.

must **morati**

Domaćin koji sve organizira mora imati plan.
The host who organizes everything must have a plan.
Moram otići u banku jer nemam više novca.
I must go to the bank because I have no money.

ought **morati**, **trebati**

On bi trebao to znati. He ought to know that.
Oni bi se morali ponašati bolje. They ought to behave better.

have to **morati**

Moram Vam priznati da ste me iznenadili.
I have to confess to you that you surprised me.
Moramo sve napraviti sami.
We have to do everything by ourselves.

be able to **moći**

Ja neću moći nositi sve kofere sama.
I won't be able to carry all the suitcases myself.
On ne može popraviti računalo.
He is not able to fix the computer.

dare **smjeti**

Tko smije spavati do deset kada imamo tako mnogo posla?
Who dares sleep until ten when we have so much to do?
Kako smiješ pušiti u bolnici?
How dare you smoke in the hospital?

The verb **trebati** and the verb **morati** are very close in meaning. While they are sometimes both translated as *ought*, there is a slight difference in meaning: **trebati** indicates a necessity, while **morati** indicates obligation. When the verb **trebati** designates a need, it is followed by an object or pronoun instead of a verb.

To remind yourself of how this verb is used in conjunction with the dative see p. 129.

3. Adjectival prefix pre-

If **pre-** is prefixed to a comparative form of an adjective, the resulting word corresponds to an adjective preceded by *too* in English. Thus the two forms that appear in this lesson **premlad** and **prevelik** mean *too young* and *too big* respectively. Because of their frequency, one should also memorize **premalo** *too little* and **previše** *too much.*

4. Collective nouns

Of several nouns in Croatian with irregular plurals, the most common one is **čovjek** *man*, with the plural **ljudi** *people*.The category of words such as **braća** *brothers*, **djeca** *children*, and **gospoda** *gentlemen* are irregular in that these nouns are *feminine singular nouns* although they have a *plural meaning and require a plural verb*:

Moja braća su u Bostonu.	My brothers are in Boston.
Dala sam darove svojoj djeci.	I gave presents to my children.

Several other collective nouns are neuter in gender and take a singular verb. As a rule, they also have a regular plural, but there is a difference in meaning between an ordinary plural form and that of the collective noun. While the regular plural emphasizes a group of individual items, the collective plural views the object as a whole. Here are some of the most frequent examples of this very small group of nouns:

singular	regular plural	collective plural
cvijet flower	**cvjetovi**	**cvijeće**
drvo tree	**drva**	**drveće**
grana branch	**grane**	**granje**
list leaf	**listovi**	**lišće**
kamen rock	**kamenovi**	**kamenje**

Several nouns, such as **novine** *newspaper*, **vrata** *door*, and **kola** *car* (colloquially) are always in the plural form.

5. Verbs of body position and movement

The concepts of sitting, lying, and standing are each expressed in Croatian through the use of three separate verbs: an imperfective verb for a stationary position, and two other verbs designating motion, one perfective and another imperfective. The first person singular, the third person plural, and the imperative forms are listed below:

to sit
sjediti (*I*, **sjedim**, **sjede**; **sjedi**) to be sitting
sjesti (*P* **sjednem**, **sjednu**; **sjedni**) to sit down once
sjedati (*I* **sjedam**, **sjedaju**; **sjedaj**) to sit down repeatedly

Be careful not to confuse this verb with **sijediti** (*I* **sijedim**, **sijede**; **sijedi**) *to turn gray.*

to lie (down)
ležati (*I* **ležim**, **leže**; **leži**) to be lying
leći (*P* **legnem**, **legnu**; **lezi**) to lie down
lijegati (*I* **liježem**, **liježu**; **liježi)** to lie down repeatedly

Be careful not to confuse this verb with **lagati** (*I* **lažem**, **lažu**; **laži**) *to lie* (not tell the truth).

to stand
stajati (*I* **stojim**, **stoje**; **stoj**) to stand
ustati (*P* **ustanem**, **ustanu**; **ustani**) to stand up, to get up
ustajati (*I* **ustajem**, **ustaju**; **ustaj**) to stand up or get up repeatedly

Be careful not to confuse this verb with **stati** (*P* **stanem**, **stanu**; **stani**) *to stop or to cease moving.*

6. Neuter *-en* and *-et* nouns

Just as some neuter nouns that we've already learned add **-en** (**ime** *name*, **vrijeme** *time, weather*, see Lesson 2) in cases other than the nominative and accusative, a few neuter nouns add **-et** in the singular of these cases. The most frequent ones are **dijete** *child* and **jaje** *egg*. This change also reduces **-ije** to **-je** in the word **dijete** (thus: **djeteta**). As noted above, the word **dijete** has an irregular plural, **djeca**.

	vrijeme (time, weather)	
	singular	**plural**
nom./acc.	**vrijeme**	**vremena**
gen.	**vremena**	**vremena**
dat./loc.	**vremenu**	**vremenima**
instru.	**vremenom**	**vremenima**

	dijete (child)		**jaje** (egg)	
	singular	**plural**	**singular**	**plural**
nom./acc.	**dijete**	**djeca**	**jaje**	**jaja**
gen.	**djeteta**	**djece**	**jajeta**	**jaja**
dat./loc.	**djetetu**	**djeci**	**jajetu**	**jajima**
instru.	**djetetom**	**djecom**	**jajetom**	**jajima**

Exercises

Vježba 14.1 Form the imperative for the 2nd person singular and plural from the verbs provided below:
Example: **čitati – čitaj, čitajte**

1. ići __________ __________
2. pogledati __________ __________
3. stanovati __________ __________
4. odmoriti se __________ __________
5. vratiti se __________ __________
6. pričati __________ __________
7. pomoći __________ __________
8. skrenuti __________ __________
9. pisati __________ __________
10. vjerovati __________ __________

Vježba 14.2
A. Match the Croatian sentence to the English sentence.

1. Bolestan sam.	a. I need medication for pain.
2. Imam glavobolju.	b. Could I get a prescription?
3. Imam opekotinu na nozi.	c. I am sick.
4. Mnogo kašljem.	d. I have a burn on my leg.
5. Trebam lijek protiv bolova.	e. I had a cold.
6. Mogu li dobiti recept.	f. I am coughing a lot.
7. Imala sam prehladu.	g. I have a headache.

B. Write a sentence describing each family member indicated below.

1. otac ____________________
2. tetka ____________________
3. majka ____________________
4. sestra ____________________
5. djed ____________________

Vježba 14.3
Translate into Croatian:

<u>It's difficult to be young –Teško je biti mlad</u>

My name is Sanja and I'm nine. It is not easy to be a child. Everyone tells you what you have to do, what you may and may not do. The first thing I hear in the morning is "Drink your milk," and then "Hurry up so you're not late for school." In school I hear "Children, write and don't talk." After that the teacher [učiteljica] says "Let Sanja read a new lesson." When I come home, my mother says "Wash your hands and eat lunch," and my father gets angry: "Be quiet, I have a headache." After that he asks me "Tell me the truth, have you gotten a bad grade [ocjena]?" My brother listens to music and says "Leave me alone!" When my friend Tina comes, we have a good time. Therefore I tell her "Come often!"

____
____
____
____
____
____
____
____
____
____
____
____
____

Vježba 14.4 Translate the following commands into Croatian using the verbs given below:

1. Be good! biti

   ____

2. Count the money! brojiti

   ____

3. Wait for him! čekati

   ____

4. Read your book, not mine! čitati

____

5. Please give me that bag! dati

____

6. Meet them at the train station! dočekati

____

7. Do not look at me that way! gledati

____

8. Do not go over there! ići

____

9. Eat your salad! jesti

____

10. Please buy me a new coat! kupiti

____

11. Do not buy cigarettes! kupovati

____

12. Do not think about that! misliti

____

13. Carry this to my house! odnijeti

____

14. Write him an e-mail! napisati

____

15. Do not leave yet! otići

____

16. Do not ask her anything! pitati

____

17. Look what they are doing! pogledati

____

18. Help me! pomoći

____

19. Pay the bill. No, you pay it! platiti

____

20. Do not do that! raditi

____

21. Do not listen to him! slušati

____

22. Put this book in that bag! staviti

____

Vježba 14.5 Create a dialogue using at least **10** of the words below.

odlazak	pogledati	mobitel	glazba
zgodan	zajedno	braća	pjevač
sin	dogovoriti	opekotina	Hrvat
karta	popiti	stric	super
knjiga	žena	noge	mnogo
računalo	umoran	boljeti	putni

____

____

____

____

____

____

____

____

____

____

____

____

Vježba 14.6 Translate the following sentences using verbs of body position and movement:

1. I like to sit down when I'm tired.

   ____

2. Lie down on that bed.

   ____

3. For how long have you been standing here?

   ____

4. She was sitting next to me.

   ____

5. He's been lying the whole day and not doing anything.

   ____

6. When I sit down, I don't like to get up.

   ____

7. I lie down every night at 10 p.m.

   ____

Vježba 14.7 Sažetak/Summary
Read the following text and insert the missing words:

Marijana je bila ________jer je vrijeme njezinog boravka u Hrvatskoj prošlo _______. Bližio se kraj _________. Dok je bila u Hrvatskoj, došla je do nekih ___________, ali u Americi su je čekali teški _________. Ivan joj je ________ da sada odlično govori _________, mnogo bolje nego što on __________ engleski.

Ivan i Marijana su odlučili ___________ po Tkalčičevoj ulici do Gornjeg grada. Tamo se ___________ crkva Svetog Marka i hrvatski Sabor. Darko __________ na Gornjem gradu, pa su poslije htjeli svratiti _______ njega. Marijana je ________ kupiti nekoliko darova za _________ obitelj i prijatelje u Americi. Da bi to napravila, prvo je trebala promijeniti __________ u mjenjačnici. Poslije toga, ona i Ivan su otišli u ___________ suvenira. Srećom, prodavaonica još nije bila _________ i u njoj je bio veliki izbor ___________. Marijana je kupila četiri stvari koje su _________ 575 kuna. Za majku je kupila __________, za ___________ kapu, za brata CD s hrvatskom narodnom ___________, a za _____________ knjigu o Hrvatskoj. Prijateljica bi htjela ___________ Hrvatsku. Ivan nije __________ da Marijana __________ brata. Njezin brat je ___________ i radi kao računalni programer. Ivanova ________ nije udana. Ona __________ pravo i ima dvadeset i jednu __________.

Ivan i Marijana su dugo __________, pa su se umorili. Marijana je htjela da ___________ Darka i kažu mu da će uskoro doći k njemu, ali Ivan je __________ da negdje sjednu. To je bila dobra __________ jer su tako imali priliku porazgovarati ___________ prije Marijaninog ___________.

Missing words:

oženjen
brzo
novac
tužan
predložiti
dar
govoriti
reći
nazvati

bluza
glazba
putovanje
zatvoren
zadatak
ideja
prijateljica
nasamo
hrvatski

odlazak
prošetati
studirati
kod
hodati
godina
stanovati
koštati
otac

željeti
zaključak
svoj
sestra
nalaziti
znati
prodavaonica
imati
posjetiti

Lekcija 15
Marijana se vraća u Ameriku

Lesson 15
Marijana returns to America

Lekcija 15: Marijana se vraća u Ameriku

Prvi dio

Darko: Marijana, jesi li gotova s pakiranjem?

Marijana: Evo, samo još nekoliko sitnica. Dobila sam mnogo darova za svoju obitelj, a neke sam i sama kupila, pa je sada kofer prilično težak.

Darko: Kada bi ostavila ovdje sve što ti neće trebati u Americi, imala bi manje prtljage.

Marijana: Ali, Darko, to sam i napravila! Nije strašno, samo jedan kofer!

Darko: Mislio sam da je gore! Ivan i ja odvest ćemo te u zračnu luku, a u Bostonu će te sigurno netko dočekati.

Marijana: Bez brige, brat će doći po mene. Razgovarala sam s njim sinoć. Rekao mi je da je dobio lijepe fotografije s našeg putovanja po Hrvatskoj koje sam mu poslala poštom.

Darko: Je li on ikada bio u Hrvatskoj?

Marijana: Davno, a i moji roditelji već dugo nisu bili ovdje. Ako budu htjeli, mogu me svi posjetiti iduće godine.

Zvoni Darkov mobitel.

Darko: Halo, Ivane, da, spremni smo. Evo, odmah silazimo!

Marijana (*tužno*): Blago tebi, ti ne moraš nikamo. Ivan je stigao?

Darko: Da, tu je. Provjeri imaš li putnu kartu, putovnicu i novčanik, pa onda idemo.

Marijana: Darko, molim te, drži moju torbu.

Darko: Čekaj, Marijana, ja ću nositi kofer, a ti torbu. Kofer je teži.

Lesson 15: Marijana returns to America

Part I

Darko: Marijana, are you finished packing?

Marijana: Here, just a few more small things. I got a lot of presents for my family and some I've purchased myself so my suitcase is quite heavy now.

Darko: If you left everything that you won't need in America here, you would have less luggage.

Marijana: But Darko, I have already done that! It is not too bad, just one suitcase!

Darko: I thought it was worse! Ivan and I will drive you to the airport, and in Boston there will certainly be someone waiting for you.

Marijana: Don't worry, my brother will wait for me. I spoke with him last night. He told me that he received the nice photographs from our trip across Croatia which I sent by mail.

Darko: Has he ever been to Croatia?

Marijana: Long ago, and my parents, too, have not been here for a long time. If they wish, they can all visit me next year.

Darko's cellphone rings.

Darko: Hello, Ivan, yes, we are ready. We are coming down immediately.

Marijana (*sadly*): Lucky you, you don't have to go anywhere. Ivan's come?

Darko: Yes, he's here. Check that you have your airline ticket, passport, and wallet, and then we can go.

Marijana: Darko, please hold my purse.

Darko: Wait Marijana, I'll carry the suitcase and you will carry the purse. The suitcase is heavier.

Malo kasnije u zračnoj luci.

Marijana: **Dečki, budite ljubazni i počekajte me nekoliko minuta. Idem potvrditi kartu i predati prtljagu.**

Darko: **Desno su domaći dolasci i odlasci, a lijevo međunarodni.**

Službenica: **Molim Vas, kartu i putovnicu. Je li to sve što imate od prtljage?**

Marijana: **Da. Izvolite.**

Službenica: **Želite li sjedalo uz prozor ili do prolaza?**

Marijana: **Uz prozor, molim.**

Službenica: **Vaš let polazi na vrijeme. Proći ćete prvo kroz kontrolu, a potom idite na izlaz broj 6. Želim Vam ugodan let!**

Marijana: **Hvala lijepa.**

Drugi dio

Marijana prilazi Ivanu.

Marijana: **Gdje je Darko?**

Ivan: **Tu je negdje. Vratit će se za nekoliko minuta.**

Marijana: **Uzbuđena sam jer ću uskoro vidjeti svoju obitelj i prijatelje, ali i tužna zato što odlazim. Bilo mi je vrlo lijepo u Hrvatskoj. Ti i Darko ćete mi vrlo nedostajati. Osobito ti Ivane.**

Ivan: **Nedostajat ćeš i ti meni, Marijana. Nemoj biti tužna jer će tih nekoliko tjedana začas proći. Ako ne budeš previše zauzeta, pošalji mi poruku s vremena na vrijeme. I ja ću tebi pisati. Tako će nam vrijeme brže proći.**

Marijana: **Ako nemaš ništa protiv, možemo se čuti i telefonski. Vremenska razlika je samo šest sati. Mogla bih te zvati navečer po hrvatskom vremenu. Znaš da moram vježbati hrvatski jezik.**

Ivan: **Svakako! To je izvrsna ideja! Šteta što je odmor tako brzo završio.**

A little later in the airport

Marijana:	Guys, be so kind and wait for me for a few minutes. I will first go to confirm my reservation and check in my luggage.
Darko:	To the right are domestic arrivals and departures, and to the left are the international.
Clerk:	Your ticket and passport please. Is that all you're checking in?
Marijana:	Yes. Here you are.
Clerk:	Would you like a window or an aisle seat?
Marijana:	Next to the window, please.
Clerk:	Your flight is leaving on time. First you will go through security and passport control, and afterwards go to gate number 6. Have a nice flight.
Marijana:	Thanks.

Part II

Marijana approaches Ivan.

Marijana:	Where is Darko?
Ivan:	Somewhere here. He will be back in a couple of minutes.
Marijana:	I am excited because soon I will see my parents and friends, but I am sad because I am leaving. I had a really nice time in Croatia. I will really miss you and Darko. Especially you, Ivan.
Ivan:	And I will miss you, Marijana. Do not be sad because these few weeks will pass in a flash. If you are not too busy, send me a message from time to time. And I will write you. That will make the time pass faster.
Marijana:	If you don't have anything against it, we could be in touch over the phone. The time difference is only six hours. I can call you in the evening according to Croatian time. You know that I must practice the Croatian language!
Ivan:	Of course! That is an excellent idea! Pity the holidays are already over.

Stiže Darko i čuje se obavijest preko razglasa: Molimo putnike na letu 461 Croatia Airlinesa za Frankfurt da se upute prema izlazu broj 6.

Marijana:	To je moj let! Dajte da se pozdravimo!
Darko:	Draga moja rođako, želim ti sretan put i da nam se što prije vratiš. Javi se čim stigneš u Boston.
Ivan:	Kako bih ti rekao ... tako mi je drago što smo se upoznali. Da sam znao da će biti ovako, otišao bih s tobom čak i u Ameriku. Jedva čekam da te opet vidim. Sretan put!
Darko:	Kakva je to ljubav?! Zar se nećete zagrliti i poljubiti? Evo, ja ću gledati na drugu stranu!
Marijana:	Ah, moram požuriti da ne bih zaplakala. Hvala vam na svemu. Pišite, zovite i vidimo se za nekoliko tjedana!
Darko i Ivan:	Doviđenja, Marijana!

Darko arrives and the announcement can be heard over the loudspeaker:
We ask passengers on Croatia Airlines flight 461 to Frankfurt to head to gate number 6.

Marijana:	That is my flight! Let's say goodbye!
Darko:	My dear cousin, I wish you a good journey and come back as soon as possible. Call as soon as you get to Boston.
Ivan:	How could I put this … I am so glad we got to know each other. If I had known that it would be like this, I would have gone all the way to America with you. I can hardly wait to see you again. Have a good trip!
Darko:	What kind of love is this?! Won't you hug and kiss one another? Here, I will look the other way!
Marijana:	Ah, I must hurry so that I don't start crying. Thank you both for everything. Write, call, and we will see each other in a few weeks!
Darko and Ivan:	Goodbye, Marijana!

Vocabulary

aerodrom airport
čim as soon as
davno long ago
dečko guy, boy
dolaz*a*k arrival
domaći domestic
izlaz exit
kofer suitcase
kontrola control
let flight
ljubav *f.* love
ljubaz*a*n kind
međunarodni international
navečer in the evening
obavijest announcement
osobito especially
pakiranje packing
preko over
prema toward
prolaz aisle, passage
protiv against
prozor window
prtljaga luggage
putni *adj.* travel
putnik passenger
razglas loudspeaker
razlika difference
sjedalo seat
službenica *f.* clerk
svakako by all means
uzbuđen excited

Verb List

dobiti (*P* **dobijem**, **dobiju**) to get, to obtain
dočekati (*P* **dočekam**, **dočekaju**) to meet, to wait for
držati (*I* **držim**, **drže**) to hold
javiti se (*P* **javim se** , **jave se**) to call, to get in touch
nedostajati (*I* **nedostajem**, **nedostaju**) to miss
nositi (*I* **nosim**, **nose**) to carry
odlaziti (*I* **odlazim**, **odlaze**) to leave
odvesti (*P* **odvezem**, **odvezu**) to give a ride
pakirati (*I* **pakiram**, **pakiraju**) to pack
počekati (*P* **počekam**, **počekaju**) to wait awhile
polaziti (*I* **polazim**, **polaze**) to leave, to set off
poljubiti (*P* **poljubim**, **poljube**) to kiss
poslati (*P* **pošaljem**, **pošalju**) to send
potvrditi (*P* **potvrdim**, **potvrde**) to confirm
pozdraviti (*P* **pozdravim**, **pozdrave**) to greet, to say farewell
predati (*P* **predam**, **predaju**) to drop off, to submit, to surrender
prilaziti (*I* **prilazim**, **prilaze**) to approach
proći (*P* **prođem**, **prođu**) to pass through, to pass by
provjeriti (*P* **provjerim**, **provjere**) to check

silaziti (*I* **silazim**, **silaze**) to descend
stizati (*I* **stižem**, **stižu**) to arrive
uputiti (*P* **uputim**, **upute**) to head, to direct
vježbati (*I* **vježbam**, **vježbaju**) to practice, to exercise
zagrliti (*P* **zagrlim**, **zagrle**) to embrace, to hug
zaplakati (*P* **zaplačem**, **zaplaču**) to cry

Useful Expressions

blago tebi lucky you
doći po nekoga/nešto to wait for someone/something [*lit.*: come get somebody/something]
budite ljubazni be so kind
domaći dolasci i odlasci domestic arrivals and departures
međunarodni odlasci international departures
Molim Vas, kartu i putovnicu. Your ticket and passport please.
Je li to sve što imate od prtljage? Is that all you're checking in?
Želite li sjedalo uz prozor ili do prolaza? Would you like a window or an aisle seat?
Vaš let polazi na vrijeme. Your flight is leaving on time.
Vaš let kasni. Your flight is late.
Proći ćete prvo kroz kontrolu. First you will go through security and passport control.
Idite na izlaz broj 6. Go to gate number 6.
začas proći to pass in a flash
s vremena na vrijeme from time to time
Ako nemaš ništa protiv . . . If you don't have anything against it . . .
Vremenska razlika je samo šest sati. The time difference is only six hours.
po hrvatskom vremenu according to Croatian time
Molimo putnike da se upute prema izlazu broj 6. We ask passengers to head to gate number 6.
Sretan put! Have a good trip!
Dajte da se pozdravimo! Let's say goodbye!
Hvala vam na svemu! Thank you for everything!
Vidimo se! See you!

Grammar

1. Future II

In addition to the future tense already discussed, Croatian has another future tense, the so-called *future II* or the *future exact*. This tense is typically used in compound constructions. It consists of the present perfective of the verb **biti** *to be* and the active past participle (the so called **l** participle).

Future II
pisati (to write)

	singular	plural		
	masc.	**fem.**	***masc.* & mixed**	***fem.***
1st	**budem pisao**	**budem pisala**	**budemo pisali**	**budemo pisale**
2nd	**budeš pisao**	**budeš pisala**	**budete pisali**	**budete pisale**
3rd	**bude pisao**	**bude pisala**	**budu pisali**	**budu pisale**

The future II is generally used together with another tense in order to indicate an action in the future that will precede some other future action:

Javit ću ti se kada *budem došao.*
I'll give you a call when *I arrive. (when I shall have arrived)*

Kada *budem dobila* novac, kupit ću novo računalo.
When *I get* the money, I'll buy a new computer. (*when I will have gotten the money)*

The future II is translated into English as the present simple but the meaning is future, as in the examples above: *when I shall have arrived* and *when I will have gotten the money.*

The same meaning can be expressed by using the perfective verb in the present tense:

Javit ću ti se kada *dođem.*
I'll give you a call when *I arrive.*
Kada *dobijem* novac, kupit ću novo računalo.
When *I get* the money, I'll buy a new computer.

The future II can also indicate two concurrent actions of which one is longer and the other one shorter in time:

Ako *budeš imao* vremena, dođi na kavu.
If *you have* time, come for a coffee.
Kada *budem putovao* po Hrvatskoj, posjetit ću Split.
When *I'm traveling* in Croatia, I'll visit Split.

2. *If* clauses

If or *conditional* clauses are used for situations in which the performance of a specific action depends on the performance of another action. As in English, there are three categories of *if*-clauses, those involving real conditions, possible conditions, and those which cannot be achieved. They are differentiated on the bases of the type of condition they express: real, possible, and unattainable.

Unlike in English, in which these types of sentences can be easily identified through the presence of the conjunction *if*, in Croatian there are several conjunctions, which all have the meaning of *if*:

ako	used in real conditions
kada, **ako**	used for possible conditions
da	used in unattainable conditions

Type I – real condition:

- **Ako budu htjeli, mogu me svi posjetiti tijekom iduće godine.**
  If they wish, they can all visit me in the course of next year.[1]
- **Ako ne budeš previše zauzeta, pošalji mi poruku s vremena na vrijeme.**
  If you are not too busy, send me a message from time to time.
- **Ako nemaš ništa protiv, možemo se čuti telefonski.**
  If you don't have anything against it, we could be in touch over the phone.

Type II – possible condition:

- **Kada/ako bi ostavila ovdje sve što ti neće trebati u Americi, imala bi manje prtljage.**
  If you left everything that you won't need in America here, you would have less luggage.

Type III – unattainable condition:

- **Da sam znao da će biti ovako, otišao bih s tobom čak i u Ameriku.**
  If I had known that it would be like this, I would have gone all the way to America with you.

---

1. Sometimes the same meaning is expressed by inversion and omission of **ako**: Budu li htjeli, mogu me svi posjetiti…

Aside from the different conjunctions, the most difficult problem for a native speaker of English is that the tenses used in Croatian *if*-constructions do not correspond to those in English.

The following chart is a summary of tense relations in *if*-clauses in English and Croatian, with the category *modal* indicating modal verbs such as *may*, *can*, *must*, *need*, etc.

	English		**Croatian**	
	subord. clause	**main clause**	**subord. clause**	**main clause**
Type I	present	future/modal	present/future II	future/modal
Type II	past	conditional	conditional	conditional
Type III	pluperfect	future perfect	past/present (*subjunctive meaning*)	conditional

Here are several more examples:

Type I – real condition:

- **Ako pročitate ovu knjigu, znat ćete sve.** (*present–future*)
  If you read this book, you will know everything.
- **Ako hoćete ovu knjigu, možete je odmah uzeti.** (*present–modal*)
  If you want this book, you can take it right away.
- **Ako dobijem novac, otići ću u kino.** (*present–future*)
  If I get money, I will go to the movies.
- **Ako budem dobio novac, otići ću u kino.** (*future II–future*)
  If I get money, I will go to the movies.

Type II – possible condition:

- **Kada biste pročitali ovu knjigu, znali biste sve.** (*conditional–conditional*)
  If you read this book, you would know everything.
- **Ako bih dobila novac, otišla bih u kino.** (*conditional–conditional*)
  If I got money, I would go to the movies.

Type III – unattainable condition:

- **Da ste pročitali ovu knjigu, znali biste sve.** (*past–conditional*)
  If you had read this book, you would have known everything.
- **Da sam dobila novac, otišla bih u kino.** (*past–conditional*)
  If I had gotten the money, I would have gone to the movies.
- **Da sam na tvom mjestu, potražio bih novi posao.** (*present–conditional*)
  If I were in your place, I would look for another job.

3. The expression *jedan drugi* (one another/each other)

While in English the expression *one another* or *each other* is fixed, in Croatian it changes depending on the verb with which it is used and takes the gender and the number of the subject.

The first part of the expression **jedan** meaning *one* can have the following forms:

jedan *m. sg./mixed sg.*	**jedni** *m. pl./mixed pl.*
jedna *f. sg.*	**jedne** *f. pl.*
jedno *n./mixed sg.*	**jedna** *n. pl.*

When the subjects are of mixed gender the default choice is masculine or neuter.

The second member of the pair **drugi** *other* takes the gender and number of the subject as well as the case required by the verb. Any required preposition is placed in between these two words. In some cases the same meaning *each other* can be expressed using the reflexive form of the verb.

Zar nećete zagrliti i poljubiti *jedno drugo*? (*mixed sg.*)
Zar se nećete zagrliti i poljubiti? *(reflexive verb)*
Won't you hug and kiss one another?

Mi vidimo *jedni druge*. (*m. pl./mixed pl.)*
Mi se vidimo. *(reflexive verb)*
We can see each other.

One često pišu *jedna drugoj*. (*f. sg.*)
They write to one another often.

Oni govore *jedni o drugima*. (*m. pl./mixed pl.)*
They are talking about each other.

Vi zovete *jedan drugog* svaki dan. (*m. sg.*)
You call one another every day.

4. Compound conjunctions

Certain types of prepositions in Croatian serve also as conjunctions that introduce subordinate clauses. Take these examples:

prep. + noun/pronoun:

Dođi *prije* puta.	Come *before* the trip.
Dođi *prije* mene.	Come *before* me.

prep. as conjunction + sub. clause:

Dođi *prije* nego što otputuješ.	Come *before* you depart.
Dođi *prije* nego što ja dođem.	Come *before* I come.

In the first set of examples above, in both Croatian and in English the preposition is followed by a noun or a pronoun. In the second set, it is followed by a *subordinate clause*, but in Croatian several *connecting* words—**nego što**—are added in addition to the preposition **prije** *before*.

The combination **nego što**, used to compare two actions, never changes:

On piše bolje *nego što* ona piše. He writes better *than* she does.

Here is a list of several *compound conjunctions* using the word ***što*** (meaning *than* in this context):

nego što than
On pliva bolje *nego što* ona pliva.
He swims better *than* she does.

prije nego što before
***Prije nego što* otputuješ, otiđi u muzej.**
Before you depart, go to the museum.

nakon što after
***Nakon što* je došao kući, otišao je na spavanje.**
After he came home, he went to sleep.

zato što because
Pitam te *zato što* mi ništa nije jasno.
I'm asking you *because* I don't understand anything.

While **zato što**, **zbog toga što** and **jer** (all meaning *because*) express cause, **zato** used *alone* expresses a purpose or reason.

Njoj je rođendan i *zato* su joj kupili dar.
It's her birthday and *therefore* they bought her a present.

tek što just, as soon as
***Tek što* je završio pisati jedan referat, već je morao početi drugi.**
As soon as he finished writing one paper, he had to start another one.

to što what, that which
Nije istina *to što* mi govoriš.
What you are telling me is not true.

Several conjunction phrases require that the demonstrative particle **to** take the genitive form **toga**. Thus *before that* and *after that* in Croatian are **prije toga** and **poslije toga**, respectively. Two other of the most important examples include:

zbog toga što because *(interchangeable with **zato što** and **jer**)*
Pitam te *zbog toga što* mi ništa nije jasno.
I'm asking you *because* I don't understand anything.

osim toga što in addition to, except for
***Osim toga što* je bio dobar student, on je i radio.**
In addition to being a good student, he also worked.

Appendix: The Pluperfect & Past Conditional Tenses

Pluperfect

The pluperfect is one of the several past tenses in Croatian (along with the rather archaic aorist and imperfect, which will not be discussed in this book) whose frequency of use is diminishing. The pluperfect is rather simple in terms of its formation. It consists of the past tense of the verb **biti** *to be* and the past participle (the **l participle**) of the given verb. The pronoun can be omitted, but in that case the auxiliary form of **biti** cannot occur in the initial position in the sentence. As in English, it is used to indicate an action that took place before some other action in the past.

Here's the example for *had bought*:

had bought
past of **biti** (to be) + **l participle** of **kupiti** (to buy)

	masculine *sg.*	**feminine *sg.***
1st	**bio sam kupio**	**bila sam kupila**
2nd	**bio si kupio**	**bila si kupila**
3rd	**bio je kupio**	**bila je kupila**

had bought
past of **biti** (to be) + **l participle** of **kupiti** (to buy)

	m.* & mixed *pl.	***f. pl.***
1st	**bili smo kupili**	**bile smo kupile**
2nd	**bili ste kupili**	**bile ste kupile**
3rd	**bili su kupili**	**bile su kupile**

Bio sam kupio auto, pa sam ga onda prodao.
I had bought the car and then I sold it.
Ja sam već bila otišla kada je on došao.
I had already left when he arrived.

Past conditional

In regard to Croatian *if*-clauses, type III (unattainable condition) allows for the use of a past tense in the subordinate clause, and the past conditional in the main clause. This type of sentence emphasizes the temporal frame and the fact that the unreal condition took place in the past. The past conditional consists of the conditional form of the verb **biti** *to be* and the past **l participle**: **bio bih kupio/bila bih kupila** *I would have bought.* As this combination of tenses is less frequently used, here is one example, solely for illustrative purposes:

Da sam dobila novac, bila bih otišla u kino. (*past–past conditional*)
If I had gotten the money, I would have gone to the movies.

Exercises

Vježba 15.1 Answer the following questions:

1. Što ćete raditi kada bude ljeto?
2. Što ćete kupiti kada budete imali novca?
3. Koje ćete gradove posjetiti kada budete u Hrvatskoj?
4. Što ćete raditi kada budete imali vremena?
5. Kada budete išli u kino, koji ćete film pogledati?
6. Hoćete li učiti hrvatski kada večeras budete kod kuće?
7. Što mislite, što će Marijana raditi kada bude u Americi?
8. Što će raditi Ivan dok bude čekao Marijanu?
9. Što će se dogoditi kada Marijana i Ivan budu ponovo zajedno u Hrvatskoj?

Vježba 15.2 Translate the following sentences using the future II.

1. I will read the newspaper while I'm eating lunch.

2. When he is traveling through Croatia, he should travel to the South.

   ____

3. When you have finished writing the report, come and we'll watch a film.

   ____

4. When you're buying bread for yourself, please buy 1kg for me too.

   ____

5. Don't be scared while you're speaking with her.

   ____

6. When we arrive, everything will be all right.

   ____

7. When they are at college, they can (will be able to) live in a dorm or in their own apartment.

   ____

8. When you speak Croatian well, nobody will know that you're American.

   ____

9. While I am driving to Pula, I'll listen to good music and I won't be bored.

   ____

10. When you're in Split, by all means visit Diocletian's palace.

    ____

Vježba 15.3
Translate into Croatian:

<u>Unreliable colleague – Nepouzdani kolega</u>

If Hrvoje calls, tell him that I'm not at home. I'm very angry. One moment he is here, another he is not. As a matter of fact, he is never here when I need him. If he had brought the materials on Wednesday, I would have finished the project [projekt]. This way I have a big problem. What will my boss think? He will not be satisfied, that's for sure. He will say "When you finish your projects on time [na vrijeme], you will get a raise [p<u>o</u>višica]. Nothing until then." Whose fault is this? No way is it mine, but rather Hrvoje's. One [čovjek] can't count on him at all. If he wishes, he can apologize to me. If he does that, maybe I'll speak with him again.

____

____

____

____

____

____

____

____

____

____

____

____

Vježba 15.4

A. Find the matching pairs:

1. Ako mi kupiš ručak danas	a. ne bismo zakasnili na vlak.
2. Da si došao na vrijeme	b. mogao bih kupiti kuću.
3. Ako nas nazovu danas	c. sada ne biste lutali.
4. Ako ikada budete putovali u Rim	d. sigurno bi otišla tamo na odmor.
5. Kada ona dođe	e. svakako posjetite arenu.
6. Ako biste htjeli ići na Hvar	f. reci joj da otiđe u trgovinu.
7. Ako bih dobio novi posao	g. ja ću te odvesti u kino.
8. Da ste poslušali Marka i uzeli plan grada	h. moći ćemo se o svemu dogovoriti.
9. Da ona zna kako je lijepo na Jadranu	i. mogli bismo otići na izlet zajedno.

B. Translate into English:

1. If you had passed the exam, you could have gone to the party.

   ____

   ____

2. If you wish, you can sleep.

   ____

   ____

3. If you love me, you'll buy me everything.

   ____

   ____

4. If he had come, she would have seen him.

   ____

   ____

5. If they had done it, we would not have had a problem.

____

____

6. If you ask him to come, he will come.

____

____

7. If she invited me, I would visit her.

____

____

8. If she gets the letter, she will know that we are in Zagreb.

____

____

9. If they speak on the phone today, he will know that we left.

____

____

10. If we had traveled to Split, we would have spent the holidays better.

____

____

11. If you just followed the map, this trip would take far less time.

____

____

12. If I ever have some free time again, I will write a novel.

____

____

Vježba 15.5 Practice the expression **jedan drugi** *each other*. Replace *we* with *you* and *they* and change gender.

1. We see one another.

____

____

2. We are writing to one another.

____

____

3. We are cooking lunch for one another.

4. We congratulated one another.

5. We spoke to one another.

6. We bought a present for one another.

7. We like one another a lot.

8. We ask one another lots of questions.

9. We call one another every week.

Vježba 15.6 Provide context (3–4 sentences) for the following situations:

1. Da ste položili ispit, mogli biste na zabavu.

2. Kakva sreća! Da nisi nazvao, zaspao bih i zakasnio na avion.

3. Imamo iste interese. Kada bismo potpisali ugovor, mogli bismo svi zaraditi mnogo novca.

4. Tko se koristio mojim računalom?!? Ako ga pronađem, morat će mi objasniti zašto ništa ne radi!

   ____

   ____

5. Ma ne mogu vjerovati! Jesi li to ti? Da sam otišla odavde samo pet minuta ranije, ne bih te vidjela.

   ____

   ____

6. Hladnjak je opet prazan! Ako stignem, otići ću u samoposluživanje. Ako ne stignem, morat ćeš otići ti.

   ____

   ____

7. Baš Vas nisam očekivala sada! Da ste mi se javili prije, pripremila bih sve materijale.

   ____

   ____

8. Rado bismo se opet vidjeli s vama! Ako budete mogli, svakako nas posjetite u Americi.

   ____

   ____

Vježba 15.7 Sažetak/Summary
Read and insert the missing words:

Marijana je ____________za odlazak. Dobila je mnogo ____________ za __________ obitelj, a neke je i sama ____________, pa je kofer prilično ___________. Darko predlaže da ostavi stvari koje joj neće _______________ u Hrvatskoj. Marijana je to i napravila i zato ima samo jedan _______________. Ivan i Darko će je _______________ na aerodrom, a u Bostonu će je __________ brat. Brat je dobio lijepe ____________ s Marijaninog _____________ po Hrvatskoj koje mu je _______________ poštom. On dugo nije __________ u Hrvatskoj, pa će posjetiti Marijanu _____________ se ona vrati u Zagreb. Možda će _____________ i njezini roditelji.

Ivan je nazvao __________ telefon da kaže Marijani i _____________da je stigao. Marijana ______________ ima li ____________ kartu, putovnicu i _______________. Poslije ____________ona i Darko silaze. Darko nosi kofer, a Marijana __________ jer je torba lakša od __________. Kada su došli u zračnu __________, Marijana prvo odlazi ____________ kartu i predati ____________. Darko joj pokazuje gdje su ________________ odlasci. Marijana daje ______________ svoje isprave i prtljagu. Njezin let polazi na ______________.

Marijana kaže Ivanu da je ______________ jer ću uskoro vidjeti svoju obitelj i prijatelje. Ali ona je i ________________ zato što odlazi. Bilo joj je _________ u Hrvatskoj, a Darko i Ivan će joj vrlo _____________. Osobito Ivan. Ivan je isto tužan, ali kaže da će tih nekoliko _____________ proći začas. On predlaže ______________ da mu šalje poruke ako ne bude previše ______________. Marijana želi da se oni čuju _____________ jer ona mora _____________ hrvatski jezik! Ona sigurno želi ______________ s Ivanom i iz drugih razloga!

Uskoro ____________ Darko i čuje se obavijest ____________ razglasa. Marijana mora otići na ___________ broj 6. Svi se pozdravljaju. Darko želi Marijani __________ put i da se što prije vrati u ____________. Ivan bi htio reći mnogo toga, ali kaže samo da bi rado ___________ s Marijanom u Ameriku kada bi ___________. Darko kaže da se Marijana i Ivan moraju ____________ i poljubiti. On sve razumije i šali se kao i uvijek. Marijana žuri da ne bi _______________. Oni će pisati i zvati jedni ____________ i vidjet će se opet za ________________ tjedana.

Ključ za Vježbe – Key to the Exercises

Lesson 1

Vježba 1.2
A. 1) Dobar; Da 2) Ne, ja sam student. 3) Tko 4) Vaš 5) zovete 6) zovem; zove
B. Vi; dan; mi; moj; Kako; se; Nisam

Vježba 1.3
1) *f.*, airport; 2) *m.*, friend; 3) *f.*, American; 4) *m.*, cousin; 5) *neu.*, place

Vježba 1.4
1) sam; 2) smo; 3) on; 4) ti; 5) su; 6) ste; 7) je; 8) ja; 9) on; 10) nisi; 11) mi; 12) niste

Vježba 1.5
A. 1) Kako se zoveš? 2) Jesi li ti student ili turist? 3) On je moj prijatelj. 4) Jesi li ti Amerikanac (Amerikanka)? 5) On ne zna jesam li ja student. 6) Oni znaju da ti radiš. 7) Drago mi je. 8) Svi smo mladi. Ja sam tvoj hrvatski rođak.
B. Zovem se Petra. Mlada sam. Nisam Amerikanka. Govorim hrvatski. Ja sam studentica i ne radim. John je moj prijatelj. On je student kao i ja. On govori engleski.

Vježba 1.6
1) noun; 2) adjective; 3) verb; 4) noun; 5) verb

Vježba 1.7
1) Da, ja sam turist. 2) Ne, ne govorim engleski. 3) Da, već radim. 4) Zovem se Ana. 5) Odlično! A Vi?

Lesson 2

Vježba 2.1
Informal address: 1) Kako 2) kamo, putuješ 3) roditelji, Amerikanka, Hrvat 4) razumiješ, govoriš 5) možeš, ponoviti
Formal address: 1) Kako ste? 2) kamo, putujete 3) roditelji, Amerikanka, Jeste li Vi Hrvat ili Amerikanac? 4) Razumijete, govorite 5) Oprostite, možete li ponoviti?

Vježba 2.2
1) Nitko ništa ne razumije. 2) Ništa nije dobro ovdje. 3) Nigdje ne vidim moj auto. 4) Ne radim kao ekonomist.

Vježba 2.3
beginning–početak; Croatia–Hrvatska; now–sada; žedna–thirsty; pomalo–a little bit; well–dobro; or–ili; very–vrlo; zbunjen–confused; like–kao; excellently–odlično; language–jezik; life–život; loše–badly; moguće–possible; velik–big; to love–voljeti; place–mjesto; turist–tourist; odmor–vacation; what–što; day–dan; often–često;

key–ključ; happy–sretan; regrettably–nažalost; there–tamo; mladi–young; sigurno–definitely; gdje–where; zajedno–together; nastavak–continuation

Vježba 2.4

1) govorim, govori, govore; 2) idem, ide, idu; 3) šalim se, šali se, šale se; 4) živim, živi, žive; 5) znam, zna, znaju; 6) mogu, može, mogu; 7) zovem, zove, zovu; 8) putujem, putuje, putuju; 9) pišem, piše, pišu; 10) oprostim, oprosti, oproste

Vježba 2.5

A. 1) To je moj omiljeni grad. 2) To je moj auto. 3) Mislim da počinje jedna lijepa priča. 4) Kako si? 5) Gdje su moji ključevi?
B. 1) The story is good. 2) And where do you live? 3) Do you speak English? 4) I am very thirsty and hungry. 5) I constantly hurry and always work.

Vježba 2.6

1) vremena; 2) majke; 3) auta; 4) gradovi; 5) turisti; 6) muževi; 7) studenti; 8) žene; 9) knjige; 10) vlakovi; 11) Splićani; 12) počeci; 13) starci; 14) pjesnici; 15) Amerikanci

Vježba 2.7

1) A: Dobar dan, da se upoznamo. Ja sam XY. B: Drago mi je. Ja se zovem ZW. A: *Baš lijepo što ste ovdje.*
2) A: *Dobar dan, kako ste?* B: Dobro, a Vi? A: Ja sam odlično!
3) A: Kako ste? B: *Tako-tako.* Ne znam gdje su moji ključevi. Kako ste Vi? A: Ja sam dobro. Ključevi su ovdje. B: Ah, da, hvala lijepa.
4) A: *Oprostite,* govorite li engleski? B: Ne baš dobro. A: Znate li gdje je zračna luka? B: Zračna luka je tamo.
5) A: Kako ste? B: *Dobro, a Vi?* A: Loše. Stalno žurim i uvijek radim. To nije dobar život. B: Hrvatska je odlična zemlja za odmor. A: Slažem se. Tamo ne radim.
6) A: *Kako si?* B: Odlično. Kako si ti? A: Nije loše. B: Ovo je moja rođaka Marijana. B: Drago mi je. Ja sam XY.
7) A: Dobra večer, kako ste? B: *Loše!* Ne znam što mogu raditi. A: Vi se šalite! Možete putovati i pisati. Zašto ništa ne radite? Ja uvijek nešto radim!
8) A: Kako ste danas? B: *Hvala, dobro.* Hrvatska je odlična zemlja za odmor. A: Slažem se! Ja sam Amerikanac, ali često sam ovdje.

Lesson 3

Vježba 3.1

također–also; friend–prijatelj; or–ili; highway–autocesta; grad–city; radije–preferably; place–mjesto; quite–prilično; price–cijena; kada–when; dan–day; žut–yellow; dugo–long; zelen–green; new–nov; naravno–of course; extraordinary–izvrstan; blue–plav; već–already; nigdje–nowhere; jeftin–cheap, inexpensive; exam–ispit; easy–lako; driver–vozač; beginning–početak; interesting–zanimljiv; nešto–something; sunčano–sunny; posao–job; osobina–trait; prijevoz–transportation; godina–year

Vježba 3.2
A. film *m.* Čiji je to film?.; knjiga *f.* Koja je to knjiga?; noć *f.* Kakva je ova noć?; student *m.* Koji student je Amerikanac?; ispit *m.* Kakav je to ispit?; boja, *f.* Koja je Vaša omiljena boja?
B. 1) Kakvo; 2) Koji; 3) Čiji; 4) Koji; 5) Koji/čiji

Vježba 3.3
1. Oni ekonomisti su pametni. 2. Tko je taj mršavi student? 3. Ovo je zanimljivo mjesto. 4. Kako se zove tvoj visoki rođak? 5. On je novi vozač. 6. To je težak ispit. 7. Danas je hladan dan. 8. Hrvatski nije lak jezik. 9. Mali ključ je moj, a veliki je njegov. 10. Ovo je sretna priča.

Vježba 3.4
1) odličan; 2) star; 3) dobro; 4) vrlo loš; 5) nova

Vježba 3.5
A. 1) pisma; 2) dani; 3) vozači; 4) poslovi; 5) problemi; 6) gradovi; 7) vremena; 8) ispiti; 9) cijene; 10) Zagrepčani
B. 1) Ja danas pišem dugo *pismo.* 2) Danas je lijep *dan.* 3) Tko je ovdje dobar *vozač*? 4) Volite li novi *posao*? 5) Benzin nije jeftin i to je europski *problem.* 6) Je li ovo veliki *grad*? 7) Kada je *vrijeme* sunčano, ja šetam. 8) Jesu li teški *ispiti* sada gotovi? 9) Povoljna *cijena* je važna kao i model. 10) Je li *Zagrepčani* dobro žive?

Vježba 3.6
A. 1) beautiful; 2) old; 3) big; 4) rich; 5) excellent; 6) interesting; 7) young; 8) bad; 9) sweet; 10) good
B. 1) *lijepo* mjesto; 2) *star/i* prijatelj; 3) *velik/i* auto; 4) *bogata* žena; 5) *odlična* priča; 6) *zanimljiv/i* ispit; 7) *mlada* Hrvatica; 8) *loše* vrijeme; 9) *sladak/slatki* pas; 10) *dobro* pitanje

Vježba 3.7
1) adverb; 2) adjective; 3) adverb; 4) adjective; 5) adverb; 6) adjective

Lesson 4

Vježba 4.1
1) Molim Vas; 2) Keep the change; 3) Jeftino je; 4) Thank you very much; 5) Molim Vas, račun; 6) Tako-tako; 7) So nice that you're here. 8) Oprostite; 9) Dobro jutro; 10) I would like to order.

Vježba 4.2
1) Taj auto je *lijep* i *nov*. Imam *lijepi novi* auto. 2) To *vino* je *bijelo*. Imam *bijelo vino.* 3) To su *sretni studenti*. Vidim *sretne studente*. 4) Ta *hrana* je *dobra* i *skupa*. Želim *dobru skupu hranu*. 5) Taj *konobar* je *spor* i *tužan*. Ne volim *sporog tužnog konobara.*

Vježba 4.3
1) to go; idem, ideš, ide, idemo, idete, idu; 2) to drink; pijem, piješ, pije, pijemo, pijete, piju; 3) can, be able to; mogu, možeš, može, možemo, možete, mogu; 4) to wish, to want; želim, želiš, želi, želimo, želite, žele; 5) to see; vidim, vidiš, vidi,

vidimo, vidite, vide; 6) to ask; pitam, pitaš, pita, pitamo, pitate, pitaju; 7) to have; imam, imaš, ima, imamo, imate, imaju; 8) to come; dođem, dođeš, dođe, dođemo, dođete, dođu; 9) to walk; hodam, hodaš, hoda, hodamo, hodate, hodaju; 10) to hurry; žurim, žuriš, žuri, žurimo, žurite, žure

Vježba 4.4
A. 1) Idemo *na* odmor. 2) Vidimo se *u* srijedu! 3) Ta juha je *za* mene. 4) Kada putujete *u* Zadar? 5) Hodam *kroz* vrt.
B. 1) Knjiga je za tebe. 2) Vidim ih. 3) Ona ga poznaje. 4) Posjećujemo ju često. 5) Moji prijatelji misle na mene. 6) Ima li nešto za nas? 7) Imam ga/je.

Vježba 4.5
1) Zovem, zoveš; 2) mi, zovem, ribu; 3) pijem, auto, dobro; 4) ideš, idem Pulu; 5) juhu i ribu; 6) palačinke, ih, dobre; 7) dođe, petak; 8) Želim jesti meso na žaru, mineralnu vodu; 9) hranu, Marijanu i Ivana; 10) nemaš, auto, ključeve; 11) filmove, knjige, filmove; 12) ništa ne, znaju

Vježba 4.6
A. 1) brz – d. spor; 2) bučan – e. tih; 3) nizak – c. visok; 4) lijep – a. ružan; 5) sretan – b. tužan; 6) jak – g. slab; 7) pametan – f. glup
B. 1) naručiti; 2) u; 3) dobro došla; 4) kažeš 5) pametnog

Vježba 4.7
A. 1. Nemate vruću juhu? 2. Imaju novi jelovnik. 3. Nemaš brzi auto. 4. Imam odličnog prijatelja. 5. Profesor ima pametne studente. 6. Imamo dobre autoceste. 7. Koji grad ima jeftin javni prijevoz?
B. 1. Jesi li siguran/sigurna da nisi umoran/umorna? 2. Pitamo se da li razumiju povijest./Pitamo se razumiju li povijest. 3. Želim da on vozi. 4. Da jedemo meso na žaru? 5. Idem u Šibenik da vidim prijatelje. 6. Budući da govorim hrvatski, želim vidjeti tu zemlju. 7. Kada da dođem?

Lesson 5

Vježba 5.1
1) c. problema; 2) c. bez; 3) c. tisuća; 4) c. mene; 5) c. vodu; 6) b. auto; 7) b. njih; 8) b. ju; 9) c. moje sestre; 10) c. centra

Vježba 5.2
1) without; Ne mogu *bez* tebe.; 2) by, at someone's place; *Kod* njega je bučno.; 3) after; Što radiš poslije ručka?; 4) from; Jeste li *iz* Zagreba ili *iz* Dubrovnika?; 5) to; Idemo *do* centra, a kamo Vi idete?; 6) around; Hodam *oko* kuće i ne nalazim ključeve. 7) after; *Nakon* filma idemo na večeru. 8) near; Žive li oni *blizu* željezničkog kolodvora?; 9) between; Što se nalazi *između* tebe i njega? 10) from; *Od* Zagreba do Splita nije daleko.

Vježba 5.3
A. 1) knjige; 2) muževa; 3) tramvaja; 4) zgrada; 5) studenata; 6) katova; 7) pisama; 8) stvari; 9) oglasa; 10) zadataka; 11) prozora; 12) profesorice

B. 1) Ako preporučuješ tu *knjigu*, sigurno je dobra. 2) Vidim tvojeg *muža*, ali ne vidim mojeg. 3) Nema niti *tramvaja*, niti autobusa. 4) *Zgrada* je dobra, ali je daleko od centra. 5) Imaš puno *studenata* jer si dobar profesor. 6) Treći kat, a nema dizala! 7) Ja volim duga i kratka *pisma*. 8) Ili imaš ili nemaš tu stvar. 9) Danas je nedjelja, pa ima puno *oglasa*. 10) Je li to moj ili tvoj *zadatak*? 11) *Prozor* je tamo, a krevet je ovdje. 12) Ona je *profesorica* i ona odlično govori hrvatski.

Vježba 5.4

A, Imam mnogo prijatelja. Gabriella je iz Italije, ali njezina majka je iz Engleske. Igor je iz Rusije, ali njegov otac je iz Grčke. Andrew je iz Kanade, a Soomi je iz Južne Koreje. Ines je iz Argentine, a Nino iz Portugala. Moji hrvatski prijatelji su iz Starog Grada, Pule, Vukovara i Gospića.
B. Ima li bijelog vina/slatkih kolača/odlične hrane/tople juhe/skupe ribe/dobrog mesa/hladne vode/zelene salate?

Vježba 5.5

1) It also has a nice courtyard. 2) I am afraid of that professor. 3) To je loša cijena za ovu lokaciju. 4) Želim čašu vode i miješanu salatu. 5) I see your friend's car. Is he a student or does he work? 6) On je zauzet danas, ali lijepo od njega što hoće pomoći.

Vježba 5.6

1) What is there and what isn't there? Ovdje ima novina, ali nema knjiga. 2) Where is x? Here is x! Gdje je ormar? Evo ormara! 3) What are you doing before lunch? Prije ručka radim. 4) What are you doing after lunch? Poslije ručka tražim novi stan. 5) Who has the keys of my new car? Ključevi od mojeg novog auta su kod Darka. 6) Where are you from? Ja sam iz San Francisca. 7) How far is it from your house to the center? Od moje kuće do centra ima pet minuta pješke. 8) What is in front of you? Ispred mene je profesor. 9) What is behind you? Iza mene su studenti. 10) Whose book are you reading? Čitam Marijaninu knjigu. 11) What can you not [be] without? Ja ne mogu bez hrane i vode. 12) Of what/whom are you afraid? Ne bojim se ničega.

Vježba 5.7

A. Želim kupiti malo kruha i nekoliko sitnica. Živim blizu centra i ne trebam tramvaj. Idem pješke. Dan je lijep. Srećem Marka i idemo na pivo. Gledamo nogometnu utakmicu. Dugo sjedimo ispred televizora. Poslije toga, kada dođemo u trgovinu, više nema kruha. Nema ničega. Ovo nije dobro jer sam gladan. Što sada? Kažem „Može se živjeti bez piva, ali ne bez kruha." Marko se ne slaže: „Ne, ne može se živjeti bez piva." On se voli šaliti. Smije se i kaže: „Idemo kod mene. Ja sam odličan kuhar."
B. Moj stan je velik i lijep. Imam dvosoban stan. Nalazi se blizu centra. Zgrada je nova i čista i ima dizalo. Moj stan ima puno prozora i sunčan je. Gleda na ulicu, ali ta ulica nije prometna. Stan je tih. Ima malu kuhinju i dvije velike sobe. Tamo su stol, stolice, krevet, ormar i veliki televizor. Ormar je do kreveta, a televizor je ispred kreveta. Ja volim svoj stan.

Lesson 6

Vježba 6.1
1) devet stanova; 2) jedan hladnjak; 3) jedanaest jabuka; 4) četiri paketa; 5) dvadeset pet računa; 6) dvadeset dvije strane 7) trideset četiri tržnice; 8) trideset sokova 9) pedeset jedno dizalo; 10) sto stolova

Vježba 6.2
1) deveti; 2) prvi; 3) jedanaesti; 4) četvrti; 5) dvadeset peti; 6) dvadeset drugi 7) trideset četvrti; 8) trideseti 9) pedeset prvi; 10) stoti

Vježba 6.3
1) Rođen sam dvadesetog šestog/lipnja tisuću devetsto osamdeset i pete godine. 2) Danas je dvanaesti devetog/rujna dvije tisuće i šeste godine. 3) Putujemo petog prvog/siječnja. 4) Rođena sam tridesetog petog/svibnja tisuću devetsto šezdeset devete godine. 5) Danas je drugi jedanaestog/studenog.

Vježba 6.4
1) It's two o'clock now. 2) Sada su tri sata i dvanaest minuta. 3) It's half past four now. 4) Sada je petnaest do deset. 5) It's twenty to two.

Vježba 6.5
1) krevete; 2) ormara; 3) stanovi; 4) cijena; 5) studenata; 6) mjesece; 7) godine; 8) oglase; 9) konobare; 10) studentica; 11) ribe; 12) ljude; 13) sniženja; 14) vremena; 15) ekonomisti; 16) Amerikanci; 17) auta; 18) odmore; 19) osobina; 20) noći

Vježba 6.6
1) sira / kobasica / kruha; 2) petak / srijedu / 3 sata; 3) čašu vode / zelenu salatu / miješano meso; 4) mojeg brata / moje majke / moje rođake; 5) mjesec dana / pet godina / tri tjedna

Vježba 6.7
A. 1) Marijana danas mora kupiti namirnice i neke stvari za stan. 2) Samoposluživanje je blizu. 3) Ispred trgovine se nalazi tržnica. 4) Marijana i Darko moraju sve završiti do četiri sata. 5) Marijana kupuje sir, salamu, sok, kruh, kolače, dva kilograma šećera, sedam litara mineralne vode, paket kave, jedan deterdžent, jedan šampon i tri sapuna. 6) Darko traži sok. 7) Svega ima, samo nema jogurta. 8) Blagajna je kod izlaza. 9) Poslije toga Marijana kupuje jabuke i grožđe. 10) Sutra Marijana želi razgledati neke znamenitosti. Ona želi vidjeti Hrvatsko narodno kazalište i Muzej Mimara.
B. 1) Ja obično kupujem kruh, jogurt, mineralnu vodu, meso i salatu. 2) Više volim male trgovine. 3) Hrana nije skupa. 4) Danas je devetnaesti kolovoza dvije tisuće i sedme. 5) Putujem u Tokyo šesnaestog siječnja. 6) Moj rođendan je dvadeset i osmog travnja. 7) Sada pišem na hrvatskom jeziku. 8) Sada je deset sati i šest minuta. 9) Obično ručam u dvanaest i trideset. 10) Obično idem spavati u petnaest do dvanaest.

Vježba 6.8
1) deset do šest; 2) dvadeset do jedanaest; 3) dvanaest i petnaest; 4) sedam sati; 5) tri sata i trideset minuta; 6) pet minuta do pet; 7) devet sati; 8) petnaest do dva; 9) dvanaest i trideset

Lesson 7

Vježba 7.1
1) toward; Idem *k* njima. 2) toward; Idem *prema* izlazu broj osam. 3) all over, apiece, according to; Oni su hodali *po* ulici. 4) in, at; *U* gradu je bilo mnogo velikih zgrada. 5) opposite from; *Nasuprot* mojoj zgradi je samoposluživanje.

Vježba 7.2
1) u kupovini; 2) u kinu; 3) na brodu; 4) na/u zrakoplovu; 5) na predstavi; 6) na večeri; 7) na stadionu; 8) u kući; 9) na ulici; 10) u gradu; 11) u restoranu; 12) na fakultetu; 13) na koncertu; 14) na autocesti; 15) na poslu

Vježba 7.3
1) U utorak putujem u Boston. Sada sam u Bostonu. 2) Danas idem u Vinkovce. Danas sam u Vinkovcima. 3) Tko ide u Karlovac? Tko je u Karlovcu? 4) Želim putovati u Rijeku. Sada sam u Rijeci. 5) Tko vozi u Dugo Selo? Ja sam u Dugom Selu. 6) Kada ideš u London? Već sam u Lodonu. 7) Kada on dođe u Zagreb, idemo u kino. On je sada u Zagrebu, pa idemo u kino. 8) Putujem u Washington u prosincu. Sada je prosinac i ja sam u Washingtonu. 9) Sutra idem u Split. Imam veliki stan u Splitu. 10) Često putujem u Portland. U Portlandu je lijepo.

Vježba 7.4
A. 1) mi; 2) se; 3) Tebi; 4) na; 5) idući; 6) im; 7) sastanak; 8) nam, mi; 9) zar ne; 10) mojem
B. 1. Čita mi se nešto. 2. Ništa mi se ne jede. 3. Ne čeka mi se. 4. Ide mi se kući. 5. Ne razgovara mi se.

Vježba 7.5
A. 1) velikoj knjizi; 2) lijepoj zemlji; 3) zagrebačkom fakultetu; 4) malom brodu; 5) starom kazalištu
B. 1) velikim knjigama; 2) lijepim zemljama; 3) zagrebačkim fakultetima; 4) malim brodovima; 5) starim kazalištima

Vježba 7.6
1) Njemu je uvijek dosadno u školi jer je vrlo pametan. 2) Što tvoj otac sada radi? Treba mi! 3) Dosta mi je! Idem kući. 4) Darko hoda prema nama. Tamo je, nasuprot Ivanu. 5) Žao mi je, ali imam važni poslovni sastanak. 6) To mu je vrlo teško! 7) Ne radi mi se sada. 8) Hladno mi je! 9) Što ti radi prijatelj? 10) Sviđa mi se taj auto.

Vježba 7.7
Ja sam poduzetnik. Zovem se Anton Lučić. Rođen sam u Zadru. Imam trideset šest godina. Meni se sviđaju stare kuće, pa ih popravljam. Volim putovati, ali Zadar je moj omiljeni grad. To je vrlo stari grad na moru. Ima zanimljivu arhitekturu. Ja

nemam ženu, ali imam brata i sestru. Moj brat je arhitekt, a sestra je prevoditeljica. Ja i moj brat često radimo na projektima zajedno. On mi mnogo pomaže. Ja volim svoj posao.

Lesson 8

Vježba 8.1
A. 1) Kakav lijep *dar*! Ovo će mi stvarno dobro doći! 2) Ne sviđa mi se bučna *glazba*! Moj omiljeni kompozitor je Mozart. 3) Bez brige! Danas ništa ne moramo raditi. Danas je *blagdan*. 4) *Dosadno* mi je! Ali, imate pravo, idemo u kino zajedno! 5) Kakvo iznenađenje! Drago mi je što ste ovdje! Idemo na *piće*!
B. 1) Želim kupiti veliki *rječnik* s *gramatikom*. 2) Dolazite li u *Zagreb autobusom*? 3) *Moja tetka* nikada ne ide u kazalište sa mnom. 4) *Vikendom* obično priređujem *zabavu*. 5) Uvijek pijem *kavu* sa *šećerom*.

Vježba 8.2
1) zaboravljam, zaboravljaš, zaboravlja, zaboravljamo, zaboravljate, zaboravljaju; 2) spavam, spavaš, spava, spavamo, spavate, spavaju; 3) učim, učiš, uči, učimo, učite, uče; 4) stignem, stigneš, stigne, stignemo, stignete, stignu; 5) brinem, brineš, brine, brinemo, brinete, brinu

Vježba 8.3
A. 1) Boston; 2) vikenda; 3) obično; 4) pišem; 5) idem
B. 1) mnom; 2) svojim; 3) tobom; 4) Vama; 5) njim

Vježba 8.4
A. 1) pod/za; 2) s; 3) pred; 4) poda; 5) nad
B. 1) ispod stola; 2) – 3) ispred vrata; 4) ispod mene; 5) iznad grada

Vježba 8.5
1) Ima li itko olovku? 2) Nikada te ne vidim. 3) Možeš li naći ikakav auto? 4) Ovo nije ničija kuća. 5) Ne idem u kino ni s kim. 6) Ne mislim ni o čemu. 7) Nitko ga ne vidi. 8) Putujete li ikada u Hrvatsku ljeti? 9) Ona nikada nikamo ne putuje. 10) Oni ne govore ni o kome.

Vježba 8.6
1) Ponedjeljkom završavam vježbe iz hrvatskog jezika. 2) Na posao obično idem autom, jer je moja tvrtka daleko. 3) Obično pišem olovkom. 4) Sutra idem na večeru sa svojom prijateljicom. 5) Preko vikenda idem u kino sa svojom rođakom. 6) U samoposluživanju obično plaćam kreditnom karticom, a nekada i novcem. 7) Volim kavu s puno šećera. 8) U Europu putujem zrakoplovom. 9) Često šetam parkom. 10) Već godinama planiram kupiti novi auto.

Vježba 8.7
A. Često putujem u Hrvatsku zrakoplovom. Tamo imam mnogo prijatelja i poslovnih suradnika. Ponedjeljkom obično razgovaramo telefonom. Ovog puta tamo putujem sa ženom. Obećavam joj već godinama da idemo tamo na odmor. Konačno imamo vremena za to. Idemo u Zagreb i Zadar. Sviđa joj se ta ideja. Putujemo

osamnaestog lipnja. Ne govorimo ni o čemu nego o putu. Čini mi se da je ovo baš lijep dar za našu godišnjicu.

B. Marijana i Darko idu k Ivanu na zabavu. Marijana brine jer misli da nema prikladnu odjeću za zabavu i da ne govori hrvatsko dobro. Darko joj kaže da ne brine. Ne može naučiti hrvatski ako ni s kim ne razgovara. Kod Ivana ima mnogo prijatelja. Tu su Sanja, Mario, Željko i Petra. Ima također mnogo hrane, pića i dobre glazbe. Pred njima je lijepa večer. Ivan obično organizira zabavu petkom poslije položenih ispita. Ali razlog ovoj zabavi je nešto drugo: Marijanin rođendan. Darko i Ivan daju Marijani zajednički dar, veliki rječnik hrvatskog jezika s gramatikom i CD s glazbom hrvatskih pop-grupa. Marijani se dar vrlo sviđa. Ona misli da su Darko i Ivan pravi prijatelji.

Lesson 9

Vježba 9.1

1) mislio je, mislili su; 2) jeo si, jele su; 3) prošlo je, prošle ste; 4) planirala si, planirali su; 5) čekala sam, čekali ste; 6) obećale smo, obećali ste; 7) napravio si, napravila sam; 8) posjetio je, posjetila sam; 9) plesali smo, plesali ste; 10) rekla sam, rekli su; 11) vidio si, vidjela je; 12) mogla sam, mogao je

Vježba 9.2

1) Nisam studirala na fakultetu u Kaliforniji. 2) Nije ti planirao doći u Ameriku. 3) Nisu joj pisali poruku o novom filmu. 4) Nije predložio ručak, ni muzički centar. 5) Nismo imali auto. Auto nije bio pokvaren. 6) Nije čekala da on dođe.
7) Prošle godine nisam putovao u Australiju.

Vježba 9.3

1) Ona se bojala, ali ja nisam. 2) Jučer sam došla u New York i otišla u kino.
3) Nije bilo knjiga u toj knjižnici. 4) Rekli su da će otići na more u kolovozu.
5) Pet studenata je primljeno na doktorat na Harvardu. Pedeset dva studenta su očekivala posjetiti Harvard u rujnu. 6) Prošlog tjedna sam gledala četiri dobra filma.
7) Mojih pet rođaka je stiglo u Texas.

Vježba 9.4

A. 1) u 2) rekli 3) sam/je 4) ga/sam 5) na

B. 1) Mi se nismo upoznali u Budimpešti. 2) Oni mi nisu rekli da imam pravo.
3) Jučer nisam / nije kupio šešir. 4) Nisam je čekao u stanu/Nije ga čekao u stanu.
5) Nisam išla na stadion u Zagrebu.

Vježba 9.5

1) Ništa se više nije moglo promijeniti. 2) Ona je saznala sve što je trebalo.
3) Bilo je kasno, a njima se nije spavalo. 4) Mi smo se vratili prošlog tjedna iz Pariza. 5) Darko je vozio Ivanov auto od Zagreba do Splita. 6) Nismo htjeli otputovati na odmor bez naših prijatelja. 7) Ona nikada nije bila u Varaždinu.

Vježba 9.6

A. 1) za, sa; 2) u, na, u; 3) – , kod; 4) iza, ispred; 5) u, kod, do

B. 1. mi; 2. mnom; 3. me; 4. me; 5. mene; 6. mi; 7. mnom; 8. mi; 9. mene; 10. mi; 11. meni; 12. mi; 13. mene; 14. me; 15. mi

Vježba 9.7
A. Zovem se Krešimir i imao sam veliku gužvu prošlog tjedna. Prvo na poslu, pa onda s mojom djevojkom. Što se dogodilo na poslu manje je važno od toga što se dogodilo s mojom djevojkom. Bila je hladna večer i šetali smo po Zrinjevcu. Njoj je bilo dosadno. Nju ne zanima romantika. Ona je htjela da idemo na koncert, a poslije na neku zabavu. Ali nije više bilo karata za koncert. Predložio sam da otiđemo negdje na večeru, ali ni to nije bilo dobro. Hodali smo tako i ni o čemu nismo razgovarali. Ona je bila ljuta i rekla je da sam se mogao sjetiti nečeg boljeg. Ah, kakva večer! Idućeg dana se ispričala, ali sada uopće ne znam što da mislim o njoj.
B. Dragi Tomislave,
Kao što znaš, ja sam ovog ljeta u Hrvatskoj. Već dva mjeseca putujem i vidio sam mnoge gradove na sjeveru i jugu zemlje. Hrvatska je vrlo lijepa zemlja. Sada imam mnogo prijatelja ovdje i već govorim hrvatski odlično. Ovdje mi se sviđa i ne znam koliko dugo ću ostati. Hrvatska je zemlja u usponu. Razmišljam o tome da otvorim svoju tvrtku. Ovo je jedinstvena prilika. Već sam razgovarao s poslovnim suradnicima u Zagrebu. Postoji velika mogućnost da se ovo dogodi. Nadam se da si ti dobro i da tvoj posao ide prema planu. Ako možeš, posjeti me. Mislim da će ti biti zanimljivo. Srdačno te pozdravlja Ante

Lesson 10

Vježba 10.1
1) Ja ću otići u samoposluživanje kupiti sendvič i kilogram kruha. Otići ću u samoposluživanje kupiti sendvič i kilogram kruha. 2) Ja ću pročitati pet knjiga ovog mjeseca. Pročitat ću pet knjiga ovog mjeseca. 3) Ja neću napisati pismo svojoj majci, ali nazvat ću je na telefon. Neću napisati pismo svojoj majci, ali ću je nazvati na telefon. 4) Hoćeš li doći sa mnom na more ovog vikenda? – 5) Koliko dugo ćeš živjeti u Bostonu? – 6) Znam da ćeš se složiti. – 7) Kamo ćemo putovati u Hrvatskoj? –

Vježba 10.2
A. 1) Bit će toplo danas. 2) Nije bilo vode. 3) Ovdje ima puno problema. 4) Ovdje nema ništa. 5) Dosadno mi je.
B. 1) Ja nisam bio u Splitu s Ivanom. Bio sam tamo s Marijanom. 2) Ne idem na kavu i neću čitati novine. Moram otići na fakultet jer imam ispit. 3) Nisam dobio novca prošle godine. Sada sam siromašan student i imam stari auto. 4) Ja neću spavati u hotelu koji je vrlo jeftin. Ja volim skupe hotele. 5) Ovaj čovjek nije kupio kuću u Splitu, pa neću biti tamo idućeg tjedna. Mislim da ću ići u Dubrovnik.

Vježba 10.3
1) U *restoranima* u *Dalmaciji* može se jesti dobra *riba*. 2) Ovog *vikenda* idem na *izlet* u *kuću* mojeg prijatelja. 3) *Vrijeme* je lijepo, pa nam u *goste* dolazi *obitelj* mojeg rođaka. 4) U *kafiću* ništa ne mogu *čuti* od bučne glazbe, a želim razgovarati *na miru*. 5) Ako nam *se* želiš *pridružiti*, imamo *dobar plan* za večeras.

Vježba 10.4

Zovem se Tomislav i ravnatelj sam jedne velike tvrtke. Idućeg mjeseca imat ću mnogo poslovnih sastanaka. Gospodarstvo je malo u usponu, malo u padu. To će donijeti mnogo problema, u to ne sumnjam. Teško je reći hoće li biti loše ili dobro. Mislili smo da ćemo otvoriti pet novih poslovnica i dvije tvornice. Kako sada stvari stoje, morat ćemo počekati. Da vam pravo kažem, ja više neću brinuti o tome. Neću više čitati novine. Neću gledati vijesti. Neću čitati poslovna izvješća. Odlučio sam da ću biti sretan i da ću živjeti bez stresa, pa kako bude.

Vježba 10.5

1) koji; 2) čija; 3) kojoj; 4) kojim; 5) čemu; 6) u kojoj; 7) koje; 8) koji; 9) koja; 10) u kojoj

Vježba 10.6

A: Dobar dan! Kakvo iznenađenje! Kako ste? B: Dobar dan! Odlično, a Vi? A: Hvala, dobro. Baš mi je drago što ste došli. Čime Vas mogu ponuditi? B: Jednu kavu, molim Vas. Zvao sam Vas prije nekoliko dana na telefon, ali dobio sam pogrešan broj. A: Ah, oprostite, imamo veliki problem s telefonom. Moram zvati telefonsku tvrtku. B: Slažem se, probajte to popraviti. Ali srećom, ipak smo vas pronašli! A: Možete li ostati kod nas nekoliko dana? Ima mjesta za sve! Ovo je jedinstvena prilika da vidite otok Hvar. B: Vrlo lijepo od Vas. Vi ste izvrstan domaćin!

Vježba 10.7

A. Marijana wants to travel to the seashore. She needs a vacation. She wants to think about everything because there has been a lot going on in the last few weeks. Darko thinks that she will be bored alone in Dalmatia. He knows that Ivan is going to visit his family for the holidays. He suggests that all of them travel together. They call Ivan on the phone because they want to discuss it with him. Ivan agrees. He says that he will have nice company for the trip. He suggests that they go in his car. They can all stay with his parents because they have a big house at the seaside. Ivan's mother likes to cook and always cooks something special when Ivan comes home. Ivan has a plan because he is the host. He says they can go sightseeing in Split and go on a trip. Marijana looks forward to the trip. They are leaving at 9 in the morning and will arrive in Split at 1 in the afternoon.

B. 1) Marijana želi otputovati na more. 2) Njoj treba odmor, a također želi o svemu razmisliti. 3) Ona mora razmisliti o tome što se dogodilo u prošlih nekoliko tjedana. 4) Darko misli da će Marijani biti dosadno samoj. 5) Darko također zna da Ivan planira posjetiti obitelj za blagdane. 6) Ivanova obitelj živi na moru. 7) Darko predlaže da svi otiđu zajedno na jug. 8) Oni zovu Ivana na mobitel. 9) Ivan se slaže s Darkom. 10) Oni će putovati u Dalmaciju Ivanovim autom. 11) Marijana i Darko neće biti u hotelu. Oni će biti kod Ivanovih roditelja jer tamo ima mjesta za sve. 12) Ivanova majka uvijek kuha nešto posebno kada Ivan dođe. 13) Oni će razgledati Split, a navečer će ići van. 14) Iz Zagreba kreću u 9 ujutro, a u Split će doći u 1 popodne.

Lesson 11

Vježba 11.1

A. 1) both; 2) both; 3) pogledao/gledao; 4) kupila; 5) nastaviti

B. 1) Idem popiti kavu. Molim te, možeš li mi kupiti novine i pridružiti mi se u kavani? 2) Gledao sam loš film prošlog tjedna u tom novom kinu. 3) Policija će me obavijestiti ako netko pronađe moj novčanik. 4) Ne mogu vjerovati da sam izgubio putovnicu. Nikada ništa ne gubim. 5) Ne volim piti alkohol dok jedem večeru u skupom restoranu.

Vježba 11.2

A. 1) čekati *I* – dočekati *P*; 2) putovati *I* – otputovati *P*; 3) ući *P* – ulaziti *I*; 4) voziti *I* – dovesti *P*; 5) platiti *P* – plaćati *I*; 6) naći *P* – nalaziti *I*; 7) gubiti *I* – izgubiti *P*

B. 1) Idem kući! Dosadilo mi je čekati. 1a) Hoću li ikada dočekati da vidim Mexico? 2) Mladi ljudi vole putovati. 2a) Želim otputovati u Mexico. 3) Kada sam ušla u hotel, vidjela sam da je sve novo. 3a) Dok sam ulazila u hotel, razgovarala sam na mobitel. 4) Ne volim voziti velike automobile. 4a) Tko te je dovezao kući? 5) Tko će platiti večeru? 5a) Ivan uvijek plaća piće Marijani. 6) Teško je naći vremena za sve. 6a) Svaki dan Ivan je nalazio nove razloge za vidjeti Marijanu. 7) Ne volim gubiti stvari. 7a) Ako izgubite novac, ne možete na put.

Vježba 11.3

1) *Policajac* je pomogao Marijani pronaći novčanik *izgubljen* kada je ona kupovala *sendvič*. 2) *Profesor* je rekao da moramo *pročitati knjigu*. 3) *Marijana* ne voli *kupovati kavu* u *trgovini*. 4) Policajac je obećao da će joj pomoći *pronaći isprave*. Rekao je "*Nema na čemu*" kada mu je Marijana rekla hvala. 5) Marijana i njezini prijatelji će *doći* u *Dubrovnik* za *sat vremena*.

Vježba 11.4

1) Koliko košta? – c. Pedeset kuna. 2) Hvala Vam na pomoći. – d. Nema na čemu. 3) Kupio sam ti dar. – a. Puno ti hvala! Ovo će mi stvarno dobro doći. 4) Moram ići. Kasnim. – e. Bez brige! Stići ćeš. 5) Treba mi odmor! – b. I meni!

Vježba 11.5

Pišem referat već osam dana, ali ga još nisam napisao. Spremam i veliki ispit iz ekonomije, ali ga još nisam spremio. Učim hrvatske glagole, ali ni njih još nisam dobro naučio. Čitam veliku knjigu iz povijesti, ali pročitat ću je do kraja tek u srijedu, a ispit je u ponedjeljak. Imam i pokus iz kemije koji završavam već pet tjedana i još ga nisam završio. Mnogo radim, ali ima toliko toga za uraditi! Svaki dan govorim „Danas ću sve završiti," a posla je sve više. Čini mi se da nikada neću biti gotov!

Vježba 11.6

A: Jučer smo bili u centru grada. Htjela sam kupiti novi rječnik, ali izgubila sam novčanik. B: To je strašno. Što je sve bilo u novčaniku? Nadam se da nisi izgubila sve isprave! A: Nije bilo puno novca, ali je bilo puno isprava, na primjer moja vozačka dozvola i dvije kreditne kartice. B: Jesi li bila na policiji? A: Ne, pronašla sam policajca na ulici koji mi je pomogao. Bio je vrlo ljubazan, ali nismo imali sreće. Nismo našli novčanik. B: I što ćeš sada? A: Ispunila sam formular. Nadam se da će me policija obavijestiti u slučaju da netko vrati moj novčanik. B: Ah, kakav loš dan! Baš šteta!

Vježba 11.7

A. Darko, Ivan and Marijana have been driving for three hours without a break. Marijana wants to stop. Darko says that he will stop soon because he has to buy gas. Ivan is hungry. He wants a sandwich and newspapers. Marijana usually doesn't buy food on the highway but the sandwiches do not look bad. She is hungry and she buys a sandwich as well. After he has bought gas, Darko wants to have a coffee. Marijana and Ivan order juice. They did not have time for breakfast before the trip.

Marijana wants to treat everyone but she lost her wallet. She never loses things. Marijana is angry and sad. Darko tells her to calm down because she had her wallet when she was buying her sandwich. She thinks that she put it in her bag. Darko suggests asking a policeman to help them. He tells the policeman what was in the wallet: 750 kunas, an American passport, $100, a driver's licence, and credit cards. If they don't find the wallet, Marijana will have to fill out a form, says the policeman. This way the police will be able to inform Marijana if the wallet is found. The policeman goes with Marijana to the store where she bought a sandwich. He finds the wallet under the counter. Marijana is very happy.

B. 1) Oni se voze već tri sata. 2) Jer Darko mora kupiti benzin. 3) Oni kupuju sendvič i novine. 4) Nitko nije pojeo doručak prije puta. 5) Marijana želi sve počastiti kavom. 6) Ona ne može ništa kupiti jer je izgubila novčanik.
7) Marijana nikada ne gubi stvari. 8) Darko joj kaže da se smiri. 9) Ona misli da je novčanik stavila u torbu. 10) Darko predlaže da pitaju policajca da im pomogne.
11) U novčaniku su bili novac i isprave. 12) Da je policija može obavijestiti ako pronađu novčanik. 13) Oni idu u trgovinu. 14) Pronašli su novčanik ispod pulta.

Lesson 12

Vježba 12.1

1) zbirke, zbirke; 2) pitanja, pitanja; 3) ostanci, ostanka; 4) odgovori, odgovora; 5) crkve, crkve; 6) prognoze, prognoze; 7) obale, obale; 8) mogućnosti, mogućnosti; 9) centri, centra, 10) stoljeća, stoljeća

Vježba 12.2

1) Na prvom semaforu skrenite desno, a onda ravno Ulicom slobode. Kada dođete do Dubrovačke ulice, na križanju skrenite lijevo. Poslije toga idite samo ravno i vidjet ćete crkvu čim prođete Gupčevu ulicu, s desne strane. 2) Idite ravno Dubrovačkom ulicom i kada prođete Branimirovu ulicu, kino će biti s Vaše lijeve strane. 3) Prijeđite Teslinu ulicu, a potom idite ravno Ulicom Tina Ujevića još 300 metara. 4) Idite Dubrovačkom ulicom do Ulice slobode, pa skrenite desno. Kada dođete do semafora, prijeđite na drugu stranu i knjižnica će biti ispred Vas. 5) Prijeđite Dubrovačku ulicu i idite Ulicom slobode ravno do semafora. Kod semafora skrenite desno i idite još malo Teslinom ulicom. Samoposluživanje je s lijeve strane. 6) Idite ravno Teslinom ulicom do trgovine odjećom. Kolodvor je s lijeve strane na

Glavnom trgu. 7) Idite tramvajem broj 3 Primorskom ulicom, pa Ulicom slobode. Siđite na šestoj stanici. To je Dubrovačka ulica i kino je tamo. 8) Kada dođete do semafora, skrenite lijevo i idite ravno Ulicom slobode do Dubrovačke ulice. 9) Prijeđite Dubrovačku ulicu i prođite kroz park. Kada dođete na drugu stranu parka, vidjet ćete Teslinu ulicu. Prijeđite Teslinu ulicu i kazalište će biti ispred Vas. 10) Idite ravno Teslinom ulicom i telefon je odmah iza samoposluživanja s lijeve strane.

Vježba 12.3
A. 1) može, mogu; 2) uzme, uzmu; 3) hoda, hodaju; 4) boli, bole 5) puši, puše 6) zaboravi, zaborave; 7) skrene, skrenu; 8) postoji, postoje; 9) stane, stanu; 10) jede, jedu
B. 1) čekanje; Čekanje je dosadno. 2) kupovanje; Kupovanje darova nije uvijek lako. 3) voljenje; Za voljenje treba dvoje. 4) pisanje; Pisanje pisama nije više popularno jer svi koriste računalo. 5) viđenje; Tvoje viđenje situacije i moje viđenje situacije se ne slažu.

Vježba 12.4
Moja kuća je izgrađena davno. Oko nje je zabranjeno voziti. Zaštićena je kao spomenik. Vidi se da je to stara zgrada. Nalazi se u centru grada. Čitajući povijest Zadra, shvatio sam koliko je ova zgrada važna. Govori se da mnogo košta, ali moje mišljenje je da ona vrijedi više od ikakvog novca. Vidjevši koliko mi znači, moja žena je odlučila da se ne selimo iz Zadra.

Vježba 12.5
A. 1) imperfective, pijući; 2) imperfective, šetajući; 3) perfective, kupivši; 4) perfective, napravivši; 5) perfective, pronašavši; 6) imperfective, tražeći; 7) imperfective, studirajući; perfective, studiravši; 8) perfective, razmislivši; 9) imperfective, gledajući; 10) imperfective, dolazeći
B. 1) Pijući kavu, Tanja je vidjela da nema šećera. 2) Polako šetajući, došli su do centra grada. 3) Kupivši hranu, spremili su dobar ručak i pozvali prijatelje. 4) Napravivši sve, otišli su u kino. 5) Pronašavši izgubljeni novčanik, Marijana je mogla nastaviti putovanje. 6) Tražeći dar za sestru, Ivan je našao dar i za Marijanu. 7) Studirajući jezike, čovjek uči o kulturama raznih zemalja. 8) Razmislivši o svemu, Marijana je odlučila zaboraviti svog dečka Andrewa. 9) Gledajući Dubrovnik, Marijana je mislila kako je to lijep grad. 10) Dolazeći u Hrvatsku, mnogi turisti planiraju provesti nekoliko dana na moru.

Vježba 12.6
1) čekan; The long-awaited bus did not come. 2) posuđen; The borrowed car drove well. 3) napunjen; A filled refridgerator is better than an empty one. 4) viđena; She was seen in the city center yesterday. 5) napisano; The letter [which was] written was long. 6) izgubljen; The lost wallet was blue. 7) zauzeto; This place is occupied. 8) prodan; The sold apartment brought them a lot of money. 9) zabranjeno; Who knows where it's forbidden to park? 10) unajmljen; Marijana's rented apartment in Zagreb was not expensive.

Vježba 12.7

A. Ivan will be the tour guide through Split because he knows the city very well. Marijana, Darko and Ivan first go to the center to see the palace of the emperor Diocletian. To get there one goes straight and then at the first traffic light to the left. After that they need to go past another two streets and then turn right. They will park the car and continue on foot. It is forbidden to drive in the center.

Split is a very old city. Its center was built by the emperor Diocletian at the end of the third and beginning of the fourth centuries after Christ. The palace is now a monument of world cultural heritage. People continue to live in it. There are many shops, cafés, and galleries. The steps lead from the main square of the palace, which is called Peristil, to the seashore. At the seashore there is a promenade with a lot of cafés. People usually sit there, talk, and look at the sea and the islands.

Marijana wants to go to some island. Ivan says that they have to go to Trogir. Trogir is famous for an old cathedral with the portal [made by] the master [craftsman] Radovan. The weather forecast says that he it will be nice and sunny. Marijana, Darko and Ivan will go to the island of Hvar or Brač. It is all the same to Ivan where they will go because he could travel around the world in such company. Everyone is tired from sightseeing. Darko sat down in a café on the seashore. Ivan and Marijana will walk for a bit because Ivan forgot to show something to Marijana.
B. 1) Oni se nalaze u Splitu. 2) Ivan je rođen u Splitu i grad mu je zato dobro poznat. 3) Oni prvo idu razgledati palaču cara Dioklecijana. 4) Do centra se ide ravno, a onda kod prvog semafora lijevo. 5) U centru je zabranjeno voziti. 6) Split je vrlo stari grad. Ima palaču iz trećeg stoljeća u centru. 7) Dioklecijan je bio rimski car. 8) Na obali se nalazi šetnica. 9) Marijana želi otići na neki otok. 10) Trogir je poznat po katedrali s portalom majstora Radovana iz trinaestog stoljeća. 11) U Hrvatskoj je ljeti vrijeme lijepo i sunčano. 12) Ivanu je svejedno: i Brač i Hvar su dobri. 13) Svi su umorni, ali Ivan i Marijana kažu da idu prošetati. 14) Ivan nije ništa zaboravio reći Marijani. On želi biti sam s njom.

Lesson 13

Vježba 13.1

A: Danas je sunčano. Idemo nekamo! B: Tko će biti naš turistički vodič? Gdje se nalazi galerija? A: Ovo je jedinstven grad, ali mi nije poznat. Imaš li kartu?
B: Imam nekoliko karata, ali ne znam gdje smo. A: Baš zanimljivo! Sigurno smo se izgubili. B: Da pitamo nekog koliko ima od ove ulice do galerije? A: To je izvrsna ideja. Ali ovdje ne vidim nikoga. Nema ni ljudi ni prometa. B: Joooj, nema ni mojeg novčanika! To znači da nema ni mojeg novca ni kreditnih kartica! A: Kako je to moguće? Stavio si novčanik u torbu. B: Ne, stavio sam novčanik na džemper.
A: Tu je! Pao je na pod! B: Ah, baš ti hvala. Već sam se zabrinuo. A: Možemo i sutra u galeriju ako hoćeš. Ja bih ostala ovdje još malo. Ovo je vrlo lijepo mjesto.
B: Naravno! Nema problema.

Vježba 13.2

Zovem se Katarina. Volim lijepu odjeću. Htjela bih kupiti novi kaput i nove cipele. Kada bih birala između kazališta i kupovine, izabrala bih kupovinu. Bila bih vrlo sretna kada bi moj muž shvatio da lijepa odjeća nije luksuz, već potreba. Žene su sretnije i ljepše kada imaju modernu odjeću. Moj muž i ja bismo htjeli provoditi više vremena zajedno, ali svaki vikend ja idem u kupovinu, a on igra tenis sa svojim prijateljima. Ja mu kažem da je tenis skuplji od cipela. On se smije i pita me bih li otišla u kino s njim. On meni oprašta cipele, a ja njemu tenis. Kako bi bilo da nije tako! Mi smo odličan par.

Vježba 13.3

A. 1) Ja bih kavu, molim Vas. Darko, je li vrijeme na Hvaru uvijek tako lijepo? 2) Koliko košta karta do Mljeta? Prošle godine jedna karta je koštala samo pedeset kuna. 3) Moram se vratiti u Ameriku na nekoliko tjedana, ali poslije toga ću doći u Hrvatsku živjeti s tobom. 4) Ako bi mi pomogao učiti za ispit, mogli bismo otići plesati večeras. 5) Mislim da je ovdje ljepše i imam bolje prijatelje nego u Americi.
B. 1) Idućeg vikenda htjela bih mnogo spavati. 2) Htio bih otputovati u Varaždin jer tamo još nikada nisam bio. 3) Kupio bih crni sportski auto. 4) Danas bih htio jesti meso na žaru. 5) Htio bih pogledati Maršala Vinka Brešana jer je to smiješan i dobar film. 6) Htjela bih pročitati neku knjigu Miljenka Jergovića. 7) Htio bih upoznati Gorana Ivaniševića jer je odličan tenisač.

Vježba 13.4

A. 1) više, najviše – a lot; 2) draži, najdraži – dear; 3) ljepši, najljepši – beautiful; 4) bliži, najbliži – close, near; 5) gori, najgori – bad, evil; 6) veći, najveći – big; 7) žedniji, najžedniji – thirsty; 8) stariji, najstariji – old; 9) tiše, najtiše – quietly; 10) bolji, najbolji – good
B. 1) Najviše novca imaju Darkovi roditelji. 2) Tko vam je draži, Ivan ili Darko? 3) Marijana je ljepša od drugih djevojaka. 4) Darko živi najbliže centru. 5) To je najgori čovjek kojeg sam ikada upoznala. 6) Koji je najveći grad u Hrvatskoj? 7) Danas sam žedniji nego jučer jer je vrlo vruće. 8) Tko je stariji, ti ili ja? 9) Ova ulica je tiša od tvoje. 10) Vi ste moji najbolji prijatelji.

Vježba 13.5

A. 1. tijesan, tješnji; 2) najduži; 3) brz, brži; 4) tužan, tužniji; 5) najteži; 6) tvrda, tvrđi; 7) gluplji; 8) mlađi, najbolji, najbolja; 9) najluđa; 10) jeftiniji; 11) najpoznatiji; 12) sretnija; 13) skup, skuplji; 14) najkraći; 15) najviše, najzanimljivije.
B. 1) misliš; 2) kako, želiš; 3) razumjela; 4) svi; 5) meni, sviđaju, reći, draži

Vježba 13.6

1) biste/bi; 2) bi; 3) biste; 4) bismo; 5) biste; 6) bih/bi; 7) biste; 8) bi; 9) bi; 10) bi

Vježba 13.7

A. Marijana was packing because she, Darko, and Ivan were traveling to the island of Hvar and Dubrovnik. Into her bag she put pants, T-shirts, a swimsuit, underwear, socks, a sweater, shirts and shoes. She was not sure whether she also needed a nice dress. Darko said that she did not need anything else because she already had the biggest bag. He was sure that Ivan was going to like all her clothes. Marijana did not understand what Darko wanted to say. But there was no time for details. It seems to Darko that Ivan had fallen in love with Marijana. She herself noticed something.

In the ferry port Ivan bought three one-way passenger tickets and one ticket for the car. The tickets were a bit more expensive than last year. The cashier told him that the ferry "Tin Ujević" was leaving exactly at 2 o'clock. When they arrived to Hvar, they went to the hotel. They had reserved two rooms there. Marijana told Ivan that there are nice beaches also in America but she liked the beaches in Croatia better. She likes Zagreb too, but she thinks that the smaller places are better for vacation because they are quieter. While Darko was swimming, Marijana and Ivan were talking. Ivan told her that he would like her to stay in Croatia. Marijana explained to him that she was still there on business. She has to return to America to sort out some work and personal things. After that she will spend a whole year in Croatia.

After Hvar, Marijana, Ivan and Darko traveled to Dubrovnik by ship. They saw the islands of Korčula and Mljet. Traveling by ship was a real pleasure. In Dubrovnik they saw the Sponza Palace, Franciscan Monastery and they took a walk on the city walls.

B. 1) Zašto se Marijana pakirala? Jer su ona, Darko i Ivan putovali na otok Hvar i u Dubrovnik. 2) Što je stavila u torbu? U torbu je stavila svoju odjeću i cipele. 3) Što je Darko rekao o njezinoj torbi? Darko je rekao da Marijana ima najveću torbu. 4) Što je on rekao o Ivanu? Darko misli da se Ivan zaljubio u Marijanu. 5) Koliko karata je Ivan kupio u trajektnoj luci? Kupio je tri karte. 6) Jesu li karte bile skuplje ili jeftinije nego prošle godine? Karte su bile malo skuplje nego prošle godine. 7) Kamo su Marijana, Darko i Ivan otišli kada su stigli na Hvar? Oni su otišli na plažu. 8) Kakva mjesta Marijana voli za odmor? Marijana voli mala mjesta jer su tiha. 9) Kakve plaže ona najviše voli? Ona najviše voli hrvatske plaže. 10) O čemu su Marijana i Ivan razgovarali dok je Darko plivao? Oni su razgovarali o Marijaninim planovima. 11) Zašto se Marijana mora vratiti u Ameriku? Ona mora srediti neke poslovne i privatne stvari. 12) Kamo su Marijana, Darko i Ivan otišli nakon Hvara? Oni su otputovali u Dubrovnik. 13) Kako su došli do Dubrovnika? Do tamo su došli brodom. 14) Koje su otoke vidjeli? Vidjeli su Korčulu i Mljet. 15) Što su radili u Dubrovniku? Razgledali su znamenitosti i šetali po gradskim zidinama.

Lesson 14

Vježba 14.1

1) idi, idite; 2) pogledaj, pogledajte; 3) stanuj, stanujte; 4) odmori se, odmorite se; 5) vrati se, vratite se; 6) pričaj, pričajte; 7) pomozi, pomozite; 8) skreni, skrenite; 9) piši, pišite; 10) vjeruj, vjerujte

Vježba 14.2

A. 1) Bolestan sam – c. I am sick; 2) Imam glavobolju – g. I have a headache; 3) Imam opekotinu na nozi – d. I have a burn on my leg; 4) Mnogo kašljem – f. I am coughing a lot; 5) Trebam lijek protiv bolova – a. I need medication against pain 6) Mogu li dobiti recept? – b. Could I get a prescription? 7) Imala sam prehladu – e. I had a cold.

B. 1) Moj *otac* je ekonomist i radi u velikoj tvrtki. 2) Moja *tetka* živi na otoku Pagu i ima dvoje djece. 3) Moja *majka* pravi najbolje kolače. 4) Moja *sestra* voli dobre knjige. 5) Moj *djed* ima osamdeset godina.

Vježba 14.3
Zovem se Sanja i meni je devet godina. Nije lako biti dijete. Svatko ti govori što sve moraš napraviti, što smiješ, a što ne smiješ. Prva stvar koju čujem ujutro je „Popij mlijeko," pa onda „Požuri da ne zakasniš u školu." U školi čujem „Djeco, pišite i ne razgovarajte." Poslije toga učiteljica kaže „Neka Sanja čita novu lekciju." Kada dođem kući majka kaže „Peri ruke i jedi ručak," a otac se ljuti „Budi tiha, boli me glava." Poslije toga me pita „Reci mi istinu, jesi li dobila lošu ocjenu?" Brat sluša glazbu i kaže „Pusti me na miru!" Kada dođe moja prijateljica Tina, onda nam je lijepo. Zato joj ja kažem „Dođi mi često!"

Vježba 14.4
1) Budi dobar! 2) Broj novac! 3) Čekaj ga! 4) Čitaj svoju knjigu, a ne moju! 5) Molim te, daj mi tu torbu. 6) Dočekaj ih na željezničkom kolodvoru. 7) Ne gledaj me tako. 8) Ne idi tamo. 9) Jedi salatu! 10) Molim te, kupi mi novi kaput. 11) Ne kupuj cigarete! 12) Ne misli o tome. 13) Odnesi ovo do moje kuće. 14) Napiši mu poruku. 15) Nemoj još otići! 16) Ne pitaj je ništa. 17) Pogledaj što rade! 18) Pomozi mi! 19) Plati račun. Ne, ti ga plati! 20) Ne radi to! 21) Ne slušaj ga! 22) Stavi ovu knjigu u tu torbu.

Vježba 14.5
A: Približio se odlazak. Kupili smo putne karte i odlazimo za tjedan dana. B: Odmor je prošao tako brzo! Je li Vaša braća i Vaš sin isto odlaze? A: Da, i moja žena također. Ali dogovorili smo se da dogodine ostanemo ovdje duže. B: Možete i ovdje raditi ako imate mobitel i računalo, a možete se i odmarati. A: Da, to i planiram. Ja sam već umoran od hodanja. Bole me noge. B: Želite li da sjednemo i popijemo nešto zajedno? A: Naravno! Ova kavana ima tihu glazbu, možemo tu sjesti. B: Odlično!

Vježba 14.6
1) Volim sjesti kada sam umorna. 2) Lezi na taj krevet. 3) Koliko dugo već stojiš tu? 4) Ona je sjedila do mene. 5) On je ležao cijeli dan i nije radio ništa. 6) Kada sjednem, ne volim ustajati. 7) Liježem svake noći u deset sati.

Vježba 14.7
tužna, brzo, putovanja, zaključaka, zadaci, rekao, hrvatski, govori, prošetati, nalazi, stanuje, kod, željela, svoju, novac, prodavaonicu, zatvorena, darova, koštale, bluzu, oca, glazbom, prijateljicu, posjetiti, znao, ima, oženjen, sestra, studira, godinu, hodali, nazovu, predložio, ideja, nasamo, odlaska

Lesson 15

Vježba 15.1
1) Kada bude ljeto, putovat ću po jugu. 2) Kada budem imao novca, kupit ću novi stan. 3) Kada budem u Hrvatskoj, posjetit ću Pulu i Zadar. 4) Kada budem imao vremena, čitat ću knjige i ići na koncerte. 5) Kada budem išao u kino, pogledat ću film „Karaula" hrvatskog redatelja Rajka Grlića. 6) Kada budem kod kuće, učit ću hrvatski. 7) Kada Marijana bude u Americi, posjetit će svoje roditelje. 8) Dok Ivan

bude čekao Marijanu, on će učiti. 9) Kada Marijana i Ivan budu zajedno, oni će biti sretni.

Vježba 15.2

1) Čitat ću novine dok budem jeo ručak. 2) Kada bude putovao po Hrvatskoj, mora otputovati na jug. 3) Kada budeš gotova s izvješćem, dođi i pogledat ćemo film. 4) Kada budeš kupovala kruh za sebe, molim te, kupi kilogram i za mene. 5) Ne boj se kada budeš govorila s njom. 6) Kada budemo došli, sve će biti dobro. 7) Kada budu na fakultetu, moći će živjeti u studentskom domu ili u vlastitom stanu. 8) Kada budeš govorio hrvatski dobro, nitko neće znati da si Amerikanac. 9) Kada budem vozila u Pulu, slušat ću dobru glazbu i neće mi biti dosadno. 10) Kada budeš u Splitu, svakako posjeti Dioklecijanovu palaču.

Vježba 15.3

Ako Hrvoje nazove, reci mu da me nema kod kuće. Jako sam ljuta. Jedan trenutak je tu, a drugi ga nema. Zapravo nikada ga nema kada mi treba. Da mi je donio materijale u srijedu, završila bih projekt. Ovako imam veliki problem. Što će misliti moj ravnatelj? Sigurno neće biti zadovoljan. Reći će „Kada budete završavali projekte na vrijeme, dobit ćete povišicu. Do tada ništa." Čija je ovo greška? Nikako nije moja, nego Hrvojeva. Čovjek uopće ne može računati na njega. Ako bude htio, može mi se ispričati. Napravi li to, možda ću opet razgovarati s njim.

Vježba 15.4

A. 1) Ako mi kupiš ručak danas – g. ja ću te odvesti u kino. 2) Da si došao na vrijeme – a. ne bismo zakasnili na vlak. 3) Ako nas nazovu danas – h. moći ćemo se o svemu dogovoriti. 4) Ako ikada budete putovali u Rim – e. svakako posjetite arenu. 5) Kada ona dođe – f. reci joj da otiđe u trgovinu. 6) Ako biste htjeli ići na Hvar – i. mogli bismo otići na izlet zajedno. 7) Ako bih dobio novi posao – b. mogao bih kupiti kuću. 8) Da ste poslušali Marka i uzeli plan grada – c. sada ne biste lutali. 9) Da ona zna kako je lijepo na Jadranu – d. sigurno bi otišla tamo na odmor.
B. 1) Da ste položili ispit, mogli biste na zabavu. 2) Ako želiš, možeš spavati. 3) Ako me voliš, kupit ćeš mi sve. 4) Da je došao, ona bi ga vidjela. 5) Da su to napravili, ne bismo imali problem. 6) Ako mu kažeš da dođe, on će doći. 7) Kada bi me pozvala, ja bih je posjetio. 8) Ako dobije pismo, znat će da smo u Zagrebu. 9) Ako budu razgovarali na telefon danas, on će saznati da smo otišli. 10) Da smo otputovali u Split, ljepše bismo proveli blagdane. 11) Kada bi gledao kartu, trebalo bi nam daleko manje vremena za ovaj izlet. 12) Ako ikada opet budem imao malo slobodnog vremena, napisat ću roman.

Vježba 15.5

1) Vidimo jedan drugog. 2) Pišemo jedno drugom. 3) Kuhamo ručak jedan za drugog. 4) Čestitale smo jedna drugoj. 5) Razgovarali smo jedan s drugim. 6) Kupile smo dar jedna drugoj. 7) Vrlo se sviđamo jedni drugima. 8) Pitamo jedan drugog mnogo pitanja. 9) Zovemo jedna drugu svakog tjedna.

Vježba 15.6

1) Niste dovoljno učili i ništa niste znali na ispitu. *Da ste položili ispit, mogli biste na zabavu.* Sada morate ostati kod kuće i opet učiti. 2) Sinoć sam otišao kasno na

spavanje jer sam bio van s prijateljima. *Kakva sreća! Da nisi nazvao, zaspao bih i zakasnio na avion.* Imam važan poslovni sastanak i ne bi bilo dobro da zakasnim. 3) Vaša tvrtka je nova i uspješna. *Imamo iste interese. Kada bismo potpisali ugovor, mogli bismo svi zaraditi mnogo novca.* Vi imate dobre materijale, a mi imamo dobre radnike. 4) *Tko se koristio mojim računalom?!? Ako ga pronađem, morat će mi objasniti zašto ništa ne radi!* Kada me nema, netko se uvijek koristi mojim stvarima. Nitko me ništa ne pita. Baš sam ljut! 5) *Ma ne mogu vjerovati! Jesi li to ti? Da sam otišla odavde samo pet minuta ranije, ne bih te vidjela.* Nismo se vidjele već dvije godine. Radim i stalno žurim, pa nemam vremena ni za što. Gdje radiš i kako živiš? 6) *Hladnjak je opet prazan! Ako stignem, otići ću u samoposluživanje. Ako ne stignem, morat ćeš otići ti.* Danas imam puno posla jer je petak i moram sve završiti. Jesi li ti vrlo zauzet? 7) *Baš Vas nisam očekivala sada! Da ste mi se javili prije, pripremila bih sve materijale.* Sada ćete morati malo počekati. Još nije sve gotovo. 8) Bilo nam je vrlo lijepo u vašem društvu. Vi ste odlični domaćini! *Rado bismo se opet vidjeli s vama! Ako budete mogli, svakako nas posjetite u Americi.* Mi bismo željeli da i vi budete naši gosti.

Vježba 15.7

spremna, darova, svoju, kupila, težak, trebati, kofer, odvesti, dočekati, fotografije, putovanja, poslala, bio, kada, doći, na, Darku, provjerava, putnu, novčanik, toga, torbu, kofera, luku, potvrditi, prtljagu, međunarodni, službenici, vrijeme, uzbuđena, tužna, lijepo, nedostajati, tjedana, Marijani, zauzeta, telefonom, vježbati, razgovarati, dolazi, preko, izlaz, sretan, Hrvatsku, otišao, mogao, zagrliti, zaplakala, druge, nekoliko

Appendix I: Declension Table—Endings

Nominative Singular (tko? što?)

	adj.	noun	
m.	various/	various	**dobar radnik**
	-i for long form		**dobri radnik**
neu.	-o/e	-o/e	**teško pitanje**
f.	a	-a	**sretna djevojka**
f.Ø	-a	Ø	**hladna noć**

NB: *f.Ø* stands for feminine zero ending nouns.

Nominative Plural

adj.	noun	
-i	-i	**dobri radnici**
-a	-a	**teška pitanja**
-e	-e	**sretne djevojke**
-e	-i	**hladne noći**

NB1: short *m.* nouns add **-ovi/evi** thus **stol-ovi, oč-evi** (**-evi** is added if word ends in **š,ž,č,ć,dž,đ,nj,lj,j,c**).
NB2: **kgh** before **-i** changes to **czs** (**jezik-jezici**).

Accusative Singular (koga? što?)

	adj.	noun	
m. inan	same as nom.		**veliki grad**
m. anim.	-og/-eg	-a	**dobrog radnika**
neu.	same as nom.		**teško pitanje**
f.	-u	-u	**sretnu djevojku**
f.Ø	-u	Ø	**hladnu noć**

Accusative Plural

adj.	noun	
-e	-e	**velike gradove**
-e	-e	**dobre radnike**
-a	-a	**teška pitanja**
-e	-e	**sretne djevojke**
-e	-i	**hladne noći**

Genitive Singular (koga? čega?)

	adj.	noun	
m.	-og/-eg	-a	**dobrog radnika**
neu.	-og/-eg	-a	**teškog pitanja**
f.	-e	-e	**sretne djevojke**
f.Ø	-e	-i	**hladne noći**

NB: a few *neu.* nouns (**dijete, vrijeme**) insert **-et/en** before singular case endings other than *nom.* & *acc.* The root vowel also shortens. Thus: **djeteta, vremena.**

Genitive Plural

adj.	noun	
-ih	-a	**dobrih radnika**
-ih	-a	**teških pitanja**
-ih	-a	**sretnih djevojaka**
-ih	-i	**hladnih noći**

NB: some *f.* **-a** nouns can also behave like *f.Ø* nouns (**majki, gužvi**).
NB2: insert **-a** if stem ends in two consonants other than **st/št/šć/šč/zd/žd/žđ** (thus **pisama, djevojaka,** but **pošta**).

Dative/Locative Singular (kome? čemu?) / **Dative/Locative Plural**

	adj.	noun		adj.	noun	
m.	-om/em	-u	**dobrom radniku**	-im	-ima	**dobrim radnicima**
neu.	-om/em	-u	**teškom pitanju**	-im	-ima	**teškim pitanjima**
f.	-oj	-i	**sretnoj djevojci**	-im	-ama	**sretnim djevojkama**
f.Ø	-oj	-i	**hladnoj noći**	-im	-ima	**hladnim noćima**

NB: *f.* nouns change **kgh** before **-i** to **czs.** Some exceptions **(baka-baki).** Those ending in **-h** can go either way **(epohi/eposi).**

NB: As in *nom. pl., m.* & *neu.* nouns change **kgh** to **czs** before **-i** **(jezik-jezici-jezicima).**

Instrumental Singular (kim? čim?) / **Instrumental Plural**

	adj.	noun		adj.	noun	
m.	-im	-om/em	**dobrim radnikom**	-im	-ima	**dobrim radnicima**
neu.	-im	-om/em	**teškim pitanjem**	-im	-ima	**teškim pitanjima**
f.	-om	-om	**sretnom djevojkom**	-im	-ama	**sretnim djevojkama**
f.Ø	-om	-i/u	**hladnom noći**	-im	-ima	**hladnim noćima**

NB: *f.Ø* nouns ending in **-ost/-est** or soft stem can take **-i (mladosti, riječi) or -u** with softening **(mladošću, riječju).**

Vocative Singular / **Vocative Plural (same as *nom. pl.*)**

	adj.	noun		adj.	noun	
m.	-i	-e/u	**dobri radniče**	- i	- i	**dobri radnici**
neu.	-o/e	-o/e	**teško pitanje**	-a	-a	**teška pitanja**
f.	-a	-o	**sretna djevojko**	-e	-e	**sretne djevojke**
f.Ø	-a	-i	**hladna noći**	-e	-i	**hladne noći**

NB: *Neu.* & *m.* nouns change **kgh** before **-e** to **čžš (momak-momče).**
NB2: *Neu.* & *m.* nouns ending in soft stem take **-u (prijatelju).**

Appendix II: Declension Table—Examples

NOMINATIVE

	m. sg.	*m. pl.*	*f. sg.*	*f. pl.*	*neu. sg.*	*neu. pl.*
tko	**mlad vozač**	**mladi vozači**	**visoka žena**	**visoke žene**	**mirno more**	**mirna mora**
što	**moj pas**	**moji psi**	**moja sestra**	**moje sestre**	**moje selo**	**moja sela**
	Vaš muž	**Vaši muževi**	**Vaša ljubav**	**Vaše ljubavi**	**Vaše ime**	**Vaša imena**
	ovaj Amerikanac	**ovi Amerikanci**	**ova stvar**	**ove stvari**	**ovo slovo**	**ova slova**
	kakav spasilac	**kakvi spasioci**	**kakva radost**	**kakve radosti**	**kakvo pitanje**	**kakva pitanja**
	čiji stan	**čiji stanovi**	**čija cijena**	**čije cijene**	**čije pismo**	**čija pisma**
	sav zadatak	**svi zadaci**	**sva vježba**	**sve vježbe**	**sve vino**	**sva vina**

ACCUSATIVE

	m. sg.	*m. pl.*	*f. sg.*	*f. pl.*	*neu. sg.*	*neu. pl.*
koga	**mladog vozača**	**mlade vozače**	**visoku ženu**	*like nom.*	*like nom.*	*like nom*
što	**mojeg psa**	**moje pse**	**moju sestru**	"	"	"
	Vašeg muža	**Vaše muževe**	**Vašu ljubav**	"	"	"
	ovog Amerikanca	**ove Amerikance**	**ovu stvar**	"	"	"
	kakvog spasioca	**kakve spasioce**	**kakvu radost**	"	"	"
inan.	**čiji stan**	**čije stanove**	**čiju cijenu**	"	"	"
	sav zadatak	**sve zadatke**	**svu vježbu**	*like nom.*	*like nom.*	*like nom.*

GENITIVE

	m. sg.	*m. pl.*	*f. sg.*	*f. pl.*	*neu. sg.*	*neu. pl.*
koga	mladog vozača	mladih vozača	visoke žene	visokih žena	mirnog mora	mirnih mora
čega	mojeg psa	mojih pasa	moje sestre	mojih sestara	mojeg sela	mojih sela
	Vašeg muža	Vaših muževa	Vaše ljubavi	Vaših ljubavi	Vašeg imena	Vaših imena
	ovog Amerikanca	ovih Amerikanaca	ove stvari	ovih stvari	ovog slova	ovih slova
	kakvog spasioca	kakvih spasilaca	kakve radosti	kakvih radosti	kakvog pitanja	kakvih pitanja
	čijeg stana	čijih stanova	čije cijene	čijih cijena	čijeg pisma	čijih pisama
	sveg zadatka	svih zadataka	sve vježbe	svih vježba/vježbi	sveg vina	svih vina

DATIVE/LOCATIVE

	m. sg.	*m. pl.*	*f. sg.*	*f. pl.*	*neu. sg.*	*neu. pl.*
kome	mladom vozaču	mladim vozačima	visokoj ženi	visokim ženama	mirnom moru	mirnim morima
čemu	mojem psu	mojim psima	mojoj sestri	mojim sestrama	mojem selu	mojim selima
	Vašem mužu	Vašim muževima	Vašoj ljubavi	Vašim ljubavima	Vašem imenu	Vašim imenima
	ovom Amerikancu	ovim Amerikancima	ovoj stvari	ovim stvarima	ovom slovu	ovim slovima
	kakvom spasiocu	kakvim spasiocima	kakvoj radosti	kakvim radostima	kakvom pitanju	kakvim pitanjima
	čijem stanu	čijim stanovima	čijoj cijeni	čijim cijenama	čijem pismu	čijim pismima
	svem zadatku	svim zadacima	svoj vježbi	svim vježbama	svem vinu	svim vinima

INSTRUMENTAL

	m. sg.	m. pl.	f. sg.	f. pl.	neu. sg.	neu. pl.
kim	mladim vozačem	*like dat./*	visokom ženom	*like dat./*	mirnim morem	*like dat./*
čim	mojim psom	*loc. pl.*	mojom sestrom	*loc. pl.*	mojim selom	*loc. pl.*
	Vašim mužem	"	Vašom ljubavi	"	Vašim imenom	"
	ovim Amerikancem	"	ovom stvari	"	ovim slovom	"
	kakvim spasiocem	"	kakvom radosti	"	kakvim pitanjem	"
	čijim stanom	"	čijom cijenom	"	čijim pismom	"
	svim zadatkom	"	svom vježbom	"	svim vinom	"

VOCATIVE

m. sg.	m. pl.	f. sg.	f. pl.	neu. sg.	neu. pl.
vozaču	vozači	ženo	žene	more	mora
psu	psi	sestro	sestre	selo	sela
mužu	muževi	ljubavi	ljubavi	ime	imena
Amerikanče	Amerikanci	stvari	stvari	slovo	slova
čitaoče	čitaoci	radosti	radosti	pitanje	pitanja
stanu	stanovi	cijeno	cijene	pismo	pisma
zadače	zadaci	vježbo	vježbe	vino	vina

Appendix III: Personal Pronoun Declension Tables

Where two forms exist, the short ones are given first. Short forms are never used at the beginning of a sentence or after a preposition.

SINGULAR

	1st	2nd	3rd *m.*	3rd *f.*	3rd *neu.*
nom.	ja	ti	on	ona	ono
acc.	me, mene	te, tebe	ga, njega	je/ju, nju	ga, njega
gen.	me, mene	te, tebe	ga, njega	je, nje	ga, njega
dat.	mi, meni	ti, tebi	mu, njemu	joj, njoj	mu, njemu
loc.	meni	tebi	njemu	njoj	njemu
instru.	mnom	tobom	njim	njom	njim

PLURAL

	1st	2nd	3rd *m.*	3rd *f.*	3rd *neu.*
nom.	mi	vi	oni	one	ona
acc.	nas	vas	ih, njih	ih, njih	ih, njih
gen.	nas	vas	ih, njih	ih, njih	ih, njih
dat.	nam, nama	vam, vama	im, njima	im, njima	im, njima
loc.	nama	vama	njima	njima	njima
instru.	nama	vama	njima	njima	njima

Appendix IV: Prepositions

bez	*gen.*	without
blizu	*gen.*	near
do	*gen.*	to, next/up to
ispod	*gen.*	under
ispred	*gen.*	in front of
iz	*gen.*	from
iza	*gen.*	behind
između	*gen.*	between
iznad	*gen.*	above
k/ka	*dat.*	to/ward
kod	*gen.*	at/on someone ('s place), by
kroz	*acc.*	through
među	*instru.*	between
na	*acc.*	on/to (in conjunction with motion)
na	*loc.*	on, at (in conjunction with location)
nad	*instru.*	above
nakon	*gen.*	after
nasuprot	*dat.*	opposite from
o	*loc.*	about
od	*gen.*	from
oko	*gen.*	around
po	*dat.*	according to, all over
po	*acc.*	to get something, to meet somebody
pod	*instru.*	under
pored	*gen.*	next to, by
pred	*instru.*	in front of
preko	*gen.*	over, across
prema	*dat.*	toward
protiv	*gen.*	against
s/a	*instru.*	with
s/a	*gen.*	from, off and down from
u	*acc.*	in/to (in conjunction with motion)
u	*loc.*	in, at (in conjunction with location)
uz	*acc.*	next to, alongside
za	*acc.*	for
za	*instru.*	behind

HRVATSKO-ENGLESKI RJEČNIK S LISTOM GLAGOLA

Croatian-English Glossary with Verb List

An italicized *a* indicates a *fleeting -a*; for less predictable forms the genitive and/or the plural is provided. Underlining marks the stress only in words of more than three syllables. In two-syllable words, the accent falls on the first syllable.

A

a and, but
adresa address
aerodrom airport
ako if
ali but
Amerika America
Amerik*a*n*a*c *m.* American *(man)*
Amerikanka *f.* American *(woman)*
analiza analysis
apartman vacation condo, hotel suite
auto, automobil car
autobus bus
autocesta highway
avion airplane
avionski *adj.* airplane

B

balkon balcony
banka bank *(financial institution)*
bar bar *(tavern, pub)*
barem at least
baš really, exactly, quite
baština heritage *(historical or cultural)*
bazen swimming pool
benzin gasoline
bez without
bijel white
blagajna cash register
blagajnica *f.* cashier
blagdan holiday
bliz*a*k close, near
blizu near
bluza blouse
bogat rich, wealthy
boja color
bok hi (*informal*)
bolest*a*n sick
bolje better
bolnica hospital
borav*a*k stay
Bostonka *f.* Bostonian
brak marriage
brat brother
briga worry
brod ship
broj number
brz fast
brzo quickly
buč*a*n noisy
budući da since
budućnost *f.* future

C

car emperor
carina customs
cent*a*r center
cijel whole
cijena price
cipela shoe
crkva church
crven red

Č

čak even
čarapa sock, stocking
čast *f.* honor
čaša glass
čest frequent
često often
četvrt*a*k Thursday
čim as soon as
čist clean
čitatelj reader
čizma boot
čokoladni kolač chocolate cake
čovjek/ljudi *pl.* man
čud*a*n strange
čvrst firm

D

da yes; *conj.* that
dalek far, distant
daleko *adv.* far
dalje continuously, further
Dalmatin*a*c *m.* Dalmatian *(man)*
dan/dani *pl.* day
danas today
dar present
datum date
davno long ago
debeo/debelog *gen.* fat, thick
dečko boyfriend, boy, guy
definitivno definitely
dekagram decagram
desno right
detalj detail
deterdžent detergent
dijete/djeteta *gen.*/**djeca** *nom. pl.* child
dio/dijela *gen.* part
divno wonderful
dizalo elevator
djelatnik *m.*/**djelatnica** *f.* employee, worker
djevojka girl, girlfriend
do to, next/up to
dob*a*r good
dobro *adv.* well
dobro došla *f.*/**dobro došao** *m.*/**dobro došli** *pl.* welcome
dodatni additional
dogovor appointment, agreement
doj*a*m impression
dok while
dok ne until
doktorat doctorate
dolaz*a*k/dolaska *gen.* arrival
domaći domestic, homemade
domaćin host
doruč*a*k breakfast
dosadno boring
dosta quite, enough
doviđenja good-bye
dovoljno enough, sufficient
drag dear, favorite
drago mi je I am pleased
drugačije *adv.* differently
drugdje elsewhere
drugi other, second
društvo company, society
dug long
dvokrevetna soba double bedroom
dvorište courtyard
dvosob*a*n one-bedroom apartment

Dž

džemper sweater

E

ekonomist *m.*/**ekonomistica** *f.* economist
era era
europski European
evo here it is/are

F

fakultet college
formular form

G

galerija gallery
gdje where
glad*a*n hungry
glava head
glavni main

glazba music
glup stupid
glupost *f.* stupidity
godina year
gor*a*k bitter
gospodarstvo economy
gospodin Mr.
gospođa Mrs.
gospođica Miss
gost guest
gotov finished, ready, done
gotovina cash
grad city
gramatika grammar
greška mistake, fault
grijanje heating
grožđe *pl.* grapes
grub rough, coarse
gužva crowd, busy place, uproar

H

hajde/hajdemo let's do it *(informal)*
haljina dress
hitna pomoć ambulance, emergency response unit
hlače *pl.* pants
hlad*a*n cold
hladnjak refrigerator
hodanje walking
hotel hotel
hrana food
Hrvat *m.* Croatian *(man)*
Hrvatica *f.* Croatian *(woman)*
Hrvatska Croatia
hrvatski *adj.* Croatian
hvala thank you

I

i and
i meni me too
ideja idea
idući next
ili or
ime/imena *pl.* name
inače otherwise, generally
ipak nonetheless, still
isključen turned off, excluded
ispit exam
ispod under
isprava document
ispred in front of
istina true, truth
isto same
iz from
iza behind
izbor choice
izgrađen built
izgubljen lost
izlaz exit
izlet trip
između between
iznad above
iznajmljivanje renting
iznenađenje surprise
izvješće report
izvolite *(formal)* here you are
izvoz export
izvrst*a*n/izvrsnog *gen.*/**izvrsna** *f.* excellent, extraordinary

J

jabuka apple
jak strong
jako very
jas*a*n clear
javni public
jed*a*n one, a
jedinstven unique
jedno i drugo both
jednokrevetna soba single room
jednosob*a*n studio
jedva hardly
jeftin cheap, inexpensive
jelo dish, meal, food, course
jelovnik menu
jer because
jesen fall
jezik language
jogurt yogurt
još more, another, still, in addition
jučer yesterday
jug south

juha soup
juha od povrća vegetable soup

K
k/ka to, toward
kada when
kak*a*v what kind of, such
kako how
kamo where to
kao like
kapa cap
kaput coat
karta ticket
kasno late
kat floor
katedrala cathedral
kava coffee
kavana café
kazalište theater
kćer daughter
kilogram kilogram *(2.2 lbs.)*
kino movie theater
ključ key
knjiga book
knjižara bookstore
knjižnica library
kod at someone's, in someone's possession, near, by
kofer suitcase
kolač sweet, cake
kolega *m.*, **kolegica** *f.* colleague
koliko how much/many
komad piece
konačno finally
konobar waiter
kontrola control
kostim woman's suit
košulja shirt
kraj end, region
krat*a*k short, brief
kravata tie
kreditna kartica credit card
krevet bed
kriv crooked, guilty
križanje crossing
kruh bread
kuća house
kuda where to
kuhinja kitchen
kuna Croatian currency
kupaće (gaće) swimming trunks
kupaći kostim swimming suit
kupaonica bathroom
kupovina shopping

L
laboratorij laboratory
lagan light
lak *adj.* **lako** *adv.* easy
let flight
lift elevator
lijek medication
lijen lazy
lijep beautiful, lovely
lijepo *adv.* nicely, beautifully
lijevo left
litra liter *(.26 gallons)*
lokacija location
loš bad
loše *adv.* badly
lud crazy
luka port
luksuz luxury

Lj
ljekarna pharmacy
ljeto summer
ljubav *f.* love
ljubaz*a*n kind
ljudi people
ljut angry

M
majica T-shirt
majka mother
majstor master, repairman
malen, mali small
malo a little, little
maloprije a little bit ago
manje less, fewer
materijal material
među between

međunarodni international
meni to me
meso meat
meso na žaru grilled meat
miješan mixed
milijun million
mineralna voda mineral water
minuta minute
miris smell, scent
mirno *adv.* peaceful
mišljenje opinion
mjenjačnica currency, exchange office
mjesec month
mjesečno monthly
mjesto place, space
mlad young
mlijeko milk
mnogo a lot
mobitel cell phone
moder*a*n fashionable, modern
moguće possible
mogućnost *f.* opportunity, possibility
moj my
molba request
molim Vas/vas please
more sea
možda maybe
mršav slim, skinny
muzej museum
muzika music
muž husband

N

na on, onto
na primjer for example
„na ti" to use informal address
nad above
nadaren creative
najprije firstly, first of all
nakon after
namirnice *pl.* groceries
namjera intention
napojnica tip
naprijed forward
naravno of course
narodni folk
nasamo *adv.* alone, in private
nastanjen inhabited
nasuprot opposite from
natrag back
navečer in the evening
Nazdravlje! Cheers! *(also* **Živjeli!***)*
nažalost regrettably, unfortunately
nečiji someone's
nedjelja Sunday
negativ*a*n negative
negdje somewhere
nego than
nehotice by chance
nekada once, at some time
nekako somehow
neki some
nekoliko several
nepouzdan unreliable
nešto something
netko somebody
nevjerojatno incredibly
ni/niti neither, nor
ničiji no one's
nigdje nowhere
nikada never
nikako in no way
nikamo nowhere (with verbs of motion)
ništa nothing
nitko nobody
niz*a*k/niskog *gen.* short, low
no but
noć *f.* night
noćas tonight
noćenje overnight stay
noga leg
nogomet football
nogometni *adj.* football
nov new
nov*a*c/novca *gen.* money
novčanik wallet
novine *pl.* newspapers
novosti *pl.* news

Nj

njegov his

O
o about
obala coast
obavijest announcement
obično *adv.* usually
obitelj *f.* family
oboje both *m./f.*
obveza obligation
obzir consideration
očajan desperate
od from
odande from there
odavde from here
odgovor answer
odijelo suit
odjeća clothes
odlazak/odlaska *gen.* departure
odličan excellent
odlično excellently
odluka decision
odmah immediately
odmor vacation, break, rest
odmorište rest area
oduvijek always, since long ago
oglas advertisement
oko eye, approximately, around
omiljen *m.* favorite
onda then
opet again
ormar wardrobe
osim beside, in addition to, except for
osoba person
osoban personal
osobina trait
osobito especially
ostali remaining
ostatak remnant, remaining part
otac/oca *gen.*/**očevi** *nom. pl.* father
otkako since
otkud from where
otok island
otvoren open
ovaj *m.* this
ovaj put this time
ovako this way
ovamo this way, in this direction
ovdje here
ozbiljan serious
oženjen married *(man)*

P
pa so, therefore, then
pad decrease, fall, drop
paket package
pakiranje packing
palača palace
palačinke crepes
pametan clever
par (a) couple of, a few
pas/psa *gen.* dog
petak Friday
piće beverage
pismo letter *(postal)*
pitanje question
pivo beer
pješke on foot
plaća salary
plav blue
plaža beach
plin gas
po according to, all over, apiece, each
početak beginning
pod *prep.* under; floor
podrum cellar
pogled view, glance
pogotovo especially
pogrešan wrong
pokazatelj indicator
pola half
polako slowly
polazak/polaska *gen.* departure, leaving
polica shelf
policajac policeman
policija police
polovina half
položen passed, laid down horizontally
polupansion half board
pomalo a little bit
pomoćni ležaj additional bed
ponašanje behavior
ponedjeljak Monday
ponekad sometimes

ponuda offer
popodne [this] afternoon
pored next to, by
porez tax
portal portal
poruka message
posao/poslovi *pl.*/**posla** *gen. sg.* job
poseban special
posjet visit
poslije later
poslovan business
poslovanje doing business
poslovnica company branch
posljednji last
pospan sleepy
pošta post office
potom after that
potpuno entirely
potreba necessity, need
potrebno necessary
povijest *f.* history
povišica raise (in salary)
povoljan suitable, cost-effective
povratni return, round-trip
povrće vegetables
pozitivan positive
poznat known
pravac direction, way
pravi real
pravo right, law
prazan empty
pred in front of, before
predah break
predavanje lecture
predgrađe suburb
predjelo appetizer
preko over
prekjučer day before yesterday
prekrasan magnificent, very beautiful
preksutra day after tomorrow
prema toward
premalo too little
premlad too young
preskup too expensive
pretvoren transformed
prevelik too big
previše too much, too many
priča story
pričanje talking
prijatelj *m.* friend
prijateljica *f.* friend
prije earlier, before
prijedlog suggestion
prijevoz transportation
prikladan suitable, appropriate
prilično quite
prilika chance
primjer example
primjerak copy
primljen accepted
primorski coastal
privatan private
prljav dirty
problem problem
prodavačica *f.* salesperson
prodavaonica shop
prognoza forecast
proizvod product
prolaz aisle, passage
proljeće spring *(season)*
promet traffic
prometan busy with traffic
promjena change
protiv against
prozor window
prostran spacious
prtljaga luggage
prvi put first time
pržen fried
pult counter
pun full
puni pansion full board
puno a lot of
put way, time, journey
putnik passenger
putnički *adj.* passenger
putovnica passport

R

račun bill, receipt
računalo computer

radije more gladly, preferably
radnik worker
rado gladly
radost *f.* joy
radostan happy, joyful
ranije earlier
rano *adv.* early
raspoložen za in the mood for
rastresen scattered
ravnatelj *m.*, **ravnateljica** *f.* CEO
ravno straight *(direction)*
razni various
razglas loudspeaker
razgledavanje sightseeing
različit different
razlika difference
razlog reason, cause
razočaran disappointed
recept prescription, recipe
redovito regularly
referat paper, report (written)
restoran restaurant
rezervacija reservation
rezultat result
režije utilities
riba fish
riblja juha fish soup
riječ *f.* word
rijedak/rijetkog *gen.* rare, not thick
rijeka river
rijetko rarely
rimski Roman
rižoto risotto
rječnik dictionary
roditelj parent
rođak *m.*/**rođaka** *f.* cousin
rođen born
rođendan birthday
romantično *adv.* romantic
roštilj grill
rublje underwear
ručak lunch
ruka arm, hand
rukopis manuscript, handwriting
ružan ugly

S

s with, from/off
sada now
salama salami
salata salad
sam *m.*/**sama** *f.* alone
samo only
samoposluživanje grocery store
samostan monastery
sapun soap
sastanak meeting
sat/sati *pl.* hour
sat/satovi *pl.* clock, watch
sažetak summary
selo village
semafor traffic light
sendvič sandwich
sestra sister
siguran sure
sigurno definitely, surely
sigurnost *f.* safety, security
sin son
sinoć last night
sir cheese
siromašan poor
sitnica trifle
sitniš change *(money)*
sjedalo seat
skoro almost, soon
skroman modest
skup expensive
slab weak
sladak/slatkog *gen.* sweet
sličan similar
slika picture
slobodan free, available
slovo letter *(in alphabet)*
slučaj case
slučajno *adv.* by chance
službenica *f.* clerk
smiješan funny
smisao/smisla *gen. sg.* sense
smjer direction, way
sniženje sale
soba room
sok juice

spasil*a*c rescuer
spomenik monument
spor slow
sprem*a*n ready
sreća luck, luckily
sret*a*n happy
srijeda Wednesday
stalno *adv.* always, constantly
stan apartment
stanarina rent
stanica stop, station
stanovit certain
star old
sto hundred
stol table
stolica, **stol*a*c** chair
stoljeće century
strana side
stranka client
strašno *adv.* terrible
stručnjak expert
struja electricity
stube stairs
student *m.* student
studentica *f.* student
studentski *adj.* student
studentski dom dormitory
studij coursework *(at college)*, a course of study
stvar *f.* thing
stvarno *adv.* really
subota Saturday
sunce sun
sunčano *adv.* sunny
suparništvo competition
suradnik business partner
sutra tomorrow
suvenir souvenir
svakako definitely, by all means
svaki each, every
svečan festive
svejedno all the same
sveti holy, saint
svi, sve all
svijet world
svjetski *adj.* world
svjež fresh
svoj one's own
svuda everywhere *(with verbs of motion)*
svugdje everywhere

Š

šala joke
šampon shampoo
šećer sugar
šešir hat
šetnica promenade
širok wide
škola school
šorc shorts
šteta pity, damage
što what, that

T

tada then
tajnica secretary
tak*a*v such
tako that way
tako-tako so-so
također also, too
taksi cab
tamo there
tečaj exchange rate
tek only, barely
telefon phone
telefonska govornica telephone booth
televizor TV
tenisko igralište tennis court
teško *adv.* difficult, hard
tetka aunt
tež*a*k/teškog *gen.* difficult
tih quiet
tijekom in the course of
tisuća thousand
tjed*a*n week
tko who
točno *adv.* correctly
toliko so much/many
topao/toplog *gen.* warm
torba bag
tradicija tradition
tradicionalno *adv.* traditionally
trajekt ferry
trajektna luka ferry port

tramvaj tram, streetcar
traperice jeans
treći third
trenutačno right now, momentarily
trenutak moment
trg square
trgovina shop
trošak expenditure
tržište market *(economic)*
tržnica food market
tu here
turist tourist
turizam tourism
tužan sad
tvrtka/tvrtki *gen.* company
tvornica factory

U
u in, into
udana married *(woman)*
ugao/ugla *gen.* corner
uglavnom *adv.* mainly
ugodno *adv.* pleasantly
ugovor contract
ujutro in the morning
uključen turned on (switch, machine), included
ukratko briefly
ukupno total, totally
ulaz entrance
ulica street
umjesto instead
umoran tired
unutra inside
uopće in general, at all
upravo just
ured office
uskoro soon
uspjeh success
uspješan successful
uspješno successfully
uspon ascent
usput along/by the way
utakmica match (in sport)
utorak Tuesday
uvijek always
uvoz import
uzak/uskog *gen.* narrow
uzbuđen excited
užitak pleasure

V
valjda possibly, perhaps
van outside *(destination)*
vani outside *(location)*
važan important
večera dinner
večeras tonight
već already
velik big
veoma very
vez berth
vijesti news
vikend weekend
vino wine
visok tall
više more
vjerojatno likely
vježba exercise
vlak train
vlasnik owner
vlastit one's own
voće fruit
voda water
vozač driver
vozačka dozvola driver's license
vozilo vehicle, car
vožnja driving
vrijeme/vremena *gen. sg.*/**vremena** *pl., gen. pl.* time, weather
vrlo very
vrsta type, kind
vrt garden
vruć hot
vruće *adv.* hotly

Z
za for, behind
zabava party *(social event)*
zabranjen forbidden
začas quickly, in a flash, in a moment

zadatak task
zadnji last
zadovoljan satisfied, content
Zagrepčanin *m.* inhabitant of Zagreb
zaista indeed, really
zajednički common
zajedno together
zaključak conclusion
zanimljiv interesting
zanimljivo *adv.* interestingly
zao/zlog *gen.* evil
zaposlenik employee
zapravo actually, as a matter of fact
zaštićen protected
zašto why
zato therefore, hence
zatvoren closed
zauzet busy, occupied
završen finished
zbirka collection
zbog because of
zbunjen confused
zdravlje health
zelen green
zemlja country, land, soil
zgodno lovely, nice
zgrada building
zidine walls *(esp. city walls)*
zima winter
značenje meaning
znamenitost *f.* sight, point of interest
zračna luka airport
zrakoplov plane

Ž

žedan thirsty
želudac stomach
željeznički kolodvor railway station
žena woman, wife
Živjeli! Cheers! *(also* **Nazdravlje!***)*
življenje living
život life
žut yellow

Verb List

Aspect is indicated as *P* for perfective and *I* for imperfective. When there is an aspectual pair, the two verbs are given. For each verb, the first person singular and third person plural forms are given; for irregular verbs, the third person singular is given as well. Past tense is given (*past*) for irregular verbs in the masculine singular form. **Biti** *to be* is given in its present tense conjugation.

baciti (*P* **bacim**, **bace**; *I* **bacati**) to throw
biti (ja sam, **ti si**, **on je**, **mi smo**, **vi ste**, **oni su**) to be
bližiti (se) (*I* **bližim**, **bliže**; *P* **približiti**) to approach
bojati se (*I* **bojim se**, **boje se**; *P* **pobojati se**) to be afraid of
boljeti (*I* **bolim**, **bole**; *past*: **bolio**; *P* **zaboljeti**) to hurt
brinuti (se) (*I* **brinem**, **brinu**; *P* **zabrinuti se** = to worry, **pobrinuti se** = to take care of) to worry, to take care of
brojiti (*I* **brojim**, **broje**; *P* **izbrojiti**) to count
cijeniti (*I* **cijenim**, **cijene**) to appreciate
častiti (*I* **častim**, **časte**; *P* **počastiti**) to treat
čekati (*I*, **čekam**, **čekaju**; *P* **počekati**) to wait
čestitati (*I/P* **čestitam**, **čestitaju**) to congratulate
činiti (*I* **činim**, **čine**; *P* **učiniti**) to do
činiti se (*I* **činim se**, **čine se**) to seem, to give an impression

čitati (*I* **čitam**, **čitaju**; *P* **pročitati**) to read
čuti (*P/I* **čujem**, **čuju**) to hear
dati (*P irr.*: **dam**, **da**, **daju**; *I* **davati**) to give
davati (*I* **dajem**, **daju**; *P* **dati**) to give
desiti se (*P* **desim se**, **dese se**; *I* **dešavati se**) to happen
dobiti (*P* **dobijem**, **dobiju**; *I* **dobijati**) to get
doći (*P* **dođem**, **dođu**; *past*: **došao**; *I* **dolaziti**) to come
dočekati (*P* **dočekam**, **dočekaju**; *I* **dočekivati**) to meet
dogoditi se (*P* **dogodim se**, **dogode se**; *I* **događati se**) to happen, to occur
dodati (*P* **dodam**, **dodaju**; *I* **dodavati**) to add
dogovoriti se (*P* **dogovorim**, **dogovore**; *I* **dogovarati se**) to agree (upon)
dolaziti (*I* **dolazim**, **dolaze**; *P* **doći**) to come
donijeti (*P* **donesem**, **donesu**; *I* **nositi** = to carry) to bring
dopustiti (*P* **dopustim**, **dopuste**; *I* **dopuštati**) to allow
držati (*I* **držim**, **drže**; *P* **pridržati**, **zadržati**) to hold, to keep
gledati (*I* **gledam**, **gledaju**; *P* **pogledati**) to look
govoriti (*I* **govorim**, **govore**; *P* **reći**; **progovoriti** = to utter, **dogovoriti** = to agree) to speak
graditi (*I* **gradim**, **grade**; *P* **izgraditi**) to build
gubiti (*I* **gubim**, **gube**; *P* **izgubiti**) to lose
gurnuti (*P* **gurnem**, **gurnu**; *I* **gurati**) to push
hodati (*I* **hodam**, **hodaju**) to walk
htjeti (*I irr.*: **hoću**, **hoće**, **hoće**; *negated*: **neću**, **neće**, **neće**; *past*: **htio**) to wish, to want
ići (*I* **idem**, **idu**; *past:* **išao**; *P* **doći**) to go
igrati (*I*, **igram**, **igraju**; *P* **zaigrati**) to play (a game)
imati (*I* **imam**, **ima**, **imaju**; *negative*: **nemam**, **nema**, **nemaju**) to have
ispasti (*P* **ispadnem**, **ispadnu**; *past*: **ispao**; *I* **ispadati**) to fall out
ispričati se (*P* **ispričam se**, **ispričaju se**; I **ispričavati se**) to excuse
ispuniti (*P* **ispunim**, **ispune**; *I* **ispunjavati**) to fill out
izabrati (*P* **izaberem**, **izaberu**; *I* **birati**) to choose
izbrojiti (*P* **izbrojim**, **izbroje**; *I* **brojiti**) to count
izgledati (*I* **izgledam**, **izgledaju**) to seem, to appear
izgubiti (*P* **izgubim**, **izgube**; *I* **gubiti**) to lose
izmisliti (*P* **izmislim**, **izmisle**; *I* **izmišljati**) to invent, to fabricate
iznajmiti (*P* **iznajmim**, **iznajme**; *I* **iznajmljivati**) to rent to someone
javiti se (*P* **javim se**, **jave se**; *I* **javljati se**) to call, to get in touch
jesti (*I* **jedem**, **jedu**; *past*: **jeo**; *P* **pojesti**) to eat
kasniti (*I* **kasnim**, **kasne**; *P* **zakasniti**) to be late
kazati (*P* **kažem**, **kažu**; *I* **kazivati**) to say
koristiti + *acc.* (**se** + *instru.*) (*I* **koristim**, **koriste**; *P* **iskoristiti** *acc.*) to use, to utilize
koštati (*I* **koštam**, **koštaju**) to cost
krenuti (*P* **krenem**, **krenu**; *I* **kretati**) to set off
kretati (*I* **krećem**, **kreću**; *P* **krenuti**) to set off
kuhati (*I* **kuham**, **kuhaju**; *P* **skuhati**) to cook
kupiti (*P* **kupim**, **kupe**; *I* **kupovati**) to buy

kupovati (*I* **kupujem, kupuju**; *P* **kupiti**) to buy
lagati (*I* lažem, **lažu**; *P* **slagati**) to lie, not tell the truth
ležati (*I* **ležim, leže**; *P* **leći**) to lie
ljutiti (se) (*I* **ljutim, ljute**; *P* **naljutiti**) to anger, to get angry
maknuti (*P* **maknem, maknu**; *I* **micati**) to move
micati (*I* **mičem, miču**; *P* **maknuti**) to move
misliti (*I* **mislim, misle**; *P* **pomisliti**) to think
moći (*I irr.* **mogu, može, mogu**; *past*: **mogao**) to be able to, can
moliti (*I* **molim, mole**; *P* **zamoliti**) to beg, to ask for
morati (*I* **moram, moraju**) to have to, must
naći (*P* **nađem, nađu**; *past*: **našao**; *I* **nalaziti**) to find
nadati se (*I* **nadam se, nadaju se**; *P* **ponadati se**) to hope
najavljivati (*I* **najavljujem, najavljuju**; *P* **najaviti**) to announce
nalaziti (*I* **nalazim, nalaze**; *P* **naći**) to find
nalaziti se (*I* **nalazim se, nalaze se**; *P* **naći se**) to be situated
napraviti (*P* **napravim, naprave**; *I* **praviti**) to do, get done
napuniti (*P* **napunim, napune**; *I* **puniti**) to fill
naručiti (*P* **naručim, naruče**; *I* **naručivati**) to order
nastaviti (*P* **nastavim, nastave**; *I* **nastavljati**) to continue
naučiti (*P* **naučim, nauče**; *I* **učiti**) to learn, to master
nazvati (*P* **nazovem, nazovu**; *I* **nazivati**) to call
nedostajati (*I* **nedostajem, nedostaju**) to miss
nositi (*I* **nosim, nose**; *P* **donijeti**) to carry, to wear (*I only*)
obavijestiti (*P* **obavijestim, obavijeste**; *I* **obavještavati**) to inform
obećati (*P* **obećam, obećaju**; *I* **obećavati**) to promise
objasniti (*P* **objasnim, objasne**; *I* **objašnjavati**) to explain
očekivati (*I* **očekujem, očekuju**) to expect
odgovarati (*I* **odgovaram, odgovaraju**; *P* **odgovoriti**) to answer, to be suitable (*I* only)
odlaziti (*I* **odlazim, odlaze**; *P* **otići**) to leave
odlučiti (*P* **odlučim, odluče**; *I* **odlučivati**) to decide
odmoriti se (*P* **odmorim se, odmore se**; *I* **odmarati se**) to rest
odvesti (*P* **odvezem, odvezu**; *past*: **odvezao**; *I* **odvoziti**) to give a ride
omogućiti (*P* **omogućim, omoguće**; *I* **omogućavati**) to make possible
oprostiti (*P* **oprostim, oproste**; *I* **opraštati**) to forgive
opustiti se (*P* **opustim se, opuste se**; *I* **opuštati se**) to relax
organizirati (*I/P* **organiziram, organiziraju**) to organize
osjećati (*I* **osjećam, osjećaju**; *P* **osjetiti**) to feel
ostajati (*I* **ostajem, ostaju**; *P* **ostati**) to stay
ostati (*P* **ostanem, ostanu**; *I* **ostajati**) to stay
ostaviti (*P* **ostavim, ostave**; *I* **ostavljati**) to leave
ostavljati (*I* **ostavljam, ostavljaju**; *P* **ostaviti**) to leave, to abandon
otići (*P* **otiđem, otiđu**; *past*: **otišao**; *I* **odlaziti**) to go away, to leave
otputovati (*P* **otputujem, otputuju**; *I* **putovati**) to depart, to leave
otvoriti (*P* **otvorim, otvore**; *I* **otvarati**) to open
padati (*I* **padam, padaju**; *P* **pasti**) to fall

pakirati (se) (*I* **pakiram, pakiraju**; *P* **spakirati**) to pack
parkirati (*I* **parkiram, parkiraju**) to park
pisati (*I* **pišem, pišu**; *P* **napisati**) to write
pitati se (*I* **pitam se, pitaju se**; *P* **zapitati se**) to ask oneself, to wonder
pitati (*I* **pitam, pitaju**; *P* **zapitati**) to ask
piti (*I* **pijem, piju**; *P* **popiti**) to drink
plaćati (*I*, **plaćam, plaćaju**; *P* **platiti**) to pay
plakati (*I* **plačem, plaču**; *P* **rasplakati se**) to cry
planirati (*I* **planiram, planiraju**; *P* **isplanirati**) to plan
platiti (*P* **platim, plate**; *I* **plaćati**) to pay
plesati (*I* **plešem, plešu**; *P* **zaplesati**) to dance
plivati (*I* **plivam, plivaju**; *P* **otplivati**) to swim
počastiti (*P* **počastim, počaste**; *I* **častiti**) to treat
počekati (*P* **počekam, počekaju**; *I* **čekati**) to wait a while
početi (*P* **počnem, počnu**; *I* **počinjati**) to start
počinjati (*I* **počinjem, počinju**; *P* **početi**) to start
pogledati (*P* **pogledam, pogledaju**; *I* **gledati**) to look
pokazati (*P*, **pokažem, pokažu**; *I* **pokazivati**) to show
polaziti (*I* **polazim, polaze**; *P* **poći**) to leave, to set off
poljubiti (*P*, **poljubim, poljube**; *I* **ljubiti**) to kiss
pomagati (*I* **pomažem, pomažu**; **pomoći**) to help
pomoći (*P* **pomognem, pomognu**; *past*: **pomogao**; *I* **pomagati**) to help
ponoviti (*P* **ponovim, ponove**; *I* **ponavljati**) to repeat
ponuditi (*P* **ponudim, ponude**; *I* **nuditi**) to offer
popiti (*P* **popijem, popiju**; *I* **piti**) to drink
popraviti (*P* **popravim, poprave**; *I* **popravljati**) to repair, to fix
porazgovarati (*P* **porazgovaram, porazgovaraju**; *I* **razgovarati**) to talk briefly, to chat
posjećivati (*I* **posjećujem, posjećuju**; *P* **posjetiti**) to visit
posjetiti (*P* **posjetim, posjete**; *I* **posjećivati**) to visit
poslati (*P* **pošaljem, pošalju**; *I* **slati**) to send
poslovati (*I* **poslujem, posluju**; *P* **isposlovati**) to do business
postati (*P* **postanem, postanu**; *I* **postajati**) to become
postojati (*I* **postojim, postoje**) to exist
posuditi (P **posudim, posude**; *I* **posuđivati**) to lend, to borrow
potpisati (se) (*P*, **potpišem, potpišu**; *I* **potpisivati**) to sign
potražiti (*P* **potražim, potraže**; *I* **tražiti**) to look for
potvrditi (*P* **potvrdim, potvrde**; *I* **potvrđivati**) to confirm
povjerovati (*P* **povjerujem, povjeruju**; *I* **vjerovati**) to believe
pozdraviti (*P* **pozdravim, pozdrave**; *I* **pozdravljati**) to greet, to say farewell
poznavati (*I* **poznajem, poznaju**; *P* **upoznati**) to be acquainted with
pozivati (*I* **pozivam, pozivaju**; *P* **pozvati**) to invite
pozvati (*P* **pozovem, pozovu**; *I* **pozivati**) to invite
požuriti (se) (*P* **požurim, požure**; *I* **žuriti**) to hurry
prati (se) (*I* **perem, peru**; *P* **oprati**) to wash (oneself)

predati (*P* **predam, predaju**; *I* **predavati**) to drop off, to submit, to surrender, to lecture (*I* only)
predlagati (*I* **predlažem, predlažu**; *P* **predložiti**) to suggest
predomisliti se (*P* **predomislim se, predomisle se**; *I* **predomišljati se**) to change one's mind
preporučiti (*P* **preporučim, preporuče**; *I* **preporučivati**) to recommend
preporučivati (*I*, **preporučujem, preporučuju**; *P* **preporučiti**) to recommend
pretjerivati (*I* **pretjerujem, pretjeruju**; *P* **pretjerati**) to exaggerate
pretvoriti (*P* **pretvorim, pretvore**; *I* **pretvarati**) to transform, to turn into
pričati (*I* **pričam, pričaju**; *P* **ispričati**) to talk, to narrate
prijeći (*P* **prijeđem, prijeđu**; *I* **prelaziti**) to cross
prilaziti (*I* **prilazim, prilaze**; *P* **prići**) to approach
primati (*I* **primam, primaju**; *P* **primiti**) to accept
primijetiti (*P* **primijetim, primijete**; *I* **primjećivati**) to notice
pripremiti (*P* **pripremim, pripreme**; *I* **pripremati**) to prepare
priređivati (*I* **priređujem, priređuju**; *P* **prirediti**) to prepare
probati (*I/P*, **probam, probaju**; *P* **isprobati**) to try
proći (*P* **prođem, prođu**; *past:* **prošao**; *I* **prolaziti**) to pass
prodavati (*I* **prodajem, prodaju**; *P* **prodati**) to sell
promijeniti (*P* **promijenim, promijene**; *I* **mijenjati**) to change
pronaći (*P* **pronađem, pronađu**; *past*: **pronašao**; *I* **pronalaziti**) to locate, to find
proslaviti (*P* **proslavim, proslave**; *I* **slaviti**) to celebrate
prošetati (*P* **prošetam, prošetaju**; *I* **šetati**) to take a walk
provesti (*P* **provedem, provedu**; *past*: **proveo**; *I* **provoditi**) to spend
provjeriti (*P* **provjerim, provjere**; *I* **provjeravati**) to check
pružati (*I* **pružam, pružaju**; *P* **pružiti**) to stretch, to extend, to offer
pustiti (*P* **pustim, puste**; *I* **puštati**) to let
pušiti (*I* **pušim, puše**; *P* **popušiti**) to smoke
putovati (*I* **putujem, putuju**; *P* **otputovati**) to travel
računati (*I* **računam, računaju**; *P* **izračunati**) to count, to compute
raditi (*I* **radim, rade**; *P* **uraditi**) to work
radovati se (*I* **radujem se, raduju se**; *P* **obradovati se**) to rejoice, to look forward to
razgledati (*P* **razgledam, razgledaju**; *I* **razgledati, razgledavati**) to sightsee
razgovarati (*I* **razgovaram, razgovaraju**; *P* **porazgovarati**) to talk
razmisliti (*P* **razmislim, razmisle**; *I* **razmišljati**) to think through
razumjeti (*I* **razumijem, razumiju**; *past*: **razumio**) to understand
razveseliti (se) (*P* **razveselim, razvesele**; *I* **veseliti**) to make happy
reći (*P* **reknem, reče, reknu**; *past*: **rekao**; *I* **govoriti**) to say
rezervirati (*I/P*, **rezerviram, rezerviraju**) to book
ručati (*I/P* **ručam, ručaju)** to eat lunch
sadržati (*P/I* **sadržim, sadrže**; *I* **sadržavati**) to contain
sadržavati (*I* **sadržavam, sadržavaju**; *P* **sadržati**) to contain
skupljati (*I* **skupljam, skupljaju**; *P* **skupiti**) to collect
saznati (*P* **saznam, saznaju**; *I* **saznavati**) to learn, to find out
seliti se (*I* **selim se, sele se**; *P* **preseliti se**) to move house
silaziti (*I* **silazim, silaze**; *P* **sići**) to descend

sjediti (*I* **sjedim**, **sjede**; *P* **sjesti**) to be seated, *P* to sit down
sjesti (*P* **sjednem**, **sjednu**; *past*: **sjeo**; *P* **sjedati**) to sit down
sjetiti se (*P* **sjetim se**, **sjete se**; *I* **sjećati se**) to remember
skrenuti (*P* **skrenem**, **skrenu**; *I* **skretati**) to turn
skuhati (*P* **skuham**, **skuhaju**; *I* **kuhati**) to cook
slagati se (*I* **slažem se**, **slažu se**; *P* **složiti se**) to agree
slati (*I* **šaljem**, **šalju**; *P* **poslati**) to send
slušati (*I* **slušam**, **slušaju**; *P* **poslušati**) to listen
složiti se (*P* **složim se**, **slože se**; *I* **slagati se**) to agree
smijati se (*I* **smijem se**, **smiju se**; *P* **nasmijati se**) to laugh
smiriti (se) (*P* **smirim**, **smire**; *I* **smirivati**) to calm down
smjeti (*I* **smijem**, **smiju**) to be allowed to
spakirati (se) (*P* **spakiram**, **spakiraju**; *I* **pakirati**) to pack
spavati (*I* **spavam**, **spavaju**; *P* **zaspati**) to sleep
spremati (*I* **spremam**, **spremaju**; *P* **spremiti**) to prepare (exam, food), to get ready, to tidy up
srediti (*P* **sredim**, **srede**; *I* **sređivati**) to sort out
sretati (se) (*I*, **srećem**, **sreću**; *P* **sresti**) to meet
stajati (*I* **stojim**, **stoje**) to be standing
stanovati (*I* **stanujem**, **stanuju**) to reside
stati (*P* **stanem**, **stanu**; *I* **stajati**, **stajem**, **staju**) to stop
staviti (*P* **stavim**, **stave**; *I* **stavljati**) to put
steći (*P* **steknem**, **steknu**; *past*: **stekao**; *I* **stjecati**) to obtain, to acquire
stići (*P* **stignem**, **stignu**; *past*: **stigao**; *I* **stizati**) to arrive
stizati (*I* **stižem**, **stižu**; *P* **stići**) to arrive
studirati (*I* **studiram**, **studiraju**) to study
sumnjati (*I* **sumnjam**, **sumnjaju**; *P* **posumnjati**) to doubt
svađati se (*I* **svađam se**, **svađaju se**; *P* **posvaditi se**) to argue
sviđati se (*I* **sviđam se**, **sviđaju se**; *P* **svidjeti se**) to like
svratiti (*P* **svratim**, **svrate**; *I* **svraćati**) to drop by
šaliti se (*I* **šalim se**, **šale se**; *P* **našaliti se**) to joke
šetati (*I* **šetam**, **šetaju**; *P* **prošetati**) to stroll
škoditi (*I* **škodim**, **škode**; *P* **naškoditi**) to harm, to hurt
štedjeti (*I* **štedim**, **štede**; *P* **uštedjeti**) to save
tražiti (*I* **tražim**, **traže**; *P* **potražiti**) to look for
trebati (*I* **trebam**, **trebaju**; *P* **zatrebati**) to need
učiti (*I* **učim**, **uče**; *P* **naučiti**) to learn
ući (*P* **uđem**, **uđu**; *past*: **ušao**; *I* **ulaziti**) to enter
ugostiti (*P* **ugostim**, **ugoste**; *I* **gostiti**) to host
uložiti (*P* **uložim**, **ulože**; *I* **ulagati**) to invest
unajmiti (*P* **unajmim**, **unajme**; *I* **unajmljivati**) to rent from someone
upotrebljavati (*I* **upotrebljavam**, **upotrebljavaju**; *P* **upotrijebiti**) to use
upoznati (se) (*P* **upoznam**, **upoznaju**; *I* **upoznavati**) to get acquainted
uputiti (*P* **uputim**, **upute**; *I* **upućivati**) to head, to direct
uzeti (*P* **uzmem**, **uzmu**; *I* **uzimati**) to take
uzimati (*I* **uzimam**, **uzimaju**; *P* **uzeti**) to take

uživati (*I* **uživam, uživaju**; *P* **nauživati se**) to enjoy
važiti (*I* **važim, važe**; *P* **uvažiti**) to be valid, to accept (*P* only)
večerati (*P/I* **večeram, večeraju**) to dine
vidjeti (*I/P*, **vidim, vide**; *past*: **vidio**) to see
vidjeti se (*I/P* **vidim se, vide se**; *past*: **vidio se**) to see oneself, each other; to meet
vjerovati (*I* **vjerujem, vjeruju**; *P* **povjerovati**) to believe
vježbati (*I* **vježbam, vježbaju**; *P* **uvježbati**) to practice, to exercise
vladati (*I* **vladam, vladaju**; *P* **zavladati**) to reign
voditi (*I* **vodim, vode**; *P* **provesti**) to lead
voljeti (*I* **volim, vole**; *past*: **volio**; *P* **zavoljeti**) to love, to like
voziti (*I* **vozim, voze**; *P* **dovesti**) to drive
vraćati (se) (*I* **vraćam, vraćaju**; *P* **vratiti**) to return
vratiti (se) (*P* **vratim, vrate**; *I* **vraćati**) to return
vrijediti (*I* **vrijedim, vrijede**; *P* **zavrijediti**) to be valid, to be worth what indicated
zabaviti (se) (*P* **zabavim, zabave**; *I* **zabavljati**) to entertain oneself, to have fun
zaboraviti (*P* **zaboravim, zaborave**; *I* **zaboravljati**) to forget
zaboravljati (*I* **zaboravljam, zaboravljaju**; *P* **zaboraviti**) to forget
zagrliti (*P* **zagrlim, zagrle**; *I* **grliti**) to embrace, to hug
zaključiti (*P* **zaključim, zaključe**; *I* **zaključivati**) to conclude
zaljubiti se (*P* **zaljubim se, zaljube se**; *I* **zaljubljivati se**) to fall in love
zanimati (se) (*I* **zanimam, zanimaju**) to interest
započeti (*P* **započnem, započnu**; *I* **započinjati**) to start
zaposliti (*P* **zaposlim, zaposle**; *I* **zapošljavati**) to employ
završavati (*I* **završavam, završavaju**; *P* **završiti**) to finish
završiti (*P*, **završim, završe**; *I* **završavati**) to finish
značiti (*I* **značim, znače**) to mean
znati (*I* **znam, znaju**; *P* **saznati**) to know
zvati (*I* **zovem, zovu**; *P* **nazvati** = to phone, to name; **pozvati** = to call out, to invite) to call
zvati se (*I* **zovem se, zovu se**; *P* **nazvati se**) to be called
zvučiti (*I* **zvučim, zvuče**, *P* **zazvučati**) to sound
žaliti se (*I* **žalim se, žale se**; *P* **požaliti se**) to complain
željeti (*I* **želim, žele**; *past*: **želio**; *P* **poželjeti**) to wish, to want
živjeti (*I* **živim, žive**; *past*: **živio**; *P* **poživjeti**) to live
žuriti (se) (*I* **žurim, žure**; *P* **požuriti**) to rush

ENGLESKO-HRVATSKI RJEČNIK S LISTOM GLAGOLA

English-Croatian Glossary with Verb List

A

a couple of, a few par
a little, little malo
a little bit pomalo
a little bit ago maloprije
a lot mnogo, puno
about o
above iznad, nad
accepted primljen
according to, all over, apiece po
actually, as a matter of fact zapravo
additional dodatni
additional bed pomoćni ležaj
address adresa
advertisement oglas
after nakon
afternoon popodne
after that potom
again opet
against protiv
airplane zrakoplov, avion *n.*; avionski *adj.*
airport zračna luka, aerodrom
aisle, passage prolaz
all svi, sve
all the same svejedno
almost, soon skoro
alone nasamo *adv.*; sam *m.*, sama *f.*
along/by the way usput
already već
also, too također
always uvijek
always, constantly stalno *adv.*
always, since long ago oduvijek
ambulance, emergency response unit hitna pomoć
America Amerika
American Amerikan*a*c *m.*/Amerikanka *f.*
analysis analiza
and i; a
angry ljut
announcement obavijest
answer odgovor
apartment stan
appetizer predjelo
apple jabuka
appointment, agreement dogovor
approximately, around; **eye** oko
arm ruka
arrival dolaz*a*k/dolaska *gen.*
ascent uspon
as soon as čim
at least barem
at someone's, near, by kod
aunt tetka
available, free slobod*a*n

B

back natrag
bad loš
badly loše *adv.*
bag torba
balcony balkon
bank *(financial institution)* banka
bar *(tavern, pub)* bar
bathroom kupaonica
beach plaža
beautiful, lovely lijep
because jer
because of zbog
bed krevet
beer pivo
before prije
beginning poč*e*t*a*k

behavior ponašanje
behind iza
berth vez
beside, in addition to, except for osim
better bolje
between između; među
beverage piće
big velik
bill, receipt račun
birthday rođendan
bitter gor*a*k
blouse bluza
blue plav *m.*
book knjiga
bookstore knjižara
boot čizma
boring dosadno
born rođen
Bostonian Bostonka *f.*
both oboje *m./f.*; jedno i drugo
boyfriend, boy, guy dečko
bread kruh
break predah
break, rest, vacation odmor
breakfast doruč*a*k
briefly ukratko
brother brat
building zgrada
built izgrađen
bus autobus
business poslov*a*n
business partner suradnik
busy, occupied zauzet
busy with traffic promet*a*n
but ali; no; a
by all means svakako
by chance nehotice; slučajno *adv.*

C
cab taksi
café kavana
cake, sweet kolač
cap kapa
car auto, automobil
case slučaj
cash gotovina
cashier blagajnica *f.*
cash register blagajna
cathedral katedrala
cellar podrum
cell phone mobitel
center cent*a*r
century stoljeće
CEO ravnatelj *m.*, ravnateljica *f.*
certain stanovit
chair stolica, stol*a*c
chance prilika
change promjena; sitniš *n.* (coins)
cheap, inexpensive jeftin
Cheers! Živjeli! *(also Nazdravlje!)*
cheese sir
child dijete/djeteta *gen.*/djeca *nom. pl.*
chocolate cake čokoladni kolač
choice izbor
church crkva
city grad
clean čist
clear jas*a*n
clerk službenica *f.*
clever pamet*a*n
client stranka
clock, watch sat/satovi *pl.*
close bliz*a*k
closed zatvoren
clothes odjeća
coast obala
coastal primorski
coat kaput
coffee kava
cold hlad*a*n
colleague kolega *m.*, kolegica *f.*
collection zbirka
college fakultet
color boja
common zajednički
company tvrtka/tvrtki *gen.*
company branch poslovnica
company, society društvo
competition suparništvo, konkurencija
computer računalo
conclusion zaključ*a*k
confused zbunjen

consideration obzir
continuously, further dalje
contract ugovor
control kontrola
copy primjer*a*k
corner ugao/ugla *gen.*
correctly točno *adv.*
counter pult
country zemlja
coursework ***(at college)*, a course of study** studij
courtyard dvorište
cousin rođak *m.*/rođaka *f.*
crazy lud
creative nadaren
credit card kreditna kartica
crepes palačinke
Croatia Hrvatska
Croatian Hrvat *m.*/Hrvatica *f.*; hrvatski *adj.*
Croatian currency kuna
crooked, guilty kriv
crossing križanje
crowd, busy place, uproar gužva
customs carina

D

Dalmatian Dalmatinac *m.*/Dalmatinka *f.*
damage, pity šteta
date datum
daughter kćer
day dan/dani *pl.*
day after tomorrow preksutra
day before yesterday prekjučer
dear, favorite drag
decagram dekagram
decision odluka
decrease, fall, drop pad
definitely, surely potpuno, sigurno, svakako
departure odlaz*a*k/odlaska *gen.*; polaz*a*k/polaska *gen.*
desperate očaj*a*n
detergent deterdžent
dictionary rječnik
difference razlika
different različit
differently drugačije *adv.*
difficult težak/teškog *gen.*
difficult, hard teško *adv.*
dinner večera
direction, way smjer
dirty prljav
disappointed razočaran
dish, meal, food, course jelo
doctorate doktorat
document isprava
dog p*a*s
doing business poslovanje
domestic, homemade domaći
dormitory studentski dom
double room dvokrevetna soba
dress haljina
driver vozač
driver's license vozačka dozvola
driving vožnja

E

each, every svaki
earlier ranije
earlier, before prije
early rano *adv.*
easy lak *adj.*, lako *adv.*
economist ekonomistica *f.*/ekonomist *m.*
economy gospodarstvo
electricity struja
elevator dizalo, lift
elsewhere drugdje
emperor car
employee zaposlenik
empty praz*a*n
end, region kraj
enough, sufficient dovoljno
enough, quite dosta
entirely potpuno
entrance ulaz
era era
especially osobito; pogotovo
European europski
even čak

everywhere svugdje, svuda *(with verbs of motion)*
evil zao/zlog *gen.*
exam ispit
example primjer
excellent, extraordinary izvrst*a*n/izvrsnog *gen.*/izvrsna *f.*; odličan
excellently izvrsno, odlično
exchange office mjenjačnica
exchange rate tečaj
excited uzbuđen
excluded isključen
exercise vježba
exit izlaz
expenditure troš*a*k
expensive skup
expert stručnjak
export izvoz
eye, approximately, around oko

F
factory tvornica
fall jesen
family obitelj *f.*
far daleko
far, distant dalek
fashionable, modern moder*a*n
fast brz
fat, thick debeo/debelog *gen.*
father ot*a*c/oca *gen.*
favorite omiljen *m.*
ferry trajekt
ferry port trajektna luka
festive svečan
finally konačno
finished završen
finished, ready, done gotov
firm čvrst
first time prvi put
firstly, first of all najprije
fish riba
fish soup riblja juha
flight let
floor pod; kat *(in a building)*
folk narodni
food hrana
food market tržnica
for, behind za
for example na primjer
forbidden zabranjen *adj.*
forecast prognoza
form formular
forward naprijed
free, available slobod*a*n
frequent čest
fresh svjež
Friday pet*a*k
fridge hladnjak
fried pržen
friend prijateljica *f.*/prijatelj *m.*
from iz; od
from where otkud
fruit voće
full pun
full board puni pansion
funny smiješ*a*n
future budućnost *f.*

G
gallery galerija
garden vrt
gas plin
gasoline benzin
girl, girlfriend djevojka
glass čaša
good dob*a*r
good-bye doviđenja
grammar gramatika
grapes grožđe *pl.*
green zelen
grill roštilj
grilled meat meso na žaru
groceries namirnice *pl.*
grocery store samoposluživanje
guest gost

H
half pola
half board polupansion
hand ruka
happy sret*a*n

happy, joyful radost*a*n
hardly jedva
hat šešir
head glava
health zdravlje
heating grijanje
here ovdje; tu
here, from odavde
here it is/are evo
here you are ***(formal)*** izvolite
heritage ***(historical or cultural)*** baština
hi ***(informal)*** bok
highway autocesta
history povijest *f.*
his njegov
holiday blagdan
holy, saint sveti
honor čast *f.*
hospital bolnica
host domaćin
hot vruć *adj.*
hotly vruće *adv.*
hotel hotel
hotel suite, vacation condo apartman
hour sat/sati *pl.*
house kuća
how kako
how much/many koliko
hundred sto
hungry glad*a*n
husband muž

I
idea ideja
if ako
immediately odmah
import uvoz
important važ*a*n
impression doj*a*m
[to use] informal address "na ti"
in, into u
in front of ispred
in front of, before pred
in general, at all uopće
in the course of tijekom
in the evening navečer
in the mood for raspoložen za
in the morning ujutro
in no way nikako
included uključen
incredibly nevjerojatno
indeed, really zaista
indicator pokazatelj
inhabitant of Zagreb Zagrepčanin *m.*
inhabited nastanjen
inside unutra
instead umjesto
intention namjera
interesting zanimljiv
interestingly zanimljivo *adv.*
international međunarodni
island otok

J
jeans traperice
job posao/poslovi *pl.*/posla *gen. sg.*
joke šala
joy radost *f.*
juice sok
just upravo

K
key ključ
kilogram kilogram *(2.2 lbs.)*
kind ljubaz*a*n
kitchen kuhinja
known poznat

L
laboratory laboratorij
language jezik
last posljednji; zadnji
last night sinoć
late kasno
later poslije
lazy lijen
lecture predavanje
leg noga
left lijevo
less, fewer manje
letter pismo *(postal)*; slovo *(in alphabet)*

library knjižnica
life život
light lagan
like kao
likely vjerojatno
liter litra *(.26 gallon)*
living življenje
location lokacija
long dug
long ago davno
lost izgubljen
loudspeaker razglas
love ljubav *f.*
lovely, nice zgodno
low, short niz*a*k/niskog *gen.*
luck, luckily sreća
luggage prtljaga
lunch ruč*a*k
luxury luksuz

M

magnificent, very beautiful prekras*a*n
main glavni
mainly uglavnom *adv.*
man čovjek/ljudi *pl.*
manuscript, handwriting rukopis
market *(economic)* tržište
marriage brak
married oženjen *(man)*; udana *(woman)*
master majstor
match *(in sport)* utakmica
material materijal
maybe možda
me too i meni; **to me** meni
meaning značenje
meat meso
medication lijek
meeting sastan*a*k
menu jelovnik
message poruka
milk mlijeko
million milijun
mineral water mineralna voda
minute minuta
Miss gospođica
mistake, fault greška
mixed miješan
modest skrom*a*n
moment trenut*a*k
moment, in a moment začas
monastery samostan
Monday ponedjelj*a*k
money nov*a*c/novca *gen.*
month mjesec
monthly mjesečno
monument spomenik
more više
more, another, still, in addition još
mother majka
movie theater kino
Mr. gospodin
Mrs. gospođa
museum muzej
music glazba, muzika
my moj

N

name ime/imena *pl.*
narrow uz*a*k/uskog *gen.*
near blizu
necessary potrebno
necessity, need potreba
negative negativ*a*n
neither...nor ni...niti
never nikada
new nov
news vijesti *f. pl.*
newspapers novine *f. pl.*
next idući
next to, by pored
nicely, beautifully lijepo *adv.*
night noć *f.*
nobody nitko
noisy buč*a*n
nonetheless, still ipak
no one's ničiji
nothing ništa
now sada, sad
nowhere nigdje
nowhere (with verbs of motion) nikamo
number broj

O

obligation obveza
of course naravno
office ured
offer ponuda
often često
old star
on, onto na
on foot pješke
once, at some time nekada
one, a jed*a*n
one-bedroom dvosob*a*n
one's own svoj; vlastit
only samo
only, barely tek
open otvoren
opinion mišljenje
opportunity, possibility mogućnost *f.*
opposite from nasuprot
or ili
other, second drugi
otherwise, generally inače
outside van *(destination)*/vani *(location)*
over preko
overnight stay noćenje
owner vlasnik

P

package paket
packing pakiranje
palace palača
pants hlače *pl.*
paper, report (written) referat
parent roditelj
part dio/dijela *gen.*
party *(social event)* zabava
passed položen
passenger putnik *n.*; putnički *adj.*
passport putovnica
peacefully mirno *adv.*
people ljudi
person osoba
personal osob*a*n
pharmacy ljekarna
phone telefon
picture slika
piece komad
pity, damage šteta
place, space mjesto
pleasantly ugodno *adv.*
please molim Vas/vas
pleasure užit*a*k
police policija
policeman polica*j*ac
poor siromaš*a*n
port *(naval)* luka
portal portal
positive pozitiv*a*n
possible moguće
possibly, perhaps valjda
post office pošta
prefer, preferable radije
prescription recept
present dar
price cijena
private privat*a*n
problem problem
product proizvod
promenade šetnica
protected zaštićen
public javni

Q

question pitanje
quickly brzo; začas
quiet tih
quite prilično
quite, enough dosta

R

railway station željeznički kolodvor
raise *(in salary)* povišica
rare, not thick ried*a*k/rijetkog *gen.*
rarely rijetko
reader čitatelj
ready sprem*a*n
real pravi
really stvarno *adv.*
really, exactly, quite baš
reason razlog
red crven
regrettably, unfortunately nažalost

regularly redovito
remaining ostali
remnant, remaining part ostat*a*k
rent stanarina
renting iznajmljivanje
report izvješće
request molba
rescuer spasil*a*c
reservation rezervacija
rest area odmorište
restaurant restoran
result rezultat
return, round-trip povrat*a*n
rich, wealthy bogat
right desno
right, law pravo
right now, momentarily trenutačno
risotto rižoto
river rijeka
Roman rimski
romantically romantično *adv.*
room soba
rough, coarse grub
rule vladavina
round-trip, return povratni

S
sad tuž*a*n
safety, security sigurnost *f.*
saint, holy sveti
salad salata
salami salama
salary plaća
sale sniženje
salesperson prodavačica *f.*
same isto
sandwich sendvič
satisfied, content zadovolj*a*n
Saturday subota
scattered rastresen
school škola
sea more
seat sjedalo
second, other drugi
secretary tajnica
sense smisla *gen. sg.*/smisao
serious ozbilj*a*n
several nekoliko
shampoo šampon
shelf polica
ship brod
shirt košulja
shoe cipela
shop prodavaonica; trgovina
shopping kupovina
short, brief krat*a*k
short, low niz*a*k/niskog *gen.*
shorts šorc
sick bolest*a*n
side strana
sight, point of interest znamenitost *f.*
sightseeing razgledavanje
similar slič*a*n
since budući da; otkako
single room jednokrevetna soba
sister sestra
sleepy pospan
slim, skinny mršav
slow spor
slowly polako
small malen, mali
smell, scent miris
so much/many toliko
so, therefore, then pa
soap sapun
soccer nogomet, nogometni *adj.*
sock, stocking čarapa
some neki
somebody netko
somehow nekako
someone's nečiji
sometimes ponekad
something nešto
somewhere negdje
son sin
soon uskoro
so-so tako-tako
soup juha
south jug
souvenir suvenir
spacious prostr*a*n
special poseb*a*n

spring ***(season)*** proljeće
square trg
stairs stube
stay borav*a*k
stomach želud*a*c
stop, station stanica
story priča
straight ***(direction)*** ravno
strange čud*a*n
street ulica
strong jak
student student *m.*/studentica *f.*; studentski *adj.*
studio jednosob*a*n stan
stupid glup
stupidity glupost *f.*
suburb predgrađe
success uspjeh
successful uspješ*a*n
successfully uspješno
such tak*a*v
sugar šećer
suggestion prijedlog
suit odijelo
suitable, appropriate priklad*a*n
suitable, cost-effective povolj*a*n
suitcase kofer
summer ljeto
sun sunce
Sunday nedjelja
sunny sunčano *adv.*
sure sigur*a*n
surprise iznenađenje
sweater džemper
sweet slad*a*k/slatkog *gen.*
sweet, cake kolač
swimming pool bazen
swimming trunks kupaće gaće
swimsuit ***(women's)*** kupaći kostim

T

table stol
talking pričanje
tall visok
task zadat*a*k
tax porez
telephone booth telefonska govornica
tennis court tenisko igralište
terribly strašno *adv.*
than nego
thank you hvala
that da *conj.*
that way tako
theater kazalište
then onda; tada
there tamo; ondje
there, from odande
therefore, hence zato
thing stvar *f.*
third treći
thirsty žed*a*n
this ovaj *m.*
this time ovaj put
this way ovako
this way, in this direction ovamo
thousand tisuća
Thursday četvrt*a*k
ticket karta
tie kravata
time, weather vrijeme/vremena *pl.*; vremena *gen.*
tip napojnica
tired umor*a*n
to, next/up to do
to, toward k/ka
today danas
together zajedno
tomorrow sutra
tonight noćas; večeras
too big prevelik
too expensive preskup
too little premalo
too much, too many previše
too young premlad
total, totally ukupno
tourism turizam
tourist turist
toward prema
tradition tradicija
traditional *adj.*tradicional*a*n
traditionally tradicionalno *adv.*

traffic promet
traffic light semafor
train vlak
trait osobina
tram, streetcar tramvaj
transformed pretvoren
transportation prijevoz
trifle sitnica
trip izlet
true, truth istina
T-shirt majica
Tuesday utor*a*k
turned off isključen
turned on (switch, machine) uključen
TV televizor
type, kind vrsta

U
uglyruž*a*n
under ispod; pod
underwear rublje
unique jedinstven
unreliable nepouzdan
until dok ne
usually obično *adv.*
utilities režije

V
vacation, break, rest odmor
vacation condo, hotel suite apartman
various razni
vegetable soup juha od povrća
vegetables povrće
vehicle vozilo
very veoma, vrlo, jako
view, glance pogled
village selo
visit posjet

W
waiter konobar
walking hodanje
wallet novčanik
walls ***(especially city walls)*** zidine
wardrobe ormar
warm topao/toplog *gen.*
watch ***(wrist)***; **clock** sat/satovi *pl.*
water voda
way, time ***(as in two times)*****, journey** put
weak slab
Wednesday srijeda
week tjed*a*n
Welcome! dobro došla *f.* /dobro došao *m.*/dobro došli *pl.*
well dobro *adv.*
what, that što
what kind of, such kak*a*v
when kada
where gdje
where to kamo, kuda
while dok
white bijel
who tko
whole cijel
why zašto
wide širok
window prozor
wine vino
winter zima
with, from/off s
without bez
woman, wife žena
woman's suit kostim
wonderful divno
word riječ *f.*
worker radnik, djelatnik
world svijet; svjetski *adj.*
worry briga
wrong pogreš*a*n

Y
year godina
yellow žut
yes da
yesterday jučer
yogurt jogurt
young mlad

Verb List

Aspect is indicated as *P* for perfective and *I* for imperfective. When there is an aspectual pair, the two verbs are given. For each verb, the first person singular and third person plural forms are given; for irregular verbs, the third person singular is given as well. Past tense is given (*past*) for irregular verbs in the masculine singular form. **Biti** *to be* is given in its present tense conjugation.

to accept primati (*I* primam, primaju; *P* primiti)
to add dodati (*P* dodam, dodaju; *I* dodavati se)
to agree slagati se (*I* slažem se, slažu se; *P* složiti se)
to agree složiti se (*P* složim se, slože se; *I* slagati se)
to agree (upon) dogovoriti (se) (*P* dogovorim, dogovore; *I* dogovarati)
to allow dopustiti (*P* dopustim, dopuste; *I* dopuštati)
to anger, **to get angry** ljutiti (se) (*I* ljutim, ljute; *P* naljutiti)
to announce najavljivati (*I* najavljujem, najavljuju; *P* najaviti)
to answer, **to be suitable** (*I only*) *I* odgovarati (*I* odgovaram, odgovaraju; *P* odgovoriti)
to appreciate cijeniti (*I* cijenim, cijene)
to approach bližiti (se) (*I* bližim, bliže; *P* približiti)
to approach prilaziti (*I* prilazim, prilaze; *P* prići)
to argue svađati se (*I* svađam se, svađaju se; *P* posvaditi se)
to arrive stići (*P*, stižem, stižu; *past:* stigao; *I* stizati)
to arrive stizati (*I*, stižem, stižu; *P* stići)
to ask pitati (*I*, pitam, pitaju; *P* zapitati)
to ask oneself, **to wonder** pitati se (*I*, pitam se, pitaju se; *P* zapitati se)
to be able to, **can** moći (*I irr.* mogu, može, mogu; *past:* mogao)
to be acquainted with poznavati (*I* poznajem, poznaju; *P* upoznati se)
to be afraid of bojati se (*I* bojim se, boje se; *P* pobojati se)
to be allowed to smjeti (*I* smijem, smiju)
to be biti (ja sam, ti si, on je, mi smo, vi ste, oni su)
to be called zvati se (*I* zovem se, zovu se; *P* nazvati se)
to be late kasniti (*I* kasnim, kasne; *P* zakasniti)
to be seated sjediti (*I* sjedim, sjede; *P* sjesti)
to be situated nalaziti se (*I*, nalazim se, nalaze se; *P* naći se)
to be standing stajati (*I*, stojim, stoje)
to be valid važiti (*I* važim, važe; *P* uvažiti **to accept**)
to be valid, **to be worth** vrijediti (*I* vrijedim, vrijede; *P* zavrijediti **to deserve**)
to become postati (*P* postanem, postanu; *I* postajati)
to beg, **to ask for** moliti (*I*, molim, mole; *P* zamoliti)
to believe povjerovati (*P* povjerujem, povjeruju; *I* vjerovati)
to believe vjerovati (*I* vjerujem, vjeruju; *P* povjerovati)
to book rezervirati (*I/P* rezerviram, rezerviraju)
to borrow, **to lend** posuditi (*P* posudim, posude; *I* posuđivati)

to bring donijeti (*P* donesem, donesu; *I* nositi = **to carry)**
to build graditi (*I* gradim, grade; *P* izgraditi)
to buy kupovati (*I* kupujem, kupuju; *P* kupiti)
to buy kupiti (*P* kupim, kupe; *I* kupovati)
to call zvati (*I* zovem, zovu; *P* nazvati = **to phone**, **to name**; pozvati = **to call out**, **to invite**)
to call (by phone) nazvati (*P* nazovem, nazovu; *I* nazivati)
to call, **to get in touch** javiti se (*P* javim se, jave se; *I* javljati se)
to calm down smiriti (se) (*P* smirim, smire; *I* smirivati)
to carry, **to wear** (*I only*) nositi (*I* nosim, nose; *P* donijeti)
to celebrate proslaviti (*P* proslavim, proslave; *I* slaviti)
to change promijeniti (*P* promijenim, promijene; *I* mijenjati)
to change one's mind predomisliti se (*P* predomislim se, predomisle se; *I* predomišljati se)
to check provjeriti (*P* provjerim, provjere; *I* provjeravati)
to choose izabrati (*P* izaberem, izaberu; *I* birati)
to collect skupljati (*I* skupljam, skupljaju; *P* skupiti)
to come doći (*P* dođem, dođu; *past:* došao; *I* dolaziti)
to come dolaziti (*I* dolazim, dolaze; *P* doći)
to complain žaliti se (*I* žalim se, žale se; *P* požaliti se)
to conclude zaključiti (*P* zaključim, zaključe; *I* zaključivati)
to confirm potvrditi (*P* potvrdim, potvrde; *I* potvrđivati)
to congratulate čestitati (*I/P* čestitam, čestitaju)
to contain sadržavati (*I* sadržavam, sadržavaju; *P/I* sadržati)
to continue nastaviti (*P* nastavim, nastave; *I* nastavljati)
to cook kuhati (*I* kuham, kuhaju; *P* skuhati)
to cook skuhati (*P* skuham, skuhaju; *I* kuhati)
to cost koštati (*I* koštam, koštaju)
to count izbrojiti (*P* izbrojim, izbroje; *I* brojiti)
to count brojiti (*I* brojim, broje; *P* izbrojiti)
to count, **to compute** računati (*I* računam, računaju; *P* izračunati)
to cross prijeći (*P* prijeđem, prijeđu; *I* prelaziti)
to cry plakati (*I* plačem, plaču; *P* rasplakati se)
to dance plesati (*I* plešem, plešu; *P* zaplesati)
to decide odlučiti (*P* odlučim, odluče; *I* odlučivati)
to descend silaziti (*I* silazim, silaze; *P* sići)
to dine večerati (*P/I* večeram, večeraju)
to do činiti (*I* činim, čine; *P* učiniti)
to do, **get done** napraviti (*P* napravim, naprave; *I* praviti)
to do business poslovati (*I* poslujem, posluju; *P* isposlovati)
to doubt sumnjati (*I* sumnjam, sumnjaju; *P* posumnjati)
to drink piti (*I* pijem, piju; *P* popiti)
to drink popiti (*P* popijem, popiju; *I* piti)
to drive voziti (*I* vozim, voze; *P* dovesti)
to drop by svratiti (*P* svratim, svrate; *I* svraćati)
to drop off, **to submit**, **to surrender** predati (*P* predam, predaju; *I* predavati)

to eat jesti (*I* jedem, jedu; *past:* jeo; *P* pojesti)
to eat lunch ručati (*I/P* ručam, ručaju)
to embrace, to hug zagrliti (*P* zagrlim, zagrle; *I* grliti)
to employ zaposliti (*P* zaposlim, zaposle; *I* zapošljavati)
to enter ući (*P* uđem, uđu; *past:* ušao; *I* ulaziti)
to entertain oneself, to have fun zabaviti (se) (*P* zabavim, zabave; *I* zabavljati)
to enjoy uživati (*I* uživam, uživaju; *P* nauživati se)
to exaggerate pretjerivati (*I* pretjerujem, pretjeruju; *P* pretjerati)
to exist postojati (*I*, postojim, postoje)
to expect očekivati (*I* očekujem, očekuju)
to explain objasniti (*P* objasnim, objasne; *I* objašnjavati)
to fall padati (*I* padam, padaju; *P* pasti)
to fall in love zaljubiti se (*P* zaljubim se, zaljubi se; *I* zaljubljivati se)
to fall out ispasti (*P* ispadnem, ispadnu; *past:* ispao; *I* ispadati)
to feel osjećati (*I* osjećam, osjećaju; *P* osjetiti)
to fill napuniti (*P*, napunim, napune; *I* puniti)
to fill out ispuniti (*P*, ispunim, ispune; *I* ispunjavati)
to find naći (*P* nađem, nađu; *past:* našao; *I* nalaziti)
to find nalaziti (*I* nalazim, nalaze; *P* naći)
to finish završavati (*I* završavam, završavaju; *P* završiti)
to finish završiti (*P* završim, završe; *I* završavati)
to forget zaboraviti (*P* zaboravim, zaborave; *I* zaboravljati)
to forget zaboravljati (*I* zaboravljam, zaboravljaju; *P* zaboraviti)
to forgive oprostiti (*P* oprostim, oproste; *I* opraštati)
to get dobiti (*P* dobijem, dobiju; *I* dobijati)
to get acquainted upoznati (se) (*P* upoznam, upoznaju; *I* upoznavati)
to give dati (*P* dam, daju; *I* davati)
to give davati (*I* dajem, daju; *P* dati)
to give a ride odvesti (*P* odvezem, odvezu; *past* odvezao; *I* odvoziti)
to go ići (*I*, idem, idu; *past:* išao; *P* doći **to arrive**)
to go away, to leave otići (*P* otiđem, otiđu; coll. odem, odu; *past:* otišao; *I* odlaziti)
to greet, to say farewell pozdraviti (*P* pozdravim, pozdrave; *I* pozdravljati)
to happen desiti se (*P* desim se, dese se; *I* dešavati se)
to happen dogoditi se (*P* dogodim se, dogode se; *I* događati se)
to harm škoditi (*I* škodim, škode; *P* naškoditi)
to have imati (*I* imam, ima, imaju; negative: nemam, nema, nemaju)
to have to, must morati (*I* moram, moraju)
to head, to direct uputiti (*P* uputim, upute; *I* upućivati)
to hear čuti (*P/I* čujem, čuju)
to help pomagati (*I* pomažem, pomažu; *P* pomoći)
to help pomoći (*P* pomognem, pomognu; *past:* pomogao; *I* pomagati)
to hold držati (*I* držim, drže; *P* pridržati)
to hope nadati se (*I* nadam se, nadaju se; *P* ponadati se)
to host ugostiti (*P* ugostim, ugoste; *I* gostiti)
to hurry požuriti (se) (*P* požurim, požure; *I* žuriti)
to hurt boljeti (*I* bolim, bole; *past:* bolio; *P* zaboljeti)
to inform obavijestiti (*P* obavijestim, obavijeste; *P* obavještavati)

to interest zanimati (se) (*I* zanimam, zanimaju)
to invent, to fabricate izmisliti (*P* izmislim, izmisle; *I* izmišljati)
to invest uložiti (*P* uložim, ulože *I* ulagati)
to invite pozivati (*I* pozivam, pozivaju; *P* pozvati)
to invite pozvati (*P* pozovem, pozovu; *I* pozivati)
to joke šaliti se (*I* šalim se, šale se; *P* našaliti se)
to keep držati (*I* držim, drže; *P* zadržati)
to kiss poljubiti (*P* poljubim, poljube; *I* ljubiti)
to know znati (*I* znam, znaju; *P* saznati)
to laugh smijati se (*I* smijem se, smiju se; *P* nasmijati se)
to lead voditi (*I* vodim, vode; *P* provesti)
to learn učiti (*I* učim, uče; *P* naučiti)
to learn, to find out saznati (*P* saznam, saznaju; *I* saznavati)
to learn, to master naučiti (*P* naučim, nauče; *I* učiti)
to leave odlaziti (*I* odlazim, odlaze; *P* otići)
to leave, to abandon ostaviti (*P* ostavim, ostave; *I* ostavljati)
to leave, to abandon ostavljati (*I* ostavljam, ostavljaju; *P* ostaviti)
to leave, to set off polaziti (*I* polazim, polaze; *P* poći)
to let pustiti (*P* pustim, puste; *I* puštati)
to lie ležati (*I* ležim, leže; *P* leći)
to lie, to not tell the truth lagati (*I* lažem, lažu; *P* slagati)
to like sviđati se (*I* sviđam se, sviđaju se; *P* svidjeti se)
to listen slušati (*I* slušam, slušaju; *P* poslušati)
to live živjeti (*I* živim, žive; *past:* živio; *P* poživjeti)
to locate, to find pronaći (*P* pronađem, pronađu; *P* pronašao; *I* pronalaziti)
to look gledati (*I* gledam, gledaju; *P* pogledati)
to look pogledati (*P* pogledam, pogledaju; *I* gledati)
to look for tražiti (*I* tražim, traže; *P* potražiti)
to lose gubiti (*I* gubim, gube; *P* izgubiti)
to lose izgubiti (*P* izgubim, izgube; *I* gubiti)
to love, to like voljeti (*I* volim, vole; *past:* volio; *P* zavoljeti)
to make happy razveseliti (se) (*P* razveselim, razvesele; *I* veseliti)
to make possible omogućiti (*P* omogućim, omoguće; *I* omogućavati)
to mean značiti (*I* značim, znače)
to meet sretati (se) (*I*, srećem, sreću; *P* sresti)
to meet, to wait for dočekati (*P* dočekam, dočekaju; *I* čekati, dočekivati)
to miss nedostajati (*I* nedostajem, nedostaju)
to move maknuti (*P* maknem, maknu; *I* micati)
to move micati (*I* mičem, miču; *P* maknuti)
to move house seliti se (*I* selim se, sele se; *P* preseliti se)
to need trebati (*I* trebam, trebaju; *P* zatrebati)
to notice primijetiti (*P* primijetim, primijete; *I* primjećivati)
to obtain, to acquire steći (*P* steknem, steknu; *past:* stekao; *I* stjecati)
to offer ponuditi (*P* ponudim, ponude; *I* nuditi)
to open otvoriti (*P* otvorim, otvore; *I* otvarati)
to order naručiti (*P* naručim, naruče; *I* naručivati)
to organize organizirati (*I/P* organiziram, organiziraju)

to pack pakirati (se) (*I* pakiram, pakiraju; *P* spakirati)
to pack spakirati (se) (*P* spakiram, spakiraju; *I* pakirati)
to park parkirati (*I* parkiram, parkiraju)
to pass proći (*P* prođem, prođu; *past:* prošao; *I* prolaziti)
to pay plaćati (*I* plaćam, plaćaju; *P* platiti)
to pay platiti (*P* platim, plate; *I* plaćati)
to plan planirati (*I* planiram, planiraju; *P* isplanirati)
to play (a game) igrati (*I* igram, igraju; *P* zaigrati)
to practice, **to exercise** vježbati (*I* vježbam, vježbaju; *P* uvježbati)
to prepare pripremiti (*P* pripremim, pripreme; *I* pripremati)
to prepare priređivati (*I* priređujem, priređuju; *P* prirediti)
to prepare (exam, food), **to get ready**, **to tidy up** spremati (*I* spremam, spremaju; *P* spremiti)
to promise obećati (*P* obećam, obećaju; *I* obećavati)
to push gurnuti (*P* gurnem, gurnu; *I* gurati)
to put staviti (*P* stavim, stave; *I* stavljati)
to read čitati (*I* čitam, čitaju; *P* pročitati)
to recommend preporučivati (*I* preporučujem, preporučuju; *P* preporučiti)
to reign vladati (*I* vladam, vladaju; *P* zavladati)
to rejoice, **to look forward to** radovati se (*I* radujem se, raduju se; *P* obradovati se)
to relax opustiti se (*P* opustim se, opuste se; *I* opuštati se)
to remember sjetiti se (*P* sjetim se, sjete se; *I* sjećati se)
to rent from someone unajmiti (*P* unajmim, unajme; *I* unajmljivati)
to rent to someone iznajmiti (*P* iznajmim, iznajme; *I* iznajmljivati)
to repair, **to fix** popraviti (P popravim, poprave; I popravljati)
to repeat ponoviti (*P* ponovim, ponove; *I* ponavljati)
to reside stanovati (*I* stanujem, stanuju)
to rest odmoriti se (*P* odmorim se, odmore se; *I* odmarati se)
to return vraćati (se) (*I* vraćam, vraćaju; *P* vratiti)
to return vratiti (se) (*P* vratim, vrate; *I* vraćati)
to rush žuriti (se) (*I* žurim, žure; *P* požuriti)
to save štedjeti (*I* štedim, štede; *P* uštedjeti)
to say kazati (*P* kažem, kažu; *I* kazivati)
to say reći (*P* reknem, reknu; *past:* rekao)
to see oneself, **each other**; **to meet** vidjeti se (*I/P*, vidim se, vide se; *past:* vidio se)
to see vidjeti (*I/P*, vidim, vide; *past:* vidio)
to seem, **to appear** izgledati (*I* izgledam, izgledaju)
to seem, **to give an impression** činiti se (*I* činim se, čine se; *P* učiniti se)
to sell prodavati (*I*, prodajem, prodaju; *P* prodati)
to send poslati (*P* pošaljem, pošalju; *I* slati)
to send slati (*I* šaljem, šalju; *P* poslati)
to set off krenuti (*P* krenem, krenu; *I* kretati)
to set off kretati (*I* krećem, kreću; *P* krenuti)
to set off (on a trip) otputovati (*P* otputujem, otputuju; *I* putovati)
to show pokazati (*P* pokažem, pokažu; *I* pokazivati)
to sightsee razgledati (*P* razgledam, razgledaju; *I* razgledati, razgledavati)
to sign potpisati (se) (*P* potpišem, potpišu; *I* potpisivati)

to sit down sjesti (*P* sjednem, sjednu; *past:* sjeo; *I* sjedati)
to sleep spavati (*I* spavam, spavaju; *P* zaspati)
to smoke pušiti (*I* pušim, puše; *P* popušiti)
to sort out srediti (*P* sredim, srede; *I* sređivati)
to sound zvučiti (*I* zvučim, zvuče, *P* zazvučati)
to speak govoriti (*I* govorim, govore; *P* progovoriti = **utter**, dogovoriti = **agree**)
to spend provesti (*P* provedem, provedu; *past:* proveo; *I* provoditi)
to start početi (*P* počnem, počnu; *I* počinjati)
to start počinjati (*I* počinjem, počinju; *P* početi)
to start započeti (*P* započnem, započnu; *I* započinjati)
to stay ostati (*P* ostanem, ostanu; *I* ostajati)
to stay ostajati (*I* ostajem, ostaju; *P* ostati)
to stop stati (*P*, stanem, stanu; *I* stajati)
to stretch, **to extend**, **to offer** pružati (*I* pružam, pružaju; *P* pružiti)
to stroll šetati (*I* šetam, šetaju; *P* prošetati)
to study studirati (*I* studiram, studiraju)
to suggest predlagati (*I* predlažem, predlažu; *P* predložiti)
to swim plivati (*I* plivam, plivaju; *P* otplivati)
to take uzeti (*P* uzmem, uzmu; *I* uzimati)
to take uzimati (*I* uzimam, uzimaju; *P* uzeti)
to take a walk prošetati (*P* prošetam, prošetaju; *I* šetati)
to talk razgovarati (*I* razgovaram, razgovaraju; *P* porazgovarati)
to talk, **to narrate** pričati (*I* pričam, pričaju; *P* ispričati)
to think misliti (*I* mislim, misle; *P* pomisliti)
to think through razmisliti (*P* razmislim, razmisle; *I* razmišljati)
to throw baciti (*P* bacim, bace; *I* bacati)
to transform, **to turn into** pretvoriti (*P* pretvorim, pretvore; *I* pretvarati)
to travel putovati (*I* putujem, putuju; *P* otputovati)
to treat častiti (*I* častim, časte; *P* počastiti)
to treat počastiti (*P* počastim, počaste; *I* častiti)
to try probati (*I*/P probam, probaju; *P* isprobati)
to turn skrenuti (*P* skrenem, skrenu; *I* skretati)
to understand razumjeti (*I* razumijem, razumiju; *past:* razumio)
to use upotrebljavati (*I* upotrebljavam, upotrebljavaju; *P* upotrijebiti)
to use, **to utilize** koristiti + *acc.* (se + *instru.*) (*I* koristim, koriste; *P* iskoristiti + *acc.*)
to visit posjećivati (*I* posjećujem, posjećuju; *P* posjetiti)
to visit posjetiti (*P* posjetim, posjete; *I* posjećivati)
to wait čekati (*I* čekam, čekaju; *P* počekati)
to wait awhile počekati (*P* počekam, počekaju; *I* čekati)
to walk hodati (*I* hodam, hodaju)
to wash prati (se) (*I* perem, peru; *P* oprati)
to wish, **to want** željeti (*I* želim, žele; *past:* želio; *P* poželjeti)
to wish, **to want** htjeti (*I irr.*: hoću, hoće, hoće; negated: neću, neće, neće; *past:* htio)
to work raditi (*I* radim, rade; *P* uraditi)
to worry, **to take care of** brinuti (se) (*I* brinem, brinu; *P* zabrinuti se = **worry**, pobrinuti se = **to take care of**)
to write pisati (*I* pišem, pišu; *P* napisati)

Index of Grammatical and Pragmatic Categories

accommodation 238, 240, 244
adjectives 50–53
  adjectival prefix **pre-** 276–277
  attributive & predicative 50
  comparative & superlative 247–249
    comparative constructions 250–252
    most frequent forms 252–253
  pairs 49
  short & long 51–52
adverbs 53
  comparative & superlative 249–250
  verbal 227–228
alphabet & pronunciation 11–12
apartment 84
body, declension chart 271
  medical expressions 271–272
  parts of 270
cases, introduction 34
  accusative 67–72
    nouns & adjectives 67–70
    personal pronouns 71
    possessive pronouns 69
    prepositions 72–72
  dative & locative 126–132
    dative of possession 130
    dative prepositions 130
    dative usage 128–130
    locative prepositions 131–132
    locative usage 131
    nouns & adjectives 126–127
    personal pronouns 128
    possessive pronouns 127
  declension table 327–328, 329–331
  genitive 86–90
    colors 90
    countable & uncountable nouns 108
    nouns & adjectives 86–88
    personal pronouns 90
    pointer words 89
    possessive pronouns 88
    prepositions 89–90
    quantifiers 89
    rule of five 107–108
    usage 89–90
  instrumental 145–148
    nouns & adjectives 145–146
    personal pronouns 147
    possessive pronouns 146
    prepositions 146–147
    usage & expressions 147–148
  nominative 34–37
    adjectives sg. & pl. 52
    noun pl. 34–37
  vocative 72–73
clothing , articles of 243
colors 48, 90
conditional
  past 300
  present 244–246
conjunctions
  compound 297–299
  da *that* 73–74
  i, a, ali, pa, ili, ni, niti, jer, ako 91–93
country names, adjectival forms 132
dates 109–110
days of the week 72
directions, asking & giving 221–222
expressions
  I feel like 129
  jedan drugi *one another* 297
  sve/svi *all*, **takav/ovakav/onakav** *such* 169–170
family members 269
fleeting -a 35–36, 70
food
  buying 100, 102, 104–105
  restaurant 64, 66
future tense 181–183

future II 294
greetings 19
if clauses 295–296
imperative 272–275
  biti *to be* 274
  imperative & verb aspect 274–275
  negative 274
impersonal constructions
  in dative 129, 130
  in future tense 182, 225–226
  in past tense 166–167, 225–226
  with **"se"** 150
interrogative forms 23–24, 52–53
letter/message writing 158
medical expressions 271–272
money, exchanging 264
months & seasons 110–111
names, possessive forms of 91
nouns
  cases *see specific case*
  collective 277
  countable & uncountable in genitive 108
  gender 19
  neuter **-en** & **-et** 35, 278
  plural 34–37
  verbal 226–227
  zero-ending feminine 34
numerals
  cardinal 106–108
  collective 113
  in past tense 167
  ordinal 109
  other numeral forms 114
  rule of five 107–108
object
  direct 67
  indirect 126, 128
officials, interacting 194, 196
past tense 163–168
pluperfect 299
pointer words 89
prepositions
  chart 333
  na/u & locale designations 131–132
  po & particle **po** 199
  prepositional objects 149–150
  s 247
  za/na in time expressions 183
professions 126
pronouns
  demonstrative 54–55
  interrogative, affirmative, neutral & negative 148–149
  negative 38–39
  personal 19–20, 332
  possessive 20, 54
  reflexive150–152
  relative 183–186
quantifiers 89
reported speech 168
shopping 264, 266
social interaction 145
soft consonants 36
tag questions 132–133
telephone 125
telling time 111–113
ticket, buying 238
travel terminology 288, 293
verbs
  aspect 200–206
  bi-aspectual 208
  biti *to be* 22
  body position & movement 277–278
  bojati se *to be afraid of* 90
  e-type 37
  htjeti *to want* 37
  imati *to have* 67
  moći *to be able to* 21
  modal 275–276
  motion 206
  negation 23, 38
  passive 224–225
  perception & expression 208
  reflexive 39–40
  tense *see specific tense*
  transportation 207–208
  trebati *to need* 129
  sjećati se *to remember* 90
  sviđati se *to like* 128–129
  typology 20–21, 229–230
voicing assimilation 51
word order 39–40, 168

Audio Track List

Audio files available at:
http://www.hippocrenebooks.com/beginners-online-audio.html

Folder One

1. Introduction and Copyright
2. Alphabet and Pronunciation Guide—the Croatian Alphabet
3. Alphabet and Pronunciation Guide—Exercise 1.1
4. Lesson 1—Dialogue
5. Lesson 1—Dialogue for Repetition
6. Lesson 2—Dialgoue
7. Lesson 2—Dialogue for Repetition
8. Lesson 3—Dialogue
9. Lesson 3—Dialogue for Repetition
10. Lesson 4—Dialogue
11. Lesson 4—Dialogue for Repetition
12. Lesson 5—Dialgoue
13. Lesson 5—Dialogue for Repetition
14. Lesson 6—Dialgoue
15. Lesson 6—Dialogue for Repetition
16. Lesson 7—Dialogue
17. Lesson 7—Dialogue for Repetition
18. Lesson 8—Dialogue
19. Lesson 8—Dialogue for Repetition
20. Lesson 9—A Very Important E-mail Message
21. Lesson 9— E-mail Message Repetition

Folder Two

1. Lesson 10—Dialogue
2. Lesson 10—Dialogue for Repetition
3. Lesson 11—Dialogue
4. Lesson 11—Dialogue for Repetition
5. Lesson 12—Dialogue
6. Lesson 12—Dialogue for Repetition
7. Lesson 13—Dialogue
8. Lesson 13—Dialogue for Repetition
9. Lesson 14—Dialogue
10. Lesson 14—Dialogue for Repetition
11. Lesson 15—Dialogue
12. Lesson 15—Dialogue for Repetition

CPSIA information can be obtained
at www.ICGtesting.com
Printed in the USA
LVHW040611050320
649023LV00002B/2